Record, Mix, and Market Your Music from Your Mac-Based Home Studio!

MAC® HOME RECORDING POWER!

Michael Prager and Ben Milstead

Mac Home Recording Power!

Credits: Senior Editor, Mark Garvey; Production Editor, Megan Belanger; Senior Manufacturing Coordinator, Laura Burns; Copyeditor and Proofreader, Karen Annett; Technical Editor, Stan Dudinsky; Cover Design, Chad Planner, *Pop Design Works*; Interior Design and Layout, *GEX Publishing Services*; Indexing, Kevin Broccoli, *Broccoli Information Management*.

Publisher: Andy Shafran

Library of Congress Catalog Number: 2003104187

ISBN: 1-59200-051-7

5 4 3 2 1

Educational facilities, companies, and organizations interested in multiple copies or licensing of this book should contact the publisher for quantity discount information. Training manuals, CD-ROMs, and portions of this book are also available individually or can be tailored for specific needs.

MUSKA & LIPMAN

Muska & Lipman Publishing,
a Division of Course Technology
25 Thomson Place
Boston, MA 02210
www.muskalipman.com
publisher@muskalipman.com

About the Authors

Ben Milstead

In addition to being a studio musician and composer, Ben Milstead has been tinkering with the home recording puzzle for over two decades. He has set up numerous home recording studios and recorded his own music for years. His most recent project is The Daisies, a full-length folk-rock record, which was recorded using three different home studio setups. By day, he writes software applications, video games, and video game tools for Regress Software.

Michael Prager

Michael Prager has been involved in music technology for more than ten years. As a graduate of many fine technology-driven campuses, Michael has had the privilege to work with such companies as Steinberg, Spectrasonics, Sony Classical, Q Up Arts, and Disney Interactive. Michael also co-founded VirtualStudioWorx.com and is a private consultant in the Los Angeles area. In 2002, Michael began work on a series of Artist Pro instructional DVDs, aimed at the professional and non-professional music market. With his wide knowledge of both PC- and Macintosh-based software, Michael is currently completing production of these videos to be released within the first quarter of 2003.

Dedications

Ben Milstead

To the 4-Track Cassette Recorder. Long live its place in the Smithsonian.

Michael Prager

To my parents for their enduring advice and love over the years and encouraging me to follow my musical ambitions. And to my "better half," Jeannie, for her love and support, which makes everything possible.

Acknowledgments

Ben Milstead

Thanks to Mike Prager, whose talents as a writer and an audio professional have made this book a real resource for Mac users, and the team at Course Technology for making this book possible, particularly Mark Garvey for his manuscript development and editing expertise. Thanks also to Diane, Summer, Alex, Laddie, Matt, Nick, Andreas, Duane, Denis, and all the others who have been there for me when I needed them most, personally and professionally.

Michael Prager

Thanks to Kevin, Andy, and Mark at Course Technology for giving me such a wonderful opportunity. It was a real treat to write this book, and I wish all the best to everyone involved. My thanks also to Ben Milstead, who has provided such wonderfully written material to help make this book a reality. I would also like to thank Stan Dudinsky for his technical editing skills and of course, for being such a great and honest friend over the years. To all of my other professional buddies for their advice and help over the years; Greg, Dee, Richard, Eric, Russ, Adam, Joel, Neal, Laurie, and all the others (the list could probably fill another book). The programs used in this book would not be possible without the tireless efforts of software developers. My thanks to Steinberg for their years of knowledge and support, to VirSyn for the best software synth ever, and to Bias for making one of the best Mac-based audio editing programs on the planet. You guys Rock!

And to you, the reader, for buying and reading this book. I hope it will help you realize your dreams and potential as an artist, and I wish you the best of luck in all your endeavors.

Contents

Introduction

Mac Home Recording Power! is devoted to empowering the budding home recording artist that lurks inside of every musician. This book shows you how to take your music from idea to CD. Not only do we teach you how to set up a Mac-based home recording studio and create a recording from scratch, but we also give you useful mastering tips and show you how to get your music out to the eagerly waiting public. Most importantly, *Mac Home Recording Power!* shows you how to do all this on a realistic budget.

What You'll Find in This Book

- Tutorials on digital recording using Mac OS X, Cubase SL, EQ, and digital recording and mixing
- Hands-on examples with illustrations that show you how to work with synthesizers, guitars, drums, MIDI, microphones, mixers, CD-R media, and more
- Tips on how to make your studio and your music work for you—not against you
- Techniques on how to create stunningly good mixes
- In-depth knowledge on the recording and mixing process in both the analog and digital domains
- Recommendations of computer hardware, recording software, sound modules, virtual and hardware synths, and studio gear that will give you professional results
- Timesaving tips for how to market, promote, and distribute your music
- Recording tips for individual instruments from piano to brass to vocals
- Real-world information about MIDI, how it works, and how to use it effectively
- Companion website with updates, links to demo software, audio examples, and recommendations

Whom This Book Is For

Mac Home Recording Power! is for anyone who is considering setting up a Mac-based home recording studio or who already has one. If you're just getting started, this book can help you make smart choices about what you need for your individual home recording situation and put those choices into action. If you already have a home studio, you'll learn how to fine-tune your recording process, how to get the most from your gear and mixes, and delve into some of the deeper aspects of audio engineering and digital recording.

This book is for any Mac enthusiast who craves real-world, no-bones-about-it knowledge, with in-depth tips and techniques to show you not only the ropes of recording and mixing your work, but also marketing and promoting it so that it can be heard. At the end of the day, *Mac Home Recording Power!* enables you to realize more of your potential as an artist.

How This Book Is Organized

Mac Home Recording Power! is divided into eighteen chapters plus an appendix. The appendix contains Web links and information on additional, quality resources online.

- **Chapter 1, "So You Wanna Be a Star?"**—This chapter gets you started examining who you are as a recording artist, what you want to achieve with your music, and what you can expect as you gear up for home recording in terms of commitment, effort, and cost. You'll learn the difference between recording devices and how to plan a home studio equipment list.
- **Chapter 2, "Choosing Your Space"**—This chapter focuses on how to set up your recording space. You'll learn how to evaluate your room's sound, use soundproofing properly, set up monitors, and know what kinds of cabling and connectors to use. You'll find a compromise you and your pocketbook can live with.
- **Chapter 3, "Assembling Your Digital Studio"**—The only way to truly and affordably achieve anything resembling a good sound is to use digital, computer-based home studio equipment. This chapter walks you through picking and choosing your equipment to get it set up for use right away. You'll choose a sound card, learn how audio software works, and connect all the components.
- **Chapter 4, "Listen to You"**—If you plan on recording vocals, this chapter is for you. You'll learn how to select the right microphone(s), understand your capabilities as a singer, use vocal effects effectively, and achieve stellar vocal mixes.
- **Chapter 5, "Keyboards and Synths"**—The synthesizer has come a long way from the Telharmonium, and you'll discover how and why. You'll learn how synthesizers work, what's available in both hardware and software, and how to select the right synth for your style of music; you'll be a synth-head in no time without geeking out.

- **Chapter 6, "Getting the Guitar Sound"**—This chapter helps you turn otherwise amateurish-sounding guitar tracks into recordings you can be proud of, by showing you how to get the most out of your setup. The key is evaluating your playing style, learning how to properly mic both electrics and acoustics, and how and when to record direct.
- **Chapter 7, "No More Drummer Jokes, Please!"**—This chapter is not about "percussion" in the traditional sense; it's about working with a standard drum kit (hi-hat, kick, snare, cymbals, and toms) in the ways you need to get "the drum sound." You'll not only learn how to get that sound, but also how to best integrate drum kit pieces into your style. MIDI, sample-based, and loop techniques are also covered.
- **Chapter 8, "All Kinds of Other Instruments"**—Though most of this book focuses on electronic instruments, the chapter goes into both recording popular acoustic instruments, as well as emulating different instruments using sampling technology. Bass, acoustic piano, and faking it all with Steinberg's HALion Software Sampler are discussed in detail.
- **Chapter 9, "Wading in MIDI"**—Although it's possible to be a home recording artist without it, MIDI is a powerful tool that can save you time and money, and it can make it easier for you to write and record your compositions. This chapter is an introduction to MIDI, guiding you through the ins and outs of hardware and software synthesis, hooking up MIDI devices, common configurations, and basic sequencing.
- **Chapter 10, "Diving Deeper into MIDI"**—This chapter is an in-depth discussion about the internals of MIDI and MIDI messages. You'll understand the types of MIDI messages and what they do, as well as learn how to record and edit tracks using Cubase, all centered around practical knowledge of how the MIDI file format specification really works.
- **Chapter 11, "Fun-Da-Mental Audio"**—This chapter teaches you the fundamentals of audio and sound in terms you can grasp and put to use. It takes you to the heart of what makes a great-sounding recording by distilling the science of audio. You'll learn about the differences between analog and digital recording, choose the solution that works best for your music, and be led through the process of installing a sound card on your computer. You'll actually understand what a sound card really does before you finish the chapter. Headphone use and techniques are covered as well.
- **Chapter 12, "Serious Audio"**—From the AIFF file format to understanding what audio buffer data is, this chapter is an introduction to some of the advanced topics of audio and sound. Concepts such as oversampling, dithering, and effects are presented in practical terms—without the math!

- **Chapter 13, "Recording and Mixing"**—There is both a science and an art to recording and mixing, and you'll learn both in this chapter. The chapter begins with recording and mixing fundamentals and moves on to monitoring, cabling, the actual mixing process, and EQ. Tips for pushing your software to the limit and using effects are covered in detail.
- **Chapter 14, "Step-By-Step: Your First 8-Track Song"**—This chapter is a single tutorial that steps you through recording, mixing, and mastering a simple 8-track song in Cubase. Each section step in the process, from setting up your recording preferences to exporting the finished product as an AIFF file master, is covered.
- **Chapter 15, "Tracking Tips and Techniques"**—This chapter offers special tips and techniques for planning your recording session, an EQ "cheat sheet" for quick EQ, using a patchbay, and mastering.
- **Chapter 16, "Pack It and Ship It"**—This chapter takes you through the world of CD-R and CD-RW media for mastering and storing your audio data and master mixes. Available software and hardware are discussed without too much technical jargon, as well as the types of media you can use for both audio masters and computer storage. Putting together sleeves, liner notes, and graphics are here, too.
- **Chapter 17, "Wired for Sound: The Internet"**—The Internet is still the biggest thing to happen to music in a long time, and after reading this chapter, there is no way you'll miss out on it. You'll learn about the differences between online audio file formats, how to set up your music website without becoming an HTML programmer, and how to protect your music online.
- **Chapter 18, "Promoting and Marketing Your Music"**—If you want your music to be heard, you have to tell people about it. This chapter is a wealth of knowledge on where and how to market your music on the Web, including how to get in on advertising and affiliate programs that will get your music out there.

Keeping the Book's Content Current

Everyone involved with this book has worked hard to make it complete and accurate. But as we all know, technology changes rapidly and a small number of errors may have crept in. If you find any errors or have suggestions for future editions, please contact Muska & Lipman at this website:

www.muskalipman.com

You can also find updates, corrections, and other information related to the content of this book.

1

So You Wanna Be a Star?

This chapter is designed to get you started examining who you are as a recording artist, what you want to achieve with your music, and some of what you can expect as you gear up in terms of commitment, effort, and cost. You may want to skip this one if you're already comfortable with the direction you're headed as an artist or if "the ropes" are all too familiar to you, in which case Chapter 2 is a better place to begin.

For the rest of us, we attempt to cover (but not limit ourselves to) the following topics:

- Your audience and the music you have to offer
- The realities of "professional" studios
- The differences between analog recording and digital recording
- Developing a home studio equipment list

Giving the Audience What You Have

There's an old saying that goes something like this: "The man is just as hitched to that plow as the mule." Though at first glance you may not think this has much to do with the process of recording your music, the fact is (unless your goal is to create music in a vacuum) that you are producing something that is tied to other people—other people's expectations and entertainment, their time, and perhaps even their money. In other words, your audience is almost as important to your music as, well, the music.

Who Is Your Audience?

Who listens to your stuff? Or, who *will* listen to your stuff? Put on your marketing cap for just a moment: Is there a market for your music? Who are they, and what do they expect? In order to answer these questions, you'll need to do one of two things:

1. Hire a market research firm or ad agency to conduct focus groups and telephone surveys about you and your music. Cost: around $100,000 for a decent firm and a handful of focus groups.
2. Identify ten other artists who are most like you, principally in terms of their music, but also their vibe, image, and lyrical style. Cost: the price of each artist's CD, unless you already own it.

If you can afford (1) above, then you probably don't need this book. Give it to one of your musician friends who can really use it.

Choice (2) is where it's at. One of the best ways to understand your intended audience is to examine other artists whose listeners might one day be your own. Though it's not a hard-and-fast rule, generally, people tend to like a particular genre of music and/or a certain vibe or lyrical style best. If your musical style is Progressive Rock, then you should be listening closely to that genre and registering the quality of the recordings (as well as how the CDs are packaged). On the other hand, if your singing and lyrical style are more like the Counting Crows than Yes, then you should study the recording style and quality of the Crows' CDs. The bottom line is, you can get a feel for what kind of quality and the types of songs people expect from popular artists who have sold lots of records.

For example, you don't have to listen to an entire Crows' album to know that people who like their music are probably a little less concerned with lush production and a little more concerned with melody, intelligent lyrics, and raw emotion. Conversely, the production on a Queen album is completely different, and people who like Queen expect Queen to sound like Queen: swanky production values, bright tones, and ironic lyrics. If your music sounds a lot like Queen's, your recording requirements and values are going to be different than if you write songs like those of Adam Duritz.

What's the Point?

Maybe it's simpler just to "do what you do" and not worry about the audience. After all, you're an artist at your core and, ultimately, it's whatever you have to say and/or your tunes that define your artistry. Right?

Don't believe it. There's lots more to the story.

When you make the jump to becoming your own engineer, producer, manager, and marketer, you've got to ante up and do the work required of those jobs. If you don't, chances are good that no one is ever going to hear your music, because it's not going to get recorded, mixed, distributed, or marketed. Music in this day and age has taken on a serious dichotomy—on one hand, it's ultimately the performance and material that provide something valuable to listeners; on the other hand, it's a business full of details. As a home recording artist, you're going to have to manage the details, wear the hats, and make it happen.

That means creating an end product that lives up to the expectations of your audience. Can you do it with home studio equipment? Ten years ago, the answer to the question would have been damn close to "No." Today, it's "Yes," but that doesn't mean it's effortless.

Got Milk? Go Professional!

One of the things you have going for you is the ability to create what your audience expects, although there is no shortage of professional engineers and producers whose primary audience is other professional engineers and producers—not your listeners. This is not said to suggest that there aren't a number of highly competent, well-run studios who truly understand their clients. There are, and they do. And they will, rightly, charge you a small fortune to do it. If you've got the milk, they'll dip cookies for you all day long. If you *don't got* the milk—or if your tastes are running a little more toward no-fat than latte these days—then that's what this book is for!

Over the past decade, the cost of recording gear has fallen, while better, relatively inexpensive new technology has gone gangbusters. This has enabled nearly anyone to equip a personal studio for a few hundred to a few thousand dollars and to record their tunes with all the comforts of home.

As more and more home recording artists are born, there has been a great deal of discussion and dialogue between the "amateurs" and the "professionals." Devote an evening to reading newsgroups like **rec.audio.pro** and **rec.music.makers.songwriting**. Aside from gaining some wonderful and helpful tips from some very knowledgeable folks, you'll also enjoy some great—and sometimes petty—debate over the merits of home recording vs. commercial recording studios.

Without doubt, both the home studio and commercial studio have their own place in recording-dom. High-end recording gear, experienced engineers, and acoustically marvelous spaces are the main advantages of commercial studios—and they are big advantages.

In addition to the cost, commercial studios are businesses that operate on strict schedules, and even if you do have a little money to burn, you're going to feel some pressure to get in and out of the studio. You're forced to do your best with a short time window, and you cannot play around and experiment with the songs, instruments, arrangements, and tracks. In a few situations, this can be an advantage—sometimes, we all need a little forced discipline to get things accomplished. The other 95 percent of the time, we need the ability to play whenever we want, without a time clock, free to create, explore, discover—and screw up—and then start all over again. Sound a little like the creative process in general? Sometimes, it can be a nightmare, but most of the time, it's the intuitive glue that keeps us married to our creations.

In short, if you want to spend money in a commercial studio, go for it, but that's not what this book is about. This book is about helping you to achieve semiprofessional to professional results and still retain the creative freedom that fuels your music.

Analog vs. Digital Audio

A fundamental question you'll have to answer is what kind of home studio you want. There are two choices, really: analog or digital (or some combination of the two). Which is better? The answer has been hotly debated for some time, particularly among professional engineers, and both will get you where you want to go. For the home studio, however, digital is a better choice, for three key reasons: money, space, and quality.

Unless you just inherited all of Uncle George's cool studio equipment—his 64-track vintage mixing board, all his effects racks, and his $20,000, 2-inch reel-to-reel—you are not going to produce the sound quality you can get with digital equipment for the same money using analog. A four-track tape recorder won't cut it; neither will a 4-track, quarter-inch reel without superior mixing and effects capabilities.

Even if you do have your hands on vintage, high-quality analog equipment, you've got to have three to five times the space to house it and keep it in running order. Contrast that to a typical digital setup, which you can set up in a space the size of your half-bath.

KEEPING YOUR POCKETBOOK IN MIND

There are several "home studio" books on the market that are actually books that show you how to spend all the money you don't have on studio equipment. Many of these books have excellent sections on mixing and recording, because they're often written by engineers or producers who run large, expensive studios. There's nothing wrong with these books; however, most of them are not written with the economy or reality of a home studio in mind.

Why Is Digital So Hot?

On the surface, recording sound as digital audio is not unlike recording sound using an analog tape recorder—in fact, you'd be hard pressed, on first glance, to tell the difference—but in reality, it's much different. Recording audio digitally means you are recording numbers on a computer, not a pattern on analog, magnetic tape. The difference is profound; the numbers are usually far more accurate than the tape, unless you can afford very high-quality, expensive tape, the equipment it takes to use it, the cost to maintain it, and a space to put it in.

THE DAT ALTERNATIVE

DAT, or digital audio tape, is a medium that can store digital audio in its digital form, much like a computer's hard drive. There are a number of DAT machines and components available, including some that use the ADAT standard, which allows you to store multiple tracks (usually eight per tape).

DAT is a workable—if not optimal—alternative to hard disk recording, and it is more difficult to integrate with your software and/or computer. It is also slower than a hard drive. That said, DAT tapes are fairly cheap, which makes DAT another alternative to mastering your recordings, in addition to burning to CD-ROM.

The numbers that are recorded digitally are called *samples*, and, depending on how many samples you record and how large the numbers are, you can have different levels of audio quality. For example, CD-quality digital recordings are based on a standard, which means that 44,100 samples are generated for each second of sound recorded. Put it another way: The *sampling rate* for CD-quality audio is 44,100 samples per second.

Likewise, the *bit depth* for CD-quality audio is 16 bits. This simply means that each one of those 44,100 samples represents a number 16 bits in length, which, in the computer programming world, is a commonly used variable. The actual value of each of those numbers carries the information that describes the audio, so that it can be converted from the digital domain to an analog waveform.

ADDING UP THE BITS

The idea of a *bit* is simple: A bit represents either 0 or 1. By combining bits, computers produce much larger numbers. For example, 8 bits is nothing more than 2^8, which yields a range of numbers from 0 to 255 (256 numbers), whereas a range from 0 to 4,294,967,295 (or -2,147,483,648 to 2,147,483,647) is 32 bits.

A 16-bit number has a range of 65,536 different values, from 0 to 65,535, or, in some cases, -32,768 to 32,767. It's a pretty good-sized number, about the same as the salary of a junior-level, second engineer in LA at the time of this writing.

Because sound is analog by nature, an audio wave pattern must first be converted to numbers before a computer or other digital recording device can record those numbers as a representation of your music. The piece of hardware that does this is called an analog to digital converter—or ADC for short.

AD TERMINOLOGY

In many cases, the computer chip that does the digitizing also handles the analogizing. Hence, you'll see DAC/ADC or ADC/DAC or DA/AD or even AD/DA. You'll also see both types of converters referred to as simply an "A/D converter."

Similarly, there is a DAC, or digital to analog converter, which converts the numbers back to an analog audio signal you can hear during playback. Why? Because, so far, no human has gained the ability to hear numbers! In addition, digital recorders often employ filters to cut off unwanted sound data above or below frequencies that are of interest to human ears. For example, white noise or radio frequencies are often discarded during the ADC process to produce cleaner results.

A digital recorder stores all the samples—and the timing of each sample—that it receives. If the digital recorder is on a computer motherboard or a sound card, the amount of data it can store is limited only by the size of the hard disk(s) on the computer. If it's on a digital audio workstation (DAW), then it's limited by the fixed hard disk in the DAW and its onboard memory.

To recap, here's the process, as shown in Figure 1.1:

1. The digital recorder uses an ADC to convert an electronic signal from an audio device (such as a microphone or your guitar).
2. The ADC process converts the signal into numbers called samples, which are stored on a hard disk.
3. The recorded samples are then sent to the DAC part of the digital recorder, which converts them back into an electronic signal.
4. The electronic signal is routed to your amplifier, which boosts the signal to audible levels.
5. The signal is sent to your speakers, so you can hear all the mistakes you're making on this take.

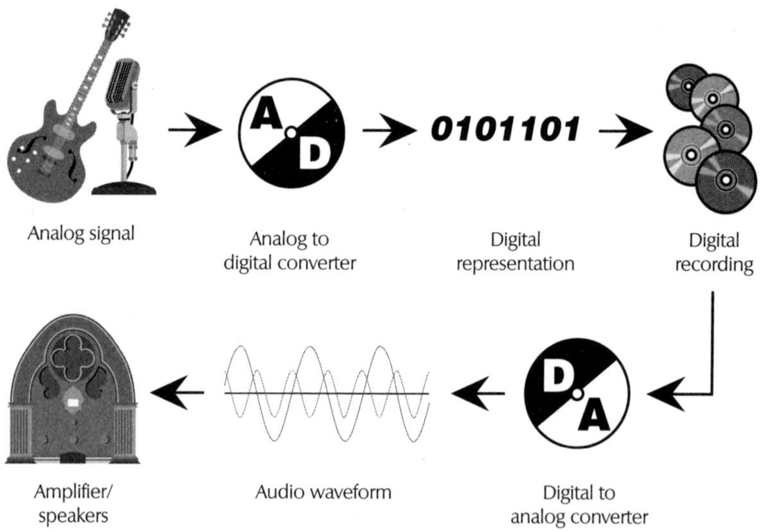

Figure 1.1
The ADC/DAC process is actually quite simple

Yeah, But Analog Is *Cool*

But isn't analog the warmest, sweetest sound around? Digital sounds cold, doesn't it? Maybe. Maybe not. There was a time when digital recording wasn't up to the accuracy of analog tape recording, but things have changed. Processors have gotten much faster—and cheaper—and dozens of professional-quality sound cards, as well as DAWs, are on the market today that didn't exist a few years ago.

However, analog still has its merits. Let's take a look under the hood.

The most simplistic explanation of sound is that it is a series of vibrations. A guitar string produces vibrations, as does a human voice. Your eardrum vibrates in response, which is the reason you can hear sound at all.

Because of this, it makes sense to record sound by capturing vibrations, in a fashion not that dissimilar from the way your ears do it. Early attempts at capturing sound had to do with recording the movement of a needle that vibrated at the frequencies of sound waves in its vicinity; tracing the needle back across the path it recorded would cause the needle to vibrate just as it did when the original sound was present. That's where the word "analog" comes from: The recording of the needle created a sound analogous to the original sound.

Today, analog is chiefly a reproduction of sound on magnetic tape, facilitated through the routing of an electrical signal received from a source sound, such as a microphone or your keyboard. At some point, amplifier circuitry adds energy to the source signal and boosts it enough that it can be filtered, effected, equalized, and so on, so that the result is a recording that is, typically, clean and warm at its core. To record this signal, the electrical signal must be saved in some manner. Recording to magnetic tape, the electrical signals are turned into magnetic pulses, and as the magnetic tape passes over a recording magnet (head), the tape is magnetized.

This approach has some limits. First, the amplified signal-turned-magnetic energy is never transferred in a smooth, wavelike fashion to the tape, but in pulses, and so the resulting recording is not a completely accurate representation of the source sound. Second, the tape itself is physically limited to just how much magnetic energy it can store.

Even with these limits, for mastering, you can record sound between 5 Hz and about 45 kHz with high accuracy (with good equipment). However, every time you run the stored signal through electronics in order to listen to it, or rerecord the signal, some of the signal is lost due to imperfections in electronic circuits, the tape, and electrical loss in wires and cables. To make matters worse (much worse), when you record a track and use that recording as part of another recording, the result is a second-generation recording of the original track. Continued rerecording of a track accumulates loss at a rapid rate, and your original pristine recording eagerly begins its journey to the Ninth Circle of tape-noise Hell.

Is this cool? Yes, actually, if you can afford the equipment to keep you in the lower circles of overdubbing. Otherwise, it makes a strong case for going digital.

More Power Means More Responsibility

In analog recording, there is some overhead for missing audio information yet still obtaining (permitting?) a fairly accurate recording. Overall, the process isn't as accurate as it is in the digital domain, but it's very reliable. In the world of digital recording, there is less room for error: The cost of doing digital business means understanding that you're dealing with purer electronics, and this means you have to get right with the idea that, though errors are few and far between, when they happen, they usually ain't small.

Data will become lost. Hard drives will crash. Unexpected, mysterious strange happenings will sometimes occur without notice. You need to accept this as a given. One remarkable aspect of digital equipment is that it ultimately requires less maintenance than analog circuitry, but it can be temperamental—especially when dealing with computer sound cards and their associated hardware drivers.

At a microlevel, most digital architecture does some interesting things to avoid problems. For example, when writing digital data, it's possible to write an extra bit of information to allow the circuitry to know if the number being read should be an even number or an odd number. This is known as a parity check. If the number is even, and the parity bit designates odd, there is an error, and the data is either reread or deleted as an error.

Another type of error check, meant to handle larger errors in which entire chunks of information are missing, is known as a CRC error (cyclical redundancy check). This is the same type of error handling performed by computer modems when sending and receiving data over a phone line. A mathematical check is completed on the data being transferred and periodically matched to an expected result. Any result other than the expected result is a CRC error. To limit the amount of data that might "drop out," data is written in a non-sequential pattern. If three blocks are lost, they are not necessarily in order, and the cyclical redundancy check can try to replace the missing data with the data it expected to receive. Sometimes, correct approximations can be inferred from the previous and next bits of data and a reasonable approximation put in place of missed data.

Digital recorders do a multitude of other interesting things behind the scenes to keep their activities reliable, and you're probably thanking the author of this book right now for not going into them—but the point is this: Don't buy the cheapest thing you can get your hands on, and be ready for the occasional out-of-the-blue crash (which invariably happens at the most inopportune time). Take that attitude, and you're on your way to producing home studio recordings that sound damn good.

Getting Ready for Your Home Studio

This book focuses on a digital home studio setup. Here and there, you'll see a note or tip that is directed at external components other than a mixing board, but for the most part, the emphasis is on a Mac-based, digital home studio setup with an external mixer. That said, this section is a quick rundown on the hardware, software, space, and external gear options that make the most sense at the time of this writing. These recommendations are made with value in mind—the most equipment you can get for your money. Most of these options are covered elsewhere in the book in more detail.

As a minimum, depending on the kind of music you do, the following are must-haves for a successful home studio:

- **Space**. A quiet, comfortable space in which to record is essential. Chapter 2, "Choosing Your Space," covers this in detail, and you'll find out that a bad space can make even the best equipment sound bad.
- **A good microphone**. There are almost as many microphones to choose from as there are singers (and instrumentalists) to use them. One of the best values on the market today is the Rode NT1 (around $200) or its slightly more expensive cousin, the NT2. If you're on the slimmest of budgets, a Shure SM58 ($100) will do in a pinch. For instrument miking, you just can't beat

the Shure SM57 ($100). Do not underestimate the importance of a good-sounding mic—it's one of the major advantages commercial studios have had in the past, because they can afford to pay thousands of dollars for high-quality large condenser mics such as Neumann's U 87 and U 89 series. These days, you can buy a large condenser mic (like the NT1) that will come very close to the expensive Neumanns.

- **Mass storage for your master recordings**. This book focuses on using CD-ROM and CD audio as a primary means of storage (see Chapter 18, "Promoting and Marketing Your Music"), but you can also use a DVD burner or an external hard drive to great effect. Any way you look at it, you have to have a reliable, lossless way to keep track of your tracks.
- **Mixers**. Behringer or Mackie are good choices or Alesis in a penny-pinching pinch.
- **Computer systems**. A preconfigured Mac computer can be purchased at any Apple Store or Apple Authorized Reseller.
- **Sound cards**. The Apple Sound Manager will do as a bare minimum to play back audio; however, you'll want to purchase a professional-quality board with higher bit depth, as well as multiple inputs and outputs. See Chapter 11, "Fun-Da-Mental Audio," for more details on the right sound cards to use.
- **Processors**. A G3 processor will be fine as a bare minimum to start, but try to purchase a G4 if you can. The bigger your processor, the better your track count in Cubase.
- **Memory**. Use a minimum of 256 MB of RAM, but consider having your Apple Technician pop in some more (512 MB would be a good amount). Don't skimp on RAM quality unless you're already a hardware geek and you know what you're doing. The extra $10 or $15 savings is not worth the potential headaches.
- **Hard drives**. Although your Mac will come with a good, fast hard drive, you might consider installing a second hard drive for your recording purposes. Talk with your Apple Technician about how to do this.
- **Operating system**. Make sure your Mac comes with OS X installed.
- **Digital recording software**. This book focuses on Cubase and uses Cubase in all its examples; it's currently by far the most bang for your buck. Logic, Digital Performer, Bias Deck, and Digidesign Pro Tools are also proven choices.

2

Choosing Your Space

On the seventh day, while God was resting, he was approached by the spirit of the Buddha himself:

God: "What's up, B?"

Buddha: "I could really use some help. I'm getting complaints about meditating too loudly. I need to build a perfectly soundproofed studio for chanting."

God: "Well, it's my day off, and there is no such thing as 'perfect sound.' How much money do you have?"

Although everyone has an opinion about what constitutes a bad mixer, a bad microphone, or a bad set of speakers, most people agree about how a bad-sounding room sounds. In all likelihood, both your home studio space and your savings account are less than optimal for creating near-perfect sound, so this chapter shows you how to find a compromise you can live with, including topics on how to:

- Choose your space
- Evaluate your room's unique sound
- Make your space sound better
- Use soundproofing techniques
- Locate your equipment
- Monitor it all
- Choose cabling and connectors

Choosing Your Space

You've pretty much got two choices when it comes to where your home studio will be: Either commandeer an existing room in the house (or the garage) or build a new room.

In terms of space, what would a home studio cost to build? At the time of this writing, basic partitions (studs with sheet rock and no insulation), cheap carpeting, and suspended acoustic ceilings in an existing shell totals somewhere near $50 per square foot. Not cheap—but much cheaper than, for example, the cost to build a stand-alone room, which ranges these days anywhere from $125 to $250 per square foot, depending on where you live. In fact, commercial recording studios average about 30 percent more than that!

Do the math: As a bare minimum, a full conversion of your 400-square-foot garage to a real studio space is going to cost you at least $20,000, and probably at least a year out of your life to manage the project. If you've got the money, the time, and the dream, it's one alternative. If you don't have the money and the time, but you do have the dream, you'll have to compromise a bit, by appropriating an existing room and making targeted changes to that space to achieve a level of audio fidelity you can live with.

Commonsense Considerations

First, there are some fundamental pieces to the home studio space puzzle that you'll have to keep in mind. The most important considerations are:

- **Isolation**. You will want to keep noise filtering in from outside your studio to a bare minimum, and at the same time not be a nuisance to your neighbors. If possible, choose the room that's the most isolated from neighbors and external noise. Also remember that *isolating* sound is an entirely different topic than *getting* a good sound. It's soundproofing vs. sound acoustics (more on that later).
- **Doors and windows**. These are almost always problems in any type of studio. Check for acoustical "leaks" behind door casings and window jambs; it's not uncommon for the shims that are used to square doors and windows to leave gaps behind the moldings. These types of sound leaks are deceptive and can make your other sound-absorption methods doubly hard.
- **Acoustic treatments**. For walls, floors, and ceilings, this is perhaps the most critical part of your studio space.

The degree to which you focus on these core aspects of setting up your studio has to do with the kind of music you'll be recording as well. For example, if your primary need is to have a place to play your drums, then your soundproofing needs will probably take precedence over equipment layout and, to some extent, sound quality. Conversely, if your music is mostly soft acoustic ballads, less soundproofing is fine, as is more natural ambience in the room, which may actually be an advantage, because atmosphere, as well as equipment placement, will probably be critical.

In any case, you're going to have to deal with the room's acoustics at some level, so it helps to know something about spatial acoustics.

The Complexities of Room Acoustics

Though there is no perfect-sounding room, sound waves travel and strike the walls in a room in predictable ways. What's not quite as predictable is the way sound is reflected back into a room once it hits the walls.

To put it another way, reflected sound is the most inaccurate aspect of room acoustics, and controlling it is the key to making your studio space sound good to you. Of course, there is control and there is control. *Real* control is *real* expensive and involves spending a lot of money and finding the right people to build your studio for you; with real *money* and real *time*, you could turn a high school gym or dormitory shower into a world-class studio. The other kind of control involves educating yourself a little bit and making a few key decisions about your recording space. With a lot less money and time, you can significantly improve the quality of your space. You won't get as near to perfection as you might if you had Bill Gates' money, but the goal of this chapter is to put you on the path to enlightenment, not make your home studio space perfect.

Absorption and Diffusion

Controlling the amount and kinds of sounds that are reflected from the walls of your home studio allows sound that is truer to that of the instrument or voice (or monitor speaker) to come through. Controlling reflection is done by adding materials to your space that either absorb or diffuse sound. Material that absorbs sound attempts to quickly stop the sound waves from vibrating—effectively making the sound go away. Diffusing materials works a bit differently, by scattering the sound waves to reduce reflections.

To understand how best to absorb and diffuse a room's sound, you should know a thing or two about reflection itself. There are three basic kinds, or modes, of reflection: axial, tangential, and oblique (and there are frighteningly complex physics equations to boot, from which you are, most happily, spared). They sound all highfalutin, but the basic idea is pretty simple:

- Axial mode means reflection from two surfaces of a room.
- Tangential mode means reflection from four surfaces of a room.
- Oblique mode means reflection from six surfaces of a room.

The worst of these is axial mode; sound that is being reflected from floor-to-ceiling or wall-to-wall usually produces the most obvious, often unwanted, reverberation and mangling of sound frequencies.

CORNER TROUBLE

A room's corners can be a trouble spot, too. Corners create "pseudo-bass," by deceptively boosting bass frequencies in a room by as much as three to four times their actual levels. "Smoothing out the corners" is an important part of improving a room's sound.

On the Surface

The degree to which any of the modes of reflection manifests itself is mainly dependent on the kinds of surfaces in the room. If you've ever been to a basketball game or have sung in the shower, you already know that the hardest room surfaces, such as paneling, concrete, vinyl, and hardwood, are to blame for the worst reflections. Generally, the smoother, harder, and less porous the surface, the better (and more unpredictably) it reflects sound waves.

It's a mistake to think that making a room's surfaces completely absorbent is the only way to make a room sound best, though. Although it's true that covering the walls and/or ceiling with 2-inch or thicker foam and carpeting the floor might create a better sounding space, you can do a more effective job by strategically placing materials that diffuse sound in addition to materials that absorb sound.

In fact, some of the best-sounding spaces tend to be ones with a proper blend and placement of good absorption and diffusion, and a little natural ambience is often preferable. The trick is to work with the room's dimensions and space, along with your equipment, rather than blindly spreading out absorbing material around the room. That's not to say that installing a base layer of acoustical foam evenly around the room, for example, is a bad idea. However, in some cases, you'll get better results by putting most of your absorbing material on one or two walls (or focusing on the ceiling and floors) while placing diffusing materials where it makes sense—for example, in the corners of the room.

For example, if your music is heavy on electric guitars or any other live, amplified instruments, then facing the amps toward one wall that is covered with a diffusion/absorption combination (such as eggshell-type acoustical foam) is a far more effective method for getting a good sound—and volume levels you can deal with—than trying to deaden the room by installing thick foam or carpet on all of the walls.

EGGSHELL MANIA

Acoustical foam products from companies such as Sonex and Technifoam are the most common commercial means of getting good sound absorption and noise reduction over a fairly wide range of frequencies. These "eggshell" foam sheets are sold in a variety of sizes and styles and typically range in thickness from 2 to 6 inches.

Acoustical foam has been a popular way to achieve good sound for a number of years, and there have been as many different eggshell and placement configurations as there have been recording studios. An average installation covers anywhere from 40 percent to 60 percent of wall space, in addition to carpeted floors and randomly spaced eggshell treatments attached to different areas of a drop ceiling.

Eggshell-type patterns absorb echoes bouncing back into the room to control reverberation, while diffusing some frequencies to prevent overdeadening. The standard, cheaper types of foam usually have fewer color choices and don't line up all nice and pretty at the seams, whereas the more expensive lines come in a huge range of designs and colors.

Acoustical foam, when used in moderation, can give you better sound by helping you to control unwanted reflections; however, treating the entire room can sometimes make the room sound *worse*. Although foam does an effective job on midrange and, to a greater extent, upper frequencies, it takes an impractical amount of it to control reflections in the low and lower-mid ranges. This means that if you cover the entire room with 2-inch or 4-inch acoustical foam, you're losing the highs but leaving the lows, effectively deadening your mixes. A totally dead room usually means a totally dead mix.

A great website for getting the specifics on pricing and styles is **www.acousticfoam.com**.

SOUND ABSORPTION FOR LITERARY TYPES

A cheap way to get noticeable absorption and diffusion is to use bookcases along the wall with randomly stacked books. It's an effective way to get rid of harsh reflections without killing your overall sound.

Speaker Placement

If you're able, using decent speakers and placing them properly can make all the difference. If you don't already know why, here are the reasons:

- **Bass response**. You cannot get accurate bass response from a set of headphones. Though high frequencies are heard primarily through your ears, bass is heard through your ears and just about every other part of your body.
- **Flat response**. If you do not have particularly "flat" speakers—ones that do not boost or cut frequencies due to their own construction—at least learn where they are not flat and figure out a way to compensate during mixdown. Ideally, flat response should lie between 40 Hz and 16–18 kHz.
- **Imaging**. Live stereo sound has to deliver the left and right sides of the mix to both your left and right ears, whereas headphones only go L-L and R-R. The result is that it's hard to get the same mix in air that you can get on headphones, and vice versa.
- **Phase**. All stereo signals contain frequencies that are out of phase, as well as phase cancellation. Because sound coming out of speakers mixes in the air before reaching your ears, these sounds will diminish before they reach you. With headphones, there is no phase degradation. This can, again, deceive you into thinking you have a better, or worse, mix than you really do.

A WORD ABOUT SPEAKERS

"Multimedia" speakers might be okay for playing a round of Unreal Tournament, but for music recording, you really need a clean power amp and a pair of good reference speakers.

If your music uses a lot of deep bass, then you'll definitely want to focus on a subwoofer (preferably matched to your other two monitors). If your space is limited, look at Bose's satellite systems, with one big woofer that sits on the floor and two or more tiny tweeters. A better choice is a pair of "nearfield" reference monitors. Nearfield monitors are typically small cabinets with very good fidelity designed to be listened to in smaller, lower-volume situations and at close range. Yamaha NS-10s are hands down the most popular nearfields (they're very flat above 100 Hz), but Tannoy and Event are also very good. As for a power amp, get the cleanest-sounding amp you can afford. You can also use powered nearfield speakers (such as the Alesis M1); however, they are generally expensive.

An important aspect of achieving a balanced sound when placing speakers is symmetry. A pair of speakers, for example, should be the same distance from you as they are from each other, and they should also be equidistant from the walls to either side of them. Picture an equilateral triangle. Speakers should also be at ear level and at least 4 feet from you to avoid phase problems. In addition, putting speakers too close to corners tends to emphasize bass frequencies (often in unpredictable ways), so, if you can, keep the speakers out from the corners—even if you catty-corner them.

Size Matters

Room dimensions play a big role in how a room behaves acoustically. Depending upon the size of the room, certain frequencies can sound louder than others, because some frequencies will resonate at louder levels as *standing waves.*

A fundamental idea in physics is that "two objects cannot occupy the same space at the same time." However, sound waves seem to violate this idea, because they can pass through each other and continue on. This is known as *superposition.* When two sound waves of identical amplitude and wavelength are going in opposite directions, they can create a superposition of a standing wave. Figure 2.1 shows three waves: Wave 1 is traveling to the left, while Wave 2 is traveling to the right. Together, they produce a standing wave. The standing wave is the result of adding the amplitude of Wave 1 with Wave 2; it is called "standing" because it, in a sense, does not move—it's constantly being re-created by the other two sound waves.

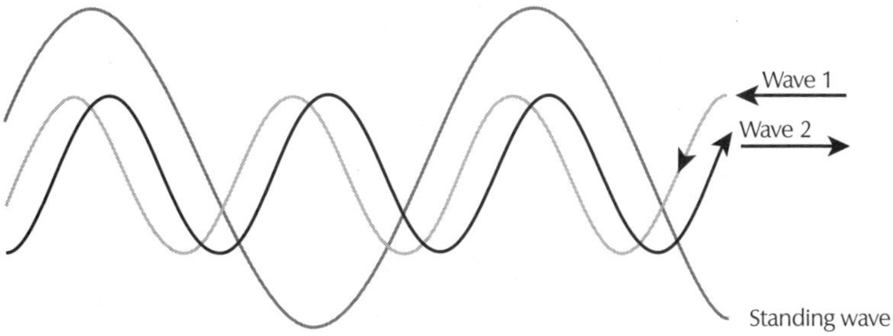

Figure 2.1
Standing waves can fool you into thinking you've got more—or less—going on than what's really there

The size of your room will tell you at what frequencies you will tend to get standing waves. There's actually a little math here, in the form of an equation:

S = 1,130 / 2L

where 1,130 is the speed of sound in feet per second, and L equals the length of the room. For example, if your room is 15 feet long, you will get a standing wave at around 38 Hz (1,130 / 30). Also, multiples of your room's standing wave frequency will result in more standing waves, though they diminish in volume and are less pronounced the higher they get. In the previous example, the next standing wave will be around 76 Hz, then 114 Hz, then 152 Hz, and so on.

If you calculate where your room's standing waves exist, then you can make adjustments by using equalization, speaker placement, or acoustical materials, which will increase how accurately you perceive your audio mixes. In the case of a standing wave at a low 38 Hz, for instance, an effective solution might be as simple as a strategically placed, four-foot bookshelf in one of the room's corners.

FREQUENCIES FLYING ALL OVER THE PHASE

Low-frequency signals have very long waves and seem to exist just about anywhere. In other words, they're omnidirectional. As a result, depending on the size of your room, the low frequencies may not be fully developed when they hit a wall, and they could cancel out or boost a portion of a subsequent or other diminishing sound wave.

As frequencies climb, things change. Mid- to high-range frequencies, for example, tend to have very short wavelengths, and so they are usually fully developed by the time they strike a surface and start reflecting. The result is that fully developed waves can reflect back to your ears and into the mix along with the sound coming from your speakers. This is called "early reflection," and you cannot tell the difference between most early reflections and the sound coming from your speakers. This can affect tone, as well as cause more inaccuracy in your perception of the stereo image.

THE DISPERSION ANGLE

Get your speakers' dispersion angle. It's in the manual or, likely, in the documentation on the manufacturer's website. You can then measure sound wave impact points by stretching string from the center of your speaker at the correct dispersion angle. Where the string touches the wall is where your room's sound will benefit from acoustical foam.

Soundproofing

A good sound is not the same thing as a "noiseless" sound. In other words, getting a good sound is altogether different from soundproofing. Acoustical foam will not keep your neighbor's new riding lawn mower from making its way into your new song's intro any more than it will it keep your neighbor from calling the police in response to your 30-minute Keith Moon altar-call. Even if you lined the room with 6-inch solid foam, you wouldn't hear a significant effect on the transmission of sound into or out of the studio.

To properly soundproof, you've got to cover a different set of bases:

- **Space in your space**. If you add a layer of drywall, for example, to the existing walls, you'll gain virtually nothing. On the other hand, if you build a new wall even a couple of inches out from the existing wall, the air pocket between the new wall and the old wall will dramatically decrease amplitude.
- **Tiny leaks cause big problems**. Even small holes, such as the gap between a doorjamb and the door, will do serious damage to your sound-blocking efforts. Airtight seals are critical.
- **The denser the better**. Dense materials have more mass and, hence, don't vibrate as much as less-dense or springy materials. Particleboard is a tad better than plywood, which is a bit better than drywall, which is better than acoustical foam for soundproofing.

Unfortunately, properly soundproofing can potentially be one of the most expensive aspects of putting your space together, because the most effective way to attenuate sound is to put a solid wall in its way. That usually means construction of some kind. Unless you're an experienced carpenter, it's going to take time and money.

One tip is to use multiple walls, rather than one wall or partition. Two or more walls with an air gap in between them will always give better results than a single wall of double or even triple the thickness, and the wider the gap, the better the sound isolation, particularly at low frequencies.

Cabling Basics

An oft-overlooked aspect of most home studios is proper cabling. Learn here from the mistakes of tens of thousands of home studio engineers before you: Don't use cheap cable or connectors.

Good connectors will have low contact resistance and hold up for years. Brands such as Switchcraft and Neutrik have been industry standards for some time, and you generally can't go wrong with either one of these brands. In general, stay away from Radio Shack, though their gold-plated connector types will do in a pinch.

Cables play an even bigger role in the quality of your audio signal. Even if the diameter, gauge, and construction are similar, two cables may have significantly different electrical properties—such as their respective resistances, capacitances, inductances, shielding density, tensile strength, jacket friction, and so on. This means you should look at your cable's specifications and keep them as consistent as possible.

Perhaps the most critical part of good cable is shielding. The best kind of shielding is foil shielding, but there is a downside: Foil-shielded cables are not the strongest, and they don't flex very well. Use foil shielding where cable movement is minimal—with racks and effects boxes, for example.

Braided and wrapped cables are a better choice for mic and instrument cables. Use cables with good-quality and stable insulation, with a tightly braided shield that is held firm by the outer jacket so the shield itself doesn't become loose when the cable is flexed.

BALANCED IS BETTER

In any recording environment, balanced connections are, absolutely, the only way to go. Balanced connections are far less likely to pick up interference from other cables, and the redundancy of two signal conductors in a balanced connection usually yields better quality audio. Balanced connections use two conductors carrying the same signal but with the polarity of one of them reversed.

KEEP 'EM SEPARATED

Audio cables can be particularly susceptible to interference from power cables. It's *very good* practice to keep the cables carrying your signal away from the cables carrying the electricity! One of the ways to accomplish this is by using a *snake*, which is a bundled set of audio cables inside additional insulation. Snakes are a bit more expensive than buying separate cables, but they will save you interference—and organizational—headaches down the road.

CABLE SPECS

The *impedance*, *resistance*, and *capacitance* of your cables and your equipment are probably the most important, and most confusing, part of a strong audio signal.

When you connect headphones to an amplifier, for example, the load (headphones) will draw some current from the source (amp). How much current is drawn depends on the impedance of the load in ohms. An ohm is a unit of resistance, reactance, or impedance, depending on the type of load; some loads are resistive and some are reactive, while impedance is a combination of both resistance and reactance.

Look for cable that has the least resistance and the lowest capacitance; resistance is usually measured per thousand feet, and good cable will be under 100 ohms per 1,000 feet.

With gear, the closer the impedance (the ohms) of the equipment being driven is to the source impedance of the device that's driving it, the more powerful the signal. It doesn't have to be perfect (and never is), but the closer the better.

In the Garage: A Dream Setup

This section briefly describes an example of a home studio space that requires some money, time, and careful planning. The idea behind this "dream studio" is to give you a glimpse of what you're getting into. The following list comprises just the fundamentals for a sound-isolated, pristine-sounding home studio space in the garage to be used as a music studio. Measurements of garage: 20 × 20 × 12, approximately 400 square feet.

- Professional, acoustically treated walls, ceiling, and floor so that maximum sound frequencies will be contained inside the studio and not disturb family members in the house, persons outside, or in nearby houses.
- Separate air conditioning/heating unit for the studio. Use of silencers, filters, and so on, so that incoming/return air ducts do not leak sound out of the studio. Incoming air should be silenced enough to enable recording without ventilation noise.
- Track lighting with quiet, nonfluorescent bulbs.
- Acoustically sound doors and windows: one door going into the house and one going outside to the driveway. The doors should have appropriate acoustical seals in order to contain as much sound as possible inside the studio.
- Dedicated electrical circuits and several sets of duplex (grounded) electrical outlets along each wall. Outlets must handle electric current fluctuations and noise caused by home appliances, air conditioning, and lighting, as well as radio, TV, and cordless/cell phone frequencies.

- Telephone outlet, cable TV outlet, thermostat control panel, light switches, and a high-speed Internet connection for zipping off mixes to clients or quickly uploading files!
- Acoustic wall around appliances, such as furnaces or water heaters, with acoustically treated pipe inserts into the wall so that sound will not leak through.
- Custom control room for mixer, computer, amp, and other control gear.

Total cost and time: Your mileage will vary, but figure at least $20,000 and around one year of project management.

In the Garage: A Practical Example

Another way to look at a garage studio is to figure out how to make small improvements that will increase sound quality while doing some minimal soundproofing. This example looks at the same garage as the one in the previous section: a typical garage with measurements 20 × 20 × 12, approximately 400 square feet.

- $10-per-square-yard carpet over a thick pad on the floor, covering the main studio area, about 12 × 12.
- Gaskets added to the doors so that isolation from the rest of the house is much improved. Noise from the street coming through the garage window is an occasional problem helped through the judicious use of extra-thick drapes purchased at the local thrift store.
- Speakers located to each side of the window, because speakers tend to move drywall as well as air. Because they are nearfield monitors, they're not right up against the wall. Hang them about 4 feet from the floor, equidistant from a 4 × 8 card table that will do as the main control table for the studio.
- Speakers about 8 feet apart, putting the sweet spot 8 feet from the wall along the center line of the room.

REFLECTION CHECK

You can check for reflections and phase interference by using a mirror and a flashlight. Set a mirror in the area of the mixer or on the mixing table (about where your head and ears would be during mixing), and then aim a flashlight from each speaker at the mirror. If a light beam falls back near the speakers, there is a potential reflection problem.

CHAPTER 2

- To combat reverb and standing wave problems, 2 × 6 R-19 fiberglass placed on the walls near the monitors to clean up short reflections and drastically improve the sound quality between the monitors. Adding a couple of panels along one of the side walls practically eliminates any standing waves; this also cuts down some of the low-frequency reflection coming from the corner.
- Two 4 × 8 particleboard bookshelves on the facing wall to the R-19. With a few strategically placed books, the bookshelves dramatically improve sound quality by diffusing and absorbing sound, while also adding some additional sound isolation benefits.

Total cost and time: About $300 and a weekend.

3

Assembling Your Digital Studio

Make no bones about it: The only way in this day and age that you're going to affordably achieve anything resembling a good sound is to use digital, computer-based home studio equipment. There are a few other places in this book that (hopefully) do an effective job of convincing you of this, but this chapter is not one of them. This chapter presumes that you are on board. It presumes you're sold on digital recording, and you need a little advice on how to pick and choose your equipment and get it all set up. To that end, in this chapter you'll learn:

- Which parts of a digital recording setup you'll use the most
- How much the hardware costs
- What constitutes a good system configuration
- How to choose a sound card
- How audio software applications work
- How to connect and route the studio components, choose cabling and connectors, and plan for wiring

Computing Audio

This is a curious time in the history of home recording. Thanks to market forces, improvements in manufacturing and distribution, and the proliferation of the Internet, the barrier of high costs has been all but eliminated for digital home studio recording. Digital recording for the home recording artist has never been more powerful or affordable.

What are the features? You can work much faster, easily edit waveforms, cut and paste to your heart's content with all the ease of a word processor, and keep all of your work in the pristine fidelity of the digital domain.

What are the benefits? You save time, money, and achieve audio quality that ten years ago was possible with only the most expensive equipment available. Your guitar sound will be better, your vocal performances cleaner, and your composition a lot closer to what was in your head when you wrote the piece. In short, you're a lot closer to the vibe—to the "right on"—today than you've ever been. Here's a quick list of some of the most "right on" aspects of your digital recording studio:

- Most upgrades to your "equipment" will be newer versions of existing software or new software products, and software is almost always less expensive than new, expensive outboard gear.
- You can cut and paste audio data in the same way that you can cut and paste text in a word processor. This is called nonlinear editing, and it significantly decreases the amount of time you must spend doing routine and mundane tasks. This also means you can easily play with multiple arrangements and tracks, and the only limit to the number of tracks you can record is the capacity of your hard drive and the speed of your processor.
- Software effects and audio enhancements are almost always cheaper—and easier to use—than their stand-alone counterparts. There are even virtual software synthesizers available that sound just as good or even better than the harder to find and very pricey hardware versions.
- Your audio stays in the digital domain all the time, meaning that you will rarely—if ever—experience a degradation in audio quality.
- The amount of space a computer-based system takes up, including an outboard mixer, is miniscule compared to using all external, analog equipment.
- Though noise can still be an issue, depending upon the type and quality of the system you use, it has become less and less of a concern due to advances in component cases and power supplies.

Sound too good to be true? Well, it's not! Order now for *rush delivery*! Seriously, there is another aspect of your digital studio that you're going to have to deal with—the learning curve. Unless you're already computer-audio savvy, there is really no way around it. Here are some of the most important points:

- If you're using a Macintosh system and other musicians you write or exchange jams with are using a Windows-based system, you may experience some incompatibility problems. This is less of a problem these days, because many Mac programs can now use the Windows Wave file (.WAV) format, but it is a potential problem to be aware of.
- Using the mouse and coordinating data on the computer screen takes some getting used to. If most of your experience has been with analog gear, you'll find using a mouse to be awkward and it will feel limiting to you. Since its introduction five years ago, the Cubase Virtual Studio has provided a graphical environment that is very similar to studio hardware, and you even have the ability to design custom console layouts to use for interfacing with real-world equivalents; furthermore, monitor resolutions,

colors, and mouse technology provide you with a lot of options. In general, though, using a mouse will never be as intuitive as turning a real knob, but you will acclimate to it with some practice. But cheer up, mixing board companies have recently released consoles that can control virtually every function of Cubase and its competitors via MIDI. So, turn that frown upside down!

- As you become more and more computer savvy, you are going to gradually become aware of the basic components of a Macintosh. Processors, RAM, and hard drives will invariably become a part of your audio vocabulary, because, as newer versions of software are produced (or conceived), you'll want to upgrade and take advantage of future technology and features. Don't be afraid of these components. There is nothing magical about them, and learning how to upgrade any of the parts in your computer requires only a little patience and time. This ain't rocket science!
- Above all else, remember that patience is truly a virtue when it comes to learning how to use a computer. It is like learning a new instrument, and, being a musician, you know that this takes a little time to get it under your thumbs.

Real-World Costs

Though component costs are currently at an all-time low, you're going to have to spend some of your cash. In other words, it may be cheap, but it ain't free.

At the time of this writing, the average costs for computer hardware, a mixing console, software, a CD-R or CD-RW drive to archive your music, and monitors are shown in Table 3.1. This table also shows comparable costs for a stand-alone digital audio workstation, or DAW.

WHAT'S A DAW?

The acronym "DAW" is also used, with more and more frequency, to describe any general digital audio setup, including a computer-based setup. In this book, you will always see it used to refer to a stand-alone, separate component—such as the Roland 2480 (see **www.rolandus.com**)—that typically includes a mixer, built-in effects, and a hard drive onboard.

Table 3.1
The basic costs of doing digital

Component	Computer	DAW
Computer	$999–4,600	-
Mixer	Starts at $199	-
Software	$329–800	-
Recording hardware/sound card	$149–1,000	$1,000–3,000
Monitors	$150–1,000	$250–1,000
Mastering/archiving	$99–200	$500–1,000
Total	$2,000–8,000	$1,750–5,000

Perhaps the most interesting thing about Table 3.1 is just how close the total price is to that of a DAW—yet the storage capacity of a computer hard drive vs. a DAW is typically much, much bigger (ten to twenty times bigger). And also remember, when you purchase a DAW, that is all you get. There is no expandability, which is really the name of the game when it comes to recording on a computer-based system.

Add to that the ability to use your computer for other tasks, such as word processing, e-mail, and the Internet to distribute and advertise your work, and there really is little contest.

A DEDICATED COMPUTER?
A few years ago, a dedicated computer for audio recording would have been practically your only option, due to slow processors and hard drives and expensive RAM. Today, it's not at all necessary, though it is still ideal. Having a dedicated machine for your studio will still minimize potential hardware conflicts. If you can't even think about the extra money for a separate system right now, having a separate hard drive dedicated to recording has some speed advantages as well.

The Software, Uh, Really Works Now!

Audio recording software has grown in leaps and bounds just in the last five years. This book focuses on Cubase SX/SL (see Figure 3.1), as well as Peak (see Figure 3.2) for some additional mastering and final mixdown tasks, but there are a number of other excellent programs available to do the same thing. Logic and Spark are two fine examples. All of these software applications handle both audio recording and MIDI sequencing to various degrees (Cubase actually has the best mix of both worlds).

Figure 3.1
Steinberg's Cubase SX/SL is the most full-featured value for Mac-based home studio recording today

> **A VARIETY OF VERSIONS**
>
> Just to get any confusion out of the way, there are two versions of Cubase available for the Mac. The basic version of the software, Cubase SL, is a fine, affordable program that has the real "meat and potato" features you need to get a song started and finished. Its more expensive brother, Cubase SX, contains slightly more robust features and is aimed a little more towards postproduction projects. The same goes for Peak, as there is a light version of Peak called Peak LE and a full-blown, more expensive version just called Peak. For more details on these different versions of the software, just visit the company websites: **www.steinberg.net** for Cubase and **www.bias-inc.com** for Peak. Rest assured, I will note any differences between the different versions along the way.

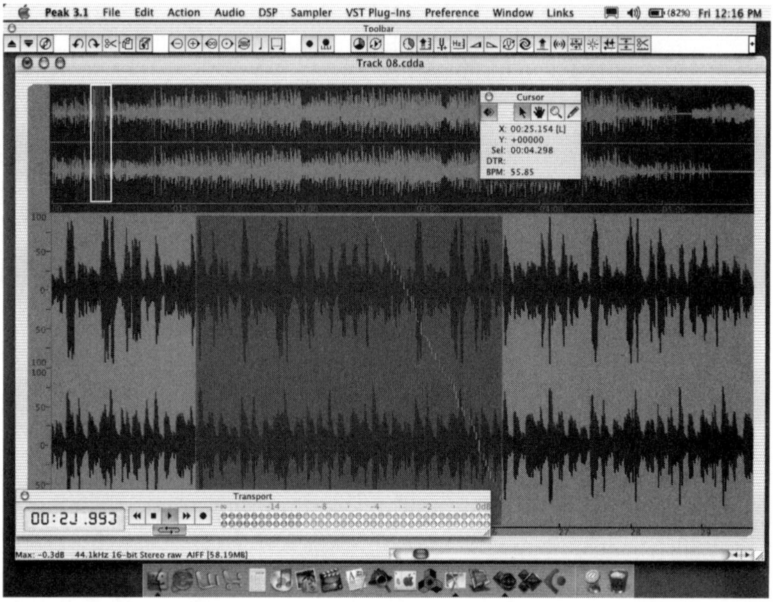

Figure 3.2
Bias' Peak is an excellent audio editing application for mastering stereo tracks

VST Plug-Ins–The Secret Ingredient

When Steinberg introduced their first original audio recording program called Cubase VST (Virtual Studio Technology), Steinberg also introduced their own original effect processor format called simply VST plug-ins. This original format gave users access to professional-sounding effects, without having to purchase very expensive internal processing cards or DSP cards (see the following note). The special feature about VST plug-ins is that they are designed to run based on the processing power of your Macintosh computer. As Macs have become faster and more efficient, so has the processing potential of VST plug-ins.

Since their introduction, VST plug-ins have taken on a life of their own. Because Steinberg released the source code as an open format, other companies started writing their own commercially available plug-ins. Even well-known hardware companies, such as TC Electronics and SPL, began releasing software versions of their very high-end hardware counterparts. At current count, there are over two hundred commercially available VST plug-ins to purchase. Even better, there are free plug-ins that have been released by well-known programmers. These can be found by going to websites such as **www.kvr-vst.com** or **www.harmony-central.com**.

TDM AND RTAS

Before the introduction of VST plug-ins, the standard format that software developers wrote for was a platform known as TDM (Time Division Multiplexing). This format was introduced and maintained by a company called Digidesign and is used in a very popular and widely used program called Pro Tools.

Although this format was and still is very popular, it is not very economical for home recording, because the required hardware is extremely expensive, not to mention the plug-ins. Digidesign has solved this problem by introducing yet another format called RTAS (Real Time Audio Suite). This can be found in their consumer-based products, such as the Digi001, 002, and the Mbox. As these pieces of hardware have become quite popular, so has this format, and you can be sure to find many software companies offering a multiplatform compatible version of their fine software.

VST plug-ins can save you time and money and rival results you can achieve from an entire rack of hardware. Not only do they sound fantastic, but they also have the ability to automate within Cubase. Figures 3.3, 3.4, and 3.5 are examples of popular plug-ins. Think of just about any effect—from any reverb type you can think of to a lush chorus to multi-tap delay to pitch correction—and it's most likely available as a plug-in.

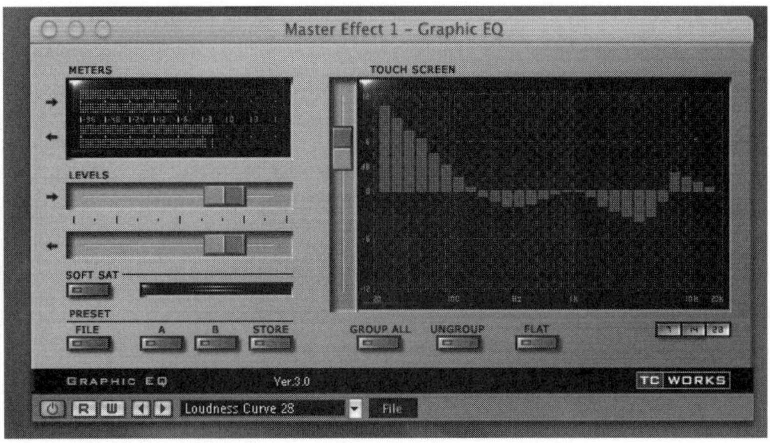

Figure 3.3
TC Works' Graphic EQ is the cat's meow of equalization

Figure 3.4
Steinberg's Reverb A comes included with Cubase SX and is a 32-bit plug-in with a truly unique sound

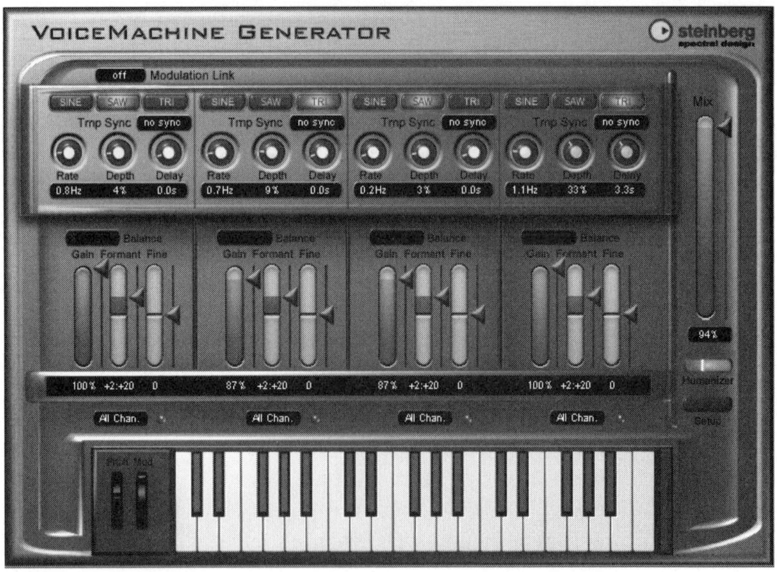

Figure 3.5
Don't have any back-up singers in your band? Not a problem—Steinberg's VoiceMachine can take a lead vocal and harmonize it via MIDI notes.

In a nutshell, VST plug-ins can:

- Literally replace any number of hardware racks, generally costing thousands of dollars, at a fraction of the cost.
- Avoid additional noise problems that can commonly be found in hardware effect processors.

- Work with any VST-compatible host-supported audio software you choose.
- Save you development time by giving you the ability to preview effects in real time before you commit them to your audio files. You can turn the effect off or on at any given time to "A-B" the effected track.

Let's look at that first bullet point in a little more detail. Plug-ins are very flexible when combined with your audio software; in terms of cost, there is no comparison. If you buy a good hardware reverb, for example, you will spend at least $200 for one box. With a plug-in, you're going to spend about half that amount, but when you need a different reverb mix for eight different tracks, all you need to do is load additional instances of the plug-in into memory. It's like having eight reverbs for the price of one. To make the deal even sweeter, most software companies provide plug-in bundles that include just about every kind of audio processor you can imagine—filters, distortions, flangers, delays, and even completely unique and unheard-of effects that just scream creativity. This *is* the way to go!

But Shouldn't I Be Using a PC?

The Windows platform is a wonderful operating system for home studio recording. If you use a PC or intend to, more power to you. However, this is not the platform this chapter—or this book—focuses on. Why? There are several reasons, and management thought you might like to know:

- **Value**. Five years ago, Macintosh computers were nearly impossible to afford unless you took out a second mortgage on your house. But now with great systems such as the impressive iMac starting at very reasonable prices, the Mac is not only a professional solution, but it is also a competitive consumer solution.
- **Power and flexibility**. One of the things that I really enjoy about using a Macintosh is that it is a nearly self-contained machine. Most commercially available "off-the-shelf" Macs come with just about everything you need. You have a great CPU, a fast hard drive, a Mac manufactured and approved motherboard, a good amount of RAM to get started, and in most cases your new Mac comes complete with a CD or DVD burner. All you have to do is purchase a more professional audio card. With PCs, you have to worry about every little component that is installed into the system, and whether or not all of these components will conflict with each other. Although most of these specifications can be easily tweaked to your liking, a Macintosh system is a welcome change of pace when you consider how much thought goes into designing, purchasing, and putting together a competitive PC-based computer.
- **Software**. Cubase SX/SL is the recommended recording software used in this book because it is the best *value* on the market today for a Mac-based digital home studio. But the good news is that Cubase is and has been available for many years on the PC as well.

- **Operating System**. The true lifeblood of the computer is the operating system, which is what runs the computer and the programs that you use. On a PC, the most commonly found operating system is Windows, for which there are several different versions available. This can become extremely confusing when you are a "newbie" to technology. With Macintosh systems, it gets a lot easier, as the most current operating system is Mac OS X, which is probably one of Apple's most streamlined and sexy looking operating systems ever. It is completely different from any previous Mac OS and is the system that we use for this book.

HOME RECORDING POWER! FOR PC

If you have a PC or intend to use one for audio recording, you will be happy to know that this book exists in PC-based form as well. *Home Recording Power!* for PC focuses on the Cakewalk program SONAR and Sonic Foundry's Sound Forge.

Macintosh, and the Wide World of Computer Geekdom

The first thing to be aware of in the Mac universe is the relationship between the computer itself and the sound card. This is an important relationship, because these two pieces are the heart of your system.

Briefly, the Computer

Obviously, no computer, no audio. The Mac you use for digital audio recording needs to be relatively powerful, and the three most important components—processor, RAM, and hard drive—can vary widely in power and cost.

For example, as this book goes to press, the most powerful processors are the G4 1.25 GHz chips. These processors are much more expensive than, for example, G3 chips that start around the 700 MHz range.

If the question is, "Do I need a dual processor G4 system?" then the answer really is "No." This is different than the question, "Can I use a dual processor G4 system?" to which the answer is probably "Yes."

The reason has everything to do with the way audio is processed on a computer, or any electronic device, for that matter. The faster the processor, the more quickly algorithms for effects and audio processing can occur. This is important for things like adding real-time reverb to your tracks as you record them, for example. The reality is that today's bare minimum G3 processor found on an iBook or iMac is around 700 MHz to start, and that's more than capable of recording and playing back a large number of simultaneous tracks. However, if you can afford a faster processor, get it. Buy a system that you can grow with over time. It will only decrease your processing overhead and allow you to more comfortably take advantage of new effects algorithms and plug-ins as they become available, as well as decrease the amount of time it takes for audio processing to occur. This means you could, for example, apply a larger number of effects at the same time. There is nothing quite as disappointing as having to stifle your creativity right in the middle of recording or mixing your new song because your computer can't keep up.

RAM, or random access memory, also plays an important role, but it has a lot less to do with effects processing than your processor. RAM is most important for recording and playing back lots of tracks simultaneously. Generally, the more you have of it, the better. A bare minimum of 128 MB will work for you to get started, but 256 MB or more will make your day. Because RAM prices are so reasonable these days, invest in as much of it as you can afford.

Hard drive speed is even more critical—because of the way in which Macs manage loading programs into memory from a hard drive, and because of the rate at which audio accesses that memory. Recording audio onto your hard drive takes roughly 5 MB per track per minute (when recording at 16 bit), and at that rate, space gets used up in a hurry. In addition, the more hard drive space you have, the more room you have to store tracks as well as mastered songs after they're mixed. Let me give you another of many "real world" examples that you will find throughout this book. If you have a five-minute song and you are playing back or recording up to 32 tracks of 16-bit audio, you can expect to use around 800 MB of hard drive space, plus you will need 50–60 MB in addition for the audio mixdown, because this also takes up hard drive space. Now, even though hard drives have increased in size and speed over the years, you can see that you need to get a hard drive that is *large and in charge*. The good news is that the hard drives provided on Macs are plenty fast for audio recording; you just need to decide on the size.

At a minimum, here is a system configuration that will give you lots of pleasure for years to come:

- iMac or iBook with a G3 700 MHz processor or higher
- 30 GB or larger hard drive
- 256 MB RAM or higher
- CD-R or CD-RW for archiving finished projects (this comes with most Macs now)
- Supported sound card, 16 bit or higher

MY OWN SYSTEM

I'm sure that after reading through all of these system specifications, you are wondering what kind of a Macintosh I (MP) use in my studio and what I used as a reference to write this book. The truth is that I used an off-the-shelf iBook as my sole computer for this project. After increasing the RAM to its maximum potential, I found that I had a decent computer to do some recording and mixing. As much as I would love to purchase that dreamy new Quicksilver G4, my pocketbook (not too mention my wife) felt it was a little too rich for our blood at the moment. But this is a good thing for you as a reader to know that the performance and processing that I will mention throughout this book is based off of what Apple considers to be one of the slower computers in its current catalog.

So, here is a quick breakdown of my iBook:

- G3 processor running at 700 MHz
- 640 MB of RAM
- 20 GB hard drive
- DVD/CD-RW drive
- M-Audio Quattro USB audio card and MIDI interface

The Sound Card

So, what about your sound card? A supported sound card allows you to listen to previously recorded tracks and record new tracks at the same time, and this is absolutely essential for overdubbing. Sound cards that come built-in the iBook, iMac, and eMac are only capable of playing back previously recorded tracks, such as drum loops. The good news is that there are many great sound card solutions for your ideal home recording studio, thanks in part to the introduction of audio cards that work with either USB (Universal Serial Bus) or FireWire. To select the right audio card, you've got to decide which features are most important to you. These include:

- **Inputs and outputs**. There is a wide variety of audio cards that support multiple inputs and outputs, which is fantastic for recording large ensembles or a full drum kit. With that thought in mind, there are also quite a few audio cards that have just a stereo pair of audio inputs and outputs. This is more useful to that singer/songwriter type of musician who is just planning to record him or herself and no one else. Although the latter might be the ideal solution for you now, try to imagine yourself expanding your studio a few months or years down the road. Try to anticipate the kind of recording that you plan to do in the future. You may very well want to consider an audio card that supports at least four ins and four outs, as they are quite reasonably priced. For best results, quarter-inch input jacks should give you not only the best audio quality, but also the most reliability.

- **Bit-depth**. It is impossible to find an audio card for the Mac that does not have at least a 16-bit recording potential. In fact, most cards today have at least a 20-bit to 24-bit recording potential. Why is this important? Simply put, it gives you an ample amount of headroom, so your recorded audio does not distort. Plus, you can achieve a much richer and more professional sound.
- **Interfaces**. Different sound cards have different types of additional interfaces, such as MIDI, ADAT, or S/PDIF. MIDI is important if you plan to sequence (see Chapters 9 and 10 "Wading in MIDI" and "Diving Deeper into MIDI," respectively); ADAT is important if you plan to use a digital mixing console that supports it or if you use Alesis ADAT machines. S/PDIF is only useful if you have a mixing board or external gear that can take advantage of it, such as a DAT machine. MIDI inputs are generally found on an add-on component to the sound card—called the breakout box—and, frankly, they are more of a convenient way to input MIDI data quickly than using an additional MIDI interface. ADAT, for most sound cards, uses optical connections built onto the actual card itself that interface with very delicate and expensive optical cable. S/PDIF inputs for most sound cards use coaxial-based RCA connections that use an electrical digital signal—instead of an optical signal—to transmit audio data.
- **Software support**. Stable software drivers are essential for satisfactory sound card performance. Make sure that the audio card has an ASIO driver. This is Steinberg's original driver standard that makes it possible to use this card with your Mac and Cubase. In addition to the recommendations that you will read in these pages, the local music store technical salesperson is another good source of information. Remember, they are musicians too, and in all likelihood, they will have tried a wide variety of the available cards. As this is the age of the Internet, don't forget to visit the company website of the sound card you are considering. Make sure they offer technical support. They might even have user forums where you can post questions, and other users around the world can offer solutions. And just one other word of caution—if the company does not have a released and working ASIO driver for the Mac, but they have a Beta driver, *do not buy it.* Beta drivers are test drivers that companies release to the public to get their opinions and feedback. They are not meant to be fully developed and tested drivers.

The section "Choosing and Installing a Sound Card," in Chapter 11 "Fun-Da-Mental Audio," goes into a lot of detail about choosing and setting up your sound card. Suffice it to say, a cheap sound card is something you should try very hard to avoid.

If the Computer's the Heart, the Mixer's the Brain

There are actually *two* brains—the mixing capabilities of your software and an external mixer, if you use one. Should you use an external mixer? There are two schools of thought on this one.

Nearly Virtual Mixing

If you buy a sound card that has enough inputs and outputs (8/8 as a minimum), you may not need an external mixer at all. You can use the inputs and outputs on the sound card and do your mixing within Cubase, for example. There are even sound cards that double as both a sound card and a mixer, such as the Event Electronics EZBus, the US428 from Tascam, and the SI24 from Roland. These are good solutions, as they also have direct support for Cubase or similar programs and can access their virtual mixers. Another workable solution is the incorporation of MIDI fader controls. These are hardware units that look and act like hardware mixing boards, but they are set up to access the virtual mixer within the recording application by sending MIDI data. As they do not process audio, like a hardware mixer, they are an affordable solution for those of us who still want a tactile controller for our audio. This has been a growing trend over the past couple of years, and there are many available by name brand mixing board companies, such as Mackie, Roland, and Behringer. Steinberg has even gotten in on the game by releasing their virtual mixer, known as the Houston, as shown in Figure 3.6. Now that we have looked at the pros of the MIDI fader control setup, let's look at the cons as well, just to be fair.

Figure 3.6
The Steinberg Houston is a MIDI mixer that can access every function of Cubase via USB

The first issue with this mixing setup is an ease-of-use problem. Depending on the sound card you use, you will either have a breakout box (a separate box hooked up to the sound card, with quarter-inch jacks, and usually rack-mountable), or you will be dealing with cables coming directly from the card. If you don't have a breakout box, you will find it difficult to manage the different cables and keep track of which instrument is plugged into which input.

If your sound card uses a breakout box, then you're in much better shape. However, depending solely on the inputs and outputs of the box means that you have no pre-fader control over the input signal, and you'll lose at least one of your outputs, because you'll need a pair of outputs for monitoring left and right channels. That brings you to three stereo channels or eight mono channels on an 8/8 sound card! In addition, you lose the ability to mix down a piece of stereo equipment, such as the stereo outputs of a keyboard, to a mono input pre-fader, which can be frustrating if you don't want to lose both signals in the original sound or instrument.

Mixing the Old School Way

The second solution makes a bit more sense: Use an external mixer in addition to your sound card, unless you choose to purchase an all-in-one sound card/mixer solution. You can then use the software mixer to submix tracks, if you have more audio tracks than mixer outs, and take advantage of pre-fader adjustments to volume as well as some basic analog equalization, via the mixer, if needed.

In addition, you can use the mixer as your monitoring system and take advantage of features such as XLR connections for your microphones and onboard phantom power for mic(s). If you can afford a digital mixer, then you can even keep everything in the digital realm, too, but a digital mixer is not critical. The amount of signal loss you will experience by using a good Mackie or Behringer mixer is minimal compared to the ease of use and flexibility of the board.

You've Got to Have Connections

Properly connecting your equipment is, frankly, mostly common sense. You need to know the kinds of connectors and the lengths of the cables you'll be needing, because at some point you'll need to power it all up.

Cables

In order to keep cable lengths as short as possible, lay out your equipment beforehand, measure the distances between the needed connections, then plan and buy accordingly. This isn't just a cosmetic thing: Cables that are too long may cause additional hum in the signal path, whereas cables that are too short are too easy to accidentally pull out or trip over.

WATCH OUT FOR INDUCTANCE

Choosing appropriate cable lengths also ensures that you aren't coloring the tone of the signal running through the cable any more than necessary. Cable *inductance*—how much the cable signal changes and when—often varies depending on how the cable is lying; usually, the more bunched-up it is, the higher the inductance. This is not good, because the higher the inductance, the more likely it will alter the tone of the audio signal.

Buy decent-quality cables. Don't scrimp unless you're on the slimmest of budgets and have no choice. Most music stores, even ones catering to professional musicians and audiophiles, sell an assortment of everything—from the low-end junk cables to the very high-end, expensive wires. The best route is to take a look somewhere in the middle. You'll be hard-pressed to find significant sonic differences between the midrange-priced cables and the high-end stuff.

If you can, go with stock wire and buy your connectors separately. It's a bit more of a pain to solder connectors in, but in the long run, it's less expensive and easier for you to maintain consistent quality.

Cable prices vary, depending mostly on capacitance and resistance, and the rule is the lower the better. Low resistance means a stronger signal, and low capacitance means better frequency response. Cable with good resistance is under 100 ohms per 1,000 feet, whereas capacitance is typically under 100 pf (picofarads) per foot.

LOW IMPEDANCE CONNECTIONS

Most, but not all, semiprofessional and professional microphones (the Rode NT1, for example) are "low impedance," which means the mic is designed to connect to a preamp with an impedance of under 1,000 ohms. Conversely, there is "high impedance," which runs from 20,000 ohms on up and covers just about all guitars and electronic instruments.

Make sure you match impedances. Low impedance connections are quieter and can use fairly long runs of cable of 50 feet or more, whereas high impedance connections should use the shortest cable possible—usually less than 25 feet.

The connection between the cable and its plug is responsible for about 95 percent of all cable failures—it's rarely a short or a break in the middle of the cable somewhere—so this step is critical. Look for:

- **Metal casings**. Forget about the cable if the connectors do not use metal covers.
- **Heat-shrink tubing surrounding the wire underneath the connector**. You can check for this by unscrewing the connector.
- **Connectors that appear to be solid and heavy duty**. Flimsy connectors are a recipe for trouble.

> **WATCH OUT FOR SHODDY CONNECTORS**
>
> Generally speaking, cables with premolded connectors are a bad idea. Plugs that have tight, plastic molded ends may look pretty but will fail, and fail fast, at the junction of the wire and connector. Many premolded cables also use poor shielding and are very high capacitance, making them less efficient at delivering low-noise sound.
>
> Cables that are spiral wound are also a no-no (most of them, anyway: There are some high-end cables that are self-retracting, but they are very, very expensive).

The cable itself should be fairly heavy, up to a quarter-inch thick for high impedance cables, and almost as thick for low impedance XLR cables. Check for a manufacturer's warranty as well—it can come in very handy, and a number of midrange cables offer lifetime warranties.

Figures 3.7, 3.8, and 3.9 show low impedance, high impedance, and speaker cable, respectively. Note that speaker cable differs most from the other two types in that it is not shielded. This is typically the case, and it is fine for the speaker cables connecting to your monitors. All other audio cables should always be shielded—either low impedance or high impedance, depending on the piece of equipment. No exceptions to this: Never use unshielded cable for anything other than speakers.

Figure 3.7
A low impedance cable is a balanced connection with two main wires and shielding

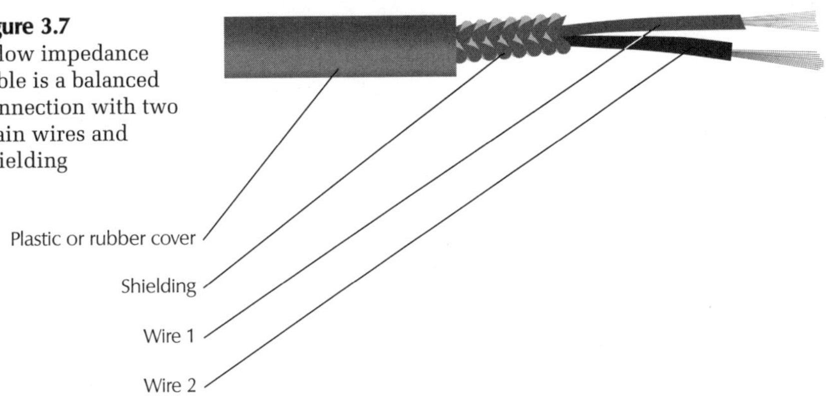

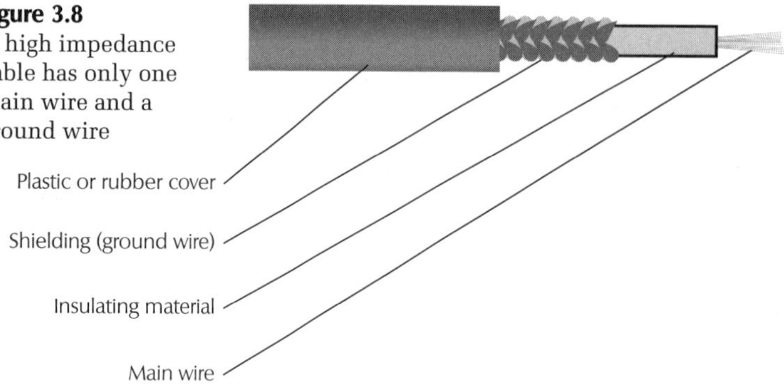

Figure 3.8
A high impedance cable has only one main wire and a ground wire

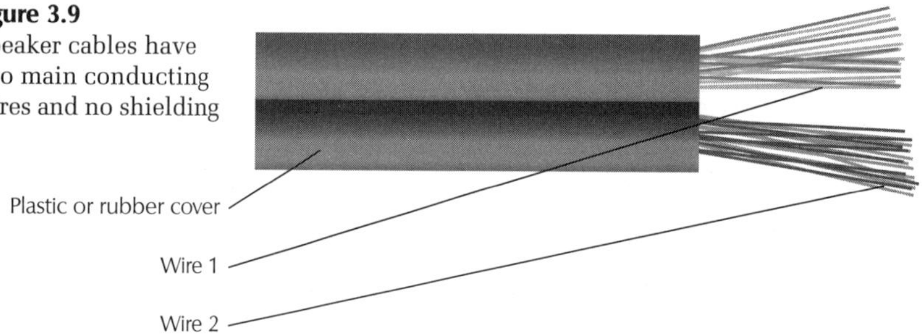

Figure 3.9
Speaker cables have two main conducting wires and no shielding

Connectors

You also need to determine the types of connectors you'll need; most likely, they will fall into one of three categories: quarter-inch phono plugs, XLR, or RCA.

- **Quarter-inch plugs**. These are the most common in any home studio, and you'll use them to connect most of your gear. Switchcraft (**www.switchcraft.com**) is pretty much the industry standard, but they aren't cheap. They are, however, far superior to connectors purchased from the likes of Radio Shack and other hardware retailers. This is not to knock Radio Shack: They are the only game in town on a Sunday at 4:30 in the afternoon, and thank Buddha for 'em, but you do get what you pay for. A quarter-inch plug will have a ring tip, which is the main signal wire, while the rest of the plug is the ground.
- **XLR connectors**. These rugged plugs are used in mics as well as in some PA systems. Mic cables that use XLR connections at both ends typically have a male connector at one end and a female connector at the other, and with low impedance gear, can be easily strung together for increased distance. XLRs have three pins—two for the main signal wires and the third (along with the rest of the plug) for the ground. Make sure when you wire

an XLR cable that you mark which pins go to what, to avoid wiring it backwards.

- **RCA plugs**. RCA connectors are the least common type of connector in most studio gear, but you will invariably have to deal with them. If you have to move RCA-based cables around too much, they will quickly become, for the most part, unpredictable and noisy. If you use gear with RCA plugs, it's not a bad first place to check if line noise suddenly pops up out of nowhere.

THE JOY OF SOLDERING

To do all this cabling and connecting stuff right, you're going to have to splurge for a soldering kit and learn how to use it. (*Hint*: Read the kit's manual.) Don't just jump right into it—you want to *avoid* damaging connectors and wire when you work on your cables.

To keep the frequency of expletives down, don't forget to put connector covers on the cable *before* you solder the connector to the cable. That way, you won't have to un-solder what you just soldered. Make sure you put the cover on facing the right direction, too.

In addition to solder, use electrical tape liberally—for instance, around the wires you solder to the connector and any potential stress areas in the cable itself.

Actually, the most difficult part of soldering is probably not the soldering: It's stripping the wire and dealing with braided shielding, but over the long haul, you'll save money and get consistently better sounding recordings, hands down.

The only downside to becoming the soldering expert mother always wanted you to be is that the activity itself spews out poisonous chemicals, such as salicylic acid and pinene. Breathing in these fumes has been known to cause headaches, nausea, eye diseases, and worse. Proceed with caution.

Electric Studioland

In addition to cabling and connectors, don't forget about the electrical outlets you'll be plugging everything into. The physical location of your gear should be as close as possible to an outlet, and you should use outlets—a dedicated circuit, if possible—that are not being used for other appliances or electrical sources in the house.

In fact, one of the most common causes of electrical fires is the improper use of extension cords. If you're using a typical-quality household extension cord and running it from an outlet to all of your studio equipment, for example, ten to twenty devices or more, spend a few bucks on a halogen fire extinguisher, which is specially designed to put out electrical fires.

In addition, if you're the kind of person who makes performance art with power strips, then make sure you buy strips with built-in circuit breakers or surge protection—the kind that will shut down in the case of a short. And if any of your gear has internal fuses (power amplifiers, older synthesizers, speakers), use only the fuses recommended by the manufacturer. A spare fuse or two ain't a bad idea, either.

In short, use the best surge protection, electrical-related components, and extension cords you can afford.

If you don't have relatively easy access to an outlet, or if your recording space is in need of power or rewiring, do yourself a favor: Hire an electrician to do whatever needs to be done. Unless you are totally comfortable with electrical wiring or have significant experience with wiring, don't mess with it. You probably wouldn't defend yourself in court, nor would you perform open heart surgery on yourself. Fooling around with anything electrical without knowing precisely what you are doing is just as serious, if not more so.

Finally, if you can hook up all of your gear so that you can power it all up with one switch, you'll find the process of getting started with any session (especially those spur-of-the-moment creative impulses) much easier than if you have to power up every single piece of equipment while the bell tolls. This goes for your cable connections, too. All this is facilitated through the use of a good patch bay, which is discussed in detail in Chapter 13, "Recording and Mixing."

4

Listen to You

If you plan to record vocals, this chapter is for you. Heck, even if you have a master plan to conquer the classical music world, this chapter is for you. Why? Because the human voice is just about one of the hardest things on earth to record well, so knowing a thing or two about vocal recording techniques will spill over into any recording you do.

This chapter covers the following topics:

- Evaluating your own vocals
- Selecting a vocal microphone
- Grouping vocal recordings and background vocals
- Vocal mixes and effects

Your Voice

Let's start by taking a quick look at the physical mechanics of a singing voice. If you "don't sing" (kind of like the way some musicians "don't dance"), you may feel the need to skip over this section and go on to "Selecting a Microphone." But stick with this one for a bit, because understanding a little about how a singing voice works will go a long way toward helping you understand how to record it.

That said, it should be noted that the human voice is a complex topic unto itself and is the subject of countless books, university courses, and, these days, websites. This chapter, let alone this book, can in no way cover the subject in detail. In fact, there are a number of techniques for learning to sing well and some of them are quite different in their approach. Most of them start with the same fundamental concepts, though, so we'll cover them briefly here and try to interpret them in a way that makes sense.

Posture

Good posture is a big deal for an opera singer and probably a bit less of a big deal for a rock singer, but it winds up being important in either case. The bottom line is that you'll generally sing better if you're relaxed and don't feel tension in your upper body. Try not to slump your shoulders too much or stick your chin up (or out), but stay relaxed.

Breathing

Breathing properly when singing is always critical, but unless you practice your breathing for a long time, it's difficult to understand just how it helps. After all, it's an involuntary gig to begin with, as we all remember from our sixth-grade health class. At a minimum, the more easily and comfortably you breathe, the better your singing will be. This means not singing when you have a lung infection or after your second pack of Marlboro Lights. Keeping your sternum lifted up so that your diaphragm moves more easily is the general rule of thumb.

Support

"Support" refers to how you control the air pressure in your lungs in order to hold the note or maintain accurate pitch. It's also how loudly or softly you're singing and, to some extent, your tone. All this relates to how much air you're pumping in and out of your lungs; the key is to stay relaxed and consistent to keep from producing sudden bursts of air.

Registers

The idea of a "register" varies widely, but what most vocal coaches (and listeners!) agree on is that breaks, or noticeable transitions between notes, in a singer's register are not pretty. For example, if your voice cracks, you are "breaking up" and it generally doesn't sound good. The idea (or ideal—both work in this case) is to maintain a consistent sound, which, practically speaking, often means simply singing within your range and knowing how far you can push yourself during a performance.

Resonance

Resonance often has more to do with what happens as the air is on its way out of your mouth and into the microphone. How you move your jaw and tongue, a nasal inflection, the movement of the soft palate, and even the larynx itself all have a great deal to do with resonance. Doing your Bob Dylan impersonation is an example of changing how your vocal sound resonates.

Expressing Yourself

Expression is the most subjective part of singing and also the most critical. The "dynamics" of your voice, its unique tone, the speed with which you sing, how clearly you sing the words, and the interplay of the lyrics with the notes are the things that ultimately have the most impact on your singing. This has as much to do with the material itself as it does your emotional state when you sing.

No one can tell you how to express yourself, because that's your unique vibe, what you bring to the table as a singer (and sometimes as a recording engineer recording the singer). At the moment of expression, you aren't typically thinking about your posture, breathing, or resonance—or any of the other physical elements that are helping you to express yourself in song.

In fact, that's the whole point of this section—that your expression should be *your* expression, not something else. What's "something else?" Well, it could be your impersonation of Bob Dylan, which, unless you're a stand-up comedian or a singer in a cover band, is *Bad* with a capital "B."

Above all, you should strive to be yourself, to sing how you sing (whatever that is) and not imitate someone else. This is one of the biggest problems with singers and has been the cause of many a band's demise, because often singers who keep trying to emulate their favorite rock stars end up being unable to get in touch with the material they're singing. Though imitation might be the sincerest form of flattery, it is also a sure-fire way to sing off-key, out-of-range, and in a completely different emotional direction than the song itself demands. This makes for mediocre performances and, in most cases, mixdown nightmares.

Don't fudge on the one thing you've got that nobody else has—you. Even if you're covering a song, it's your interpretation of the song and your own expression of it that matter, not your attempt to try to sound like the singer who has already brought his or her own unique vibe to the song.

End of soapbox. High horse dismounted. Let's move on to something you *should* imitate as much as your wallet will allow—the intelligent selection and acquisition of a damn good microphone.

Selecting a Microphone

When it comes to recording vocals, as a home recording artist, you have fewer choices and less flexibility than a professional studio engineer. First, in a home recording setup, you are less likely to use a microphone for anything other than vocals (with the possible exception of guitars and live drums—see Chapters 6 and 7, "Getting the Guitar Sound" and "No More Drummer Jokes, Please!," respectively. Second, as a home recording artist, you may not be able to afford the space, instruments, or multiple microphones necessary to make a lot of live recording very worthwhile.

That said, the growth of home recording over the last several years has brought with it an explosion in the number of cheap microphones available as well as cheap microphone preamps. Manufacturers have responded to budding musicians and home recording artists everywhere by creating lots of low-end models that, when you get down to the nitty-gritty, all sound about the same and give you the same horrible results.

WHAT'S A PREAMP FOR?

A microphone preamp is an amplifier that takes the microphone output signal (sometimes with the aid of a small DC 48-volt voltage circuit) and amplifies that signal from around –60 to –50 dbV to an acceptable recording level of either –10 dbV or +4 dbU. This is necessary because most microphones don't have enough signal amplification built in. The term "preamp" rather than just "amp" is used because the level of amplification is not typically enough to be heard clearly, but it is enough for an external preamp or mixer to amplify further. Yeah, you guessed it: "Preamp" stands for "preamplification."

USE YOUR PREAMP

Never record your vocals by plugging a mic directly into the 1/8-inch jack on your sound card. Use the mic inputs in your external mixer or a separate external mic preamp. The frequency response of a typical sound card's microphone input is not hot enough to give anything resembling a good performance.

Microphone Types

There are two fundamental types of microphones (there are a few others, such as ribbon microphones, but we won't cover them here): dynamic and condenser. Although dynamic microphones are cheaper, they don't pack anywhere near the punch of (usually more expensive) condenser mics for vocal recording.

Dynamic Microphones

Dynamic mics use a wire coil suspended over a magnet to pick up sound waves (see Figure 4.1). The coil moves in response to sound over the magnet, and produces voltage that is the electronic equivalent of the sound. Dynamic mics output a reasonably accurate reproduction of sound, but their accuracy is determined more by fluctuations in voltage rather than in the source sound, for example, your singing.

Small diaphragm dynamic microphones are far and away the most popular mics used for live recording and live performance. Because of their simple design, they can withstand a lot of abuse and they don't require a voltage source to work properly. Two of the most commonly used dynamic mics are the Shure SM58 and SM57 models, but there are many other, similar dynamic mics from companies such as Audio-Technica, Sennheiser, AKG, and Sony. At the time of this writing, most of them can be bought for less than $100.

AVOID ULTRACHEAP MICS

Those cheap Radio Shack mics that you can buy for $10 or the generic computer mics you've seen at the checkout stand are dynamic, small diaphragm mics, too. Unless you are on the slimmest of all possible budgets, don't touch them. No matter how good your voice or your singer's voice sounds, these mics will never give you a good sound.

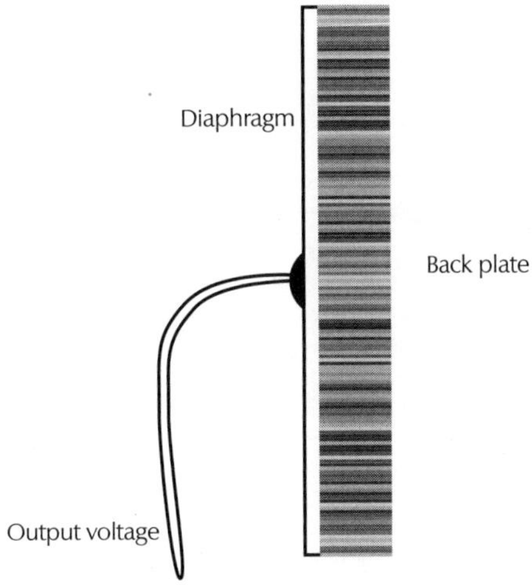

Figure 4.1
A dynamic microphone operates like a speaker "in reverse;" the "diaphragm" is moved by the air waves from sound

There are also large diaphragm dynamic mics. Though less common, they are used for very loud, bass-heavy instruments, such as kick drums, bass amp speakers, brass instruments, and, in some cases, guitar amps—no pun intended! They are not best for recording vocals, however (unless all your vocals are spoken word only). A very popular large diaphragm dynamic microphone is the ElectroVoice RE20, which has been a favorite among broadcasters and engineers (for drums) for many years, as has the Shure SM7.

The bottom line with dynamic microphones and vocal recording in the home studio is that, although you will get a fairly accurate general vocal reproduction, you will rarely achieve a warm, rich sound while accurately conveying the midrange and high-range frequencies—and the mids and highs are typically the most important part of a vocal performance. For truly killer vocal recording, you've got to consider a condenser mic—there's just no way around it.

Condenser Microphones

Condenser (or capacitor) mics capture sound a bit differently than dynamic mics. As shown in Figure 4.2, a condenser mic uses a stretched diaphragm running parallel to a thin, charged plate. Electrical current is sent through both the diaphragm and the plate, and fluctuations in the diaphragm create slight changes in current, producing an output signal. The charge itself typically comes from a DC voltage source—either a battery or, in the case of a mic preamp or mixer, 48-volt "phantom power."

The key to the condenser mic is its two-piece design and its plate, which is always charged. The diaphragm can also be made quite thin, so condenser mics tend to be much more accurate than dynamic mics, particularly in the mid and high frequencies. These are exactly the places you want accuracy when recording vocals.

The flip side is that condenser microphones are not usually as rugged as dynamic mics, which makes them difficult to maintain for stage use. However, with a minimal amount of care, they are perfectly suited to a studio environment.

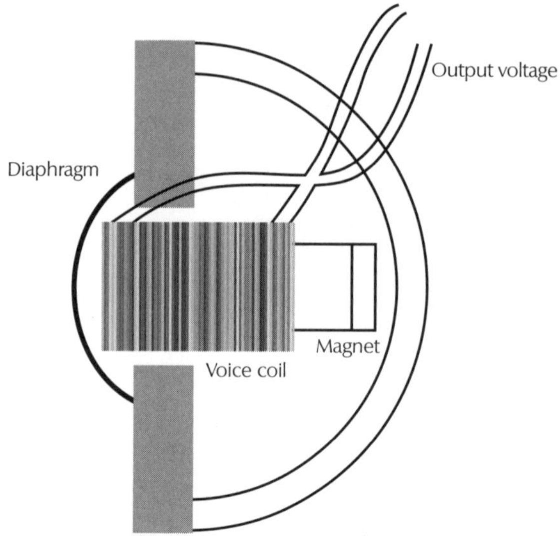

Figure 4.2
Air pressure from sounds against a thin diaphragm causes a condenser microphone to pick up detailed frequencies

Of course, just like dynamic mics, there are both small and large diaphragm condenser microphones. Small diaphragm condenser mics have great high-frequency response and are excellent for drums and cymbals, acoustic guitars, or just about any other stringed instrument for which high frequencies are critical.

For vocals, however, large diaphragm condenser mics are as good as it gets. With a large diaphragm, you achieve a fuller, warm sound, but you have all the advantages of a condenser mic's design—meaning the mids and highs are accurate and rich.

A number of condenser mics are worth mentioning. German-made Neumann condenser microphones are highly popular, from the vintage sound of a U 87 or U 89 to Neumann's recent tube mics, the M 147 and M 149. These are very good choices. AKG is another company that produces sterling-quality, large-diaphragm condenser mics. Their fairly recent C12VR model and the C-414 series are excellent condenser microphones and are popular in professional studios (as are the Neumanns).

Of course, the Neumanns and the AKGs of the world share one thing in common: They are not only expensive new (well into the thousands of dollars) but are also, in many cases, more expensive used (particularly the original, vintage U 87s and U 89s).

Thankfully, there are a few good, low-end choices that are, remarkably, very close in sound quality to the expensive mics. These economical large-diaphragm condensers have become quite popular just in the last few years. The Rode NT1 and NT2 are excellent examples of very high, yet affordable, quality. At the time of this writing, for example, an NT1 can be found for less than $200. The mic lacks some of the frills of expensive large diaphragm condenser mics—such as multiple response patterns, a pad, a roll-off filter—but that's just fine, because you don't need these accessories to get a stellar vocal sound with the NT1.

(That, incidentally, is why we're not covering these kinds of features in any depth.) Other good choices on the low end of the condenser cost spectrum include the AKG C3000B and the Shure SM87.

Response Patterns, AKA "Pickup Patterns"

Every microphone possesses a particular response, or "pickup," pattern—meaning the ability of the mic to capture all or some of the sound in the space surrounding it. (Note: Many large diaphragm mics feature dual diaphragms that can be switched between different patterns.) Although there are actually several different kinds of pickup patterns, most of them are based on three fundamental patterns.

Omnidirectional

A good omnidirectional mic is great for capturing sound in open spaces, making it ideal for acoustic instruments or live background vocals. An omnidirectional pickup pattern, as shown in Figure 4.3, is able to pick up sounds coming from all sides of the microphone.

Figure 4.3
An omnidirectional pattern is ideal for capturing ambience and sound in open spaces

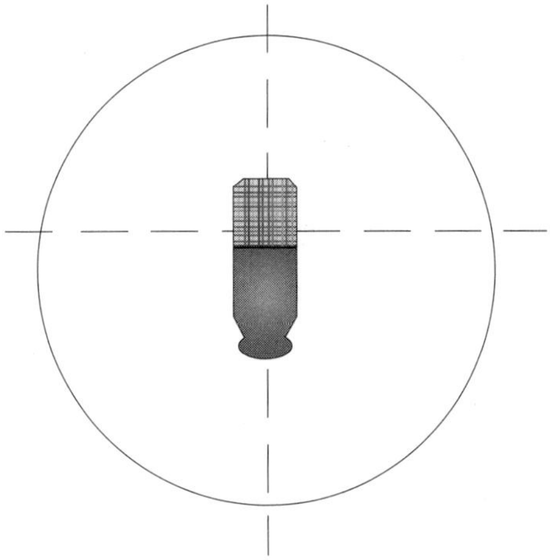

Cardioid (Unidirectional)

A cardioid mic pattern (see Figure 4.4) detects sound coming from directly in front of the mic, whereas sounds to either side are barely detected, and sounds behind the mic are ignored.

The cardioid mic pattern is an excellent pickup pattern for vocal recording in the home studio. Because sound from the back and sides of the mic come close to being ignored altogether, you'll pick up less unnecessary noise in a studio that isn't fully soundproof, while the front of the mic is dedicated to picking up your vocal performance. Cardioid mics are useful for live stage sound for the same reasons.

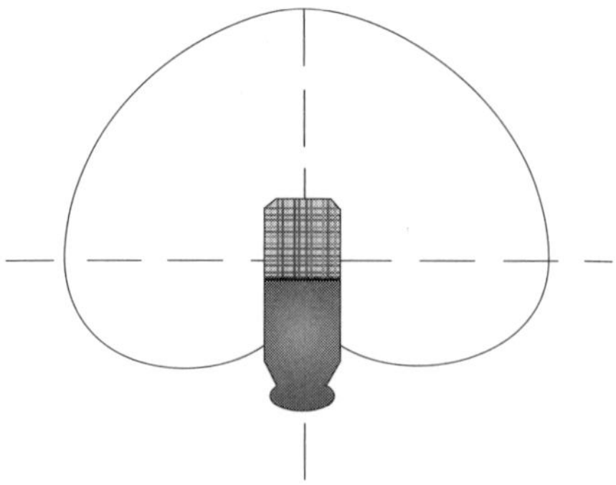

Figure 4.4
The cardioid pattern is heart-shaped (hence its name); its pattern of response makes it the all-around best choice for multipurpose recording in the home studio

Figure-8 (Bidirectional)

Figure-8 mics have a pickup pattern shaped like—yes, you guessed it—a figure eight, and they pick up sound equally well from both the front and rear of the mic, while ignoring sounds from either side. Figure-8s work particularly well in small rooms, for live classical music, and for generating a stereo mic field (see Figure 4.5).

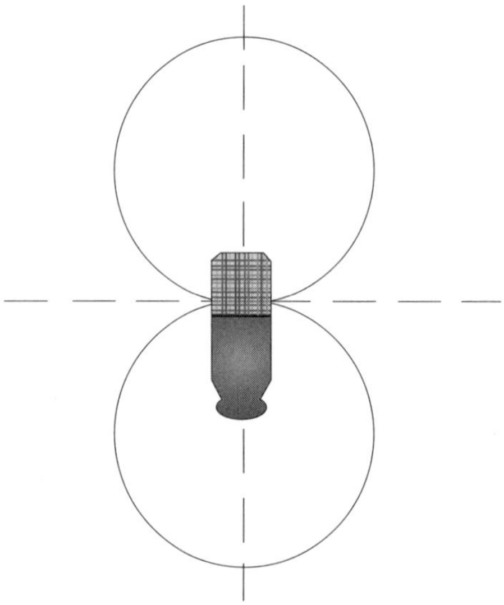

Figure 4.5
A figure eight pattern is useful for setting up a stereo mic field

STEREO MIC FIELD

A stereo mic field is probably something you won't be dealing with in the home studio, because you can achieve all of your stereo effects in the mixdown. It's most useful in a live recording situation in which you want to create a live stereo mix.

Vocal Microphone Placement

With a condenser mic, you're already one up on much of the home recording competition, because you've opened the door to capturing a vocal performance with a very high degree of accuracy, thanks to the high sensitivity of the condenser's design.

This does, however, bring up one small problem—a problem that exists in any case but is most certainly a problem with a condenser microphone—placement of the microphone in your home studio setup.

In Chapters 2 and 3 ("Choosing Your Space" and "Assembling Your Digital Studio," respectively), you learned about the important parts of putting together space and equipment that work with your budget, musical goals, and recording style. You learned that how you set up every piece of the equipment in the studio can greatly affect your performance and mixdown process. This is especially important when recording vocals.

This is a good place to put on your finicky, particular, anal-retentive hat; stressing over mic placement is actually going to be healthy for you in the long run, because the results will be worth it. Ask yourself the following questions:

- What's my singing style (or the singing style of the vocalist(s) I'll be recording)?
- How close to the mic do I like to get?
- How much soundproofing do I have in the studio?
- Am I using headphones or monitors?

Singing Style

How do you move when you sing? Do you plant yourself in one spot and croon like Sinatra (rest his soul) or do you feel the need to do gymnastics like Mick Jagger?

If you're a mover and a shaker—and you can't seem to keep it from happening—you're going to have a few problems in the home studio, and those will affect the kind of mic(s) you choose.

You'll probably want an omnidirectional mic so that you can hear all of the performance. The downside to this is that because of its wide pickup field, an omnidirectional mic is noisier than a cardioid or figure-8. This means you need a quieter room, and that means more expense (see Chapter 2, "Choosing Your Space").

Although there are no set rules, ideally you want to sing directly into the diaphragm of the microphone, which is called singing "on-axis." Singing on-axis is going to give you the most faithful reproduction of the performance, but it may not be the most intuitive way for you to sing or "work the mic."

Working the Mic

"Working the mic" is what many experienced vocalists do. It's different for every singer, of course, but it comes down to manipulating distance and position from the mic in order to accentuate the good areas of a singer's voice and play down the bad areas.

In addition, moving closer or farther away from the mic can also have a big effect on how intimate or distant the vocal line is. An experienced singer often uses slight changes in position to make parts of the vocal more or less dramatic. Of course, a singer isn't thinking about these things during the performance, and a singer isn't typically going to calculate or script the performance beforehand to ensure that the vocal line follows the material emotionally. It's a completely intuitive thing, as it should be.

Pattern Selection and Microphone Placement

As a home recording artist, you may have to dissect the process a little bit for your own vocal style (or the style of the singer you're recording). This is not far off from what a professional studio engineer must do. A full-time professional engineer gets to see and hear it all—from the mumbling, wobbly grunge singer to a stuttering choir to the vocalist who eats the mic as much as she sings into it.

But a professional studio has the luxury of employing different types of microphones in a fully soundproofed, controlled environment. This is probably not what you've got to work with, so you'll need to select a mic that, to a large degree, is based on how you work the mic. Here are some tips:

- For most any large diaphragm condenser mic, the ideal placement is to position it slightly higher than the vocalist's mouth, with the mic pointed downward toward the singer. This arrangement puts the vocalist almost directly on the diaphragm but has the advantage of providing a bit more breathing room and a more "open" feeling for the singer.
- How "dead" the room is can be critical to vocal recording. On a limited budget, you want the room as soundproofed as it can possibly be. The "natural" reverb in the room is something that, for a home studio setup, will ultimately be more of a hindrance than a help when it comes to mixdown time. You can (and will, in many cases, depending on your vocal sound preferences) add reverb or other effects during recording for monitoring only (that is, you don't actually record the effects, just the singing), but you should always record vocals completely dry.

KEEP IT DRY

Suggesting that you circumvent the natural sound of your recording space for the driest possible vocal sound is not exactly a commandment on the professional engineer's wall. In fact, in a professional environment, it can practically be bad advice. Because a professional studio has the resources (such as a few dozen expensive microphones and $500-a-sheet soundproofing material) that you don't have, professional engineers can afford to experiment with effects during recording, as well as how different spaces sound. As a home recordist, if your aim is to get the vocal as close to authentic as possible, while preserving the performance for maximum flexibility during mixdown, always record the vocals without any effects whatsoever.

- You'll want to use a "pop filter" (also called a "windscreen") to keep the "p's" and "b's" (and a few other consonants) from ruining an otherwise good performance. A pop filter prevents unwanted air blasts coming from the pronunciation of certain words and consonants from making their way into the recording.

POP FILTER ON A BUDGET

Pop filters can be had for as little as $20 up to well over $100. Here is the $2 alternative method that, incidentally, works quite well:

1. Obtain a pair of pantyhose from your local department store. Size and quality do not matter (unless you plan on wearing them first!), so the $2 pair or the 99-cent special will do just fine.
2. Procure a metal coat hanger from your closet or from the closet of someone you love.
3. Stretch the pantyhose (just the hose part, not the cotton crotch) over the hanger and fasten with a strong tape, such as clear packing tape.
4. Secure the top part of the hanger to your mic stand, just below the microphone itself, using a pair of pliers and/or additional tape. Alternatively, you can attach the hanger to a separate mic stand.
5. Bend your new apparatus so that the triangular part of the hanger (the part with the pantyhose attached) is positioned about 6 inches directly in front of the microphone's diaphragm.
6. Test your new invention by singing "Peter Piper picked a peck of pickled peppers" to the tune of McCartney's "Yesterday" and record the results.

Getting the Right Kind of Feedback

Headphones should almost always be used when recording vocals—unless you can afford a small, completely dead room with high-quality monitors just for singing. Even then, headphones are the surest way to hear the singing and the music as clearly and flexibly as possible. And it goes without saying that you do not want to deal with feedback from monitor speakers during vocal recording. With sensitive condenser mics in particular, this is exactly what you will be dealing with.

The Headphone Mix

Getting a good headphone mix is critical, for good reason: You want the headphone mix to sound as much like the finished product as possible, because the mix of the other instruments may have a huge effect on how the vocal line is performed.

This shouldn't stop you from experimenting with changing the headphone mix as the vocal takes wear on, though. In fact, this can be crucial. When you're singing, the most important part of your performance tends to be the volume of your voice in the mix relative to the volume of the other instruments. For some singers, hearing themselves loudly and clearly is important; for others, inspiration comes more easily if the music shares equal billing or is louder.

REVERB DURING RECORDING

Adding a little reverb for warmth to a vocal headphone mix—while still recording the track dry—can often extract a slightly more passionate performance. The reverb tends to smooth out your voice so that you sound a little better than you, well, sound!

But as time wears on, changing up the volume levels of the other instruments in the mix can go a long way toward keeping a singer inspired and "into" the song. Be willing to change the volume levels to keep the inspiration high.

Headphone Mix for Multiple Vocals

When you're recording, it's not hard to distinguish a lone singing voice over a music mix, sans other vocals. It can be exceedingly difficult, however, to pick out the lead singer from a choir of other voices—particularly if you're doing the singing!

A tried-and-true technique for singing the lead vocal over backing vocals (or vice versa) is to listen with only one ear to the headphone while singing. It seems pretty obvious and works quite well—kind of like that old bend-your-ears trick you may have experimented with in third grade—but you'll want to be careful not to record audible leakage from the unused side of the headphones. Make sure the unused headphone is held tightly against your head to keep the leakage to a minimum.

That brings us to the subject of multiple vocals in general. The next section is a closer look at some techniques for recording both multiple vocal lines and backing vocals.

A Multiple Vocal Primer

As a home recording artist, adding additional vocals can be some of the hardest work you'll do—next to mixing all those vocals down (see Chapter 13, "Recording and Mixing" for more details).

Unless you're doing post-Laurie Anderson, experimental, crowd-noise, ambient music, if you intend to record more than one vocal track into the song, it's usually for one of three reasons:

1. To add vocal harmony or a countermelody to the song
2. To reinforce the vocal line by doubling (or tripling, or quadrupling) the line
3. Both 1. and 2.

Okay, so technically, it could be for three of three reasons, but you get the point: You can reinforce any sung line by rerecording it or duplicating it as many times as you want (commonly known as "stacking" vocals), or you can simply add different parts.

As you'll see, which direction you head ultimately has less to do with how the song is written and more to do with the dynamic of the song as it unfolds during both arranging and recording: Do you want big and glossy vocals or stripped-down, natural harmonies? Let's briefly look at both approaches.

Stacking Vocals

Stacking vocals—recording the same lines over and over or duplicating those lines in your audio recording software—is a common technique (think Brian Wilson). It produces a fat, somewhat glossy sound that tends to hide flat notes and pitch problems.

An important aspect of stacking vocals is rerecording the same performance rather than simply copying one track over and over using your digital recording software. Why? Because the subtle differences in the performances create bits of dissonance that give each performance a slightly different vibe. This produces that full, "wall of sound" sound. Though you may be tempted to fire up Cubase and start layering vocal tracks by copying performances to new tracks, predictable results are hard to achieve.

It follows that in the home studio, you can stack effectively by singing and recording the line over and over, but you can also achieve a very similar effect by employing a vocal "harmonizer"— an external device that works in real time or during mixdown—or by using a software effect that can transpose a vocal line to whatever pitch or part you desire. There are advantages and disadvantages to each.

Vocal Harmonizers

Vocal harmonizers work by adding on the harmony parts you specify in real time. At the time of this writing, these pieces of hardware (from small box devices to rack-mount units with more features) range in price from about $300 upwards of $2,000 or more.

A vocal harmonizer is a rather sophisticated piece of effects gear. It works by employing algorithms that transpose your voice in real time to any number of steps above or below each note you're singing.

The least expensive units typically have less capability, but they are still remarkably good. Digitech's Vocalist Performer, for example, is less than seven inches square and weighs about a pound, and it can provide up to two harmony vocals to accompany your vocal performance. It even offers three reverb presets for different room ambiances. With only six possible harmonic variations, you can combine and create hundreds of different stacks.

It also has doubling capability, which is just enough pitch transposition to create dissonance.

More expensive models are MIDI-equipped and provide almost unlimited combinations of harmonies at every half-step along the scale (they also do straight-up pitch shifting in a number of other scales and some remarkable things with dissonance). The bottom line is that a vocal harmonizer can be a very useful addition to your vocal performances if stacking the vocals suits the dynamic of the song you're recording.

> **MORE ON MIDI**
> For excessive detail on MIDI, start with Chapter 9, "Wading in MIDI."

Software Harmony

Another option is mixing the harmonies during mixdown through the use of software or VST plug-ins that alter pitch. There are numerous applications available these days that do just that, so it shouldn't come as too much of a surprise that the most significant aspect of pitch-shifting software is just how widely the quality varies.

For example, the standard pitch-shifting algorithm that comes with Cubase (see Figure 4.6) is not going to produce a realistic wall of harmonic sound, although it is a vast improvement on the earlier version. The pitch shifter in Steinberg's VoiceMachine plug-in is slightly better, but there are a number of other VST plug-ins on the market that will give you a higher-quality shift in pitch. Melodyne by Celemony (**www.celemony.com**) is probably one of the best programs for changing the pitch and length of digital audio files, but at a price tag of $999, it's not the most cost efficient way to go.

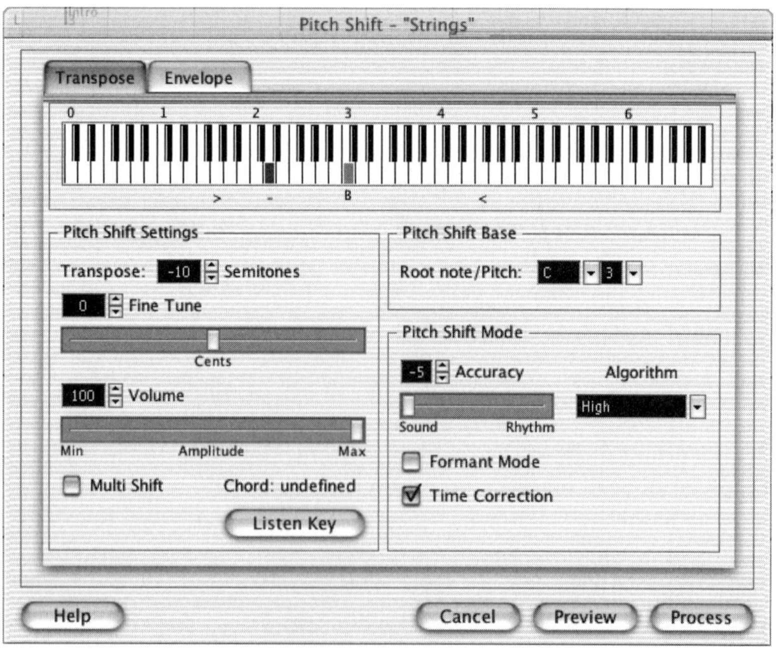

Figure 4.6
The standard pitch shifter in Cubase is great for playing around with, but it doesn't give a very realistic sound

HOW ABOUT PITCH SHIFTING THAT PITCH-CORRECTS?

If you've ever put everything you've got into a lead vocal, only to discover that you've missed the pitch mark a few times, you know the frustration that comes with trying to "fix" a vocal performance. It seems that the more you punch-in, edit, copy, and paste, the more the emotional vibe of the performance degrades. Even if you do finally get the flat spots edited out, you always seem to lose that original "special something" that was in the performance.

The Antares Auto-Tune VST plug-in (it's also available in a single rack-mount piece of hardware) is a great example of a solution to this problem. Auto-Tune is a set of very well-written algorithms that correct pitch deficiencies with great precision, in real time, at a speed as fast as 4 milliseconds (which is faster, by the way, than MIDI, which runs at around 7 milliseconds).

Auto-Tune has an automatic mode for quick and easy use and a graphical mode for more anal-retentive tweaking. The graphical mode is useful for tasks such as clearing up small, unwanted inflections, removing vibrato, or employing unusual scales.

Toward a More Perfect Harmony

If you're going for a more natural, stripped-down harmonic sound, you usually start by limiting the harmonies to one or two parts, and you rarely, if ever, double the vocal lines. The result is a more realistic harmony, something you can't achieve very easily through stacking. If you want to evoke a sense of intimacy, for example, this technique works best (think The Eagles).

In terms of backing vocals, there is another layer of reality to this approach, however. The reality is that to achieve an intimate, more natural-sounding backing vocal track, you'll need to plan on doing a minimum of effecting and/or compression to the track. This is because, rather than doubling your vocal takes for that thick, "wall of sound" vibe, you'll most likely be piecing together the best parts in the final mixdown.

This also means reevaluating the kind of mic you need as well as the sound of your recording space. In order to successfully pull together a number of recordings of the same parts and use them in different places, you want the most consistent sound you can get in the first place—otherwise, you'll have a devil of a time getting the different takes to match up, not to mention normalizing the volume of the different tracks.

By default or design, achieving a more perfect harmony is more difficult than stacking vocal tracks, and you're simply limited in how far you can go with the subject of the next section: vocal mixing.

Vocal Mixing

The reality of home studio recording is how involved you are in every aspect of a project. If you write the music, play the instruments, sing the vocals, record the tracks, and then mix it yourself, your objectivity almost vanishes. And if you have to spend hour upon hour getting the mixdown just right, you no longer have anything approaching objectivity: You have become so close to the project that an objective set of ears is impossible.

Such is life, and there's not a lot you can do about it. You don't have $300 an hour to hire a professional engineer to provide that objectivity for you, so you have no choice but to reach for it yourself.

It follows then that you want to do as little mixdown as possible, but not at the expense of denying yourself enough room to capture the right performance. It's a balancing act, and one you'll only begin to start walking once you've got a few more mixes under your belt. The next sections will help you get a feel for the kinds of vocal mixing challenges you'll be facing.

> **TRACKING**
> The word "tracking" is just another way of saying "recording a track." If you crash a party at a professional studio, use the word "tracking" and they'll think you're one of them.

Troubleshooting Vocal Mixes

Each mix is different, but you'll notice that with almost every mix, several common problems can crop up again and again. Being as close to the music as you are, you may not always notice them, though, so this section discusses what to look for and remember during vocal mixdown.

The Problem Could be Noise

Most people easily recognize distortion or unwanted noise, but knowing what causes it and how to avoid it is not always so easy.

The easiest distortion to understand and fix is the ugly crackling noise that happens when you overload an AD/DA converter during digital recording or when you've cranked up the mic's input gain way too high. The solution is obvious: Lower the mic gain until you're consistently normalizing (maximizing the strength of the audio signal with the rest of the mix) the mic's signal path. The trick is not to lower the gain so much that you introduce other kinds of noise, such as humming or RF noise.

There are two ways to approach getting the gain just right, and both of them should be utilized:

1. Check the mic's maximum SPL (sound pressure level) rating and don't exceed it. For example, the Rode NT2 has a maximum SPL of 135 db, which means that anything louder than 135 db is going to distort, period.

2. Experiment with the microphone! Get to know the mic before doing any "real" recording by putting it through several test runs, recording the tests, and playing them back to compare notes. Write it all down, and do it again. After you get to know the mic and how far you can push it with your gear, you won't need to write anything down. But until then, do the math.

There are also all kinds of other noises that make their way into your vocal mix that are not so obvious, and, of course, it's usually your other gear that's causing the distortion. Determining exactly which piece of gear is causing the problem is the difficult part. Other mics, a mic preamp, every mixer bus you use (and sometimes the ones you're not using), the computer or DAW (digital audio workstation), your other instruments—any of these can add distortion whenever their electromechanical limitations are exceeded. The only way to get a handle on all this is to understand what those limitations are, and that means experimenting with levels and cracking open a few manuals.

Because almost all manuals for any kind of recording or musical gear categorically suck, this is not an idea that will get you up in the morning, so look at it this way: If you test your gear once and take a few notes, you may never have to reach for a manual again (yeah, right).

The Problem Could be Space

One of the easiest mistakes to make in the home studio is to overcompensate for the room's sound (and lack of soundproofing) by adding too many effects to the vocals. Reverb, delay, chorus, and all those other cool, exotic VST plug-ins you just installed are great tools, and they go a long way toward adding ambience and realism to your vocal mix, but overusing them will take the life out of your performance before you know it.

Different effects have different parameters for you to control to manipulate the output of the effect; covering them all could turn out to be a very large book. The effect you'll use the most—and the one that can give you the biggest headaches—is reverb.

Reverb falls into three main areas: plate reverb, room reverb, and hall reverb. Plate reverbs usually offer shorter decay and, therefore, are best for vocals, whereas room and hall reverbs are generally best for your other instruments.

DECAY TIME

Decay is the amount of time it takes for a reverb to fade. Short decay times put a little edge back into your vocals when the lines start to bunch together in the mix, whereas long decay times create a kind of sustain effect that can be useful for dramatic transitions, such as build-up between a chorus and a bridge.

The clever way to apply reverb is to use it according to the individual need of each vocal part—not applying it to everything at once. If you overapply reverb to the entire vocal mix, you push the vocal sound further and further away from the rest of the mix, until the sound is too distant to be understood. And what you want is depth—not a misunderstanding.

Another way to compensate for a less-than-optimal recording space is to make judicious use of panning. The concept of panning is really simple: Every signal of every track you record can be placed at any point on the surface of the "stereo plane" (the audio landscape that represents your music being outputted to two or more speakers) to create variable sound positions, or a "three-dimensional" vibe to your vocals.

Experimenting with different pan settings can be quite revealing. For example, say you've recorded four similar vocal tracks, each with about the same volume and effects level. Table 4.1 suggests the kinds of variation in the mix you can generally expect by trying different pan settings.

Table 4.1
Panning variations

Pan Settings	Result
All Centered	All of the vocals are blended closely together.
1Left, 2&3&4 Centered	Vocal 1 is much more present in the mix than the other vocals.
1Left, 2Left, 3Right, 4Right	Vocals 1 and 2 blend together, as do vocals 3 and 4, but the distance between the two pairs is very wide.
1Left, 2Left, 3Left, 4Right	Vocal 4 is somewhat distant from the other three vocals, and even more distant from the music.
1Left, 2Right, 3&4 Centered	Vocals 3 and 4 tend to blend with the music, and vocals 1 and 2 tend to compete with each other for room.

Table 4.1 is a generalization—your own mileage will undoubtedly vary according to the kind of vocals you're recording and your own style of music. But you get the idea: Panning is a very effective way of accentuating vocals when they're out of control and you're pulling back on them when necessary.

The Problem Could be the Level

As we touched on earlier in the chapter, the human voice is highly prone to wide (some might say extravagant) dynamic fluctuations. Couple this with the way you or the singer works the mic, and you've got the potential for a lot of hard-to-handle level adjustments to make in the mixdown.

When this happens, compression is worth every penny you'll pay for it. A compressor can level out peaks in a vocal performance (or any other performance—bass, for example, is very commonly compressed during mixdown) by attenuating levels that go where you don't want them to. This applies to both boosting levels as well as quieting them, and smart use of compression is almost miraculous in its ability to make a molehill out of a mountain (or vice versa).

Compressors vary widely in price. You can purchase anything from a small guitar-pedal compressor for around $50 to a sophisticated, knob-ridden, rack-mount unit for thousands of dollars. There are also a number of good VST plug-in compressors on the market.

In general, a good place to start compressing is with a compression ratio of about 2 to 1, with a small release, and with the gain at around 5–7 db.

It should be noted that although using a compressor is an easy answer, it's not always the best answer. For example, the quickest and most effective technique is usually just to select the offending area of the vocal track and lower or raise the level.

The Problem Could be the Frequency

EQ can be your friend or it can be your enemy—but most of the time it's going to be your friend. Though Chapter 13, "Recording and Mixing," covers equalization in some detail, it's worth a mention here specifically with regard to vocals.

EQ is one of the more subjective aspects of listening to music. That's why even the cheapest of today's boom boxes have some form of EQ, because everyone likes to hear the music just a little bit differently. But there are a few guidelines that are useful for getting the most out of your vocal performances as they relate to the rest of the mix.

For example, in a typical pop song, the biggest concern is usually the relationship between vocals and drums. A good general tip here is to try and match the EQ levels of the lead vocal with the kick and snare drums so that they tend to dominate the song together—so that they occupy the same musical cubbyhole, if you will. Another way to even out your "wall of sound" backing vocals a little is to drop back on the 1 K to 3 K frequencies.

STOPPING SIBILANT SOUNDS

Another battle to be fought and won in mixing is the elimination of "sibilant" frequencies. These frequencies are commonly found in vocal tracks in which words start or end with the letter "S." Speaking or singing these words in succession causes a distortion in the S-frequency spectrum. To kick this problem in the butt, a company called Sound Performance Labs (or SPL) developed a piece of hardware called the DeEsser. This hardware helps hone in on the unwanted sibilance and removes it from the mix. SPL also went one step further and introduced the DeEsser as a VST plug-in for Cubase. Steinberg then took the DeEsser and included it with the Cubase SX package. If you have the Cubase SL package, you can still find the SPL DeEsser as a separate VST plug-in at your local music store.

Table 4.2 shows the general effects of boosting vocal frequencies in some of the most common ranges.

Table 4.2
EQ treatments

Frequency	Result
200–500 Hz	Warm, thick, smooth
1 K	Hollow, edgy, banging
3 K	Punchy, excited, hot
5 K	Bright, poppy, clear
7 K	Slightly brighter
10 K and above	Breathy, airy, sparkly

Of these frequencies, 5 K is the one you'll end up being concerned with the most when it comes to mixing vocals. 250 Hz or so adds more warmth to your vocal performance, and 500 Hz is sometimes very helpful when smoothing out harmonies or adding body to a lead vocal. If you're mixing backing vocals and you've already tweaked the levels to where you want them, try easing back or forward in the 5 K to 7 K range to get the most out of your EQ. If you're equalizing multiple lead vocal lines, you may also want to play with the 10 K and higher ranges to add a little spark and realism back into the performances.

PHASE CANCELLATION

If you're using more than one microphone for vocal recording, you run the risk of encountering problems with phase cancellation. Phase cancellation occurs when frequencies in one vocal performance cancel out frequencies in another, and vice versa. The amount of cancellation can vary widely. In general, the only way to prevent phase cancellation is to alter mic positions or attempt to reverse the phase by using an external adapter or your mixing console (or DAW), if it supports reversing phase.

The Zen of Microphones: Guidelines for Vocal Satori

Okay, so maybe the title of this section is a bit strong, but, hey, you want to end on a high note, don't you? The following are some quick and dirty, yet highly useful, tips to remember for recording and mixing vocals:

- Always use your best mic for vocals—for some people, this is a no-brainer, because you have only one mic!
- Monitor your vocal performances with all the effects you want, but record them dry.

- Don't overdo reverb unless you just can't sing!
- If you are using a DAW or software recording, use a high-pass filter during mixdown—it can keep the vocal from becoming too muddy.
- Use headphones when recording vocals. Sealed headphones (the Sennheiser HD25 is a good example) are much better than open designs.
- Boosting frequencies between 200–300 Hz will make almost any vocal thicker.
- A short delay of up to 50 ms (milliseconds) can boost the "size" of your lead vocals and make them sound a bit "fatter."

5

Keyboards and Synths

Make no mistake. A good synthesizer is the lifeblood of your home studio. I can vividly remember days of long ago when I vowed that I would never use a synth in my music and that I would keep it real with acoustic instruments. Well, this book is a testament to me eating those words and then some. There are so many great synthesizers on the market today, both new and old, that can provide the ideal texture or flavor that your music never previously knew. Even with guitar being my primary instrument, I still reach for my synths and drum machines to start writing a new tune first. But with all of this potential, there is a lot of mystery and confusion that comes with purchasing your first synth. This chapter shows you:

- How synthesizers work
- The differences in synth technology
- What kinds of synths are available
- An alternative to traditional synthesizers—virtual synths
- How to select the right synth
- How different genres of music use synthesizers

Key Choices

There are lots of synthesizer choices—from sampling modules to digital stage pianos to full-fledged workstations to software-based synths on your computer. The main thing—other than General MIDI—that they typically share in common is expense: Unless you're rich, you'll probably be able to afford only one, at best a handful, of these instruments or modules.

To get to the heart of the kind of synthesizer you'll really use—the kind that makes you want to play it every time you see it—there are a few things you should know. Think of them as the Three Commandments of buying a synth. If Moses had been a musician, here's what he would have brought down from the studio with him:

- Thou shalt know a thing or two about the technology of the synthesizer.
- Thou shalt know what's available, what to look for, and the common similarities and differences between synthesizers.
- Thou shalt not get so caught up playing the ultracool sounds in the music store that thou forgetest that most of those sounds will never make their way into your recordings.

If you follow these commandments, you may just find yourself in synth heaven. The rest of this chapter is a roadmap showing you how to reach that longed-for spot.

The Technology of Synthesizers

In the strictest sense of the word, a synthesizer is an electronic device that produces sound. In the common sense of the word, a synth is an electronic musical instrument.

Various synthesizers produce their sounds in different ways, and most are equipped with a piano keyboard. Though a keyboard is the most popular type of input device, a synth can use just about anything, really, such as mouthpieces, guitar strings, drum pads, or even your computer's mouse or keyboard, to control sounds. Whatever you use, the reality of what you're doing is simple: You operate a series of switches that turn sound circuits on and off.

Hence, synthesizers "synthesize" sound that can be used on stage or recorded along with natural instruments or other synthesized sounds. Some synths are used to mimic acoustic instruments, such as flutes, brass, drums, or guitar, whereas others are used as electronic sound canvasses, capable of creating unique sounds that could never be created with acoustic instruments.

Historically, one of the first known electronic synthesizers—perhaps *the first*—was the "Cahill Telharmonium" built by Thaddeus Cahill in 1902. This "instrument" used a 200-ton array of 145 Edison dynamos that produced different pitched hums according to their speed; each of these coils was about the size of a refrigerator and, together, they filled an entire floor of a building in New York City. This made the whole setup a bit hard to gig with, so the output of the Telharmonium was "broadcast" over telephone lines.

MORE ABOUT THE TELHARMONIUM

At the time of this writing, you'll find a complete write-up on the Telharmonium online at **www.obsolete.com/120_years/machines/telharmonium/index.html**.

The earliest *portable* synthesizer was a device invented in the 1920s by Leon Theremin. The theremin consists of two antennae that create an audio circuit that can be modulated by moving a hand in between the antennae—one for controlling volume and the other for pitch. Brian Wilson used a theremin to create those otherworldly sounds in the song "Good Vibrations." Although this is a very antiquated form of synthesis, it is still very sought after and has been reconceived many times over by companies such as Big Briar and Alesis. If you are really interested in learning more about the theremin, go to your local video store and check out *Theremin: An Electronic Odyssey*. It is a wonderful and at times disturbing (he was kidnapped by the KGB) biography about Leon and his groundbreaking invention.

Other early synthesizers that attempted to build complex sounds from scratch with individual analog components were too big and expensive for anything other than strictly academic purposes. They were very unstable, often drifting out of tune, but in time, engineers made them more reliable and practical to use. Most notably, Robert Moog's Minimoog synthesizer (see Figure 5.1) captured the imagination of the music world in the late 1960s. One of the standout records of the '60s was Wendy Carlos' "Switched on Bach" in which Wendy performed various classical pieces of music by J.S. Bach on Moog synthesizers. This may very well have been one of the main reasons why synthesizers became so popular, as it was then commonly found in quite a few recording studios and concert halls.

Figure 5.1
In its time, the Minimoog was revolutionary for its compact size

Oscillators

In the land of synthesizers, the primary source for generating sounds is the oscillator. An oscillator is a circuit that produces waveforms, which are types of audio waves. Early synths employed voltage-controlled oscillation, meaning they were operated by analog circuitry.

Each waveform has its own recognizable audio thumbprint; there are three basic waveforms—the sine, square, and sawtooth waves—from which almost all synthesizer sounds are produced. These are shown in Figures 5.2, 5.3, and 5.4, respectively.

Figure 5.2
Sine waves produce sounds that are pure and flute- or bell-like

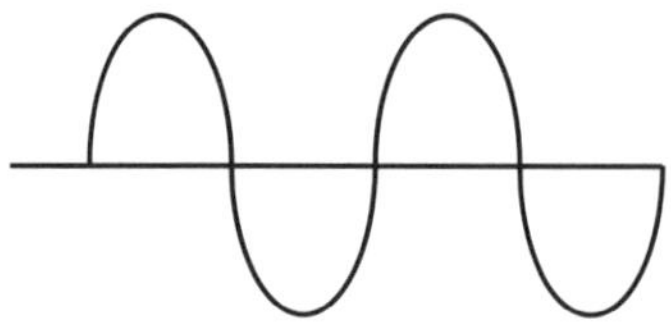

Figure 5.3
Square waves typically sound bright and hollow

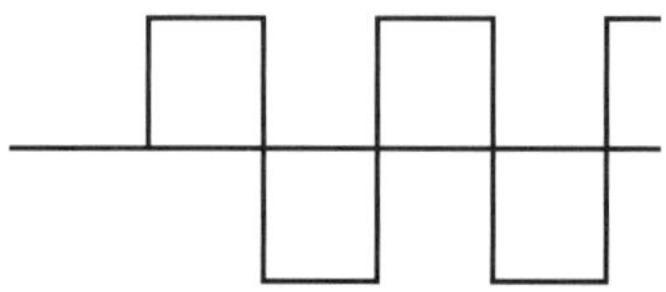

Figure 5.4
Sawtooth waves tend to sound bright and brassy

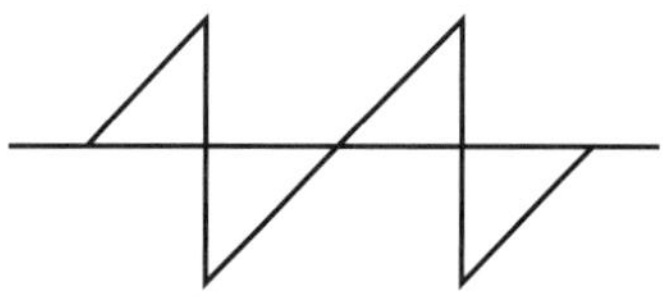

Of course, there are other types of waveforms, most notably rectangular waves, trapezoidal, and trigger waves. These, however, are essentially derivatives of the three fundamental waveforms.

MAKING NOISE

Some synthesizers feature a special source component called the white noise (or pink noise, in the case of early Moog modular synthesizers) generator. White noise is a waveform that would resemble a snow blizzard if measured on an oscilloscope. It is sometimes used to create special effects, such as wind sounds or percussion instruments that are atonal in nature.

One of the most interesting facts about waveforms is that they maintain their basic shapes irrespective of changes in frequency (pitch) or amplitude (loudness). In fact, this leads to one of the most distinguishing abilities of the synthesizer as an instrument: It can generate a perfect sine wave.

Filters

One of the most powerful modulators available on a synthesizer is the filter. By removing different ranges in a waveform's frequencies, filters can alter the quality of that waveform. In fact, a sawtooth waveform can be reshaped into a mellower sine wave with proper filtration. This approach to synthesis is called subtractive synthesis (as opposed to additive synthesis, which combines simple waves into more complex waveforms) and represents the basis of sound generation on many synths, old and new. In essence, the tone control(s) on your home stereo are just simple filters.

The way in which a filter acts upon a source waveform depends upon the type of filter employed and its "cutoff" setting. For instance, a low-pass filter "subtracts" all harmonic overtones above 1000 Hz with a cutoff at 1 kHz. Unfortunately, filters don't do their job perfectly due to extraneous frequencies, known as "rolloff," which pass through as the filter closes in on a signal.

Some of the most common filters are:

- A low-pass filter, which rejects frequencies above a cutoff setting
- A high-pass filter, which rejects frequencies below a cutoff setting
- A band-pass filter, which rejects all frequencies outside a predetermined band of frequencies
- A band-reject filter, which rejects only the frequencies within a predetermined band of frequencies

Filters can also have resonance, which refers to the slope of the filter's cutoff level. For example, when resonance is set high—meaning frequencies closest to the cutoff level are emphasized—a sort of vibrational effect occurs when any object comes in contact with the waveforms initiated by the sound source.

In general, the amount and kind of resonance is dependent on the makeup of the object. For example, the soft trailing tone of a piano after its hammer has struck has a completely different kind of resonance than what is created by your pick on a guitar string. However, on a synthesizer, the resonance created by a filter occurs at bands of frequencies usually either below or just above the cutoff level, and most synths are capable of some far-out resonances.

Envelopes

The purpose of an envelope generator is to add dynamics and flexibility to synthesized sounds, something that occurs naturally in the acoustic world but has to be made to happen in the synthesized world.

The envelope generator model evolved out of the standard low frequency oscillators that were voltage-controlled on early synths. There are four stages in the process of envelope generation: attack, decay, sustain, and release (ADSR). An envelope generator is a single ADSR oscillation that produces a dynamic contour each time a note is played or a key is struck.

ENVELOPES VS. LFOs

Technically speaking, envelopes were created to provide variable voltages set off by a single trigger as opposed to the continuously variable voltages provided by LFOs (low frequency oscillators).

Attack and Decay

Consider a banjo and a cello (not two instruments you'd likely hear playing together). The picking style of a banjo player is very different from the bowing of a cello in many ways, but one important difference is the time it takes to produce the actual source sound and bring it to full volume. A pick does so quickly, but a bow is quite slow by comparison.

In a synthesizer, the time it takes for a sound to reach its initial full volume is called the attack time, and it's the first variable piece of the process of envelope generation. The next piece is the decay time, which is how the harmonic content of a sound behaves just after it has begun. Envelope generators control the amplitude (volume) of the sound during both attack and decay, as well as the cutoff of the filter. Most often, both the volume and the filter are controlled by the same envelope generator; however, they can be controlled by separate envelopes.

Exactly how does it work? Consider an acoustic guitar: When a string is plucked, a waveform with lots of harmonic overtones is quickly produced. Then, the string is held and many of the harmonics begin to trail off. An envelope generator can replicate this event by rapidly amplifying the source signal and opening the filter connected to it (a short attack). This produces a loud signal with many frequency overtones. Thereafter, the envelope generator begins closing the filter, rejecting more and more upper harmonics (decay stage).

Sustain and Release

The point at which a guitar player holds the vibrating string with his finger corresponds to the sustain level of an envelope. During sustain, the filter stays partially open, shaping the source waveform into a desired timbre. The volume may also be affected at this point, because the level is often less than the peak level of the attack stage.

The final stage is the release. This defines how a sound behaves once the key is "released" and source waveforms stop being generated. Amplification begins to go toward zero and the filter completely closes. On an acoustic guitar, the release time is moderately fast, but this can vary depending on the resonant properties of the guitar body.

The envelope generator itself falls under the more general category of synthesis controllers. A controller is any component, analog or digital, that is applied to one or more of the primary sound generating elements: source, modulator, or amplifier. Controllers give you great flexibility by extending a keyboard's dynamic and sound shaping potential. In addition, a controller can also be the electronic keyboard or other input device itself. It "controls" the source waveform's frequency.

LFOs AS CONTROLLERS

Here is where things can get a little confusing. In the three-pronged model for sound generation, the oscillator is the chief sound-producing element. But an oscillator can also serve as a controller. For instance, a low frequency oscillator (LFO) can be applied to a signal to create a vibrato effect. The oscillator creating the waveform and the oscillator causing the vibrato effect are two separate components. In fact, the frequency required to make a waveform is much higher than the one needed to produce vibrato.

The same LFO can be applied to amplification, causing dramatic changes in volume, as if you were repeatedly turning the volume knob on your stereo up and down. In addition, some LFOs can actually be inserted into the frequency range, effectively making them HFOs (high frequency oscillators), though the results tend to be very distorted.

The key is to keep the different components as separate entities in your head. In fact, the very early experimental synths were made up of distinct pieces of hardware ("modular synths"). These massive components had to be reconfigured with patch chords to achieve the same results we enjoy today with a few simple buttons.

PATCHES

You'll sometimes hear an instrument sound referred to as "patch"—particularly by some equipment manufacturers. This comes from the days when patch cords had to be used to reconfigure components on early synths.

Digital Synthesis

Early on, Moog and others dealt in the world of analog synthesis, through direct involvement with hardwired oscillators, filters, and waveforms. Very quickly, though, a computer chip found its way into synthesizer architecture, and a whole new type of synth was born. Today, MIDI-based digital synths offer a ton of benefits, such as onboard effects, user-definable patch banks, and extended polyphony (the ability to produce lots of instrument sounds, or multiple voices, simultaneously), and they stay in tune! Ironically, a number of digital synths these days are even used to emulate the old analog sounds.

Digital synthesis comes in two basic flavors—FM (frequency modulation) and sampling, or wavetable synthesis.

GRANULAR SYNTHESIS

Another approach to synthesis is called granular synthesis. Granular synthesis gets its name from the fact that it generates thousands of short audio events, or "grains" of audio sand, which are combined to create something more interesting than static to your ears. Granular synthesis techniques produce some amazing sounds, although understanding the mathematics behind it all will eventually land you in a twelve-step program, or, potentially, one-on-one therapy.

FM Synthesis

FM synthesis uses a signal to modulate the frequency of another signal, and the result is a sound much more like that of an arcade game from the 1970s than a Steinway grand piano. Each FM voice needs at least two signal generators (called operators), and the more sophisticated FM synthesizers use several operators per voice.

Operators are the digital equivalent of oscillators, but more powerful. Operators create sine waves but can be set to a particular pitch, volume, envelope, and so forth for each key that is struck, effectively making each operator a kind of microsynthesizer in its own right. In addition, operators can either carry waves or modulate waves, depending on a number of factors, including their relationship with other operators. The relationship is based on an algorithm—a piece of computer code that sets the rules for how the operators interact.

THE YAMAHA DX7

The digital circuitry available to manufacturers eventually became so powerful that it began to change the look and feel of synthesizer interfaces. On earlier analog units, for example, dials or knobs were used to control one single function each, but digital interfaces could assign multiple functions to a single button. Eventually, programming and editing features were organized into layer upon layer of digital menus, which opened up wonderful new ways of creating synthesized sound.

First appearing in 1983, Yamaha's DX7 was one of the first all-digital synths, and it is still well-known today for many of its sounds. The DX7 was quite different from any other synth of its time, both in its interface and its sounds. The DX7 was the first popular synth to introduce the idea of buttons instead of knobs, and sported the first (very small, non-lit) LCD panel. It offered thirty-two preset algorithms for creating instrument sounds, and the results were complex and unpredictable, in many cases never-before-heard.

Other popular, groundbreaking synths in the early '80s were the Wave PPG (predecessor to the Waldorf), the Fairlight digital sampler, the EMU Emulator, NED's Synclavier, and Sequential Circuits' Prophet 5 (the first fully programmable polyphonic analog/digital hybrid).

Though FM synthesis has produced some way-cool sounds and added an entirely new sound category to music, it does have a number of limitations. Chiefly, if you're aiming to re-create the sound of an existing instrument or other sound using a synthesizer, FM just won't do it for you. The best way is to record the sound, convert it to a digital sample, and then change the pitch according to the notes you play. This is the essence of a far more powerful form of sound synthesis: wavetable.

Wavetable Synthesis and Sampling

Wavetable synthesis, also known as sample-based synthesis or sometimes simply "sampling," is the most popular form of synthesis these days and for good reason: The instrument sounds can be frighteningly realistic.

Instead of synthetically manufactured oscillators creating source waveforms, wavetable makes it possible to digitize a waveform from the natural world directly into memory or storage device. This "sampled" waveform can then be modulated and amplified in a regular synthesizer-like fashion.

The diversity and vastness of sample-based sounds available to the home recording artist is nothing short of astounding, making it possible to play a virtual orchestra in your small studio or to sample your own live instruments and then play them back however you want them, using an electronic keyboard or other input device.

A DISTINCTION

Strictly speaking, wavetable synthesis means two different things: First, it can refer to the technology behind a sound card's MIDI-based, sample playback capabilities, where samples are stored in a RAM (random access memory) "table." Or, there is the classic definition, which is to produce a sound by sequencing through a "table" of ROM (read only memory) for different waveforms in response to playing a note. For all practical purposes, though, these definitions are interchangeable.

So, how does it all work? Sample-based synthesizers and sound cards use a type of subtractive synthesis that you'll see referred to primarily as PCM (pulse code modulation), though you'll also see AWM (advanced wave memory), AWM2 (advanced wave memory version 2), and even AI Synthesis (by Korg). These terms pretty much mean the same thing: An acoustic audio signal—for example, your voice through the microphone or the sound of your Steinway grand—is sampled, or digitized, and the recording is stored in RAM or ROM. The sound can then be played back at will, using a controller device (such as an electronic keyboard), along with traditional controller functions of modulation and volume, pitch, and so on.

If a synthesizer can sample sound and store the result in RAM or to disk, it is called a sampler; if it can play back samples at different pitches, it is usually called simply a synthesizer or a sample playback synthesizer. Most samplers and sample-based synths use subtractive synthesis, although some instruments are very limited to how much processing they can perform.

PCM has become the coding technique used in almost all digital musical instruments and sound cards. Wave files also use PCM as the core technique for storing audio "buffer" data, as do a number of other common audio file formats. With most digital recording software, too, the core standard for sampling audio data is PCM.

FOR MORE ABOUT FORMATS...

See Chapters 11 and 12, "Fun-Da-Mental Audio" and "Serious Audio," respectively, for the gory details about audio file formats and digital audio.

The only drawback to digitally sampled instruments is that they offer fewer options for expressive playing. For example, you might have a killer alto saxophone sound, but playing it like a saxophonist does, using a keyboard with a limited amount of control over the final sound, isn't easy. Sampled audio is difficult to shape because of its fundamental nature—a "digital waveform" cannot so much be changed through modulation as it can be affected through a limited set of effects filters.

This isn't to say that the actual playback parameters themselves can't be modulated with interesting results; however, you won't typically find this kind of advanced control on most commercial synthesizers.

Virtual Synths

One of the most exciting options in the world of synthesizers today is the virtual synth. With accurate, usable, and affordable sounds, virtual synths won't have you sweating bullets over how to pay for that expensive vintage synth you found in the local used ads. In addition, virtual synths produce some absolutely unique and original sounds you've probably never heard before.

Virtual Synth History: The Nickel Tour

1997 saw many different things: a rising economy, Cubase VST, and even the introduction of a fake British spy named Austin Powers. But one of the most important introductions of the year was a program called ReBirth by a company called Propellerheads (see Figure 5.5). ReBirth was an all-in-one techno groove box that was completely software-based. Through a process called physical modeling, ReBirth was able to emulate and mimic the sounds and behaviors of a couple of the most sought after and expensive bass synths and drum machines for dance music, the Roland TB303 and TR808. This single program brought about a software synth revolution that to this day seems to change on a monthly basis.

Figure 5.5
ReBirth: where it all began

LET'S GET PHYSICAL

Physical modeling is an interesting form of programming that models the tonal qualities of the instrument (acoustic or electronic) that is to be emulated. The immediate benefit of physical modeling is that the performance characteristics of the modeled instrument can be emulated as well. A good example of this is a woodwind instrument that is blown too hard, causing the produced tone to play flat or sharp. Physical modeling is a simple enough concept to understand, but a lot of thought must go into formulating and creating the equations, and then they must be programmed.

As users were still accepting the basic idea and principle of software synths, many other companies attempted to shake up the music community by releasing their own software synths. Some did quite well, like GigaSampler (now known as GigaStudio and used on numerous film scores), whereas others did not fare as well, such as Reality.

Then, Steinberg once again completely took the music world by storm by releasing the specifications for VST Instruments in 1999. Unlike the software synths before them, these had a few very strong points in their favor:

- They would act and behave like VST plug-ins, except that VST Instruments could produce audio signals. This also meant that they could share your computer's audio card, because it was built into the program.
- Because they were inside the computer, there were no concerns about noisy audio signals.
- They were also sample-accurate in their playback mode, which means that they had better timing than MIDI.
- They could produce various kinds of synthesis that was simply not available in hardware synths.

As soon as Steinberg introduced VST Instruments to the music world, they immediately released a few commercially available VST Instruments, the Model E and the LM-4. The Model E emulated the look, feel, and sound of the old Moog synths that were nearly impossible to find. The LM-4 was an 18-pad virtual drum machine that was capable of playing back 24-bit audio samples. Both of these were well-received upon their release and are used quite a bit to this day.

As with VST plug-ins, Steinberg released the development code to programmers around the world, so that they would have the ability to create their own VST Instruments for Cubase. A software company called Native Instruments immediately came forward and released the groundbreaking Pro-5. This was a software emulation of the very vintage and very difficult to find Prophet 5 synth that was originally developed by Sequencial Circuits. In its day, the Prophet 5 was one of the first synths to be able to produce five notes simultaneously (also known as five-note polyphony). It was not without its fair share of problems though, as it was difficult and expensive to maintain and keep in tune. To say the least, the Pro-5 was a well-received virtual synth and has gone through many revisions since its release.

This was the beginning of a long trend of vintage synth emulations, such as the Yamaha DX7 (NI's FM-7), the Waldorf PPG Wavetable Synth, and even a couple that were not really synths at all, such as the Mellotron (GMedia's M-Tron) and the Hammond B3 Organ (NI's B4).

Not too long afterwards, most other host application companies either introduced their own specification, such as MAS (MOTU Audio System) and RTAS (Digidesign's Real Time Audio Suite), or they simply found a way to offer support for VST Instruments within their programs. Either way, it was a win-win situation for all of these companies, as there was yet again another technology that excited the user community.

Although vintage synth collectors are still clamoring for the real thing, virtual synthesizers can now offer you a unique and interesting solution for your home studio. Instead of spending a pile of cash on just one hardware synth, you can simply buy a hardware controller keyboard and supply your computer with virtual synths for the same cost or less. You can find a software synth that emulates the General MIDI sound set called the Virtual Sound Canvas (**www.edirol.com**), or you can even find a synth that produces rhythm guitar patterns that sound pretty decent (Steinberg's Virtual Guitarist).

To make things even better, Steinberg has included some basic, but great, software synths to get you started. Most notably, the LM-7 drum machine, the A1 synth (programmed by Waldorf), and the simple but useful VB-1 bass synth (see Figures 5.6–5.8).

Figure 5.6
Steinberg's LM-7 is a 24-bit drum machine that includes three drum kits

Figure 5.7
The A1 synth was actually programmed by Waldorf and can create fantastic bass and pads

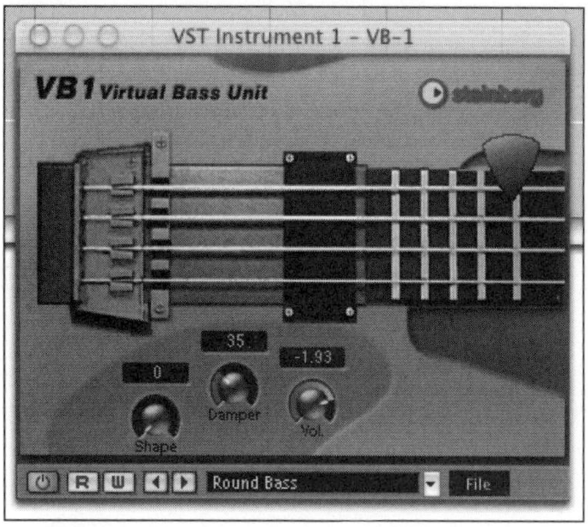

Figure 5.8
The VB-1 is a simple but very usable bass synth that produces a uniquely deep tone

Need a Better Reason Than This?

Propellerheads has gone to great lengths to create the all-in-one remixing software that gives you virtually every kind of synthesis you will ever need, plus a very user-friendly interface and sequencer that you can use with Cubase. Let's keep the group together and follow me as I take you on a tour of this gem.

As you can see in Figure 5.9, the interface of Reason is pretty straightforward. The mixer is at the top, followed by the virtual synths, and the built-in sequencer is at the bottom. The eye candy gets even better when you press the "tab" key on your computer keyboard, which reveals the routing capabilities of Reason (see Figure 5.10).

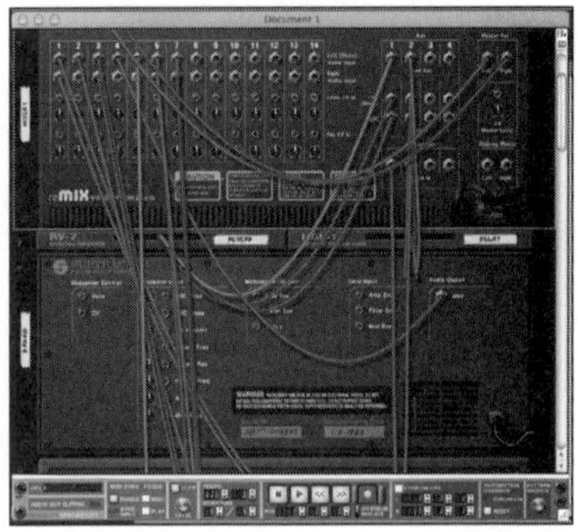

Figure 5.9 and Figure 5.10
The Reason interface, front and back

The first synth that Reason provides is a fantastic analog emulation called the Subtractor (see Figure 5.11). There are hundreds of patches to get you started, and the Subtractor is quite easy to program.

Figure 5.11
The Subtractor synthesizer

With Reason 2.0, Propellerheads decided that just one synthesizer was not enough, so they created the Malstrom (see Figure 5.12), which is a "graintable synth." This is a unique combination of both granular and wavetable synthesis that can produce tasty acid-dipped bass lines, or those fantastic "artsy-fartsy" pad sounds you'll hear on just about any ambient CD.

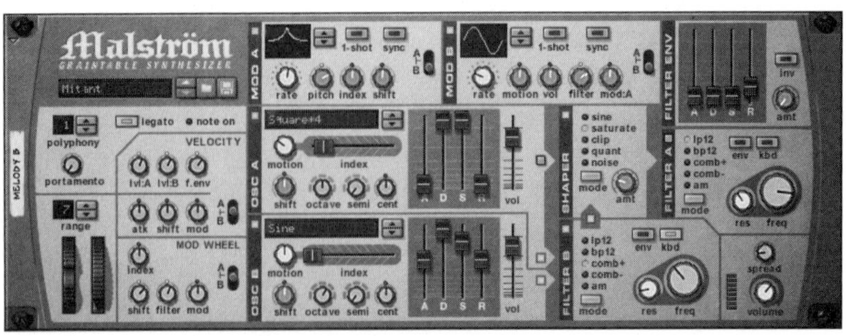

Figure 5.12
Reason's Malstrom synthesizer

Reason also includes a virtual drum machine called ReDrum. Fashioned after the good old drum machines of the '70s and '80s, ReDrum (see Figure 5.13) possesses some fantastic drum sounds ranging from acoustic drums to punchy four on the floor techno sounds.

Figure 5.13
Reason's ReDrum drum machine

What studio would be complete without a sampler? Reason provides a simple sampler (the NN-19—see Figure 5.14) that resembles the old Akai samplers, and the more complex NN-XT (see Figure 5.15), which is in a class all its own (it sports features such as multiple velocity layers on each sample and several improved editing parameters).

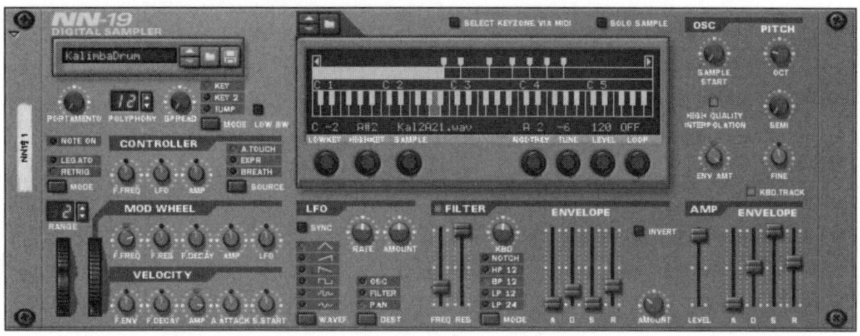

Figure 5.14
The NN-19

Figure 5.15
The NN-XT

A few years ago, Propellerheads developed a program called ReCycle that could slice up loops that were not quite in tempo with your song, and create a REX (ReCycle Exclusive) file that would import into Cubase and play at just about any tempo you desired. Reason provides a REX file player that can do that and a whole lot more with filters and modulation (see Figure 5.16).

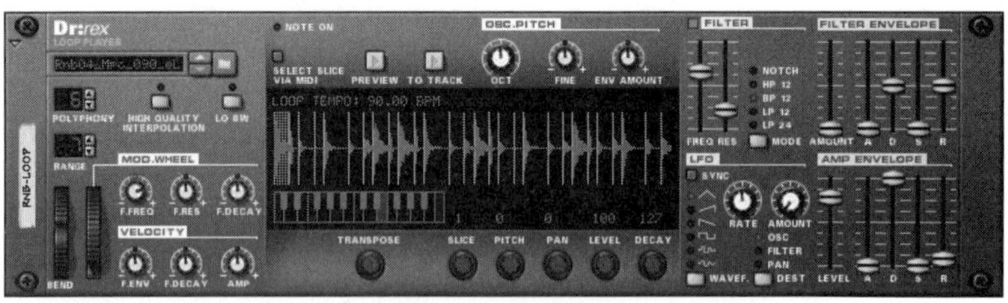

Figure 5.16
Dr:rex file player

What would remixing software be without a mixing board? Reason provides a virtual line mixer that looks a lot like the standard hardware Mackie line mixers (see Figure 5.17). In addition, Reason also supplies up to four auxillary FX sends. The real-time FX includes your standard reverbs and delays, as well as a few more creative choices, such as the Foldback Distortion and the Envelope Controlled Filter.

Figure 5.17
Reason's mixer

When you are ready to start recording your next big club hit, Reason provides a fantastic stand-alone sequencer with a lot of potential to make those creative juices flow (see Figure 5.18). Better yet, as you delve deeper into Cubase, you will undoubtedly see a striking similarity between the MIDI functions of Cubase and Reason. Isn't it great when we are all on the same page?

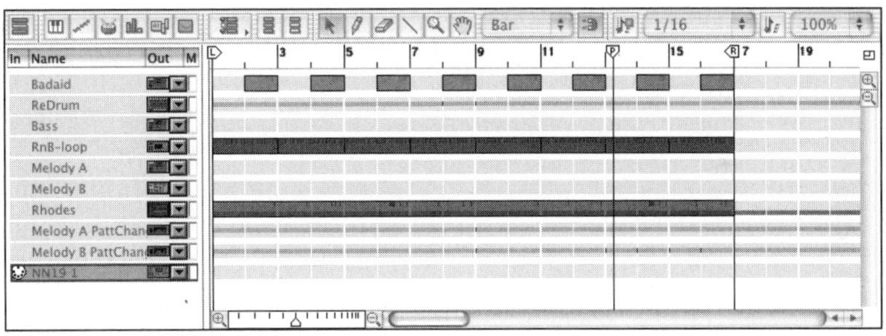

Figure 5.18
Reason's sequencer

So why should you use Cubase when there is a great program out there like Reason? Well to begin with, Reason is a MIDI sequencer that houses virtual synths, yes; however, it is not a digital recording program. But, with a few tricks, we can use Reason alongside Cubase with a technology called ReWire. This is a standard developed by Steinberg and Propellerheads, and it allows us to do two things:

- Run both programs at the same time in perfect synchronization.
- Bring up the outputs of the virtual synths of Reason into the virtual mixing console of Cubase. We can then use VST plug-ins and EQs on the synths of Reason and we can create and mix our entire song in one environment.

Making a Sound Decision

So what kind of synth should you get? If you already own a synth, does it work for what you want it to? And what are your options?

Armed with a little knowledge about wavetable, PCM, RAM and ROM, MIDI (see Chapter 9, "Wading in MIDI"), voicing, polyphony, and virtual synths, you already have a step up by knowing a bit about what synthesizers are and what they are capable of. You shouldn't be confused when the salesperson at the music store starts batting terminology around like air molecules.

You might, however, discover a little newfound emotional confusion when he starts playing on a keyboard or two, especially when he produces some incredibly cool sounds in and around some masterful playing. It's enough to make you want to just buy the whole synth department.

This calls for a little preparation, so before you head out to the music store, it helps to think about what you really want and what you'll really use—not just what sounds awesome.

Get What You Need—Not What You Want

What you need for your home studio and what your emotions tell you while you're in the music store can be two different things. It's like buying a car—you can't get that Corvette convertible out of your mind but all you really need is reliable transportation to the next gig—plus you don't exactly need to go bankrupt any time soon.

What do you want to achieve in your home studio? What sounds do you use most? Make a list. If you're a keyboard player who does jazz pieces, your needs will be radically different than if your main instrument is guitar and you do thrash metal. List the sounds that are most important to you. Are they solid drum sounds? If so, you may want to focus on a good drum machine. Realistic piano? If so, focus on digital pianos instead of regular synths or workstations. Synthetic noises? Some cheaper-quality synths and vintage models will have lots of these sounds.

Do you need a full seven octaves of weighted keys to tickle or do you need drum pads to tap? Or is a basic MIDI controller the best bet? (In which case, you may want to look at getting a controller, along with a rack-mounted module for your sounds, and/or software such as GigaStudio—see Chapter 8, "All Kinds of Other Instruments"—for your computer.) If studio space is at a premium, modules can be the golden ticket—and in many instances, modules cost less than their keyboard-ready equivalents.

The most important thing is to listen. Either bring a pair of headphones to the music store with you or ask for a pair when you get there—with everyone else in the store playing, it is hard to really hear the sounds without them, and you won't feel self-conscious in front of a new audience of other musicians. Plug the headphones into the headphone jack of the synth and spend some time with it. When you feel as though you've heard all the sounds you want to hear on a particular synth, go try another, and another. Try out synths that are way out of your price range and the cheaper home keyboard models. Listen for the differences.

LISTEN WITHOUT EFFECTS

When you're auditioning synthesizers, turn off the onboard effects, because reverb and other effects are notorious for disguising weak samples and low-quality loops! If you can't figure out how to do it, ask the salesperson. If he or she can't figure it out, you may want to seriously consider going to another music store.

When you're done sampling everything that looks interesting to you, go home. I repeat: Go home and think about it. Even if the salesperson gives you the deal of the century and you're 90 percent sure it's the synth you've always wanted, politely say, "I think we've got a deal, but can you hold it for me for one day? I need to think it over." Give yourself some time to think about what you learned in the store—unless you've got money to burn, you're going to have to live with your purchase for a long time.

Chasing Down the Right Synth

Music has been stuffed into almost every genre imaginable (Math Rock, anyone?), so although it's impossible to narrow the field of synthesizers down to a few categories, this section aims to focus on the most common genres, what's available in those genres, and what generally works for most musicians.

These are general guidelines, based to some extent on some of the most popular synths as well as some of the best values. Some of the synths in this section aren't even manufactured anymore, and the prices can vary widely. Wherever possible, the super-expensive stuff is left out. The assumption here is that you don't have an extra $5,000 in the cookie jar earmarked for a new synth, so most of these synths are generally in the $500 to $2,000 range.

SYNTH RESOURCES

A couple of wonderful resources for checking out other musicians' experiences with synthesizers (and lots of other instruments as well) are Harmony Central (**www.harmony-central.com**) and Music Player (**www.musicplayer.com**). Check out the Synth Database and Gear Databases for reviews on literally thousands of different models.

Rock/Pop

Most rock and pop songs use a synthesizer primarily for warm string pads, basses, pianos, electric pianos, percussion, and string and brass ensembles. Workstations—synthesizers that offer enormous numbers of different sounds and usually include a sequencer—are probably the most common type of instrument for rock and pop artists, particularly for gigging, because one good workstation can often do the trick. Korg, Roland, and Yamaha are the most popular brands for full-featured workstations, which also typically include onboard sequencing capabilities.

Though the warmest classic synth sounds come from analog synthesizers, sample-based synths are usually far more useful in the studio for rock/pop. Most likely, you'll need realism over expressiveness. For the times when you need a killer keyboard solo or some really bright pads, you might want to consider a used analog in addition to a sample-based synth. A Yamaha DX7 or Korg PolySix are both good choices and aren't too difficult to find used at reasonable prices.

If you are looking for a virtual, or soft synth, equivalent, you might try the VirSyn TERA (see Figure 5.19), as it is the mother of FM synthesis with 800 included patches that are sure to sparkle up any recording. Another good candidate is the PPG by Waldorf, which is distributed by Steinberg. In its hardware form, the PPG was the first wavetable synth available on the market and is about as rare as a blue ox, but now it is readily available as a virtual synth.

Figure 5.19
The VirSyn TERA (**www.virsyn.com**) is a 16-part multitimbral virtual synth that has got it all under the hood

SHOPPING ONLINE

Don't let the confines of your hometown prevent you from looking for that perfect studio synth. This is the age of the Internet, so be sure to look for mail-order websites or eBay (**www.ebay.com**), as I have found some unbelievable deals on vintage gear.

In addition, without liquidating your bank account, you can afford to look at some of the synths that have sampled some classic sounds—for example, Emu's Vintage Keys synth, the EMU Proteus series, or the Roland JV-1080.

Techno

Techno is a wide genre, but it tends to gravitate toward the analog and FM-synthesis-based sounds. A lot of techno also involves controlling filter cutoff and, in particular, resonance during a performance, so using a synth that has lots of controls (typically knobs and dials) will probably be important to you.

Some of the most popular techno synths are the x0x series from Roland; most of them are vintage units, and some of them, such as the TR808 and TB303, can get expensive.

Fortunately, there are plenty of other ways to get a similar, although not identical, sound. The TB303, for example, has been emulated by the Syntechno TBS-303. A number of other monophonic bass synthesizers will give you a TB303 sound, such as Novation's Bassstation, but also give you the ability to create a number of other deep bass sounds. Novation also makes the Drumstation, which does an effective job of emulating the TR808/909.

Lots of other analog synthesizers have been used and are popular in techno. Samplers are important, too, but you'll find some of the sample-based techno synths these days far less expressive than the analog or analog-modeled units.

Although ReBirth would seem the obvious virtual candidate here, at the time of this writing, it has not been made OS X-ready yet. So as an alternative, you might consider Reason.

Ambient

Ambient is a subtle genre of music, but it can have demanding requirements when it comes to a synthesizer. Reverb, delay, chorus, and other effects are often critical in an ambient piece, and much of ambient uses sampling as well as analog synthesis.

A sampler is probably more important than analog synthesis for ambient music, because ambient is a genre that rests on producing new and unique sounds. Analog synthesizers are also popular because of their warmth, but samplers are much more useful from a creative perspective. Make sure you look for real samplers, not just sample playback synthesizers. You'll want the flexibility of programming and really experimenting with the sounds.

That said, Brian Eno composed many songs with nothing more than a Yamaha DX7 and a lot of reverb and delay. It's the expressiveness of analog that makes it important to the ambient genre. Look at samplers first, though. In the home studio, you have more opportunities for experimenting with new sounds than you do new ways to express old sounds. For new synthesizers, look at samplers from Emu, Akai, and Kurzweil, as well as analog-emulators, such as the Nord Lead and the Prophecy. The Oberheim Matrix 1000 is also a cheap, rack-mounted warm analog synth, and it works very well for ambient music. If you want an analog with a great look, sound, and price, keep your eyes peeled for the Roland Juno-60, as it has a built-in arpeggiator and LFO trigger button.

New Age

Korg has consistently been good at making New Age sounding synths. For example, the entire 01/W and X series are excellent for all kinds of New Age music, as well as the Trinity (and TR-Rack) and the Korg Triton. The Kurzweil K2000, for example, produces some excellent swirly pads as well as solid realistic instruments—though it's on the expensive side.

On the used side, an Emulator II, Prophet 5, or Roland Jupiter 8 are also very good choices for New Age sounds.

Jazz/Blues

For traditional jazz and blues music, organ sounds are the most common, and the Hammond B3 sound is the most revered. The B3 is not really a synth, and it is rare and very expensive these days. Fortunately, many companies, including Hammond, with its XB series, have produced remarkably good synths that sound a lot like a B3 and range around the $1,000 to $1,500 mark. In addition to the B3, realistic instruments and warm pads are popular in jazz and blues, so sample-based synthesizers and sampling synthesizers will work fine as well. Semi-weighted keyboards may also be important to you if you're used to either an organ or piano feel.

If you thought there wasn't a solution for organ players, you thought wrong. LinPlug (**www.linplug.com**) has an OS X-ready VST Instrument called daOrgan, which is a physically modeled Hammond B3 organ. Honestly, synth organs can either sound really cheesy or unbelievably cool, and at $39, daOrgan certainly falls under not just the inexpensive category, but also the cool category.

Rap/Hip-Hop

Loops and more loops—that's what fuels rap and hip-hop these days. Look for samplers and a good turntable, obviously. Rap also relies heavily on drums, so focusing on a good drum machine is critical—for example, the TR808, TR909, or more likely a high-quality sampler. EMU has a fine line of fantastic drum machine/synths such as the MP-7, which can be found at a reasonable price. Some rap artists use old analog synthesizers, too (Snoop Doggy Dogg, for instance), but on a home studio budget, focus on the sampler and turntables first.

Although Reason might be the right virtual solution here, you should also check out the big brother version of the LM-7, which is called the LM-4 MkII. It sports some impressive features, including bit crushing (to get those down and dirty drums), but you can layer drum sounds according to velocity. Also, the sound reverse feature is pretty cool.

Film Scoring

If you score films or aspire to do so, you should be on the lookout for synthesizers that are highly programmable, versatile, and as expressive as possible. Synthesizers made by Korg, Kurzweil, and Waldorf, just to name three, have been the most popular among film composers for this purpose.

Weighted keys may be very important to you for expression as well as for comfortable controller options. For example, Kurzweil is well-known, and Korg is becoming known, for touch pad controllers instead of the traditional modulation and pitch wheels.

Building a home studio for film scoring can be quite expensive, with costs ranging from $1,500 for a used Trinity to well over $5,000 for a high-end Kurzweil.

KVR INSTRUMENT RESOURCES

Throughout this chapter, we have given you many virtual synths to consider as alternatives to synthesizer hardware. A lot of the information for this chapter was found at the KvR Instrument Resources web page (**www.kvr-vst.com**). At this website, you can search by the type of instrument you want (drum machine, sampler, synth), which platform (Windows, Mac), and price range. The search engine then produces a link of all available synths that match your parameters.

6

Getting the Guitar Sound

The guitar is where it's at if you're doing anything approaching rock music, and it plays a part in virtually every other popular musical genre, too. This chapter helps you turn otherwise amateurish-sounding guitar tracks into recordings you can be proud of, by showing you how to get the most out of your setup. This chapter covers:

- Evaluating your playing style
- Recording acoustic guitars
- Miking vs. pickups
- Choosing acoustic or electric guitar
- Recording electric guitars and amps
- Recording guitars direct

First Things First: Do You Like Your Guitar?

It almost goes without saying that you must have a fundamental affection for the instrument you're playing if you're going to get a good sound, a good performance, and a good recording. At the very least—if your budget prevents you from buying the guitar sound you're in love with—you should know your guitar's strengths and weaknesses and its limitations, in addition to your own.

The best way to find out what features and feel you really like is to play as many guitars as you can. If your friends have guitars, check them out, and spend a Saturday or two camping out at music stores with a wide selection. In general, ignore brand names and focus on the sound; just because a guitar has a brand name you've heard of doesn't necessarily mean it's right for you or your level of playing or playing style. For example, a Gibson Les Paul is well-known for its rich upper-end tones and sustain, but there are many guitarists who simply don't care for the sound of a Les Paul—that's why there are Fenders! In addition, different individual guitars of the same model don't always sound the same and, in some cases, may sound strikingly different. In fact, every manufacturer (even Gibson) turns out an occasional dud, and every manufacturer (including no-name brands) turns out the occasional must-have.

Cost is another factor to consider when evaluating which guitar to purchase. Both Gibson and Fender have the "expensive" version and the "affordable" version of all the well-known models. For example, the standard "Made in the USA" Stratocaster or Telecaster can start around $400, and they do sound fantastic. But, Fender also has a series of guitars known as the "Squire" models. These are the beginner to intermediate guitars that are fashioned after the same strat and tele models. The only real difference is where they are made and what material they are made from. Most of the less expensive guitars are made from a composite wood and are much lighter than their more expensive counterparts, which are made from solid pine or maple. After 15 years of playing all kinds of different guitars, believe me when I say that you get what you pay for.

Evaluating Quality: Basic Tips

What a guitar is made of has a lot to do with its sound. A cheap acoustic guitar, for instance, will probably have a top made of plywood, which over the years will pull itself apart. It won't sound too good, either, because plywood doesn't resonate well at all. A spruce or cedar top sounds much better and will last for a very long time, with care. The back, sides, and neck of an acoustic can be just about any type of solid wood; maple and mahogany are the two most popular.

Electric guitars can be made of almost anything, but the hardest woods, such as maple, ash, or walnut, are best. These types of woods are durable and provide a fair amount of sustain for a solid-body construction.

Fretboards are usually ebony, rosewood, or maple. Ebony, the most expensive, is extremely hard and durable, but rosewood runs a close second.

> **HOLD THE VARNISH**
>
> If a fretboard has been varnished, painted, or stained, it runs a greater risk of cracking, chipping, shrinking, and swelling, making the guitar difficult to play and even more difficult to keep in tune. A notable exception is Fender's popular lacquered maple fretboards, which hold up quite well.

Fretboards should contain level, even frets across the board, and none of them should stick out more than the others. A binded neck—one that is reinforced with plastic trimming around it—usually ensures this, but binding is not necessary for the frets to be level, and a warped binded neck is not unheard of. Perhaps the most important aspect of the neck is that it is straight, which is critical for intonation but also important for the frets to have the right "feel." If you hold the guitar up and sight down the neck, the fretboard may be either flat or slightly curved, but if the fretboard doesn't look level, the neck may be twisted or warped, in which case you should stay away. The machine heads, or turning keys, should also work smoothly, though this is less of a concern, because you can replace them easily on most models. On an electric guitar, all the switches and knobs should work smoothly.

How Does It Feel?

The feel of the guitar is just as important as the sound. Make sure the neck is a comfortable width for your hands. For example, Gibson and Epiphone acoustic guitars tend to have much wider necks than Fenders or Martins, so they're usually a better choice for thick fingers or big hands.

Check out the action—this is critical. Low action, meaning the strings are close to the frets, means an easy-playing guitar. However, especially in the case of acoustics, low action can often mean less resonance, less complex tone, and, in some cases, string buzzing that can be difficult to get rid of.

CHECK YOUR GAUGE

The gauge of a set of strings can also be a big factor in how the instrument can feel. When you try out a guitar at your local music store, nine times out of ten it will be strung with very light gauge strings, probably an 8 or 9 gauge set. If you are a beginner, this is a fine place to start, but as you get more experienced with your axe, you will probably want to look into strings that are a little bit heavier. When I use 8 or 9 gauge strings, I feel like I'm playing dental floss, so I prefer the tougher feel of a thicker and heavier 10 gauge when I play my electric guitars. I prefer this even more so when I play acoustics, because I am always after that nice, rich acoustic tone that can only really be achieved with a thicker string.

Make sure the body and weight are comfortable. If the body is too big or too heavy, you won't last a week with it. This includes the likes of the American made Les Paul guitar, which weighs a ton. On the other hand, if it's too light or doesn't have the right "balance" for your playing style and body size, you'll find it difficult to wring a good performance out of the guitar. If the guitar is even slightly uncomfortable, it will affect your playing in an adverse way; you'll play best when the instrument feels comfortable and balanced.

If it's an electric or acoustic/electric guitar, make sure the controls are easy to reach and use. Some manufacturers put controls in places where you can quite easily move them accidentally while you are playing. This will annoy you to no end.

Recording Guitars

Recording guitars can often be a frustrating experience, because there are so many variables. For electric guitars, duplicating the warmth and tone of different guitar amplifiers in the home studio environment is tough; for acoustic guitars, it's a bit easier, but harder still to get a simultaneously noiseless and accurately reproduced sound.

The Basics

If you're reading this chapter, then you have recorded or want to record guitar parts in your music. If you haven't already discovered it, you'll be pleased to know, first, that most songs that use guitar contain several guitar parts mixed together, and this can really give a recording a unique guitar sound. A common technique used to beef up guitar parts, especially in rock and pop, is layering.

Layering is achieved by recording several identical guitar parts to separate tracks, and then bouncing them down to two stereo tracks. This can create a virtual guitar chorus, or "wall of sound," which can work wonders for everything from thin-sounding distortion to acoustic second-strumming rhythms. A good example of heavily layered guitars is just about any release by White Zombie.

If you do layering, usually two to four separate layers are plenty, because any more than that starts straying into the "extreme lack of clarity and definition" category. For lead parts, more than two layers can present a problem, and, even then, it's most common to record the main solo line and then add a second countermelody or harmony part with the same guitar tone. The best way to hear a sample of this is to dust off those old Queen CDs and listen to the complex harmonies that Brian May achieved back in the mid '70s. Rumor has it that there were so many layered vocals and guitars on "Bohemian Rhapsody" that you could actually see through the master tape in certain places.

You also don't have to mix down to stereo. For example, if you do more-or-less standard guitar/bass rock music, mono, rather than stereo tracks, usually works just fine if you have other instruments to fill out your sound, such as synthesizers, horns, and vocal harmonies. In general, however, by mixing down to two stereo tracks, you'll achieve a richer sound and provide more flexibility for tweaking that sound during mixdown.

Stereo Separation

How you handle stereo separation and levels is important and will take a little experimentation. Here are the basic concepts:

- Pan closer to the center for more thickness, and farther left/right to hear them separately.
- Panning hard left and hard right respectively can sometimes be highly unnatural sounding and distracting to other frequencies in the mix, especially vocals; on the other hand, hard-panning for a bridge or another break in the song can exude a lot of harmonic complexity and add texture to the overall composition. In short: Judicious use of hard-panning can be very cool, and overuse can be a mess!
- Be careful when mixing together two guitar harmonies or countermelodies to either side of the stereo mix. You'll want to fold the harmony part toward the background for touching up and fullness, not blend the tones

as you would your vocals. Too much blending, and you lose the lasting impact of the melody, as well as its "punch," or the natural attack and decay of the instrument itself.

- When taking the best parts of multiple takes and combining them into one track, use short to moderate pans for transitions between the spliced tracks, essentially performing a crossfade on the two separated tracks. This makes a doubled lead, for example, more natural—as if you'd played the whole thing yourself in one shot. You'll also want to join the different tracks, either on a beat or in the middle of a long note, to more effectively mask the edit.

GET A RUNNING START

If you know you're going to be splicing guitar parts, it's always good practice to play along well before and after the part. Give yourself plenty of room to figure out the best place to make the edits.

The Acoustic Guitar Sound

Recording an acoustic guitar starts with the instrument. Either it's an acoustic that you'll need to mic, or an acoustic/electric with a pickup built in. There are advantages and disadvantages to both.

The biggest benefit to using an acoustic/electric is the clarity of the sound. You'll get a clean, noiseless recording if the electronics in the acoustic/electric are of good quality. The downside is that you'll be harder pressed to reproduce the sound of the guitar accurately. This makes complete sense when you think about it: The whole point of an acoustic guitar's design is to create sound in a natural space for human ears—not to process sound directly from the strings by way of electronics. That's why a dreadnaught is four inches thick and hollow.

If a song uses a simple acoustic guitar intro that winds up rocking after eight bars, this isn't a big concern. You'll get a sound you can live with comfortably using a built-in pickup. If, however, you're doing folk music, new age guitars, or bluegrass—anything that really depends on the character of the acoustic sound—you'll need to use a microphone.

The tried-and-true standard is the Shure SM57, which sells for around $90 new (at the time of this writing), and it will give you a good tone with enough experimenting. A good condenser mic, however, is much better. The Rode NT1 and NT2 are both good choices and are in the few-hundred-dollar range. Even Carvin has a really decent sounding condenser mic that starts at around $120 called the CM90E. But as we have discussed in a previous chapter, you can also use real-time effects to enhance the sound even further when it has been recorded.

A good condenser mic should be able to nicely reproduce all the nuances of an acoustic. Here are the guidelines:

- For a full sound, place the mic 6 to 12 inches away from the sound hole of the guitar. Generally speaking, to avoid getting a muddy sound, don't put the mic directly in front of the sound hole; put the mic either ahead of or behind the hole, yet aimed towards it.
- For a warmer, mellower tone, aim the mic toward the twelfth fret or so, at least 3 but no more than 9 inches away.
- For a really bright sound, mic closely and near the bridge.
- For capturing the sound of your space along with the guitar, move back 1 to 2 feet, or use two mics, one close to the hole and one at least 2 feet back.

Another option is to record in stereo, by placing two microphones in a crisscross ("X") pattern, with one aimed at the sound hole and the other pointing toward the bridge or neck. Be warned, though: Creating this kind of variation in the tone takes a good deal more patience than usual to master.

I have used a lot of different configurations for my mic placement over the years, when it comes to acoustic guitars. At times, I have even placed an extra condenser microphone in the middle of the room that I am recording in just because I liked the sound and feel of the room. The trick here is to let your creativity flow and don't be afraid to experiment. Some of the best sounds that you can achieve might be found by accident.

MORE ON THE RODE NT1

The Rode NT1 is discussed in more detail for vocal microphone techniques in Chapter 4, "Listen to You."

The Electric Guitar Sound

Once you're into a recording session, the last thing you want to worry about is your electric guitar sound. Ideally, you should have already decided upon the amp sound you'll use, starting with the guitar tone itself, and, having worked your way down the EQ, gains, and effects, you have a pretty good idea of how the guitar should—and will—sound.

Recording *is* the time to fine-tune how the guitar sounds fit with the other instruments and the feel of the song. The delay or chorus effect you used when practicing without the other instruments may have sounded just right, but it may not work in the final recording or it may muddle other parts or sound too muddled itself in the mix. Best rule of thumb here is: Keep it as clean as possible. Remember, we are talking about digital recording, so you can bet there are effects and tricks we can do later on to give you the best guitar tone possible.

Amplitude can also be one of the hardest pieces to get right. The most common mistake is cranking gain up so much that the guitar tracks behave more like phase cancellation effects than actual instruments. In addition, massive amounts of distortion, though it may work quite well live or during a practice jam, produce so many harmonics in your tone that it can make one note indistinguishable from the next.

In particular, if your guitar parts are intricate, a little less gain adds enough clarity to allow the notes to come through in the mix. Couple this with paying closer attention to your use of midrange frequencies on the amplifier. Though opting for little or no midrange during a live performance heads you in the direction of that "scooped" sound every time, in the studio, you'll need to pump the midrange just a bit to keep the guitar from being buried by the other instruments—particularly drums.

Miking Your Amp

The SM57 is, hands down, the most popular mic for a guitar cabinet; in fact, it's pretty much the industry standard. Condenser mics are not generally useful for getting a sound you can live with from your guitar amp, though there are a few exceptions, chiefly Audio Technica's AT4050 multipattern, large condenser.

The most important aspect of miking an amp is, well, the amp—and the speakers. Amplifier tone is one of the most subjective things on earth, and trying to corral it into a comprehensive discussion could easily take up the entire book, so it qualifies as one of those "beyond the scope of this book" topics. Here are some general tips, though:

- With most amps, the volume should be as high as you can get it (or as high as the neighbors will allow). Generally speaking, the hotter the amp, the more consistent and warmer its output, and you can add a bit of compression to smooth things out during recording.
- In a multiple speaker cabinet (2×12, 4×10, and so on), check mic placement with each of the speakers thoroughly to find the sweet spots—the spots that produce the most consistent modulation and tone that you like. Most likely, one or two of the speakers will sound better than the others.
- Keep the mic at an acute angle to the grill cloth—not perpendicular—and generally about 1 to 3 inches away. Direct the mic into the cone but not right on the center.
- As a general rule, plan to record the guitar dry and add your effects during mixdown. We'll be sure to talk about the real-time VST plug-ins you can use just on the guitar.
- If you want to add some natural reverb, stereo miking in a large room—by using a distant mic as well as one right on the grill cloth—can be quite effective. You'll have to play around with the exact distances according to the room size and natural sound, and watch out for phase cancellation—this technique can produce quite a bit of it. The solution is to keep changing the distances between the two mics. Of course, it just about goes without saying that if the room itself doesn't sound good, your amplifier isn't going to sound too good, either.

THE MATTER OF SIZE

The most common thought here is that the larger the amp, the bigger the sound. This is somewhat true, but there is also a lot to be said for just using a smaller practice amp when you are working in your home studio. You can achieve a lot of interesting effects when you record a guitar through a smaller amp. In particular, if you can construct a small padded isolation space just for the guitar amp and place a dynamic microphone right in front of it, not only can you achieve a monstrous dirty guitar sound, but you can also get a squeaky-clean guitar sound that will make heads turn when they hear you play.

Direct Signal

Recording electric guitar without using a microphone is another option for the home studio, and, with the right setup, you can achieve some interesting and desirable guitar sounds. With all but the most expensive hardware (and even then, it's no walk in the park), you need healthy doses of both patience and practice to get a good recording.

The first method is to use the preamp output from the back of your amp, routed through a direct box to match impedances and, to some extent, eliminate hum.

LEAVE THE SPEAKERS PLUGGED IN

Don't disconnect your speakers when using the preamp output. You can potentially damage the amp, your mixer, or yourself—especially with a tube amp.

Using the preamp output usually produces fairly harsh sounds, so this technique will have you doing some heavy equalization to counter the lack of warm frequencies. The tone control on the guitar itself can be quite useful when fine-tuning preamp output as well—don't ignore it.

Another approach, which, thanks to newer technologies, has gained quite a bit of popularity in the last several years is using a speaker simulator to simulate the power amp and speaker of your amp. The best units use physical modeling techniques to handle the simulation. With a fair amount of tweaking, you can achieve some highly realistic sounds.

The Pod, from Line 6 (**www.line6.com**), is one of the best values available at the time of this writing, selling for around $300. Using physical modeling techniques that Line 6 calls "Tube-Tone Modeling," the company has painstakingly analyzed the characteristics of various amps, different types of tubes, and how the sound is colored and shaped to design a software-based model of some of the most popular amps in the world. The Pod is not a sampler, but a chip/software-based device for re-creating tones. It features sixteen different models from a "Small Tweed" vintage Fender amp to "Rectified," the Mesa Boogie Dual Rectifier. The back panel features stereo inputs and outputs along with MIDI In and Out. The Pod also provides some good, basic functions, including output level, EQ, reverb, and gain.

The unit also has a built-in tuner, a noise gate, and a tap tempo button that allows you to change the speed of flanges or delay times by just tapping the button for the desired effect. The tap tempo button also lets you access additional features, such as drive and presence boost. There are even some basic effects onboard, including delays, choruses, tremolo, flange, and a killer rotary sound.

MULTIPLE PERSONALITIES

As this book goes to press, Line 6 has also released a new product—an actual guitar—which has been touted by some to be nothing short of a revolution: the Variax. The Variax is a substantive collection of highly authentic guitars in a single instrument; from a 1960 Telecaster to a '58 Les Paul Standard to '59 Martin D-28, the Variax—particularly in conjunction with the Pod—produces some amazingly accurate tones. At a street price of around $1,000, it's not cheap, but it's worth every penny.

Tricky-Dicky EQ

Probably the most important factor in creating your guitar sound is how it is equalized. Electric guitar frequencies range from around 100 Hz to about 10 K, and equalization can be added at any point during recording, from initial tracking to the final mixdown. If you have to bounce tracks, or if you have a limited number of EQ bands, it's a good idea to make changes as needed and save most of the equalization for the mixdown. Here are the guidelines:

- Boosting distortion in the 100 Hz range gets you closer to those ballsy power chords you get out of your cousin's Marshall stack.
- You can regain some clarity by making a cut at around 200 Hz.
- 400 to 600 Hz is where most of the tone exists, so tweak this area carefully.
- 3 kHz is critical, because this is where the guitar's edge typically exists. Boosting this frequency certainly makes the guitar cut through the mix, but too much gives you a serious headache.
- A boost between 5 and 7 K adds some air and sparkle to the guitar.
- Up over 10 kHz, you can experiment with small boosts to get a little more flavor and blend with vocal harmonies and cymbals.

KNOW YOUR FREQUENCIES

For acoustic guitars, the following frequencies are most important:

- Boosting 500 Hz or so typically gives you a fuller sound.
- Cutting at around 300 Hz can take some of that fullness back out.
- You get a little more pluck in the 1–3 kHz range, and a little more pick from 5–7 kHz.
- For more sparkle, boost above 10 kHz.

Finally, don't overlook the simple things. Make sure the guitar is in tune and the intonation is spot on (as much as it can be). Also, use new strings when recording, and stay loose: You can almost promise yourself that the fiftieth take isn't really going to sound much better than the forty-ninth!

LISTEN FOR YOURSELF

To give you an idea of what all of this sounds like, you can download and listen to samples of different microphone techniques from this book's web page on the Muska & Lipman website at **www.muskalipman.com**.

7

No More Drummer Jokes, Please!

This chapter is not about "percussion" in the traditional sense; it's about working with a standard drum kit (hi-hat, kick drum, snare, cymbals, and toms) in its various incarnations. The focus is on getting a good drum sound and how to best integrate drum kit pieces into your sound. Acoustic, MIDI, and sample-based drums are discussed, including:

- MIDI drums
- Looping and drum samples
- Setting up your kit
- Working with MIDI drum kits
- Rolling your own MIDI kit
- Quantization and groove editing
- Event-based MIDI editing
- Live skins
- Getting a good sound from acoustic drums

Drums for Non-Drummers (or, "Dig Those MIDI Drums!")

If you're not already a drummer with your own trap set, the ideal way to get authentic-sounding drum tracks into your recordings is to bring in a drummer and mic his kit. The "ideal way," you should note, has a few caveats:

- You need to know exactly what you want the drum parts to be; otherwise, you will waste an enormous amount of the drummer's time, and his ability to do exactly what you want will diminish accordingly.

- It almost goes without saying that you need a really good drummer—one who can catch the groove of your music, who "gets it," and can not only do exactly what you ask of him, but also make it better.
- You need money to buy enough high-quality mics to get a good sound. The best drummer in the world is worthless to you if you can't mic him properly.
- You need more money to create the space in which to record the drums (see Chapter 2, "Choosing Your Space"), one that captures the performance but is hot enough to work within your mix.
- You need even more money to soundproof the space—otherwise, your drum session will last about as long as it takes the police to arrive.

We'll deal with some of these points later in this chapter, but for now, consider some less-than-ideal ways to integrate drums into your recordings:

- **MIDI**. Though MIDI is the cheapest route, it may well be the most difficult and time-consuming.
- **Looping samples**. Using sampled drum loops, thanks to better collections of loops these days, is far easier than it once was.

MIDI Drumming

With guitar being my first instrument, one of the immediate benefits I saw in MIDI was the ability to write my own drum parts without having a drummer around. I figured if keyboard players like Kate Bush and Vince Clarke did it, so could I. However, as time went on, I came to find that I was fine at programming a basic or complex drum pattern via MIDI and Cubase (back then on a very old Atari 1040ST), but I couldn't make it sound very realistic. The fact that the drum machine I was using at that time had what I considered to be very cheesy sounds didn't help either. I concluded that in order to create better drum patterns, I would have to *think* like a drummer.

The question then became, how does one go about accomplishing this? The best way to start thinking like a drummer is to know and understand the functionality of each drum in a standard trap kit. One way to do this is to listen to jazz or rock CDs that concentrate on the drummer as a featured player. You can be sure to find great drumming on CDs by the likes of Max Weinberg (Conan O'Brian), Neil Peart (Rush), Buddy Rich, or something as simple as a good Rolling Stones CD. There, you are sure to hear the acoustic drum kit at its best. This is also where you are sure to find the greatest challenge in reproducing these styles and techniques via MIDI.

These techniques include:

- Snare rolls with strategically placed, random rim shots
- Flams inside of rolls
- Random volume, attack, and decay with cymbals

- Random volume variation with the snare, toms, and kick
- Switching between sticks, soft mallets for cymbals, and brushes
- Playing the snare behind or ahead on beats differently for each bar
- Cymbal chokes
- Hitting the snare with both sticks, one just off from the other
- Slight variations in tempo and volume on any given fill
- Following the music for certain parts of the song and leading on others

Drummers use these techniques anywhere, any time, with varying degrees of subtlety and dynamics, often without even thinking about it too much. Your task is to learn to fake these kinds of techniques using MIDI, and that involves gaining an understanding of what MIDI can do for percussion instruments.

Dynamics

A drum kit is an extremely dynamic instrument, and there isn't a MIDI drum module or keyboard in existence that gives you the dynamic range of a set of drums.

But you can get close. A relatively quick, easy way to increase the dynamics of your MIDI drumming is to edit velocity. Velocity is mostly amplitude, but it often includes some filtering to make a hard hit brighter as well as louder. You can control the dynamics of a MIDI instrument by using the event editor of your sequencer or, in the case of Cubase SL, you can introduce variation in velocity by using the Key Editor. Figure 7.1 shows the Key Editor with the velocity controller changes highlighted.

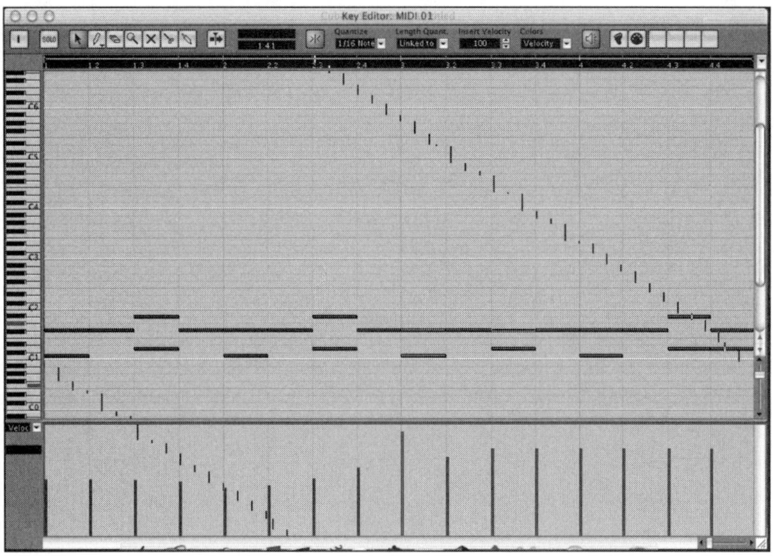

Figure 7.1
Cubase's Key Editor makes it easy for you to add dynamics to your MIDI drums

DRUM EDITOR

The problem with the Key Editor is that it's really a simple solution. You can accomplish quite a bit, but I tend to use the Key Editor as a great editing platform for synths and bass tracks. As time goes on, you'll want to sink your teeth into your drum programming even more. This is where Cubase whips out one of its best MIDI features called the Drum Editor, as shown in Figure 7.2. Within this editor, you can create a customized map of your own drum machine, or numerous drum machines within your MIDI rig. This comes in handy when you like the kick drum from your TR808, but you like the snare from the TR505, and the hi-hat from the HR16. You can also assign different note values to different pads. To have a look at this editor, just highlight the drum track and select the Drum Editor option from the MIDI pull-down menu in Cubase.

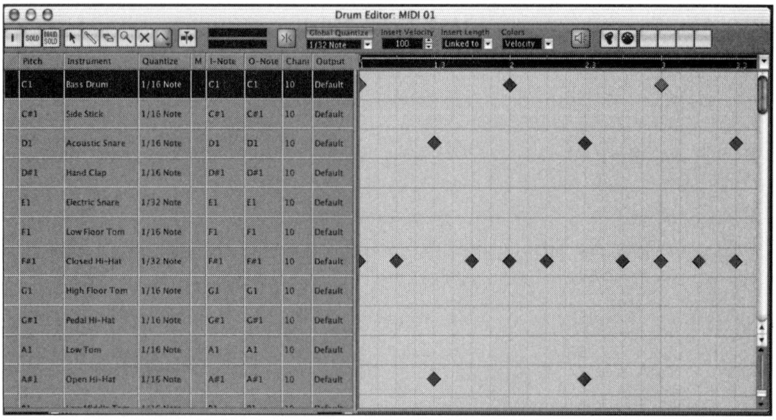

Figure 7.2
Cubase's Drum Editor is perfect for the precise editing that a drum kit requires

Octopus Syndrome

A real drummer does not have eight arms to hold you; he has only two hands and two feet, while you've got a practically unlimited palette of percussion instruments to work with in MIDI. Although it's tempting to just let the individual instruments "double up," that is, playing a fill on top of a backbeat that's already using four sounds on every beat, it does not sound realistic.

Because a drummer can only actually produce four different percussion sounds at a time, so should you. For example, when a drummer does a fill, he switches from hi-hat to pedal hat because he needs his sticks for the other skins. No drummer plays the same hi-hat pattern from the beginning to the end of a song. Neither should you, if your goal is to produce realistic drums.

THE REAL THING

A really good way to understand this concept better is to have a look at a drum pattern book. These are very easily found at your local music store in the sheet music section. This can be helpful to you, even if you don't read music, as they usually provide a tablature version, which is similar to a "cheat sheet." Here, you'll see what drummers read and play on a constant basis. Not only will you get rhythmic ideas for your next song, but you will also see how a drummer has to think in order to play. For example, if a drummer is playing a ride cymbal and wants to add a hi-hat sound as well, he would not use his left hand to play the hat, as it is always playing the snare in this position. He would instead use the hat pedal, which produces a similar and softer sound.

Varying the Snare

Different drum patterns have different feels, from "tight" to "digging" to "laid back" and so on. The feel almost always originates from where the drummer alters snare beats relative to either beats 2 and 4 or 1 and 3.

You can fool around with moving your snare beats up or back just a tad in your sequencer's note event editor. It's incredibly time-consuming, but it's a highly effective way to add some feel to your drum mixes. This technique all but eliminates that "robotic" or zombie-like precision that can occur with MIDI drums. Be sure to have a look at how this is done in Chapter 14, "Step by Step: Your First 8-Track Song."

Be a Smart Quantizer

Contrary to popular belief, quantization is almost always your friend. In fact, it's one of the most important tools you've got for doing drum sequencing. Nobody has the ability to lay down a spot-on drum groove using a keyboard, and the lack of air space and interplay between the instruments that a real drummer has at her disposal only increases the need for effective quantizing.

Be smart about it, though: Never quantize an entire drum kit together. Quantize only the individual sequences, and then work with each sequence by itself to add velocity changes and adjust the timing of individual beats.

Features such as Swing Quantize in Cubase, as shown in Figure 7.3, make this simple and relatively painless. Swing Quantize takes a rhythmic part that has been played in a straight pattern (for example, "one and two and three and four and" for an eighth note rhythm) and shuffles the individual notes by pulling them back or pushing them forward. This creates a fantastic shuffle feel that works well in R&B or hip-hop music. You can quantize in a straight mode, triplet mode, or dotted mode. Then, it's just a matter of making your swing settings and note values and you are good to go. You can preview your new groove in real time; then, when you are ready, just click Apply.

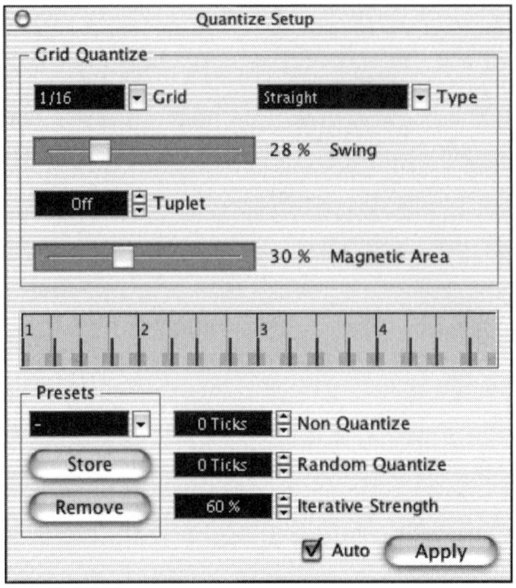

Figure 7.3
The Swing Quantize in Cubase makes it easy to create the grooves that you hear in rock and pop music every day

Using MIDI Triggers

If you've got the money, a MIDI-based trap set can be a big advantage. You get the opportunity to play like a real drummer, but you don't have to be an experienced drummer to hear some immediate benefits, because you can control "feel" and amplitude much like a real drummer, and then quantize away your errors at the end of a session.

Yamaha (**www.yamaha.com**) and Roland (**www.rolandus.com**) make some of the most popular prebuilt MIDI drum kits on the market.

Rolling Your Own MIDI Kit

A much less expensive option is to create your own MIDI trap set by using sensors to trigger MIDI notes, either adding them to a cheap acoustic set of drums or creating your own surfaces to beat on. There are almost as many ways to do this as there are types of surfaces and sensors to build it with.

One of the most inexpensive setups can be had by using PVC pipe, Remo practice pads, Radio Shack piezo audio transducers, and a drum module with trigger inputs.

There are a number of drum modules on the market, but the Alesis DM5 is one of the most popular drum modules available, has respectable sounds, and, most importantly, has twelve trigger inputs with five programmable parameters for each one, twenty-one programmable drum sets, four audio outputs, and a hi-hat switch. The unit also features an 18-bit sample rate, 540 different sounds, and random sampling capability.

You can buy Remo practice pads at just about any music or drum retailer; they run around $10 a pop. The piezo transducers are ultracheap (a buck and a half apiece, Radio Shack part number #273-073) and work quite well.

To build a frame out of PVC pipe, you'll spend around $25 or a little more, depending on how elaborate (and how big) you make the kit. One quarter-inch PVC with enough T-fittings and L-fittings to fill out your kit's design is stable, though you could buy a larger diameter PVC for a more rigid setup. A handsaw works just fine for cutting the PVC, while the Remo pads can be attached by drilling holes through the tubes and running bolts into the pads.

You'll also need to construct footswitches for the kick drum and the hi-hat; a cheap on/off switch can be had from Radio Shack for about $5, but a little actual drum hardware is better, such as inexpensive kick drum and hi-hat pedals that you can mount onto wood brackets.

The piezo transducers install as follows:

1. The piezo should be soldered to decent quality, shielded cable; check the polarity and the instructions to wire it correctly. The module-end of the cable needs to be soldered to a quarter-inch plug or whatever your module is expecting.
2. After you do the soldering, make sure to plug everything into your module first and test to ensure the piezos all work. They're fairly reliable, but because they're so cheap, buy a couple of extras just in case.
3. Next, you need to unscrew each Remo pad and cut a space in the foam for the piezo. Make sure you don't place the piezo directly against the surface of the pad, or you will get a sharp rebound sound on contact. An exception to this is if you remove the main sensor element of the piezo from its frame and install it flush with the Remo pad surface.
4. Drill a small hole into the bottom of the Remo pad to run the cable from the piezo.
5. After you get all of your Remo pads equipped, you'll want to play around a bit with the trigger settings, primarily gain and velocity.

MIDI Loops

No matter how creative you are, or how long you've been drumming, drum pattern ideas may be hard to come by from time to time. With that in mind, MIDI loops might be a good solution to your rhythmic problems. These are programmed MIDI drum loops that can be imported into your Cubase session. The loops are mapped out to emulate a "General MIDI" (see Chapter 9, "Wading in MIDI") drum kit, which is supported by a number of synth and drum machines. These loops are already quantized and grooved to perfection and have been dynamically edited as well. This brings you as close to a real-sounding drum kit as you can expect to get via MIDI. For more information, check out Keyfax Software (**www.keyfax.com**).

Virtual Synths to the Rescue (Again)

As mentioned in Chapter 5, "Keyboards and Synths," Steinberg has a fine line of virtual synths that are available at your local store, but they have also included some very good basic synths to get you started in Cubase SX/SL. This includes a great little virtual drum machine called the LM-7 (see Figure 7.4). This is a 16-pad drum machine that has an acoustic kit, electronic kit, and a hand percussion kit that is sure to rival just about any of the hardware drum machines in the $100–200 price range. Steinberg also offers a much more robust and better sounding drum machine called the LM-4 Mark II. This virtual drum module has great dynamic control over its 18 individual pads, and has multilayered drum samples that help it respond precisely to dynamic changes in drum patterns.

Figure 7.4
Steinberg's LM-7 is a 24-bit drum module that is included with Cubase SX/SL

Drum Loops and Samples

Another option is to forego MIDI altogether and use presampled loops for your drums. Thanks to the large number of sound libraries available these days, this is now a reasonably effective option. Not only can you get great sounding acoustic drums, but, undoubtedly, you can also look towards the more processed and programmed electronic percussion loops used so frequently.

The problem here is that there are literally thousands of different drum loop CDs, and it can be confusing to know which collection is right for you and worth your hard-earned cash. Make sure the CD you're interested in is in the right style and format for you. If this is your first time out, keep it simple and only select one of the following three formats:

- **AIFF**. This is the most common format for the Macintosh computer.
- **WAV**. This is the most common format for Windows-based computers. The good news is that Cubase can read both AIFF and WAV files, so you can use this format without any problems.
- **REX**. This format was discussed briefly in Chapter 5, "Keyboards and Synths." REX is a format based on Propellerhead's ReCycle Software and it involves taking an AIFF or WAV file, slicing it up, and using it in a program like Reason or Cubase. The immediate benefit is that the REX file quantizes itself to the tempo of your song in Cubase. Additionally, you can erase different slices, which can help to create a whole new sound and feel to your groove. The name of this game is definitely *versatility*.

Recording Acoustic Drums

If you own a set of acoustic drums or have recorded them before, you probably know just how tricky the process can be. The variation in tone, frequency, and volume can be a challenge (or a nightmare, depending on how you look at it).

There are two basic ways of recording real, live drums.

Close Miking

Miking each individual drum, known as *close miking*, while placing a couple of additional mics overhead for the cymbals, gives you the most control over each piece during mixdown, particularly the amplitude and stereo placement of each instrument.

You have a great deal of flexibility with this method, too. You can use different types of microphones, for example, to emphasize or de-emphasize each instrument's unique tone and timbre. You can mic both sides of a drum, change the relative positioning of mics in infinite ways, and alter the input gain of the mic for a load of different effects and sounds.

Good microphone values for close miking are the ever-reliable Shure SM57, AKG DA20, Senheiser 421 (for kick and/or floor tom), and Shure SM81. There are many other, more expensive mics, as well as specialty mics that are made for certain percussion instruments, such as a hi-hat microphone.

Having all of this freedom has its drawbacks, too: It's expensive, it's time-consuming, and it's not hard to make a career out of looking for the perfect trap sound. In addition, some engineers dislike the close-miking method, because you lose much of the soundfield interplay created by the interaction of the different drums. Still, close miking probably remains the most popular way to record acoustic drums. The next few sections offer some tips for using close miking effectively.

Kick-Butt Kick

A good kick drum mic, such as the Senheiser 421, should be placed roughly halfway into the kick and should be pointed at the beater. If you bring the mic in from the other side of the drum and angle it at the beater, you stand a better chance of avoiding leakage from the snare drum mic; you can experiment with the depth of the mic's pickup by trying different angles, but you'll want to keep the mic lined up with the beater as much as possible.

Use a pillow or sandbag in the kick drum angled toward the drum head that the beater kicks to dampen unwanted frequencies.

> **KICK EXPERIMENTATION**
>
> A few years ago, I had the unique opportunity to attend a drum clinic by the wonderful Greg Bissonette (David Lee Roth, Joe Satriani) and he talked at great length about recording techniques with producer Bob Rock. Bob's approach to recording kick drums was fairly unique in that he removed the front skin of the kick drum so that the entire drum was exposed. This produced a very large hit that sounded great. What was interesting is that Greg had to adjust his playing in order to control the amount of boom from within the kick, so it didn't bleed too much into the other microphones. It sounds a little bizarre, but this is a great example of how to experiment to get a completely unique sound out of a standard trap kit.

Trapping the Snare

The Shure SM57 is a tried-and-true mic for capturing a snare sound; you'll want to angle it at about 45 degrees, while varying the height depending on how much space you want in the sound. Be careful, though: The farther away you place the mic, the more potential you've got for phase cancellation (covered in detail later in this chapter).

> **A SECOND SNARE MIC**
>
> If you have enough additional inputs on your mixing board, you might want to consider an additional mic underneath the snare as well. This can help thicken up the sound of the snare considerably.

Tommy Guns

Miking a tom is similar to miking a snare, except you'll want to place mics farther from the drum head, usually at least 2 inches past the rim. The distance of the mic from the head has a little more range—you can go as far as 6 inches or more, but, again, watch out for dreaded phase problems.

Cymbals

For cymbals, start by placing your overhead mics anywhere from about a foot and a half to two feet out from the center of the cymbal and angle in the 45–60 degree range. Your primary goal with cymbals is to get separation from the soundfield to some extent, while reducing any bleed from the toms and snare.

Hi-hat

In most cases, you won't need a dedicated hi-hat microphone. You should get plenty of bleed-through from the other mics to provide good hi-hat. If you've got an extra mic and input, mic about 2 to 4 inches from the side of the hi-hat away from the snare, at an angle of 45–60 degrees.

Ambient Mics

If you have an opportunity to record your drums in a large hall, then you can also place a couple of microphones in another area of the room away from the kit to create an ambience effect. This can add a little more overall character to your kit sound.

Triangular Miking

Using a pair of overhead mics, along with a dedicated mic in the kick drum, works quite well for most situations and spaces. This technique is called *triangular miking*, has plenty of soundfield, is less expensive, and takes far less effort to set up.

Give the kick drum its own channel in the mix, and capture everything else using a pair of overhead mics, placed anywhere from 6 inches out from the kit and from 6 inches to several feet apart.

Start by ensuring that the overheads are placed an equal distance from the drums and that the drums are positioned so that they do not block each other from the overheads. You can capture a highly realistic, balanced, full-kit sound this way. This method isn't a walk in the park—it takes experimentation to account for the acoustics in the studio and the natural fluctuations in the resonance of the drums and cymbals. But it's the quickest way to get an authentic sound without getting stressed to imperfection!

SM81s are excellent for an overhead-only approach, as are AKG C-408s.

> **SOUNDPROOFING**
>
> Chapter 2, "Choosing Your Space," discusses an important topic regardless of the mic method you use for your acoustic drums: soundproofing.

Phase Cancellation

With either method—close miking or triangular miking—there is a strong likelihood that you'll run into some problems with phase cancellation. Phase cancellation happens when frequencies from one microphone cancel out frequencies in another, and vice versa; you'll know you've got a phase problem when frequencies drop out or seem to "shift."

When trying to correct a phase problem, the first thing you need to do is isolate the source(s) of the phase. If only part of the mic signal is out of phase (this is typically the case), moving one mic while carefully monitoring the other mics will probably fix the problem. With an overhead setup, sometimes simply changing the height of the mics is very effective.

> **CHECK IN MONO**
> When monitoring to check for instruments that may have dropped out due to phase cancellation, check each drum in mono—not stereo. Monitoring in stereo makes it difficult for you to trace the exact source of the phase.

Perhaps the most important aspect of detecting and dealing with phase is to do it before you start experimenting with different mic positions, levels, and distances. If you start out with a bunch of phase problems, things will only get worse.

All Skins Are Not Created Equal

Different percussion instruments can produce a wide range of frequencies, and the effects those different frequencies have on the mix also varies widely.

For a kick drum, the thump is usually in the 60–100 Hz range, whereas the punchiness of the kick is up a little higher, in the 100–200 Hz area. Snares are not quite as predictable, especially if you are working in the pop/rock or country music genres. Many snares tend to dominate the 1–2 kHz region, but this is by no means the rule; generally, if you need a little more bottom-end in a snare sound, you can boost around the 150 kHz range, whereas crispiness typically resides in the 2–5 kHz region. Snare sounds are sensitive to equalization, though, as well as reverb, so don't over-EQ your snare. Work with the source sound as much as possible.

Depending on the size and tuning of toms, their effective ranges run anywhere from 100 Hz to 2 kHz; to achieve clearer tom sounds, you'll usually focus on the 1–3 kHz range when it's time to EQ the mix. With cymbals, the effective ranges are about 8 kHz and above, and their overall harmonic frequency range can go well past the range of the human ear. Thankfully, during mixdown, you tend to be a little less concerned with boosting or cutting frequencies in cymbals, and more concerned with the attack and delay of the sound.

Drums and EQ

EQ can do wonders for drums; it is also terribly easy to overdo EQ, particularly if you've used triangular miking.

> **BEFORE YOU EQ...**
> Before you EQ drums, always check and play with mic placement first. Don't spend an hour playing with EQ when all you had to do in the first place was move the mic an inch to the right. Always check the placement of your mic(s) and evaluate the signal based on location first—then EQ.

If you've got everything on separate tracks (using the close-miking method discussed earlier), it's a bit easier in one sense, because you've got only each individual sound to contend with, and an isolated sound is always easier to EQ than the complexity of an entire soundfield of instruments.

Using equalization with anything is always, to some extent, a trial-and-error, roll-your-sleeves-up kind of proposition, so it's a bit difficult to predict exactly what works in every situation. However, there are some general guidelines:

- Adding more thump to the kick drum is usually achieved by boosting frequencies between 100–150 Hz. Clarity and definition like the 3 kHz region.
- The snare is always tough, but you will definitely hear a sharper, more banging snare at around 1 kHz, and the sound gets clearer and clearer as you approach 5 kHz or a little higher. Snare also responds to changes in the 100–150 kHz region—just like the kick. However, depending on how the snare is tuned, you will undoubtedly have to mess around with frequencies lower and higher than this range. In addition, at around 1–2 kHz, you'll get a more explosive, snappier sound out of the snare.

ADJUST CAREFULLY

Be careful when boosting or cutting the same frequencies across several different instruments. For example, boosting both the kick drum and the snare in the same region tends to diminish the effect you would have gotten from the boost or cut to begin with.

- For toms, you'll play around with frequencies almost exclusively in the 100–250 kHz region; if it is much higher than that, you will rapidly begin to muddy up the sound of the toms, especially the floor tom.

TOM EQ

Cutting tom frequencies around 750–850 Hz can help if you need to get rid of "boxiness." Also, if you are losing toms in the mix to guitars or synth, then add some narrow-band EQ up around 3 kHz.

- Cymbals, as well as the hi-hat, travel in roughly the same frequency range. If you cut around 180–200 Hz, you'll tend to get a subtler sound, whereas you can add tons of presence and crash if you can effectively boost around 500 Hz. For sizzle, boost in the 5–7 kHz range, and for more air, experiment with 7–10 kHz.

Reverb and Compression Are Your Friends

You can use effects with drums—acoustic, MIDI, sampled, or otherwise—just like you can with any other instrument, though you'll discover that compression and reverb are the two most valuable tools in your drum-effects toolkit.

FOR MORE INFO...

Compression and reverb are covered in more detail in Chapter 11, "Fun-Da-Mental Audio."

If you use close miking, adding effects will probably do more for your mixes than if you use triangular miking, because, presumably, you already have a good deal of natural reverberation from your recording space, and you're most likely already dealing with a relatively thick soundfield. Compression can still be helpful for a triangular-miked mix; it's rather hit-and-miss depending on the qualities of your room, but a little compression can thicken up any limp ambient qualities of a room.

With close miking, compression is highly effective for everything but the cymbals; using it judiciously evens the level of the overall kit, by squaring up the decay with the attack. In particular, compression can even the spots where some hits are louder than others.

For example, to create a gunshot snare sound, use a compression ratio of around 1:3 to 1:4 and a threshold of at least −20. Then add reverb to taste. You can also thicken the kick and the toms with a lower compression ratio, around 1:2.

For close miking, you can introduce a lot of variation by using reverb. If you use large amounts of reverb on the snare, ensure that the length of the reverb syncs up with the song's tempo, so that the reverb finishes decaying before the next snare hit. Otherwise, you'll be swimming in a sea of wishy-washy snare before you know it.

A SHARP ATTACK

When adding reverb to drums, lay off the pre-delay; otherwise, you lose the very essence of any percussion instrument—its attack.

8

All Kinds of Other Instruments

Though most of this book focuses on electronic instruments, this chapter goes into both recording popular acoustic instruments as well as emulating different instruments using sampling technology. The following topics are discussed:

- Getting a great bass sound
- Using acoustic piano techniques
- Effective miking for strings, woodwinds, and brass
- Using high-quality samples with Steinberg's HALion

Live Recording or Recording Live?

The first, most important aspects of any "live" acoustic instrument sounds are the player and the instrument. Bad player + bad instrument (or good instrument + bad player) = bad recording! Of course, you may not exactly be spending your weekends filling in for the first violin chair at the local symphony; in fact, your primary goal just might have a little more to do with that "cool horn section" in the bridge or the string sounds you need to ramp up the chorus. You may have some rudimentary skill with the instruments, but you're not an expert. That leaves you with two choices: Acquire the instrument and learn how to play it or use professional-quality samples.

If you use real instruments, you first need to consider from whence the sound comes—where the sweet spots are, and vice versa. The same qualities of an acoustic instrument of any kind that give it character and expressiveness can also sometimes be the most difficult sounds to capture on disk. Which mic to use? How closely do you mic it? From behind, to the side, square in front of it? How important is the sound of the room?

Hopefully, you're aware of the role the instrument will play in your recording. Is it sixteen bars of a pan flute intro or a four-piece string section to carry the verse? Does the composition feature the instrument or does it serve a backup role? Ask these questions and leave the experimentation for the guitar solo on your Les Paul.

For honest-to-goodness acoustic instruments, you should experiment with some recording sessions first. You'll most likely find that it takes a good deal more tinkering to get a good sound, so "roll tape" (or track, or sample—choose your own terminology) more often during practice sessions while you are working on learning the material.

Recording the Bottom End

Although the guitar is a popular instrument to learn, no mix is complete without a good dose of bass. The kick drum in a trap kit supplies some of the low end, but the bass guitar defines the overall character of the low end in a song. Throughout the '90s, producers were finding ways to bring the bass out even more in the mix, which has gone on to help shape the style of today's pop, rock, and jazz music. I'll never forget the first time I listened to Van Halen's *For Unlawful Carnal Knowledge* CD in 1992; I was blown away by the fact that not only could I finally hear Michael Anthony's bass playing, but also that he played really well.

Fast forward to today and we find that recording the bass well has never been easier, but it is also an art form in itself. With the help of some hardware and some time at your recording console, we'll have you recording bass like a pro.

First, the Bass-ics

As the bass guitar is an essential element to the rhythm section of any song, it is important to understand the bass both physically and rhythmically. So, let's start by talking about the bass itself and the different models that you are sure to run into in your recording career.

- **Electric bass.** This is the most common bass found and generally the easiest to play and record. There are several variations ranging from the standard jazz bass to the more complicated fretless bass that can produce those ever-so-cool jazzy slides.
- **Acoustic upright bass.** Although not as popular as the electric bass, the upright acoustic bass is a more revered and eclectic instrument that is used more typically for jazz music; however, on rare occasions, it has found its way onto a few rock recordings. It's a more complex instrument to record but a real pleasure to listen to.

> **BASS STRINGS**
>
> As discussed in Chapter 6, "Getting the Guitar Sound," the type of string used on a guitar can greatly change the overall action and sound, and the bass guitar is no exception to this rule. The bass guitar differs, though, in that there are not only different gauges of strings, but also different kinds of string that have different feels and textures. The most common is "roundwound," which has a rough texture and can produce very loud slide noises when moving up and down on the fretboard. The other kind of string is "flatwound," which is smooth to the touch. This kind of string is found mainly on fretless bass guitars and can be used to create noiseless slides up and down the fretboard.

Bass Recording Techniques

Recording the bass is actually pretty simple, when you compare it to the guitar. Just as with the guitar, there are two main ways to record the bass: mic it or go direct. Although both have advantages and disadvantages, there are two important rules to remember:

- Keep it simple.
- Keep it clean.

Miking Your Bass

Recording an electric bass through an amp is just as easy as recording an electric guitar, because the same rules apply. You'll want to start by selecting the proper mic to capture the best tone and frequency response from the amp. As with the electric guitar, a Shure SM57 is a good mic to accomplish this. Another personal favorite is the Samson Q2. It runs about 100 bucks and has a fantastic frequency range.

After you have selected your microphone, you need to place the mic in a proper position to get the best tone that the amp has to offer. In an ideal situation, your bass player will have an amp with just one low-end speaker, or "woofer" for you to mic. When recording with this setup, simply position the microphone 1 to 3 inches away from the speaker and angle the mic so it does not point at the direct center of the cone. Also, make sure that the amp volume is turned up as much as possible. And remember that a good way to measure the amp volume is by the intensity of your neighbors' pounding on your front door. Seriously though, keep the amp hot and you will not be disappointed with the results.

Some bass cabinets have up to four built-in speakers. In this situation, miking can require a little experimentation to reach perfection, but the same basic rules of amp mic placement apply here as well. Test each speaker to find the best tone, and then position the microphone as before. Additionally, you can choose to mic more than one speaker, but this can lead to the possibility of creating too much low end, which makes your mix sound muddy and distorted. Remember the first rule: Keep it *simple*.

Recording an acoustic bass is a real joy, as it can produce a very rich and warm tone all on its own, and becomes a centerpiece in the final mix of a recording. With that in mind, it is important that you use a good condenser microphone to complement the tone potential of this classic instrument. Don't waste time trying to use a dynamic microphone to accomplish this, because it doesn't suit the nature of an acoustic bass sound. Instead, use a condenser microphone, such as the Carvin CM90E, the Rode NT3, or even the Samson C01, to achieve a nice warm bass tone.

To get a good acoustic bass sound, start by placing the microphone 6 to 12 inches away from the bass. Although you can twist and contort most microphone stands to your liking (or until it looks like a modern art sculpture), for best results, I recommend using a very short mic stand that sits 6–12 inches tall from the floor. This allows you to point the microphone up towards the acoustic bass, so that you are sure to capture the tone a bit more accurately.

To capture the best tone of the acoustic bass, position the mic upwards and aim it between the end of the neck and lower bridge of the bass. This produces not only a warm resonant tone, but also captures the punch of the lower bridge.

PZM

A type of microphone that we have not discussed yet is the Pressure Zone, or PZM microphone. Basically, it is a flat metal plate with a microphone the size of a small pencil eraser situated near the center of the plate. Due to its unique design, it is able to handle very loud signals with minimal distortion. Although it was designed for recording meetings and conferences, a PZM can also be used to capture an acoustic instrument, such as a classical guitar or bass. It can be placed flat on the ground next to the instrument and mixed in to complement the condenser mic. Best of all, you can buy a fairly decent PZM at your local Radio Shack for well under $100.

Going Direct

The bass is often the most important instrument when recording (aside from the vocals), simply because it provides the groove to most tunes. With that in mind, many producers try to always record electric bass directly without miking amps. This results in a clean and dry bass signal; after the bass is captured in Cubase, sparkle and spice can be added with EQs and FX.

The best way to record directly is by using a "direct box." The direct box boosts the signal of a low impedance instrument, such as a guitar pickup, so that it can be recorded at a greater volume. You'll be able to find some decent direct boxes at your local guitar shop for around $50–60.

If you have been reading this book from the beginning, then you know that there are always alternatives, and directly recording the bass is no exception. If you have the means and moolah to have some fun, then you can find some fantastic bass amp simulators such as the Bass POD from Line 6. This is the bass counterpart to the Line 6 guitar POD discussed in Chapter 6, "Getting the Guitar Sound." The Bass POD is able to duplicate the sonic qualities of some of the most sought-after bass amps around. Additionally, the Bass POD comes with a boatload of presets that can make your bass player sound as though he is playing in a little hole in the wall jazz club or the great forums of arena rock.

Once you dial in your sound, you then just simply plug the POD directly into your Mac's sound card and start recording into Cubase. What could be cleaner and easier than that?

Acoustic Piano Techniques

There are almost more ways to record acoustic piano than there are pianos, which means you'll wind up experimenting a lot more with your particular room and instrument.

The first thing to consider is the piano part itself. For example, if you want to record a piano sound to back a rock tune and your instrument isn't set up for it, it probably isn't going to sound good, because rock pianos have much harder hammers than "normal" pianos and generally sound brighter than most. Similarly, you're not going to get that killer concert grand sound on the $400 Kimball in the living room.

If you're an experienced piano player who has dabbled in any studio, you probably already know these things, and you may even be prepared to shell out the dough to get the right kind of setup for the style of music you're working in. If you're serious about your keys, you've probably already done it.

After you have a setup you're comfortable with, you'll need a good mic. For rock, pop, and R&B, it's hard to beat a good condenser if you have a little bit of money to burn. The Neumann U 87 and U 89 and Shure SM81 are all good choices but still not cheap. The Rode NT1 and NT2 mics, which are covered in a couple of other places in this book, are better values in the $200–400 price range.

COSTLY MICS

Tube condenser mics, such as the Neumann U 67 or AKG C-12, are fairly common in professional studios and are excellent for piano miking of all kinds. They are very expensive, though—$2,000 or better. If you've got that kind of bread, you're probably not reading this book.

Dynamic microphones work very well for piano miking, too, and the Shure SM57 is practically the standard for stage miking. The SM58 also gives good results, although both are generally better suited to singers than instruments. Both are cheap, around $100 at the time of this writing. Their size and pickup pattern also cuts down on bleed for a recording situation in which you are using multiple acoustic instruments simultaneously.

BLEEDING MICS

Technically speaking, "bleed" occurs when microphones pick up the signals from the output of other microphones. The result can often be muddy, cause feedback, and sometimes introduce phase or phase cancellation into the mix.

Placement of a piano mic is critical. For rock or pop music, you should position the mic as close to where the hammers hit the strings as possible, and cardioid (such as the NT1 or SM57) mics are the best pickup pattern to use.

CATCHING THE ATTACK

Positioning a microphone close to where the hammer hits tends to pick up more of the dynamics of the attack of each hammer—and attack is what gives the "punchier" sound needed for most rock/pop music. To decrease the pickup of the attack and mellow the sound, experiment with moving the mic further and further down the strings until you find a spot you like.

For classical piano or jazz piano, omnidirectional pickup patterns work a little better, if you've got a room sound you really want to capture with the piano, which is typically the case. Position the mic outside the piano on the open side to allow the room and the instrument to "breathe."

Ideally, two mics (a pair of SM57s, for example) work best. A tried-and-true technique is to pan one hard left and one hard right (while checking in mono and listening carefully for any phase cancellation). With a jazz piano setup, especially if you have other musicians playing along, you'll probably want to space the mics out a bit farther from the piano to capture the live mix in the air.

Woodwinds

To record most woodwind instruments (flute, clarinet, and so on), use a microphone with a cardioid pickup pattern, usually no more than 12 inches in front of the mouthpiece. Most of the overtones of a wind instrument come out at the ends, whereas the wind tones and resonance come from the mouthpiece, so experimenting with where you position the mic relative to the mouthpiece is highly important. It's not hard to end up capturing too much air.

In addition, try to position the instrument itself equidistant from the floor and the ceiling to avoid phase cancellation.

The following steps are a good way to start experimenting:

- Start with the mic pointing more directly at the mouthpiece and a bit closer, maybe around 8 inches, then work back from there, depending on how much unwanted breath is present in the recording.
- Try a condenser mic first, if you have one. Dynamic mics make it much harder—especially for the flute—to capture a rich sound.
- Try a number of different angles to keep too much air from hitting the mic.
- Experiment with a pop filter—but not a wind screen. A wind screen will unacceptably dull most woodwind instruments.

Strings

Strings are bright. Almost always. In fact, this is where an SM57 or SM58 can work rather well, though you may find the sound too dull, depending upon the characteristics of your recording space. A tube condenser microphone, running through a tube-type preamp, also brings a warmer sound to strings, particularly smaller ensembles such as a quartet.

For placement, the bow sound is a big variable. Positioning the mic more toward the body of the instrument, a little away from the neck, and angled downward slightly is the best place to start to preserve more of the bow. Bringing the angle up tends to lose more of the bow and pointing more directly on the neck gives a fuller sound. Work with a range of anywhere from 10 to 15 inches back from the instrument.

Compressing live acoustic strings during recording almost always sounds bad, though you may find a little pre-fade EQ (see Chapter 13, "Recording and Mixing," for more details) very helpful, especially with a small or less-than-stellar sounding recording space. In general, though, start with the input levels at about two-thirds of the fader and record as dry as possible.

Brass

Ribbon microphones are popular for brass instruments and horn sections (dynamic cardioid pattern mics run a nice, close, cheap second place here, as always). A vintage ribbon model such as the RCA 44 will just blow you away, but if you have to ask about the price, you can't afford it!

More reasonable choices are mics like the Coles 4038, which has a high-end roll-off, whereas the Sony C-37 is a solid choice for a condenser mic.

> **WATCH THE MOISTURE!**
> Ribbon microphones are highly sensitive to moisture, so much so that a pop screen is practically required.

You should work with a range anywhere from 2 to 4 feet when placing the microphone, from chest to head level, depending on the instrument.

HALion–VST Instrument Solution

Another solution to consider for recording orchestral instruments is to use samples. Not only can you save a lot of money by not having to hire professional players to come into your studio, but also there are a lot of sample collections that can sound pretty close to the real deal when used properly.

As sure as a sunrise, Steinberg once again has a great solution to this problem—their very own virtual sampler called the HALion.

Although hardware samplers have been a popular choice for creating convincing piano and orchestral sounds, one of the main drawbacks to using a hardware sampler is that the information is stored in the sampler's RAM. This limits both the size and quality of the samples being used. With the introduction of faster computers over the last few years, software companies have developed the ability to play samples via the hard drive.

The result is that, with today's fast hard drives, you can play back high-quality libraries of sampled acoustic sounds with very long loops or with no looping at all, as well as record your own sounds. Additionally, you can set these samples up on their own dedicated hard drive to ensure the best performance. For all practical purposes, this means unlimited sampling capability. Although this sounds pretty expensive, the HALion is priced at $399 MSRP, which is quite affordable when you consider that a hardware sampler is at least a couple of thousand dollars.

Steinberg has also made sure to supply plenty of high-quality samples to get you started. More important than this, the HALion has the ability to import other popular sample formats, such as Akai, EMU, and even the GigaSampler format (previously available only for the PC). This gives you access to literally thousands of samples that are sure to make heads turn when they hear it in your recording project.

Let's take a brief look at how HALion can fit into your virtual studio.

Getting Started with the HALion

Upon first loading the HALion, you will see the Macro view, as seen in Figure 8.1. This is the condensed main window that allows you to control the global parameters of the HALion.

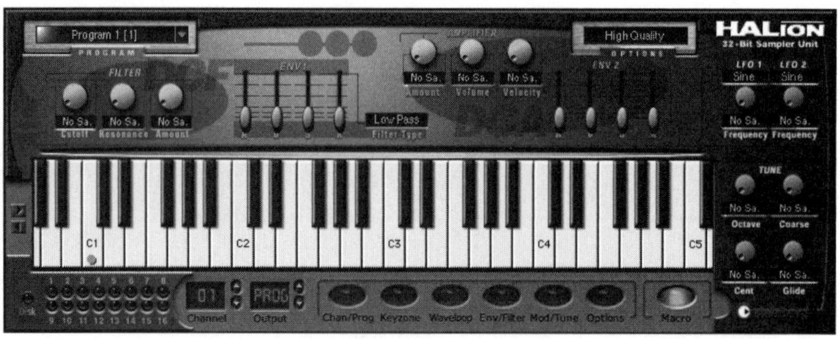

Figure 8.1
HALion's Macro view

The Macro view of the HALion is where you can edit your global parameters. These include functions such as envelopes, filters, LFOs, and the Master Tuning. You can also select the playback quality of the samples in the Macro view. This is very useful if you don't have a fast enough hard drive to stream large samples.

The virtual keyboard at the bottom of the Macro view is unique in that it is velocity sensitive. If you click with your mouse at the top of the key, HALion plays the sample back at its lowest velocity range. As you move and click downward, the samples play back at greater and greater velocities.

The HALion is a multitimbral virtual instrument. It has the ability to play back up to sixteen different instruments at one time. Even the most expensive hardware samplers don't have this ability.

A View to a Thrill

Let's move on with our tour. After you have acquainted yourself with the Macro view, you will certainly want to jump right in and have a look around. So, let's keep the group together and be sure to keep up.

The Channel view (Figure 8.2) is where you can route your samples to either stereo or mono outputs. This is also where you will notice the peculiar looking blue navigation ball in the lower-right corner. It looks a little like the interface of the HAL 9000 computer from the movie *2001: A Space Odyssey*, hence the name HALion.

Figure 8.2
HALion's
Channel view

The Keyzone view (Figure 8.3) is where you can edit both the key mapping and velocities of your samples. You can use the blue navigation ball to scroll from left to right on the keyzone, or to scroll vertically over the list of samples that you have loaded in the HALion (you can have up to 127 different programs loaded at one time). One of the lesser-known features of the keyzone is that you can drag and drop a sample into the keyzone right from your computer's desktop or anywhere else on your system. The formats supported for this function include WAV, AIFF, and REX.

Figure 8.3
HALion's Keyzone view

In the Waveloop view (Figure 8.4), you can set up and edit loop points for samples. This technique is used to help create a continuous loop for long sustained sounds, such as a sustained bass sound or a piano hit. An example of this is playing a note on your acoustic piano, holding it down, and letting the note sustain. You can achieve this same effect by setting up loop points and holding down the key on your keyboard. If set up properly, the HALion responds to this and the result is a very believable, sustained piano sound.

Figure 8.4
HALion's Waveloop view

The Envelope/Filter view (Figure 8.5) is where you can edit both the envelopes of the samples and create some very neat filter effects such as the cutoff sweep that you hear so often in dance music. There are also some unique features here, such as the "fatness" knob that beefs up the overall tone of the samples and the spread knob, which can randomly pan the sample as it plays back, creating a cool stereophonic effect.

Figure 8.5
HALion's Envelope/Filter view

The Modulation view (Figure 8.6) is truly a wonderful feature of the HALion, as there are hundreds of different combinations that can be used here to create wild modulation effects. A couple of key features to note are the Drum mode, which optimizes the HALion to play LM-4 drum kits, and the LFOs, which can be synced to the tempo in Cubase.

The Options view (Figure 8.7) in the HALion is where the preferences can be set. In the middle of this window is the "Preload into RAM" preference. This can be a little confusing because the HALion is supposed to stream the entire sample from the hard drive. This is not necessarily true, because the HALion loads only the first bit of the sample into RAM and then the rest of the sample is played out by the computer's hard drive. This is to ensure that there is not a delay between the playing and the hearing of the note.

Figure 8.6
HALion's Modulation view

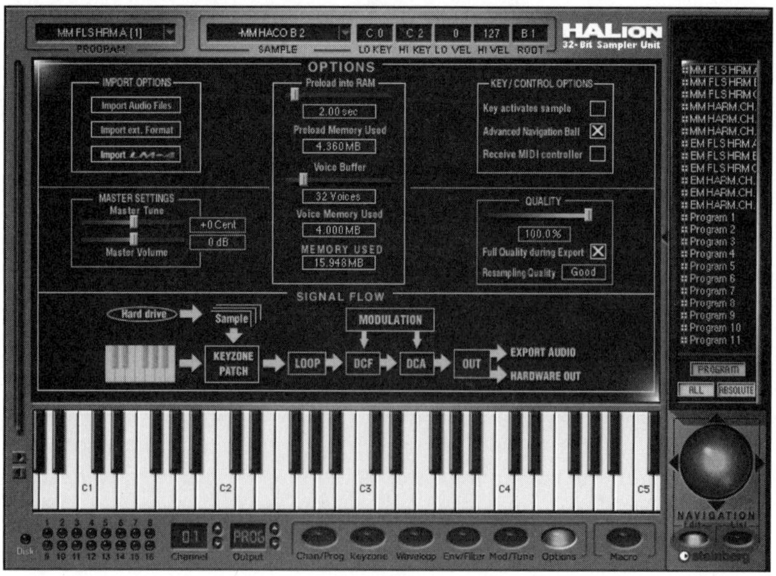

Figure 8.7
HALion's Options view

To the upper left is the "Audio Import Options," where the HALion can import standard audio files, such as AIFF, WAV, or REX. This is also where the HALion can import LM-4 drum kits and external sample formats, such as Akai, EMU, and GigaSampler files, as shown in Figure 8.8.

Figure 8.8
Audio import options

As you can see, the HALion rivals any hardware sampler on the market today, as well as just about any software sampler. When you consider the cost of hiring professional orchestral musicians, the cost and usage of the HALion is very justified and produces the versatility to accomplish very realistic performances.

9

Wading in MIDI

MIDI is unquestionably an important part of most home studios. Although it's possible to be a home recording artist without it, MIDI is a powerful tool that can save you time and money, and it can make it easier for you to write and record your compositions. This chapter is an introduction to MIDI and presumes that you have little or no knowledge about it. We cover a number of topics, including:

- What MIDI is and how it works
- FM and wavetable synthesis
- Hooking up MIDI devices
- The three most common configurations
- Channels and notes
- Sequencing
- Connecting to the Mac
- MIDI-to-wave software

What Is MIDI?

The musical instrument digital interface (MIDI) is a protocol—a standard that is agreed upon and published by a body of experts—for how electronic musical instruments interact with each other or with a computer. MIDI has been widely accepted and used by musicians and composers since it was adopted in 1983, and it has proven to be a highly creative and useful tool for writing and recording music. MIDI makes it easy for you to quickly record instruments and change tempos, keys, time signatures, instrument sounds—virtually any music editing activity.

With MIDI, you can write music that no human could ever perform, because the standard allows you to manipulate musical notes in any way you see fit. Before MIDI, the physical limitations of a keyboard and two hands made it difficult to achieve many sounds on stage that artists were coming up with in the studio. And even in the studio, there were limitations as to how much layering one could comfortably achieve and experiment with using analog tape recording techniques.

Enter a group of musicians, synth designers, and equipment manufacturers who got together to devise a way to share the sounds of electronic keyboards with each other. What they produced was the MIDI specification, which was presented at the NAMM (National Association of Music Merchants) show in Los Angeles in 1983. Suffice it to say, it took off like a rocket.

APPROACHING A STANDARD

MIDI may have taken off like a rocket, but it was not without a few disagreements between the United States and Japan (and between Yamaha and Roland). The result was that in the United States, the MMA (MIDI Manufacturers Association) was formed, and the JMA (Japan MIDI Association) was formed in Japan.

For this reason, MIDI implementation of early instruments (1983–85) was a bit dicey; for example, the Yamaha DX7 keyboard handles only a velocity range of 0–100, whereas its internal sound generator accepts up to 127—meaning the DX7 sounds a bit different when it's being controlled by another MIDI device or sequencing software.

How MIDI Works

Any device that is MIDI-enabled can communicate with any other device that speaks MIDI's language. The device is typically a synthesizer or MIDI controller keyboard, but it could also be a drum machine, a rack-mounted effects unit, an external sequencer, a computer, a guitar outfitted with a MIDI interface—the list goes on and on.

So what's the language of MIDI? On one level, it's digital—a transfer of bytes that tells each participating instrument what it can and cannot do. On another level, the information is all musical: MIDI bytes tell an instrument, a sound card, or other MIDI device when to start and stop playing musical notes. MIDI also handles other important musical elements, such as volume and modulation, pitch, pan, when to change instrument sounds, the starting and stopping points of a song, and tempo.

MIDI IS NOT AUDIO

It is important to understand that MIDI never produces or transports sound itself: It is a means by which you create and edit *data* to control the sound produced by the hardware or MIDI device.

The best examples of this are the names for MIDI sounds. On a practical level, names are just a guideline. For example, depending on your hardware, selecting the "Piano" sound from one keyboard may produce the "String" sound from another. As Freud said when asked about his family, "They're all relatives." (*Bada-bing, bada-boom*!)

A MATTER OF TERMS

Terminology in the world of MIDI can often be confusing. For example, the terms "sound," "patch," "preset," "instrument," "program," and "voice" don't always mean the same thing to every manufacturer of MIDI hardware—but often they are exactly the same thing. The terms "track" and "channel" are another example. It can be a synonym frenzy at times, so don't let it get to you, just go with it, let it happen, let it be, chill out, and take a load off.

BITS AND BYTES

A byte consists of 8 bits. A bit is the smallest "unit" of data on a computer. Because a single bit is capable of representing only two different values (typically 0 or 1), you might think that there are a very small number of things you can represent with a bit. Actually, there are an infinite number of things you can represent with a single bit, for example, true or false, on or off, male or female, right or wrong, or two different notes, such as C# and A. You can even represent two unrelated things with a bit, such as B*b* and the color white.

Because a byte is 8 bits, this means that a byte can actually represent 256 different values, or 2^8. This means MIDI can transmit a lot of data back and forth, and it does so quickly, too. In fact, MIDI operates internally at a speed of around 7 milliseconds, or 7/1000 of a second!

The bottom line is, MIDI devices communicate with each other by exchanging data. That data could instruct a MIDI device to, for instance, play a note, change pitch, or change volume. The data may even cause the device to use a different voice, so that it sounds like a completely different instrument. In the next several sections, you will discover exactly how that data does its thing. Understanding the data process of MIDI allows you to better understand the power and flexibility of MIDI.

MIDI Channels

When MIDI devices speak to each other, they always follow a certain sequence of events. For example, the first thing two MIDI devices do after shaking hands, or exchanging data, is to agree to use the same MIDI *channel*. MIDI can operate on sixteen such channels, which are actually numbered from 0 through 15. Whenever two MIDI devices communicate, they have to agree upon the channel that's going to be used for any useful musical information to be exchanged.

On a technical level, information about which MIDI channel is being used is just part of what's contained in a chunk of data, called a status byte, that's sent from one MIDI device to another. The status byte also includes the elements that define the musical note. For example, it tells when the note is being played, when it's not being played, special system exclusive (SysEx) commands, instrument changes (also called "patch changes" or "program changes"), pitch, volume, and so on.

Each of these elements also defines some of its own bytes—for example, the "Note On" byte tells the MIDI device to begin sounding a note, then "Note On" uses two other bytes itself to state the pitch (telling a MIDI device which note to play) and velocity (how loudly to play the note).

All these bytes must be handled successfully by two MIDI devices for MIDI to work. In other words, even if a particular MIDI instrument doesn't recognize the velocity byte, it still has to communicate back to the sending MIDI device or the MIDI message isn't complete.

NOTE ON, NOTE OFF

You would think that MIDI uses the Note On and Note Off commands as part of the same byte, but they are completely separate. This is because, just as Note On requires two additional bytes to indicate pitch and volume, the Note Off command needs its own two bytes to indicate pitch and volume. To put it another way: If you say, "Note On/Pitch" and "Note On/Volume" to play a note, you have to say, "Note Off/Pitch" and "Note Off/Volume" to stop playing that note.

The MIDI Interface

There are three *ports* that make up a MIDI interface: In, Out, and Thru. The In port processes incoming MIDI bytes—data coming "in" from another MIDI device—and plays the MIDI device according to the incoming data. The Out port transmits MIDI bytes "out" to another MIDI device. For example, if you play a chord on a synthesizer, all the things that define that chord on your keyboard—the notes that make up that chord, the velocity, the type of instrument sound, the value of your keyboard's pitch-bend wheel—goes out of the MIDI Out port into the other MIDI device to which the synthesizer is connected.

The Thru port operates a bit differently. Data from the Thru port is just a copy of the data that's coming in through the In port. Hence the name "Thru"—MIDI data is just passing through, and there are no changes to any of the data before it leaves the Thru port. The Thru port is useful for, among other things, hooking up multiple MIDI devices.

Hooking It All Up

Almost all MIDI-enabled devices have both an In and an Out port (although, in some cases, you'll see only an Out port, because an In port is not necessary for devices that only *send* data). To hook up two MIDI devices, you connect the In port of one to the Out port of the other, and/or vice versa. You can use both ports or either one of them when you hook up MIDI devices with one another.

THE MIDI CABLE

Most MIDI interfaces use a standard MIDI cable, a special five-pin cable to connect the ports together. The length of the cable is important: More than 50 feet between any two MIDI devices can cause problems with data transmission. Most musicians keep MIDI cable to less than 20 feet; 6- and 12-foot lengths are common.

FIVE-PIN DIN

Technically speaking, only three of the five pins of a MIDI interface are actually used. Originally, the MIDI standards proposal was to use a cannon connector—a connector very similar in design and appearance to an XLR connector, but wired a bit differently—but the five-pin din was less expensive, and a computer standard at the time.

If you connect the MIDI Out port of one device to the MIDI In port of a second, when you press a key on the first device, both devices will play. However, pressing a key on the second one causes only the second device to sound. This is because the first one is only sending MIDI data, and the second device is only receiving data—so it has no way to send its data back to the first device.

It follows that if you connect both the In and Out ports of two MIDI devices, you can send and receive MIDI data on both devices, as shown in Figure 9.1.

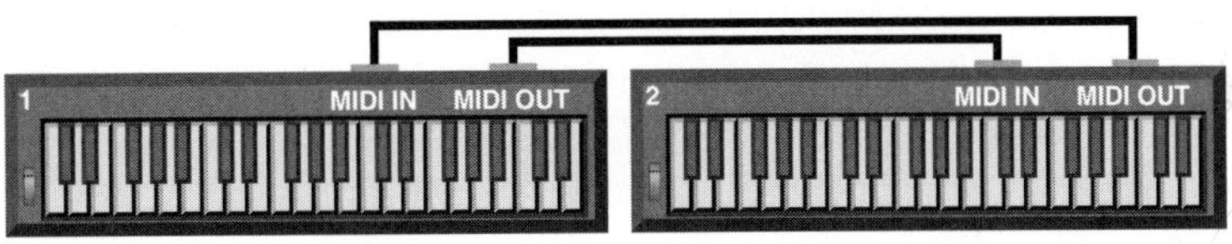

Figure 9.1
Two keyboards are connected via their MIDI ports, and can both send and receive their MIDI bytes

If you're used to using amplifiers or mixing boards, the labeling scheme that MIDI ports use can be a little confusing. It helps to think of a MIDI device the way you think of a mixing board: The MIDI In port is an input into the device and the Out port sends data to another MIDI device. Hence, the In port gets connected to the Out port and vice versa. It will not work the other way around: You cannot hook up the In port to another In port or the Out port to another Out port.

Masters and Slaves

Figure 9.1 shows a simple MIDI configuration: Both of the keyboards shown in the figure can be either the *master* or *slave*. A master is any MIDI device that sends data through an Out port, whereas a slave is any MIDI device that generates sound from the data being passed from, or through, the master.

Masters and slaves are where the Thru port becomes important. Many, though not all, MIDI devices possess a Thru port. Figure 9.2 shows a slightly more complex configuration using the Thru port. Notes played on the master keyboard are sent to the two slave keyboards, which will sound when the master is played.

Figure 9.2
Two slaves can easily serve one master using the Thru port

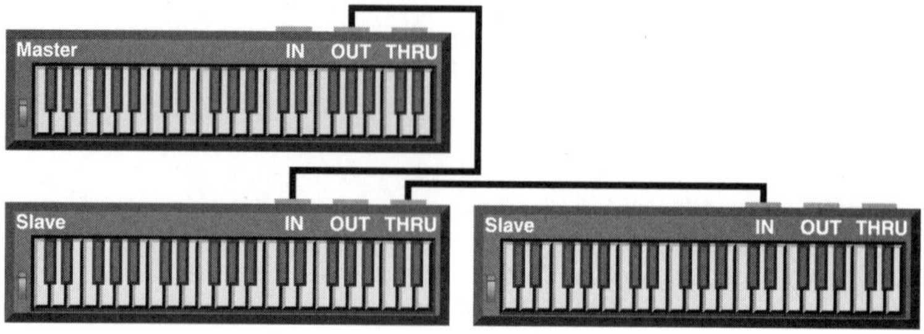

As discussed earlier, the channels of all the devices must be the same. For example, say you set one keyboard (the first slave keyboard) to a lush string sound. Then, you set a second keyboard (the second slave) to play a horn section. In order to play the string and horn sounds simultaneously from your master keyboard, you must make sure that the channel you set on both of the slaves is the same as the master channel. It doesn't matter which number you use as long as it's between 0 and 15—and it's the same.

This brings up a question: What if you want to play more than sixteen instrument sounds at once? MIDI allows you only sixteen different channels with which to transmit MIDI data, which means you can never play more than sixteen different instrument sounds at the same time. This doesn't mean you cannot play more than sixteen different slave devices—you can, by simply setting them all to the same channel.

The reason for the sixteen-channel limitation isn't too difficult to figure when you think about it: At the time MIDI was conceived, the most common type of mixing board consisted of sixteen channels. The creators of the MIDI specification presumed that, in most instances, musicians wouldn't need more than sixteen channels.

For most musicians, this limitation isn't a problem. However, there is a workaround in the MIDI specification that enables you to cheat a bit. Though you still cannot play more than sixteen sounds at once, you can switch—on any given note—instrument sounds by sending a program change that changes the instrument sound in midstream. The section "The General MIDI Standard," later in this chapter, discusses this in more detail.

POLYPHONY

"Polyphony" refers to how many simultaneous notes your electronic instrument can play. A keyboard that has 32-note polyphony simply means that it can generate up to 32 notes at once. Early synthesizers were all monophonic, as are some modern models, meaning that they could play only one note at a time. The first synth that could play more than one note at a time (five notes actually) was the Prophet 5 by Sequential Circuits.

Polyphony is important for MIDI. At some point, you are going to be limited as to how much layering or how many different MIDI parts are playing at once by the amount of polyphony in your MIDI keyboard or other device.

Hooking Up 1,000 MIDI Devices

Could you hook up a thousand MIDI devices? Theoretically, yes—but multiple MIDI connections using all three ports can quickly become very complex. For example, consider just four MIDI devices—a synth, a guitar synth, a drum machine, and a direct box for controlling guitar effects. Hooking them together using just one of their possible configurations might go something like this:

> The synth's Out port is connected to the In ports of the drum machine and guitar synth via the drum machine's Thru port. The drum machine's Out port then connects to the In port of the direct box, whose Thru port connects to the In port of the synth. A key pressed on the synth sounds the synth itself, the guitar synth, and the drum machine. A pad pressed on the drum machine plays the drum machine and nothing else. A chord played on the guitar synth sounds the guitar synth, the direct box, and the synth, whereas an effect dialed up on the direct box sounds the effect only. The drum machine does not sound when the guitar synth is pressed, because there is no direct connection between the guitar synth and drum machine. But the drum machine's note, which routes through the direct box, does make it through the synth into the drum machine, because the synth's Thru port is not connected to the drum machine. A note played on the synth does not sound on the direct box for the same reason.

Did you follow all of that? If you did, go to the head of the class, pass Go, collect $200, and the check's in the mail! If you didn't, don't worry—it's genuinely hairy stuff and not at all necessary to be a happy, MIDI-actualized composer. In fact, you can further rid yourself of this kind of complexity by making your real master your computer, as discussed in the section, "MIDI Computing," a bit later in this chapter.

MIDI Is Not Audio, Really

MIDI does not actually sample data or play back "normal" audio data—it does not work the same way as a tape recorder or digital audio hard disk recorder in this regard. For instance, you could not record live instruments or your singing using MIDI. MIDI contains only its MIDI messages, which instruct a *synthesizer* to play sounds by telling it which sounds to use, which notes to play, how loud to play each note, and so on. The actual sounds are then generated by the synthesizer itself and are limited by the quality and capabilities of the synthesizer.

A synthesizer in this context is not just a keyboard—it's any electronic device that contains a built-in set of predetermined sounds that have already been sampled and hard-coded into hardware or, more recently, into software on a computer. A number of different technologies and algorithms have been created over the years to generate sounds using a circuit board. The two most widely used are FM (frequency modulation) synthesis and wavetable synthesis.

FM Synthesis

FM synthesis uses one timed electronic signal, called a *modulator*, to control the frequency of another signal, referred to as a *carrier signal*. Modulating a carrier signal changes the timbre of the signal, which results in a theoretically unique FM *voice*. Every FM voice needs at least two signal generators, which are commonly referred to as *operators*.

The best FM synthesis techniques use more than two operators per voice, and the operators have flexible envelopes that allow you to change, for example, the signal's rate of attack and decay—the coolest knobs on a vintage Moog Sonic Six. The Sonic Six is an analog synthesizer—meaning that the way in which it passes sound around doesn't involve conversion to 0s and 1s—but most modern FM synthesis is done digitally.

To get into any more of the technical detail may cause nasty flashbacks of that physics course you dropped in school—suffice it to say, FM synthesis techniques have created some very expressive, unusual sounds and have been in popular use since the early '70s (the Yamaha DX7 being, hands down, the most popular early FM synthesis synth). FM has more recently undergone a big resurgence, which has resulted in synthesizer manufacturers producing new models and more new sounds.

FM synthesis was also the technique used for many years to reproduce instrumental sound on a computer sound card, using MIDI to play the sound card's FM-synthesized bank of sounds. The result was not exactly ear candy, and it was obvious to even the most casual listener that FM synthesis was not at all useful for accurately re-creating the sound of an acoustic instrument. In other words, it sucked for realism. In order to achieve a realistic sound, digital sample-based techniques were developed, and wavetable synthesis was born. It has become one of the best games in town.

DX7 REDUX

Native Instruments (**www.native-instruments.com**) has helped FM synthesis become popular again with the software-reissue of the classic Yamaha DX7 (although it's called the NI FM7 due to copyright and trademark laws). This is a perfect software emulation of the classic synth that sports a few improvements, and even a few built-in "secret weapons" that spark creativity in those who use it. There are also other popular software synths based on FM synthesis. Among them is the VirSyn TERA (**www.virsyn.com**), which uses both FM and Spectrum synthesis.

Wavetable Synthesis

Wavetable synthesis stores sound samples in digital format, allowing you to play those sounds on demand or via MIDI. They use a number of digital signal processing tricks, such as looping, pitch shifting, filtering, and interpolation, to whittle down the memory needed to store the individual sound samples and produce faithful reproductions of acoustic or even other electronic instruments. The word "wavetable" was coined because the samples are organized into a bank, or table, of sound waveforms that can be accessed individually.

DSP

Digital signal processing—DSP—is everywhere and can mean everything from enhancing sound in the studio by adding digital reverb to using a noise reduction filter in a cell phone. One of the most important aspects of DSP for the home studio artist is A/D and D/A conversion. This is the process of converting analog waveforms to digital format and vice versa. The algorithms and design of A/D and D/A converters can vary widely and can have a great effect on the quality and accuracy of the sound in your final recordings. DSP is covered in more detail in the next chapter, "Diving Deeper into MIDI."

Nowadays, almost all professional synthesizers, as well as computer sound cards, use some form of wavetable synthesis. Using wavetable synthesis in conjunction with MIDI, you can "play" chords and notes that would be impossible to achieve on the original instrument by yourself. Depending on the polyphony capabilities of your keyboard, for example, you could very easily layer a 24-note chord using an acoustic guitar sound that even three sets of five fingers couldn't handle. You can then use MIDI to sustain, attack, control any number of tempos and volume, and so forth, without ever having to actually play the chord.

The quality of wavetable sounds can really vary. It's often dependent upon the original quality of the sampled instruments themselves, as well as the skill of the musician who played the sample. One thing's for certain: No matter how good a wavetable instrument sounds, you have to have a way to specify the sound, play it, and remember how to access it using MIDI.

Sequencing

Being able to play back beautifully realistic wavetable sounds across your MIDI devices is one thing, but being able to record them together in one place, create a MIDI "song," and play that song back at will, is far more compelling. This is where the real power of MIDI lies.

Recording in MIDI, generally referred to as "sequencing," is more or less the process of recording all of the note events corresponding to what you play. Using an external sequencing device, an onboard sequencer, or, more commonly, sequencing software with your computer, you can record, store, play back, and edit note events.

MORE ABOUT SEQUENCING

Because software sequencing is the most common—and most powerful—way to sequence MIDI data, it's covered in more detail later in this chapter, in the section titled "MIDI Computing," which also discusses the MIDI file format.

In order to sequence MIDI data in a meaningful and organized fashion, you also need some way—other than your ear—to distinguish instrument sounds from one another. For this purpose, there is a standard called General MIDI, often referred to as simply "GM."

Though MIDI device manufacturers have come up with their own schemes over the years for categorizing which sounds are which, it wasn't until General MIDI emerged that musicians could share a common structure for which sounds go where and in what order. This is a very necessary thing if you want someone with a different instrument or sound card to hear the same MIDI piano sequence—or any other sequence—that you've recorded.

The General MIDI Standard

When a MIDI sequence begins, a Program Change message—a kind of MIDI channel traffic cop—is sent on each channel, thereby setting up an instrument's sound. The Program Change tells the MIDI device which program number, or patch number, should be used on a particular MIDI channel. If the MIDI device receiving the MIDI sequence has already preassigned its patch numbers to sounds in exactly the same way the sending MIDI device has, then the sounds of the notes will all play as expected.

However, if the sounds assigned to patch numbers on one device don't match up with the sounds assigned to those same patch numbers on another device, pandemonium ensues, because there is no way you can predict which instruments will sound. Enter the General MIDI (GM) standard, which sets up the relationship between patch numbers and instrument sounds. Any MIDI device that supports GM will usually be able to sound an instrument that corresponds to any other GM device's patch numbers.

The GM standard defines a GM sound set (a set of patch numbers—also called a patch map), a GM percussion set (percussion sounds only), and a set of other music-related capabilities, such as the number of voices and the kinds of MIDI messages that should be supported on any GM device.

GM uses MIDI channels 1–9 and 11–16 for instrument sounds, while channel 10 is reserved for percussion. Instrument sounds are grouped into families of similar sounds, as shown in Table 9.1.

Table 9.1
General MIDI instruments are parts of different families

Program Number	Family
1–8	Piano
9–16	Chromatic percussion
17–24	Organ
25–32	Guitar
33–40	Bass

Table 9.1
General MIDI instruments are parts of different families (continued)

Program Number	Family
41–48	Strings
49–56	Ensemble
57–64	Brass
65–72	Reed instrument sounds
73–80	Pipe
81–88	Synth lead
89–96	Synth pad
97–104	Synth effects
105–112	Ethnic
113–120	Percussive
121–128	Sound effects

For instrument sounds, a note number is sent via a MIDI Note On message to select the pitch of the sound that will be played. For example, if program number 1 (acoustic grand piano) is using channel 1, then playing note number 60 on channel 1 plays middle C using the acoustic grand piano sound.

For percussion sounds, a Note On message is used a bit differently: Note numbers select which drum sound will be played rather than sending pitch information. For example, a MIDI Note On message on channel 10 transmitting note number 38 plays a snare sound and could care less about the snare sound's pitch.

GM NUMBERING

Remember how MIDI channels start at 0 and are numbered from 0–15? General MIDI is similar but is a bit more complex. GM specifies sounds using program numbers 1 through 128, but the MIDI Program Change message used to select these sounds corresponds to decimals numbering from 0 through 127. Hence, if you select GM sound number 19, rock organ, a MIDI Program Change message will have a data byte with the decimal value 18. Although most sequencing software uses the numbers 1–128, you will occasionally see 0–127 used.

The General MIDI standard specifies which instrument corresponds with which patch number, but GM does not specify how these sounds are produced. The result, of course, is that the overdriven guitar sound, for example, may not sound the same on two different GM synthesizers. In fact, although the organization that sets MIDI standards (the MIDI Manufacturers Association, or MMA, as noted earlier) set guidelines for developing GM-compatible sound sets that are relatively accurate, they did not set guidelines for the quality of individual sounds. So, instrument sounds can vary significantly.

The Cost of Doing General MIDI

This section lists all the program numbers and their corresponding sounds for the GM sound set, but with a twist. The third column in Table 9.2 is a general indication of how much an accurate sound is going to cost you.

In the same way that food critics rate restaurants—with dollar signs ($) to indicate how expensive your meal is going to be—the scheme used here demonstrates that the quality of some instrument sounds can vary considerably, while others change very little. Though much has changed in the worlds of MIDI and wavetable synthesis since their inception, generally speaking, the most accurate, realistic sounds are available only on more expensive MIDI hardware (or sound cards or software synthesizers). Cheaper, less accurate sounds are stereotypical of inexpensive products, though this is not always the case. The ratings are as follows:

- **$**. A rating of one dollar sign indicates that a realistic instrument sound for this patch is inexpensive and widely available, with, for instance, an inexpensive portable "home" keyboard or a SoundBlaster Live! sound card. At current prices, this could mean anywhere from $50 to $250.
- **$$**. Two dollar signs means that you'll have to spend a little more, usually but not always on entry-level professional gear. This means you're probably somewhere over $500.
- **$$$**. Three dollar signs means that, although you probably won't have to get a loan to afford it, an accurate instrument sound is going to be reasonably expensive and available only on professional-level equipment. Plan on spending at least $1,000 (and you could easily creep up another thousand or two).
- **$$$$**. Four dollar signs means the cream-of-the-crop is necessary to get a realistic, accurate instrument sound. Plan on spending some major bucks, whether it's for a rack-mounted synthesizer, a sound card, or a software synth bank.

These ratings are, of course, subjective, as is music in any case. What might be a proper electric grand piano sound to one person may sound like elevator Muzak to another. Indeed, many musicians agree that some of the sounds in the GM sound set are *impossible* to reproduce accurately.

Use Table 9.2 as a guideline—not the last word on the subject—to give you a feeling for which end of the cost spectrum you're headed toward in order to obtain an accurate sound for a given instrument.

Table 9.2
The cost of doing GM instruments

Program Number	Instrument Sound	Cost
1	Acoustic Grand Piano	$$$$
2	Bright Acoustic Piano	$$$$
3	Electric Grand Piano	$$$
4	Honky-tonk Piano	$$
5	Electric Piano 1	$$$
6	Electric Piano 2	$$$
7	Harpsichord	$$
8	Clavi	$$$
9	Celesta	$
10	Glockenspiel	$$
11	Music Box	$
12	Vibraphone	$$$
13	Marimba	$$$
14	Xylophone	$$$$
15	Tubular Bells	$
16	Dulcimer	$$$$
17	Drawbar Organ	$$
18	Percussive Organ	$$
19	Rock Organ	$

Table 9.2
The cost of doing GM instruments (continued)

Program Number	Instrument Sound	Cost
20	Church Organ	$$$
21	Reed Organ	$$$$
22	Accordion	$$$$
23	Harmonica	$$$
24	Tango Accordion	$$$$
25	Acoustic Guitar (nylon)	$$$$
26	Acoustic Guitar (steel)	$$$$
27	Electric Guitar (jazz)	$$$$
28	Electric Guitar (clean)	$$$$
29	Electric Guitar (muted)	$$$
30	Overdriven Guitar	$$$$
31	Distortion Guitar	$$$
32	Guitar Harmonics	$$$$
33	Acoustic Bass	$$
34	Electric Bass (finger)	$$
35	Electric Bass (pick)	$$
36	Fretless Bass	$$$
37	Slap Bass 1	$$$
38	Slap Bass 2	$$$
39	Synth Bass 1	$
40	Synth Bass 2	$$
41	Violin	$$$

Table 9.2
The cost of doing GM instruments (continued)

Program Number	Instrument Sound	Cost
42	Viola	$$$
43	Cello	$$$$
44	Contrabass	$$$
45	Tremolo Strings	$$$
46	Pizzicato Strings	$$$$
47	Orchestral Harp	$$
48	Timpani	$$
49	String Ensemble 1	$$$
50	String Ensemble 2	$$$
51	SynthStrings 1	$$
52	SynthStrings 2	$$
53	Choir Aahs	$$$$
54	Voice Oohs	$$$$
55	Synth Voice	$
56	Orchestra Hit	$$
57	Trumpet	$$$
58	Trombone	$$$
59	Tuba	$$
60	Muted Trumpet	$$$
61	French Horn	$$$
62	Brass Section	$$
63	SynthBrass 1	$$

Table 9.2
The cost of doing GM instruments (continued)

Program Number	Instrument Sound	Cost
64	SynthBrass 2	$$
65	Soprano Sax	$$$$
66	Alto Sax	$$$
67	Tenor Sax	$$$$
68	Baritone Sax	$$$
69	Oboe	$$
70	English Horn	$$
71	Bassoon	$$$
72	Clarinet	$$
73	Piccolo	$$$$
74	Flute	$$$
75	Recorder	$
76	Pan Flute	$$
77	Blown Bottle	$
78	Shakuhachi	$$
79	Whistle	$
80	Ocarina	$
81	Lead 1 (square)	$$
82	Lead 2 (sawtooth)	$$
83	Lead 3 (calliope)	$$$
84	Lead 4 (chiff)	$$$
85	Lead 5 (charang)	$$$

Table 9.2
The cost of doing GM instruments (continued)

Program Number	Instrument Sound	Cost
86	Lead 6 (voice)	$$$$
87	Lead 7 (fifths)	$$$$
88	Lead 8 (bass + lead)	$$
89	Pad 1 (new age)	$$
90	Pad 2 (warm)	$$$
91	Pad 3 (polysynth)	$$$$
92	Pad 4 (choir)	$$$$
93	Pad 5 (bowed)	$$$
94	Pad 6 (metallic)	$$
95	Pad 7 (halo)	$$$$
96	Pad 8 (sweep)	$$
97	FX 1 (rain)	$$
98	FX 2 (sound track)	$$$$
99	FX 3 (crystal)	$$$
100	FX 4 (atmosphere)	$$$
101	FX 5 (brightness)	$
102	FX 6 (goblins)	$$$
103	FX 7 (echoes)	$$$
104	FX 8 (sci-fi)	$
105	Sitar	$$$$
106	Banjo	$$$
107	Shamisen	$$

Table 9.2
The cost of doing GM instruments (continued)

Program Number	Instrument Sound	Cost
108	Koto	$$$
109	Kalimba	$$
110	Bag Pipe	$$$$
111	Fiddle	$$$
112	Shanai	$$$$
113	Tinkle Bell	$
114	Agogo	$$$
115	Steel Drums	$$
116	Woodblock	$
117	Taiko Drum	$$
118	Melodic Tom	$
119	Synth Drum	$$$
120	Reverse Cymbal	$$$$
121	Guitar Fret Noise	$
122	Breath Noise	$$$$
123	Seashore	$$$$
124	Bird Tweet	$$
125	Telephone Ring	$
126	Helicopter	$$
127	Applause	$$$$
128	Gunshot	$$

The Cost of Doing GM Percussion

Following a format similar to the previous section, Table 9.3 lists the MIDI note numbers, using channel 10, which corresponds to different drum sounds. GM-compatible percussion instruments will sound the instruments according to the note number shown in the table. It should be noted that many MIDI devices add additional percussion sounds corresponding to note numbers below or above the GM-specified range, and it's not uncommon for manufacturers to offer full-fledged drum kits based on a "chord" of note combinations as well.

Percussion instruments that make up popular trap set configurations (kick drum, snare, hi-hat, cymbals, toms) are particularly difficult to estimate in terms of realism. One of the unique aspects of a drum kit in popular music is the way the different percussion pieces combine together to create ambience—the way the sounds play off one another. This makes achieving a highly realistic kit sound with MIDI percussion patches very difficult.

Table 9.3
The cost of doing drums

MIDI Note Number	Drum Sound	Cost
35	Acoustic Bass Drum	$$
36	Bass Drum 1	$$$
37	Side Stick	$$
38	Acoustic Snare	$$$$
39	Hand Clap	$$$$
40	Electric Snare	$$
41	Low Floor Tom	$$$
42	Closed Hi-Hat	$$$
43	High Floor Tom	$$$$
44	Pedal Hi-Hat	$$
45	Low Tom	$$$
46	Open Hi-Hat	$$$
47	Low-Mid Tom	$$$

Table 9.3
The cost of doing drums (continued)

MIDI Note Number	Drum Sound	Cost
48	Hi-Mid Tom	$$$
49	Crash Cymbal 1	$$$$
50	High Tom	$$$$
51	Ride Cymbal 1	$$$$
52	Chinese Cymbal	$$$
53	Ride Bell	$$
54	Tambourine	$$
55	Splash Cymbal	$$$$
56	Cowbell	$
57	Crash Cymbal 2	$$$$
58	Vibraslap	$$$
59	Ride Cymbal 2	$$$$
60	Hi Bongo	$$$
61	Low Bongo	$$$
62	Mute Hi Conga	$$
63	Open Hi Conga	$$
64	Low Conga	$$$
65	High Timbale	$$$$
66	Low Timbale	$$
67	High Agogo	$$$
68	Low Agogo	$$

Table 9.3
The cost of doing drums (continued)

MIDI Note Number	Drum Sound	Cost
69	Cabasa	$$$
70	Maracas	$$
71	Short Whistle	$
72	Long Whistle	$$
73	Short Guiro	$$$
74	Long Guiro	$$$
75	Claves	$$$
76	Hi Wood Block	$
77	Low Wood Block	$
78	Mute Cuica	$$$
79	Open Cuica	$$$$
80	Mute Triangle	$
81	Open Triangle	$$

MIDI Computing

Because MIDI devices and computers speak the same language, a computer is an ideal tool for using MIDI. To control MIDI devices from your computer, you need a MIDI interface for your computer, a cable, and MIDI software. There are many different interfaces available for almost all types of computer systems. Both Macs and PCs support MIDI in most of its current models, through a USB port. There are also a number of audio interface cards that have a MIDI I/O actually built into the hardware.

USB

USB (universal serial bus) has rapidly become the standard for hooking up devices to both Macs and PCs. There are numerous Mac peripherals that use a USB port, including joysticks, scanners, digital speakers, and digital cameras. The same goes for Mac laptops, which are both USB and FireWire ready.

USB is also fast—the current 2.0 standard runs at 60 MB per second—and you can easily chain together a large number of USB devices, typically using a USB "hub," which is a central box for routing and rerouting all the data. The ability to chain together USB devices is a lot like MIDI, except standard MIDI interfaces run at a speed of 31.5 Mbaud, which is much slower than USB.

More and more MIDI-based devices can use USB, and there are real benefits to USB for MIDI due to the speed increase: better timing accuracy, increased bandwidth, hot swapping (changing connections during data transmission), and easy expansion.

A computer functions in much the same way as any other MIDI device, but it is used a bit differently. A computer works best as the main MIDI data driver, meaning it supplies MIDI data to the rest of your MIDI-enabled instruments. To use a recording analogy, it's your (MIDI) playback console.

This works perfectly with the whole idea of MIDI channels. A computer can send MIDI bytes out on all sixteen MIDI channels simultaneously with ease. For example, if you've connected sixteen different MIDI devices to your computer and assign a different MIDI channel to each one, you can play a different part on each MIDI device and control it all from your computer. This capability has great implications for the home recording studio.

In addition to driving the MIDI data that "plays" your MIDI devices, your computer can function beautifully as the recording device that will capture your MIDI performances, too. Using MIDI software, you can receive incoming MIDI data, record it, play it back while recording new tracks, save it to your hard drive as a file, reopen it later, or share it with anyone who has the ability to play MIDI files on a computer.

You'll need to be able to connect your computer to your MIDI instruments and install software that enables you to use the computer as your own MIDI studio. The following sections show you how.

Connecting Your Computer

As shown in Figure 9.3, the easiest setup for connecting your computer to another MIDI device is a simple matter of connecting the In port to the Out port and vice versa. With both the In and Out ports in use, you can use a MIDI-enabled synthesizer, for example, to input MIDI data into the computer as well as play MIDI data using the computer to control playback.

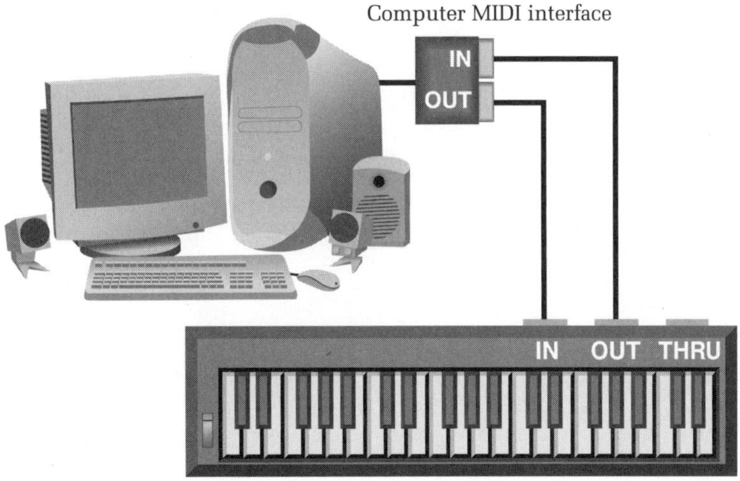

Figure 9.3
A typical MIDI connection between a keyboard and a computer is easy

Connecting slaves is also similar to the way the master/slave setup worked earlier in this chapter. Figure 9.4 shows a setup with the computer, one master keyboard, and two slaves.

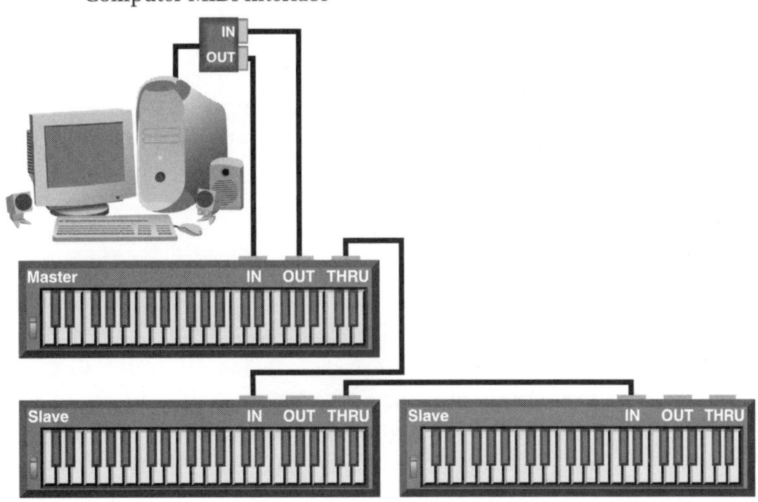

Figure 9.4
A master/slave MIDI using a computer is slightly more complex

A master/slave setup is most useful if you have one primary MIDI device you'll use to play your songs and several other MIDI devices that you want to trigger from the master, such as external sound modules, rack-mount units with additional instruments and/or effects, your computer's sound card, or software synth sounds on your computer's hard drive.

The master/slave setup is *not* the most useful way to set up your connections if you have a number of other devices you want to actually play—like a separate drum machine or electronic drum kit or a guitar synth. In this case, you'll need to be able to both send and receive MIDI data between your computer and each instrument, which is impossible to do with a standard 3-port MIDI interface for a computer. There are two ways around this.

The first way is the most cumbersome—simply disconnect the cables from one MIDI device and connect them to the next device you want to play. If you use more than one MIDI device frequently, you'll quickly tire of having to switch cables.

A much easier way is to buy a MIDI interface that supports more than one In and Out. This allows you to connect many MIDI devices at one time and they are easy to access via Cubase (see Figure 9.5).

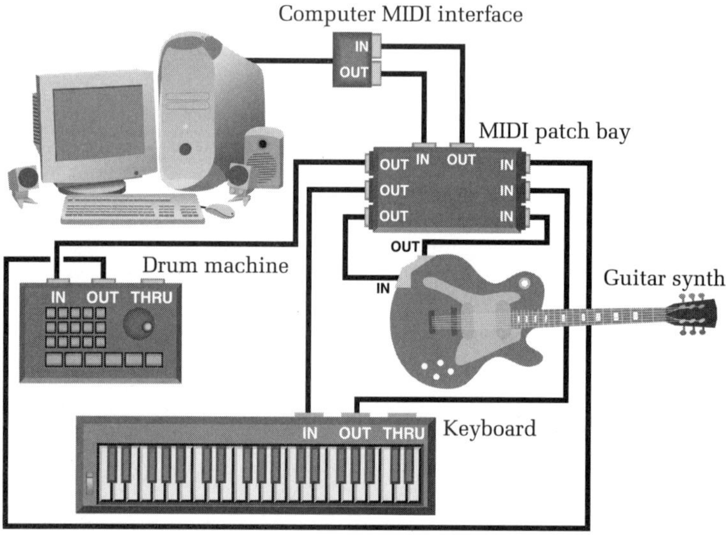

Figure 9.5
A MIDI interface with more I/Os makes it easier to attach multiple synth modules to your rig

There are several MIDI interfaces to choose from that will get the job done. In order to select the right one, you need to consider how many MIDI ports you may need and also whether you will want any extra features, such as SMPTE or Word Clock. After you have answered these questions, have a look at interfaces by companies such as Mark of the Unicorn (**www.motu.com**) and MIDIman (**www.midiman.net**). Steinberg (**www.steinberg.net**) makes a very versatile USB MIDI interface called the Midex 8. These interfaces range from $150–700, so your pocketbook has the last say in which interface you select.

SMPTE

SMPTE (Society of Motion Picture and Television Engineers) time code, pronounced "Simptee," is a time code synchronization protocol originally developed by NASA to time-stamp satellite data, then adapted for synchronizing audio with videotape.

For example, a multitrack audio tape recorder can use SMPTE to provide time code on one track to keep all the other tracks in sync, or videotape might use a cue track or one of its audio sound tracks to record and play back the synchronizing SMPTE time code.

MIDI also has its own kind of time code—MTC, or MIDI time code. It's a subprotocol within MIDI used to keep in sync two devices that control any kind of timed performance. MTC is essentially SMPTE mutated for transmission over MIDI, and it's covered in more detail in Chapter 10, "Diving Deeper into MIDI."

The MIDI File Format

MIDI has its own file format, which uses the .MID file extension, to store MIDI data. The format is a binary one, rather than text, so you cannot open it up and view it or edit it directly. The MIDI file format is very efficient compared to storing digital audio. You could create a 30-minute MIDI composition with dozens of instruments and need only a couple of dozen kilobytes on your drive to store all the MIDI information needed to play that file on a computer. Compared to a "real" audio file format like AIFF (about 10 MB per minute) or even MP3 (about 1 MB per minute), this is very small.

The MIDI file format specification actually sets up three types of MIDI files: MIDI Format 0, MIDI Format 1, and MIDI Format 2. Format 0 stores all MIDI sequence data in a single track, whereas Format 1 files store MIDI data as a collection of tracks. For home studio recording with MIDI, Format 1 is the most useful, because you can edit and view individual tracks. Format 2 can store several independent patterns and has some other nonmusical capabilities; it is generally not used or supported by most MIDI software.

MIDI SIZE

MIDI data files are extremely small when compared to digital audio files. For instance, a typical three-minute pop song in WAV or AIFF format recorded in high-quality stereo needs more than 30 MB of space on your hard drive and requires about 10 MB of data per minute of sound, whereas an average MIDI file takes up around 15 KB of space and consumes less than 10 KB of data per minute of sound.

The small size of MIDI files also makes the format very well-suited to download over the Internet; Web browsers support it, and there are hundreds of thousands of MIDI files available for download across the Net. The MIDI Farm, at **www.midifarm.com**, has a large number of MIDI files online and also has links to other MIDI file collections.

The downside is that a MIDI file does not always sound the same on a given computer—particularly so if the MIDI file is not General MIDI! This is because not all sound cards use the same synthesis techniques for reproducing instrument sounds, as discussed earlier.

In fact, there are as many differences between sound card instruments as there are between different external MIDI devices. Not too many years ago, it was much more consistent: All sound cards used FM synthesis and they all sounded consistently horrible. Today, almost all sound cards are wavetable-based, so that even the cheapest sound cards sound much better than FM. However, there are differences—sometimes major differences—between the wavetable engine and the sampled sounds (commonly called wavesets) of one sound card versus another. And it's the same rule-of-thumb when it comes to cost: For many sounds, the more you pay, the more realistic the sound, whereas some instruments sound about the same whether you paid for them in cash or mortgaged your house.

Using MIDI Software

There are dozens, if not hundreds, of software programs that manage virtually anything that can be done with MIDI. Many keyboards have sequencers built on board the keyboard itself, so that if you want to create songs using MIDI instruments, you can store them and play them back at any time. Unfortunately, most onboard sequencers cannot store anywhere near the amount of data that a typical hard drive can, and there's no easy way for you to share your work with other musicians or distribute your work to anyone else—without a computer.

In addition, MIDI software has expanded in the last several years to include digital audio recording capabilities. The converse has happened as well—most software that started out focusing on digital audio has added MIDI support.

MIDI software runs the gamut in price, from freeware programs to professional packages that run into the thousands of dollars. Rather than go into an extensive review of every imaginable MIDI program, this section briefly focuses on Cubase—the most popular and best valued, reasonably priced software package available. We also survey a few of the other MIDI applications in use today.

Cubase SL/SX

Cubase SL/SX (**www.steinberg.net**) is one of the oldest, best-supported MIDI software packages and is used by many professional musicians and engineers, from Stevie Wonder to Moby. Cubase SL/SX began as just Cubase, an Atari-based MIDI sequencer. A few years later, when recording digital audio on a computer became all the rage, Cubase Audio was introduced on the Atari Falcon, which was quickly ported over to the Macintosh. This was a fairly good program, although it relied on third-party hardware and software in order to make it work properly. In 1997, Steinberg changed the way we thought about digital audio by releasing Cubase VST (Virtual Studio Technology). This quickly became the new standard in digital audio/MIDI sequencing software and Steinberg was quick to follow this up with many new formats for FX and software-based synths. In 2002, Cubase SL/SX was released, sporting an entirely new look and feel that is causing yet another ripple in the pool of digital audio.

Cubase allows you to record an almost limitless number of MIDI and digital audio tracks. Cubase also supports 24-bit/96 kHz audio, SMPTE synchronization for film and video, automated volume, and panning. But this just scratches the surface; there are a huge number of other features, so many that an entire book could easily be written to cover them all.

> **CUBASE SX POWER!**
>
> Robert Guerin's book, *Cubase SX Power!* (Muska & Lipman, 2002), is highly recommended for those wanting to get the most out of this powerful recording/sequencing/editing software.

Cubase employs a number of different interfaces, and its main interface, as shown in Figure 9.6, is highly intuitive.

Figure 9.6
Cubase's main interface is shown along with the main audio mixer

Cubase uses a simple scheme that displays blocks of MIDI data that you can cut, copy, paste, and edit, much as you would edit text in a word processing program. You can also view the MIDI data in other ways: a rote list of all MIDI events, a "Piano Roll" view that shows you individual blocks of each MIDI note, a "Staff" view to edit notation, and several others.

These different views of MIDI data allow you to "see" your music in ways you may never have thought of before. For example, the Event List view (Figure 9.7) allows you to manage at a microlevel exactly what every note does, including where patch changes occur. This is highly useful, as mentioned earlier in the chapter, for overcoming MIDI's limit of sixteen simultaneous channels.

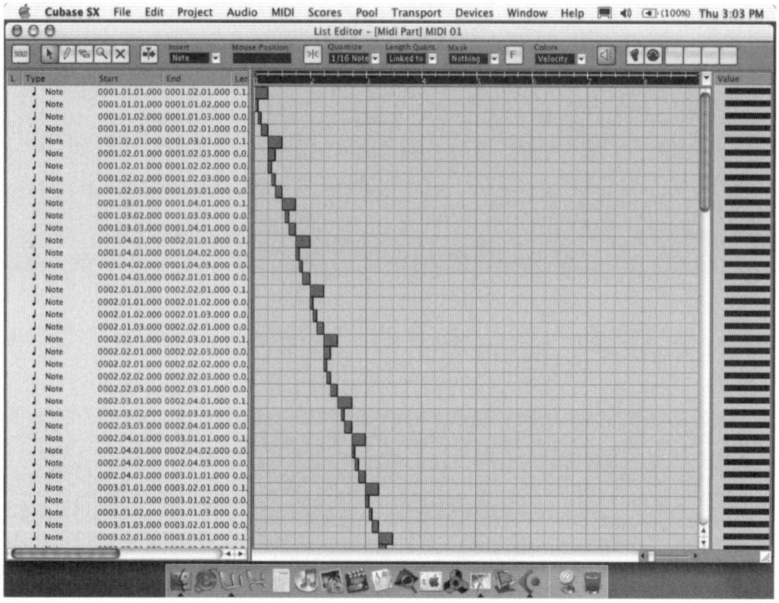

Figure 9.7
Cubase's Event List view is an easy way to make patch changes anywhere in a song

In order to use Cubase, you'll need a MIDI interface in your computer or a sound card that supports MIDI (just about all of them do). During installation, Cubase automatically detects your audio hardware and sets itself up to work with that hardware.

Although Cubase uses a couple of its own proprietary file formats for storing both MIDI and digital audio data, it also fully supports the MIDI file format. In addition to the Cubase SX Pro Audio package, Steinberg also sells a stripped-down version, called Cubase SL, which still offers full MIDI support but more limited digital audio capabilities.

Other MIDI Software

In addition to Cubase, a number of other audio software applications fully support MIDI and offer well-designed interfaces.

- Logic Audio (**www.emagic.de**) is a complete digital audio application for the Macintosh. The application is high performance, DSP-rich, and completely redesigned for version 4.0 in 1999. Logic Audio fully supports MIDI, offers 24-bit/96 kHz digital audio recording, and ships with dozens of high-end digital audio plug-ins.
- Digital Performer (**www.motu.com**) is a digital audio and MIDI sequencing production tool that handles recording, playback, and editing for both MIDI and audio data. The software includes an automated 32-bit digital mixer, reverb, effects, EQ, and compression in addition to its MIDI sequencing capabilities.

- Propellerheads Reason (**www.propellerheads.se**) is a MIDI sequencing/Virtual Synth application. Although it does not record audio, Reason contains a very powerful sequencer that bears a striking resemblance to Cubase. Reason also contains a number of fantastic virtual synths that rival most conventional hardware synths. If you want to use Reason with a digital audio program such as Cubase, Propellerheads developed an application called ReWire that allows other programs that support ReWire (such as Cubase, Logic, and Digital Performer) to easily synchronize to Reason.

10

Diving Deeper into MIDI

If Chapter 9 was learning how to drive, this chapter is understanding how the engine works. Although the basics of MIDI will take you well down the road to a more powerful home studio setup, understanding the way MIDI works under the hood puts you across the finish line. This chapter teaches you:

- How MIDI works behind the scenes using MIDI messages
- The types of MIDI messages and what they do
- How to record and edit tracks in a MIDI software sequencer
- The inner workings behind the MIDI format and where MIDI is headed in the future

Messages, Messages, and More Messages

Dissect for a minute exactly what happens when you play a line on a MIDI device: Each time you create a note, an almost instantaneous stream of digital data travels down your MIDI cable. Any MIDI device, including your computer, that is tuned to the correct MIDI channel immediately responds to each note in the stream and "renders" that note as an audible instrument sound—a bona fide analog sound wave. The analog sound is then piped through an amplifier, and then routed through a set of speakers and into the air.

THE MIDI DEVICE

A MIDI device can be anything that sends and/or receives MIDI messages. This includes everything from an electronic keyboard to a drum machine to a device that operates based on motion detection.

This chapter generally refers to a MIDI device as an electronic keyboard, which is the simplest and most common method of doing MIDI.

Hence, there are two sides: a digital side and an analog side. You can't hear something that is digital, any more than a computer or an electronic keyboard can "hear" an analog signal. In both cases, a conversion process must take place, from digital to analog and from analog to digital, commonly referred to as D/A and A/D.

In order for a stream of MIDI information to eventually reach D/A, it needs to contain meaningful bits of data that a D/A converter can use to manipulate audio data and then construct a sound wave. These bits of data are organized into 8-bit chunks, or *bytes*—meaning they are delivered 8 bits at a time—and make up what are called MIDI messages.

Bytes in the Message

Two types of bytes make up a MIDI message: status bytes and data bytes. A status byte comes first. It identifies what kind of MIDI data is being transmitted or received—for example, Note On or Note Off, Velocity, Modulation, Pitch, and so on. A data byte comes next, and it is simply the value of its associated status byte.

As an analogy, think of how a mixing board works: Imagine a board with 128 faders, each with a range of 128 different values. When you move fader 1 to the halfway position, it is like saying, "Fader 1, Value of 64." The instrument on fader 1 then changes its volume to a value of 64.

Now imagine that instead of moving a fader, you tap a note on a MIDI keyboard. When you press the key, a Note On status byte is sent, immediately followed by the data byte for that note, for example, a value of middle C. It's like saying, "Play a note. The note is Middle C." All MIDI devices receiving your MIDI messages respond by telling their D/A converters to get ready to render a note and then render it as Middle C. When you release the key, a Note Off status byte and a data byte of Middle C is sent, causing connected MIDI devices to stop playing Middle C.

Types of MIDI Messages

There are two basic types of MIDI messages: Channel messages and System messages. A Channel message is channel-specific, meaning there is always a channel number included in its status byte, whereas a System message is not channel-specific. System messages come in three different flavors: System Common, System Real-Time, and System Exclusive messages.

Channel messages can be further broken down into three groups: Voice messages, Controller messages, and Mode messages. Voice messages carry musical data, and make up most of the traffic in a MIDI data stream, whereas Controller messages allow you to affect musical data in other ways, such as panning the sound or adding vibrato. Mode messages work a bit differently: They deal only with the way a receiving MIDI device responds to Voice messages.

Voice Messages

There are several important kinds of Voice messages. They are:

- Note On
- Note Off
- Aftertouch
- Pitch Bend
- Bank Select and Program Change

Each type of Voice message is discussed in the following sections.

Note On

Note On is the most basic of all MIDI messages. Every time a key is pressed on a MIDI device, a Note On status byte is delivered, followed by pitch and velocity data bytes, which are values for the note's pitch and volume, respectively. MIDI devices don't exchange pitch information in terms of traditional letter names, such as Middle C or F#, but use numeric values between 0 and 127. This range effectively means you've got 128 different pitches at your disposal—40 more than a typical acoustic piano—although you'd be hard-pressed to find a MIDI controller with 128 keys!

Middle C is always a value of 60, hence a MIDI device that receives a Note On message and a value of 60 produces a sound with its pitch at Middle C, regardless of the instrument setting.

Velocity refers to how fast the key is struck, which more or less equates to volume. Velocity carries a value range from 0 to 127 and is obviously a critical data byte for shaping any performance.

Note Off

A Note Off message is just the opposite of Note On and must be sent to a MIDI device for it to release the note. Note Off also must be followed by messages for pitch and velocity. A Note Off/velocity message combination specifies the rate at which a key is lifted; velocity has a range from 0 to 127.

RELEASE VELOCITY

Technically speaking, a Note Off/velocity combination is called "Release Velocity," and a few instruments (Kurzweil, for example) can change voice parameters based on the rate at which you release keys. It's difficult to use, but extremely cool!

RUNNING STATUS

A Note On or Note Off message takes about one millisecond (ms) to be sent, which is quick enough that the human ear perceives multiple notes as being played simultaneously. Even if you played a 10-note chord, for example, the time between playback of the chord and when you pressed all the notes (10 ms) wouldn't be noticeable.

However, playing a large number of different parts, such as several tracks from a sequencer, could produce delays that might be noticeable. To prevent this, a technique called "running status" is often used.

Running status takes into account the fact that it's common for a string of MIDI messages to be of the same message type. For instance, when you play that 10-note chord, 10 successive Note On and Note Off messages are pretty much guaranteed to occur. So, running status doesn't change status bytes until a different status byte comes through. Running status doesn't work with all types of MIDI messages, but it does work for many important ones, such as pitch bend, which can produce a huge number of MIDI messages.

Aftertouch

An Aftertouch message is sent when any key is held and pressed harder or softer after striking the key. Not all MIDI devices support Aftertouch, and ones that do vary, responding differently depending on the type of instrument and the sensitivity of the electronic sensors built into the MIDI device.

Channel Pressure

The most common, and least expensive, type of Aftertouch is called channel pressure. Channel pressure calculates pressure sensitivity based on an average of all of the keys that you're holding down. In other words, you don't have individual control over each individual key. This type of Aftertouch is better than no Aftertouch, but is not nearly as useful as key pressure.

Key Pressure

Key pressure Aftertouch usually means that the MIDI device has a separate pressure sensor for each key or pad on the device. This means you can be much more expressive during a performance. For example, say you've written a horn section and you're playing several parts of the arrangement at the same time. At some point, you're going to want one or more of the instruments to stand out a bit more than the others while you're playing. Using key pressure, you can focus on any one note without also making the other instruments' notes brighter, which is a much more realistic horn section, because real brass instruments are capable of a wide range of subtle differences in volume and tone.

SUPPORTING KEY PRESSURE

Key pressure is more expensive to implement; therefore, many MIDI devices don't offer it. The same is true for many sound cards and MIDI sound modules. A MIDI device that supports key pressure won't do you much good if you're using a sound card that doesn't support it.

Aftertouch is not just for controlling volume. In fact, one of the most common uses of Aftertouch is for modulation or vibrato. The harder you hold down a key, the wider the resulting vibrato. This is very useful for wind and string instruments.

AFTERTOUCH SENSITIVITY

It's not uncommon for some instruments or sound patches to be overly sensitive to Aftertouch, making it difficult to play notes at high velocity with a vibrato effect, for example. You may have some luck adjusting the sensitivity of the MIDI device itself (if it offers that capability), but the easiest route is to edit the Aftertouch values using your sequencing software after recording the performance.

Pitch Bend

Most MIDI devices have the ability to bend the pitch of any given note, usually using a toggle or wheel control. Pitch Bend messages are great for accentuating the natural expressiveness of instruments such as guitar, flute, and even some percussion.

Pitch bend is measured by combining two data messages. Because a range of 0 to 127 isn't sufficient to create a convincing effect, MIDI combines two data messages to provide 16,384 possible values (128 × 128). This creates a high enough resolution to make pitch changes smooth and continuous.

Bank Select and Program Change

MIDI instruments are organized into a MIDI device's memory by numbered banks, and each bank contains individual sound patches tagged with unique ID numbers. A MIDI Bank Select message allows a MIDI device to trigger a bank change on any other device with a matching MIDI channel.

A Program Change message then brings up a sound within the bank that corresponds to the ID being sent. This seems basic enough at first glance, but it's actually quite powerful: Because a Program Change affects only an ID and not any other sound parameters, it can be applied to any MIDI-compatible device, such as an effects unit, a mixer, or even a sampler.

A STANDARD PROBLEM

General MIDI aside (see Chapter 9, "Wading in MIDI"), there is no standard for numbering patches and banks, nor is there any agreed-upon system for organizing instrument types with ID numbers. Hence, most MIDI devices are packed with sounds that are numbered well beyond the scope of the GM specification, which makes it difficult to share anything beyond GM across multiple MIDI devices.

Controller Messages

Controller messages are similar to Voice messages, but they behave a bit differently. These messages provide extended "control" over the sounds or instruments that you associate with them and are typically transmitted using a modulation wheel or other controller on a MIDI device, such as a pedal, slider, touch ribbon, knob, fader, and so on. Controller messages use a status byte just like a Voice message, but they use two data bytes, rather than just one. The first data byte is the Controller Number, of which there are 128 possible values (numbered from 0 to 127). The second byte is similar to the data byte in a Voice message—it's the actual value of a particular controller.

The idea behind MIDI controllers is that they work while the MIDI device is generating sound, in "real time," so that the effect is immediately noticeable. However, Controller messages can also be sent from within a MIDI software program, usually through virtual knobs and faders as part of the software interface or by editing a particular value directly.

Many of today's songs use controllers in creative and innovative ways to give a customized, unique expressiveness to a sequence. The next sections cover the most common types of controllers.

Modulation

Most sounds in a MIDI device respond to modulation with a vibrato effect. Vibrato is a common and useful type of modulation and can add realism to wind, string, and brass instruments if used carefully. Vibrato can also create some very nonintuitive and unrealistic sounds when applied to other types of instruments, such as piano or percussion, for example. In addition, many electronic instruments respond too abruptly to modulation, which can create unnatural and sometimes indecipherable mutations.

Devices that control modulation—such as a modulation wheel or pedal—typically control the depth of the effect, not the speed. Speed is almost always a preset parameter.

FLEXIBLE MODULATION

Modulation isn't just for wavering the pitch of an instrument, as is the case with vibrato. It can also be used to produce a trill (with a square wave) or introduce distortion, with noise as the modulation source.

Volume

This message controls a sound's volume. Just like the knob on your home stereo, a Volume message controls the overall output level. If you manipulate a Volume message using a software sequencer via a virtual knob or fader, it can create dynamic volume changes.

Volume doesn't affect a given MIDI instrument's velocity; rather, it adjusts the internal volume of any sounds using it. A good general rule-of-thumb is to set an instrument's volume to maximum and then use Volume messages to change the volume. This can be more expressive and accurate than using velocity strictly for volume control.

Pan

The Pan Controller has a value range from 0 to 127, where 0 is a full left pan and 127 is a full right pan. Most keyboards are equipped with stereo output connections. By connecting both left and right outputs to two channels of a mixer and setting the pan-pots to a corresponding hard left and hard right, automated pan moves can be performed using the Pan Controller and sequencing software.

Sustain Pedal

A critical part of getting a good piano sound is the use of a sustain pedal. The Sustain Pedal Controller manages the depressing, sustaining, and releasing of a MIDI sustain pedal that you might use during a performance. Connecting a compatible sustain pedal to a master MIDI controller and applying it during the recording of a part is usually enough to initiate Sustain Pedal messages.

Other Controllers

Each Controller message carries with it a specific number, and although there are 128 possible controller types, not all of them are predefined. Table 10.1 shows the defined controller types. Notice the gaps in the left-hand column of numbers: These gaps represent nondefined controller types, which could be just about anything a particular manufacturer wants them to be.

Not all of the defined types are implemented in every MIDI device, either, and often MIDI devices implement the defined types differently. For example, a device may recognize and respond only to controller number 1, Modulation Wheel (coarse), and not implement controller number 33, Modulation Wheel (fine), to save processing overhead.

A FINE ADJUSTMENT

The difference between "coarse" and "fine," in technical terms, is a difference in the bit-resolution of the controller itself. A fine adjustment is twice the bit-resolution, which translates to a more realistic or intuitive effect but takes more processing power.

Table 10.1
MIDI-defined controllers

Controller Number	Name	Controller Number	Name
0	Bank Select	38	Data Entry (fine)
1	Modulation Wheel (coarse)	39	Volume (fine)
2	Breath Controller (coarse)	40	Balance (fine)
4	Foot Pedal (coarse)	42	Pan Position (fine)
5	Portamento Time (coarse)	43	Expression (fine)
6	Data Entry (coarse)	44	Effect Control 1 (fine)
7	Volume (coarse)	45	Effect Control 2 (fine)
8	Balance (coarse)	64	Hold Pedal (on/off)
10	Pan Position (coarse)	65	Portamento (on/off)
11	Expression (coarse)	66	Sustenuto Pedal (on/off)
12	Effect Control 1 (coarse)	67	Soft Pedal (on/off)
13	Effect Control 2 (coarse)	68	Legato Pedal (on/off)
16	General Purpose Slider 1	69	Hold 2 Pedal (on/off)
17	General Purpose Slider 2	70	Sound Variation
18	General Purpose Slider 3	71	Sound Timbre
19	General Purpose Slider 4	72	Sound Release Time
32	Bank Select (fine)	73	Sound Attack Time
33	Modulation Wheel (fine)	74	Sound Brightness
34	Breath Controller (fine)	75	Sound Control 6
36	Foot Pedal (fine)	76	Sound Control 7
37	Portamento Time (fine)	77	Sound Control 8

Table 10.1
MIDI-defined controllers (continued)

Controller Number	Name	Controller Number	Name
78	Sound Control 9	98	Non-registered Parameter (fine)
79	Sound Control 10	99	Non-registered Parameter (coarse)
80	General Purpose Button 1 (on/off)	100	Registered Parameter (fine)
81	General Purpose Button 2 (on/off)	101	Registered Parameter (coarse)
82	General Purpose Button 3 (on/off)	120	All Sound Off
83	General Purpose Button 4 (on/off)	121	All Controllers Off
91	Effects Level	122	Local Keyboard (on/off)
92	Tremulo Level	123	All Notes Off
93	Chorus Level	124	Omni Mode Off
94	Celeste Level	125	Omni Mode On
95	Phaser Level	126	Mono Operation
96	Data Button Increment	127	Poly Operation
97	Data Button Decrement		

Mode Messages

Most MIDI devices have a mode setting, which tells the device exactly how to respond to incoming notes on each of its 16 channels. The following mode settings are common:

- **Omni mode**. The MIDI device responds to note messages on all sixteen channels.

- **Poly mode**. The MIDI device responds to note messages on the current channel only.
- **Mono mode**. The MIDI device responds to note messages one note at a time (monophony) on any combination of channels.
- **Multi mode**. The MIDI device responds to note messages on any combination of channels but maintains the messages relative to each channel.

Though a particular device's mode setting is usually set locally on the device itself, Mode messages can control the way a device responds to other MIDI events from an external master or sequencing software. The types of Mode messages are:

- Omni On/Poly
- Omni Off/Poly
- Omni On/Mono
- Omni Off/Mono

When Omni/Poly is on, a MIDI device responds to incoming MIDI data on all channels and incoming Note On messages are played polyphonically—meaning that each note is assigned its own voice, up to the maximum number of voices the MIDI device has available. The result, of course, is that multiple notes are played at the same time.

When Omni/Poly is off, a MIDI device responds only to MIDI messages on one channel. This can be useful when several MIDI devices are daisy-chained together using the MIDI Thru port, because each device in the chain can be set to play one part and ignore the information related to the other parts.

When Mono mode is selected, a single voice is assigned to each MIDI channel, so that only one note can be played on a given channel at a time.

Most MIDI devices these days default to Omni On/Poly, and, generally speaking, Omni On/Poly gives you the most flexibility and is the easiest with which to work.

All Notes Off

As the name suggests, this Mode message globally stops all notes that are currently on. This is useful to stop an entire sequence from playing back—when using sequencing software, for example.

Reset All Controllers

This Mode message resets all MIDI controllers. Most sequencing software sends a Reset All Controllers message immediately following an All Notes Off message when the Stop button is pressed or clicked.

Local Control Off

In a MIDI configuration with two or more MIDI devices, a Local Control Off message may be very useful. Local Control Off, with a data byte of 0, disables a device's ability to be operated from the device itself, which is helpful when using a software sequencer to change instrument sounds.

System Messages

MIDI System messages come in three flavors: System Common, System Real-Time, and System Exclusive. System Common messages are useful for sending information to all the MIDI devices in your setup, and System Real-Time messages are used to synchronize two or more MIDI devices. System Exclusive messages, or SysEx, are device specific and are used to relay information that might be useful only to a specific MIDI device.

System Common Messages

System Common messages are not something you'll deal with on a regular basis—they typically work behind the scenes, usually as a means of additional communication between your MIDI devices and software. The following are the most common System Common messages:

- **MTC Quarter Frame messages**. Are part of MIDI time code, or MTC, that is used for synchronizing MIDI devices with other equipment, typically audio and video tape machines.
- **Song Select messages**. Are used with sequencers or drum machines to store and recall "songs," or sequenced MIDI tracks, that have been stored in memory.
- **Song Position Pointer**. Allows for playing back a song from any point in a MIDI sequence; though it is a System Common message, it can only be used with MIDI devices or software that recognizes MIDI System Real-Time messages, because it derives its ability to keep track of note positions through the use of the MIDI clock.
- **Tune Request message**. Is useful for analog synths for retuning internal oscillators and is not typically used with digital MIDI devices.
- **End of Exclusive (EOX) message**. Indicates the end of a System Exclusive message.

MIDI TIME CODE SYNCHRONIZATION

MIDI time code synchronization is useful for synchronizing external audio or video data and for letting your software sequencer act as a slave to another MIDI device. It's essentially a way for MIDI to recognize and react to other types of time code, chiefly SMPTE time code. Time code messages are received from an external MIDI device or from a MIDI interface that generates MTC from another time code signal, such as SMPTE. Cubase, for example, uses MTC for this purpose.

Time code is nothing more than an indication of position and timing that specifies the position of data in an audio or video track and the speed of the track. Both MTC and SMPTE label position in terms of hours, minutes, and seconds, whereas speed is indicated via a frame rate calculation.

Time code is recorded onto tape using a time code generator—a process called "striping." Normally, the start of a tape stripe has a particular time, for example, 00:00:00:00 or 01:00:00:00. The actual audio or video data on the tape may start anywhere, though, after the start of the time code itself.

Most sequencing software—including Cubase—supports the most common time code frame rates, as shown in Table 10.2.

Table 10.2
Typical time code frame rates

Time Code Frame Rate	Uses
24 fps	The standard for movies and film
25 fps (also called EBU time code)	PAL/SECAM video, video, and some film in countries that use 50 Hz wall electricity
29.97 fps non drop-frame	NTSC nonbroadcast and short video in North America and Japan and some audio applications
29.97 drop-frame	NTSC broadcast and long-format video in North America and Japan
30 fps non drop-frame	Many music projects, some film in North America
30 fps drop-frame	Used only rarely for speed correction and transfer problems

System Real-Time Messages

System Real-Time messages are used to synchronize MIDI clock-based devices, such as sequencing software, synthesizers with built-in sequencers, and drum machines. To keep accurate time, System Real-Time messages are given priority over other messages, and these single-byte messages may occur anywhere in a MIDI data stream. System Real-Time messages include the MIDI Clock, Start, Continue, Stop, Active Sensing, and System Reset. Together, these messages work to keep MIDI notes and other messages in sync and in time.

System Exclusive (SysEx) Messages

System Exclusive messages allow a MIDI device to send and receive special information that pertains only to a particular MIDI device. A MIDI device that can use SysEx messages carries with it an assigned manufacturer's ID number that allows it to be distinguished from the other MIDI devices when data is sent or received. SysEx messages are used mostly to transmit custom sound patch settings to a software sequencer or proprietary patch librarian/editor. By doing so, special instrument parameters can be played, stored, or edited along with the rest of the MIDI information for a specific sequence.

Certain SysEx ID numbers are reserved for special activities, such as doing a MIDI Sample Dump, which is a way for MIDI devices to share sampled audio data between them, as well as MIDI Show Control and MIDI Machine Control.

A MIDI Sequencing Tutorial

This section takes you, step-by-step, through a MIDI sequencing session, including setting up a typical MIDI configuration, the sequencing process itself, and the editing of MIDI tracks. This tutorial uses Cubase (**www.steinberg.net**), a combination audio/MIDI software package that has been used elsewhere throughout this book. Cubase is full of professional features, is powerful and fast, and represents the best value on the market today for the home recording artist. There are lots of other software packages for the Macintosh, but Cubase is your best bang for the buck. It also has one of the easiest-to-understand graphical interfaces around.

Still, if you are using another brand of software, that's cool: Almost all software sequencers share the same basic functionality, and you generally can't break software simply by clicking a wrong button!

The Setup

The MIDI setup for this tutorial looks like this:

- Cubase SX/SL
- M-Audio Quattro USB audio card with MIDI I/O
- Roland JV-1080 synth module
- MIDIman USB MIDI controller keyboard
- LM-7 virtual drum machine
- VB-1 virtual bass module

Hooking it Together

Figure 10.1 is a diagram of how the devices in this tutorial are connected. The MIDI controller keyboard functions as the master controller for the entire studio. As it is a USB device, the controller keyboard plugs into the back of the Mac and can be easily configured via the driver software that accompanies it.

Next, the JV-1080 must be plugged into the available MIDI ports that are found on the front panel of the Quattro. The rule-of-thumb to remember here is that the MIDI In on the Quattro is connected to the MIDI Out on the JV-1080, and vice versa.

The LM-7 is a virtual drum machine that comes included with Cubase and is triggered by the controller keyboard. The VB-1 is a virtual bass guitar module that comes included with Cubase as well and is triggered in the same manner as the LM-7. The only thing you have to worry about here is installing Cubase properly.

This setup allows all three devices—the JV-1080, VB-1, and LM-7 drum machine—to receive MIDI data from Cubase on the computer. This means that, for drum parts, the pads on the virtual drum machine can be recorded and played back from the master controller, and the JV-1080 and VB-1 sounds are independent of the drum machine. These devices are easy to manage separately using Cubase.

Although this is a relatively easy and straightforward MIDI setup, as time goes on you may come to find that you will need more MIDI ports for other synth modules and drum machines. Should this be the case, you can simply use an external MIDI multiport interface, such as those made by Mark of the Unicorn (**www.motu.com**), Steinberg (**www.steinberg.net**), or MIDIman (**www.midiman.com**), to keep daisy-chaining to a minimum.

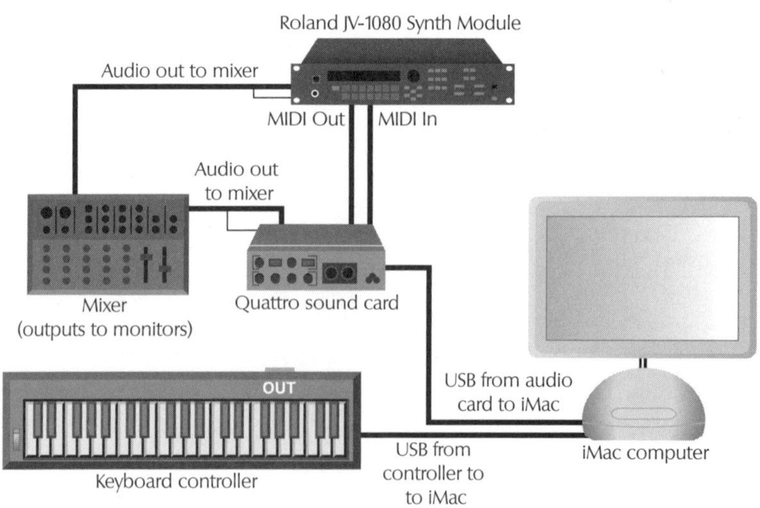

Figure 10.1
This MIDI setup is simple and allows for control of both sound-generating MIDI devices

Figure 10.1 also shows how the stereo outputs, which carry the analog audio signals from the different MIDI devices, are routed to a mixing board so that the music can be monitored while recording and playing back MIDI tracks and live performances at the same time. The mixing board, in this case, has channel inserts as well as direct outputs to handle routing output signal mixed with input signal on separate buses. (This tutorial is concerned only with MIDI; for more detail on how to set up the digital audio portion of your home studio, see Chapter 11, "Fun-Da-Mental Audio.")

The Cubase Interface

When Cubase is launched, the first thing you'll see is pretty much nothing, except for a bunch of pull-down menus. This is because a Cubase project has not been created, or opened up. If this is your first time using Cubase, you need to create a new project. It's simple to do.

1. Select File > New Project.
2. Cubase then provides a list of templates to choose from. Select 16 Track MIDI Sequencer (see Figure 10.2).

Figure 10.2
Available templates

3. You are then asked to select a Project Folder where the data can be stored. Use the Documents folder if you are new to Mac OS X, because it's easy to find (see Figure 10.3).

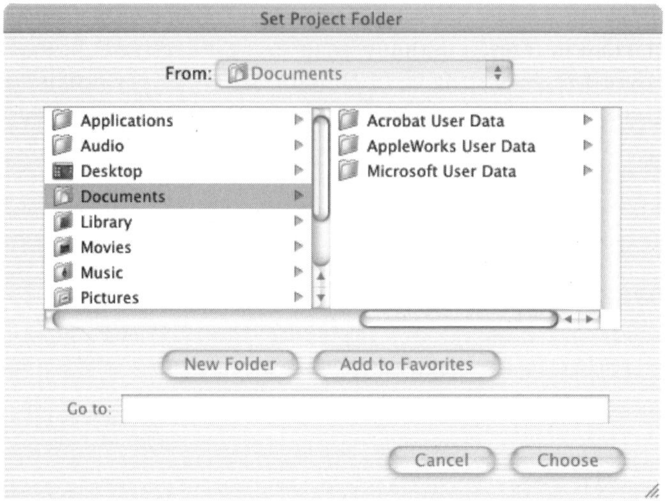

Figure 10.3
Setting the Project Folder

4. After you have selected a project folder, just give the project a name, or you can leave it untitled and Cubase's interface launches.

Toward the bottom of the screen (see Figure 10.4), you'll find the Transport bar, which controls recording, editing, and playing back MIDI sequences.

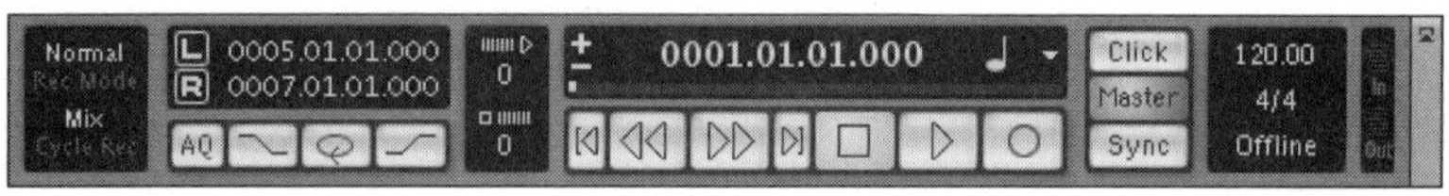

Figure 10.4
Cubase's Transport bar buttons are fashioned after traditional recording control buttons

The tool bar contains some familiar buttons, including "Play," "Stop," and "Record." It also contains basic information about the sequence being recorded or played back, such as the tempo setting, position, and time signature.

Cubase, like most MIDI software applications, derives its sequencing power from utilizing one of the System Common messages discussed earlier, the Song Position Pointer. The Song Position Pointer allows MIDI software to find the location of a sequence down to at least the nearest sixteenth note.

Enabling MIDI Tracks

The Project window displays track information as well as the recorded sequences once you've recorded them. The right side of the resizing bar contains a visual of the MIDI data coming into the computer, which makes locating notes and editing sequences of notes easy.

To record a track in Cubase, you must first map it to a MIDI device. As shown in Figure 10.5, Track 1's MIDI Out port is set to the JV-1080, and in this case it has been mapped to an instrument sound from the 1080 called "Film Score 1." The MIDI channel is set to 1, and, in this case, there is no special setting for the MIDI In port—it's designated by the "Port 1" setting, which maps the In port from the USB MIDI controller keyboard.

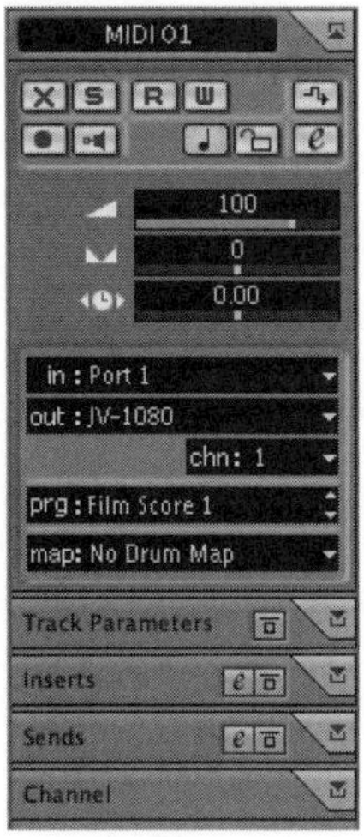

Figure 10.5
Track 1 is set to receive and send MIDI information for the JV-1080

The setup for the LM-7 drum machine is a little different, but it's just as easy:

1. Select Devices > VST Instruments
2. The VST Instruments rack appears, and it is empty, because there are no VST Instruments loaded. Just select the LM-7 from any of the empty rack spaces. The LM-7 then loads up with the default Compressor acoustic drum kit (see Figure 10.6).

Figure 10.6
Cubase is capable of loading as many as 32 individual VST Instruments in one project

3. In the Cubase Project window, select Track 2 and set the input to Port 1 and the output to the LM-7 (see Figure 10.7).

Figure 10.7
Mapping a MIDI track to a VST Instrument is a snap

4. Play the note C1 on your MIDI keyboard and you should hear the kick drum patch.
5. Repeat the same steps to load and use the VB-1.

SETTING UP CUBASE MIDI DEVICES

Although this tutorial doesn't address installation and basic configuration of Cubase, setting up a MIDI device in Cubase is very easy. Just install the MIDI device from the MIDI Device Manager from the Devices pull-down menu. After this is done, you can navigate through the sounds of your MIDI modules within Cubase. If your module is not listed, contact Steinberg to find out if there is a patch script available for your MIDI module.

The exceptions to this rule are the VST Instruments. Because they are software-based and run within Cubase, the patch list for every virtual synth is ready and waiting to be used once it is turned on in the VST Instruments rack.

The MIDI Recording Process

After you're hooked up and your MIDI ports have been set, you're ready to begin a MIDI recording session. You can play anything you want, but for the purposes of the tutorial, we'll set up the song a little beforehand.

In this case, it's a basic groove with some drums, bass, and strings—a pop ditty. We'll add a kick drum, snare, hi-hat, toms, and cymbals for the percussion, lay down a bass line, and then add some strings for melody and harmony.

You could start with any of the instruments, but in this case, we'll lay down the beat first, which provides a solid anchor for the other parts. In pop music, rhythm is critical, and it's one of the hardest things to get right using MIDI.

Here's the step-by-step:

1. Set the meter and tempo first. In Cubase, click the "4/4" on the Transport bar, and then type in the time signature that you want for this tune (if this is your first sequence, you should use 4/4). For tempo, click the text box on the Transport bar and type in the desired bpm (beats per minute). For example, you might set the time to 6/8 and the tempo to 120 bpm—both good choices for a pop tune. These settings are essential to laying down the drums properly, and, ideally, you want to know what they are before you start. However, you can easily change them later.
2. Next, you want to set up your left and right locator points so that you can create a four-bar drum loop. To do this, look to the far left on the Transport bar to find the left and right locators. Set the left to measure one and the right to measure five. Then click on the loop playback button, which is located right below the locator points on the Transport bar. The button looks like a lasso and can be activated by either clicking on it with your mouse, or simply by using the "/" key on your keyboard. Once activated, the sequence plays in a loop between the left and right locators.
3. You're now ready to record your first drum track on Track 2 with the LM-7. We're going to use cycle recording so that we can record a full drum kit on one MIDI track. Cycle record allows you to constantly overdub your MIDI performance each time the four-bar loop plays through. This way, you can record your kick drum on the first pass, then the snare, and then top it off with a little hi-hat (see Figure 10.8). If you're using a keyboard, you'll use note number 36 (C1) for the kick, 38 (D1) for the snare, and 42 (F#1) for the hi-hat.

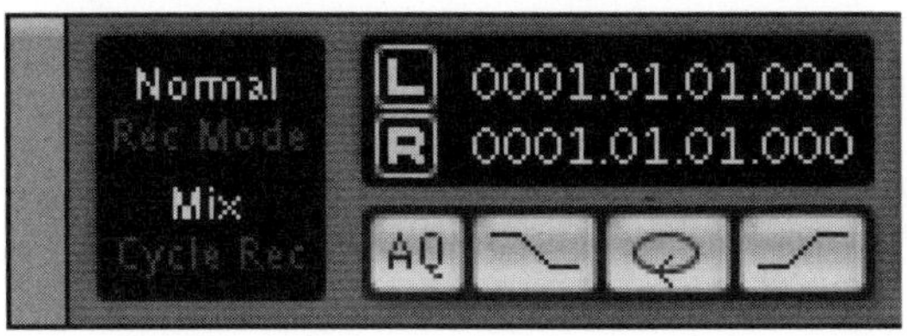

Figure 10.8
Before you record your first MIDI track, make sure the Cycle Record mode is set to "Mix" and that the Cycle mode is turned on by selecting it with your mouse or using the "/" key on your keyboard

4. To begin recording in Cubase, arm the track by clicking the Record Enable button in Track 2. Then click the Record button on the Transport bar, or press "*" on your keyboard. After you've started recording, you'll hear a metronome from your sound card to keep you in time. Lay down a kick drum sound on every beat in the four-bar loop, then record a snare, and finish up with a hi-hat. When you're finished, tap the space bar or click the Stop button on the tool bar and you should see a MIDI clip that looks similar to Figure 10.9. Voila, instant rhythmic bliss!

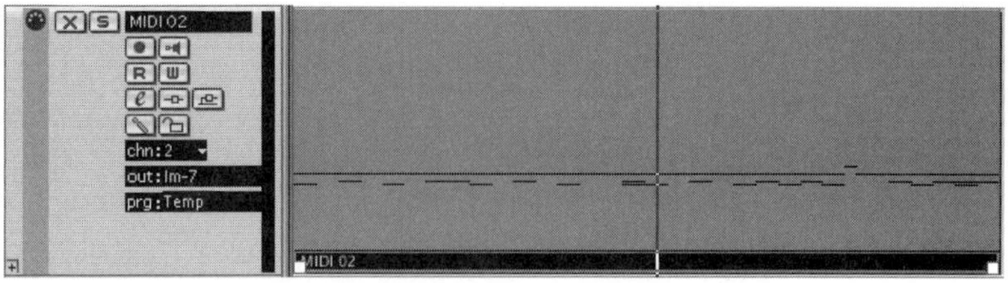

Figure 10.9
Keep it steady and now you're ready to record your first MIDI rhythm track

> **SETTING A LEAD-IN**
> By default, recording begins immediately with the sound of the metronome, but you may want to give yourself some lead-in before you start playing. In Cubase, select Metronome setup from the Transport menu, and then select the number of measures of pre-count that you want.

5. For the bass line on Track 3, you need to decide what you're going to play on your VB-1. For the tutorial, you can play a time-honored pop "walk-up" bass line, which puts the following notes at 8 beats each per measure: E, G, A, B, and E. Repeat this for several bars.
6. For strings on Track 1, lay down a melody of your choice and some backing chords for depth and harmony with the JV-1080. First, record the main line on the first pass, and then record on top of the same track to achieve a really thick and layered string section.

After you record each track, Cubase plays it back as you record subsequent tracks. The beauty of sequencing is its nonlinear design: There's no real "rewind," because you can jump later to any point in the sequence and edit individual notes.

Quantizing

Play back everything you've done so far. How does it sound? Unless you're the exception rather than the rule, your timing isn't going to be dead on. This is where quantizing comes in handy. Quantization is an incredible feature found on every modern sequencer that corrects timing to the nearest metric value that you specify.

In this example, quantizing to the nearest eighth note should correct any stray rhythm issues, though you can quantize up to a sixty-fourth of a note, as well as in triplets. Start by quantizing the drum track. In Cubase, highlight the drum track and select Quantize from the MIDI menu. Set the quantize resolution to an eighth note and bingo: You're as tight as a drum.

Many software sequencers provide additional parameters that allow you to further customize the quantization for any selection of notes. This can help with putting some of the natural feeling back into a performance. For example, in Cubase, selecting Groove Setup from the MIDI menu gives you options such as Shuffle Feel, Straight Feel, Pushing Feel, Late Snare, and so on.

Copying Tracks

One of the beautiful things about MIDI is how easily you can take one performance and layer it by copying it onto another track, and then changing the instrument sound. This was the main impetus for the creation of the MIDI specification to begin with—to be able to create rich compositions by layering sounds.

With any modern software sequencer, copying and pasting tracks is as simple as using a word processor. You start by selecting the MIDI data comprising the track you've recorded, copy it, and then paste it to a new track. After it is pasted, you simply change instruments for that track until you get something you like!

You can also edit individual notes to make the track vary from the original in any way you want, or you can change the entire track by raising or lowering all of the notes a half-step at a time, creating instant harmonies using multiple instruments.

Editing MIDI Notes

Editing individual notes is a highly useful and common feature on all modern sequencers. In most applications, including Cubase, this is achieved through the Key Editor.

The Key Edit View in Cubase, as shown in Figure 10.10, lists all of the notes for a track on a grid. The vertical axis shows a virtual piano indicating each note and its pitch, and the horizontal axis shows when and where the notes were played. Editing an individual note is as simple as highlighting the note, dragging and dropping it to another pitch, shortening or lengthening it, or deleting it to make mistakes disappear instantly.

Figure 10.10
The Key Edit view is a wonderful way to hand-edit your music without having to rerecord the performance

KEY EDIT

It's not hard to see how useful the Key Edit feature can be. Aside from having the capability to deliberately change pitch and note placement at will, you can easily correct stray notes or that perfect performance that was ruined by one or two flub-ups.

You can also smooth out volume changes using a piano roll editor. You will recall that velocity is a MIDI message that measures how fast each key is pressed. By making strategic velocity changes in percussion instruments, you can quickly add a more natural feel to the performance—or unnatural, if that's your gig! Other instruments can benefit from velocity editing—for example, adding some punchiness to the bass in the tutorial or creating a smooth string ensemble crescendo.

In fact, most software sequencers that provide a key editor allow you to graphically edit all of the Controller messages your devices and/or the software itself supports.

11

Fun-Da-Mental Audio

It's time to home in on perhaps the most critical part of successful home studio recording—the sound itself. This chapter focuses on getting to the heart of what makes a great-sounding recording by distilling the science of audio. You'll learn the most important things you need to know in order to get up and running and actually producing something. These include:

- The basic principles of audio engineering
- The difference between analog and digital recording
- The basics of digital audio file formats
- Which kind of recording gear works best for you
- How to choose and install a computer sound card
- How to choose headphones for monitoring and mixing
- The most common types of DSP

Audio Engineering 101

What makes a "good" sound? Putting the music itself aside for a moment, why is it that some recordings wring emotion out of you like water out of a sponge, while others have little effect at all? It's the sound—the realism, surrealism, or otherwise—that often does it, and, contrary to popular belief, it ain't all that complicated to understand.

A Little Math, Please

In one sense, sound is, pure and simple, a matter of math. The way sound works is a much traversed (and much ballyhooed) piece of science, and there are a number of facts about acoustics and audio that are unavoidable, especially when it comes to music. In fact, the physiology of sound has played a major role in the character and existence of music long before music was, well, music.

Here are some fundamental facts about sound and music—some of them translated for your pleasure into understandable English—from the *Audio Cyclopedia*, by Howard M. Tremaine (Howard Sams and Co., 1978, ASIN 0672206757):

- Sound is quantifiable: In humans, hearing takes place whenever vibrations of frequencies between about 15 and 20,000 hertz reach the inner ear.
- The hertz, or Hz, is a unit of frequency equaling one vibration, or cycle, per second.
- Vibrations reach the inner ear when they are transmitted through the air, and the term "sound" refers to these vibrational "waves." Some sound waves vibrate at frequencies lower and higher than what most humans can hear; for example, sounds of frequencies higher than about 20,000 Hz are called "ultrasonic."
- The human ear can easily pick out frequencies that differ by a factor of two, so most musical systems have naturally evolved around dividing notes where the frequencies of the notes in one group are a factor of two higher or lower than the notes in the other group.

A BRIEF HISTORY OF SOUND

The ancient Greeks had a great interest in music; Pythagoras, for example, discovered that an octave represents a 2-to-1 frequency ratio, and he stated the law connecting harmonic intervals with numerical ratios. (He also came up with some interesting religious ideas about sound, but that is another book.) Aristotle, too, made a fairly accurate guess concerning the nature of the generation and transmission of sound.

It wasn't until around 1600, however, that serious inroads were made into the scientific study of sound. Galileo formed many of the fundamental laws, including stating the relationship between pitch and frequency and the laws of musical harmony and dissonance. He also theorized that the frequency of sound produced by a stringed instrument depends on the length, weight, and tension of the string.

Since Galileo, there have been a number of advances in the study of sound, including developments by Heinrich Hertz (for whom the "hertz" was named) and Alexander Graham Bell (the decibel). Today, there are enough details in existence that some universities even offer Ph.D. programs in acoustics and sound engineering.

- In the system with which we're most familiar, the groups are called octaves, and an octave always contains seven major notes (C, D, E, F, G, A, and B) and five minor notes (C#, D#, F#, G#, and A#), for a total of twelve notes equally spaced on the scale.
- The American scale starts at C-0 and is located at 16.351 Hz, while the European scale ends at C10 and is located at 16,351 Hz. The C we usually consider to be Middle C is C4 on the American scale and is 261.63 Hz. In the American scale, A4, or A above Middle C, is set at 440 Hz.

There are lots of other facts, but you get the idea: The "standard notation" musical system is a finite system, which operates in a known way and is based on known facts about sound. This means that you can, to some degree, successfully predict and repeat how a performance and/or a recording will sound.

Sound Waves

A sound wave moves in a somewhat linear fashion, meaning that, as the wave motion created by a sound moves outward from the source of the sound, air molecules carry the sound parallel to the direction of wave motion. In this physical sense, a sound wave is a series of air molecules moving back and forth in the air, and after the sound wave has passed, each molecule stays in about the same location.

> **THINK SLINKY**
>
> Another way to think of the propagation of sound through air is a Slinky (you know, the toy: "a Slinky, a Slinky, it's fun for a girl and a boy"). While stretching a Slinky out on the ground, quick pulses can be sent down its length: The coils compress and expand without the Slinky actually going anywhere. These pulses in the coils are representative of how sound waves travel out from their source.

This is a bit different from other types of physical waves. For example, if you throw a rock into a pond, a cork floating near where the rock hits the water will bob up and down, moving somewhat perpendicular, rather than parallel, to the point of impact. It will show some, but very little, outward motion in the direction of the wave motion.

The way in which sound waves behave has implications for musical notes. In fact, musical notes end up with three basic characteristics that correspond to three physical characteristics:

- Pitch refers to how fast the sound wave vibrates, otherwise known as the sound's *frequency*.
- Intensity is the loudness of the sound, also known as *amplitude*.
- Timbre is the accuracy of the sound frequency, physically described as the sound's *waveform*.

> **NOTES VS NOISE**
>
> A musical note is a simple sound. Noise is a highly complex sound—a mixture of many different frequencies and/or notes that are not harmonically related and cannot be neatly described in terms of pitch, volume, and timbre.

Pitch

Pitch, or frequency, of a sound wave is a measure (in hertz) of the number of waves passing a given point in 1 second. Frequency can be controlled independent of amplitude or waveform, as in the case of the notes on a keyboard. Each note is "tuned" to a specific frequency. To illustrate this, consider the sound of a typical fire engine's siren, which consists of a rotating wheel with 44 teeth. The wheel rotates at 10 revolutions per second, with each tooth interrupting an air blast creating 440 vibrations per second, or 440 Hz.

This is equivalent to the A above Middle C on a keyboard. Though the sound of the siren is quite different in quality from that of A above Middle C, they correspond closely in pitch.

Two octaves above Middle C on the piano, A has a frequency of 880 Hz. Similarly, an A one octave below Middle C has a frequency of 220 Hz, and the next octave below has a frequency of 110 Hz, and so on. In fact, an octave, by definition, is the interval between any two notes by a factor of a 2-to-1 ratio.

EUPHONIUS INTERVALS

A fundamental law of harmony states that when two notes an octave apart are sounded together, they produce a pleasant sound to the human ear, or a *euphonious* sound.

A fifth and a major third sounded with the "root" note produces a slightly less euphonious sound. In terms of physics, an interval of a fifth consists of two frequencies at a ratio of 3 to 2, while a major third has a ratio of 5 to 4.

The general rule is that two or more notes sound sweet when played together if their frequencies reduce to small, whole numbers. Otherwise, the sound is not so sweet and produces dissonance—which, arguably, can be sweet to some ears! In addition, it's not technically possible to arrange notes on most instruments, including piano and guitar, so that all the ratios hold exactly, so some compromises are made when tuning, resulting in a somewhat altered scale known as the tempered scale.

Volume

The greater the volume, or amplitude, of a wave, the harder the air molecules strike the ear drum, and the louder the sound is perceived. The amplitude of a sound wave can be measured in several ways: the distance of displacement between the air molecules; the pressure difference in the compression and "rarefaction;" and even the actual, physical energy that's produced. Human speech, for example, produces sound energy at the rate of around one hundred-thousandth of a watt. These types of measurements are quite difficult to make, however, so the intensity of a sound is generally expressed by comparing it to a standard reference measurement, the decibel (dB).

The decibel is actually one-tenth of a *bel*, an idea developed by and named after Alexander Graham Bell. The bel is a ratio that compares the intensity of two sounds and is expressed in large, logarithmic values from 10 to 10,000,000,000. Because the bel never really falls into the range of human-perceptible sound, the decibel is used instead. The range is generally about 0 to 120 dB, with a whisper coming in at about 20 dB, a conversation at about 60 dB, and a space shuttle blasting off (or a Pearl Jam concert) around 120 dB.

Graphically, using an oscilloscope or digital editing software, amplitude is represented by how tall the waveform is. Figure 11.1 shows a waveform of a song in Cubase.

Figure 11.1
This waveform of a track in Cubase shows both the frequency and the volume of the sound

Timbre

If A above Middle C is played on a bass guitar, a piano, and a tuning fork—all at the same volume—the notes have the same frequency and amplitude, but are quite different in quality. Of these three instruments, the simplest tone is produced by the tuning fork, which is almost entirely pure sound waves having a frequency of 440 Hz. The bass guitar and piano are less pure, because they contain other frequencies—in this case exact multiples of 440, called *harmonics*—which determine the quality, or timbre, of the note. The intensity of these additional frequencies is what makes a piano sound like a piano and a bass guitar sound like a bass guitar.

Of course, the physical ear is not perfect (and not exactly the same for every person), so even the most pure tone of the tuning fork isn't going to reach the brain in pure form in any case.

Tone Reality

The human ear is most sensitive to tones in the range from A above Middle C up to A four octaves higher—so sensitive that a sound in this range can be hundreds of times fainter than a sound an octave higher or two octaves lower and still be heard. For tones of slightly different loudness or slightly different frequency, perception is, naturally, much less accurate.

For example, a difference in amplitude of just 1 dB and a difference in frequency of 30 percent (about 1/20 of a note) can be distinguished in sounds of moderate intensity at frequencies in the 1 to 2 kHz range. In this same range, the difference between the softest sound that can be heard and the loudest sound that can be heard is about 120 dB.

This is quite sensitive—but these facts refer to pure tones, such as those produced in a controlled environment by an oscillator. The reality is that, at high volume, the ear is pretty much equally sensitive to most frequencies, but at low volume the ear is much more sensitive to the middle high frequencies than to the lowest and highest notes. In other words, a recording with a lot of mid-level frequencies—not unusual for a typical pop or rock song—will seem to lose its lowest and highest tones when the volume is decreased. In fact, this is exactly why many stereos have a "loudness" switch, which boosts high and low frequencies to compensate for the perceived loss of the lowest and highest tones at low listening volumes.

This imperfection of the human ear is called *masking*, and it will be of concern to you as a home studio recording engineer. As you'll see later in this chapter and in Chapter 13, "Recording and Mixing," it can present a problem for getting a mix that will sound consistent across a number of different playback devices; in fact, properly managing the amount of "mid in the mix" can often be a bit tricky. Ample midrange frequencies usually sound great on a good stereo with the volume pumped up, but it can be almost ruinous on an inexpensive car stereo.

Analog vs. Digital Recording

When Sir George Martin started his relationship with the Fab Four, he had the technological equivalent of a 4-track tape recorder. It was the technology of the time, and it took a great ear and a lot of savvy to translate the abilities and talents of the Beatles to tape. Don't think for a second that issues of equalization, tape hiss, unpredictable equipment, bad microphone response, and inferior instruments weren't very much a part of a day in the life of Sir George.

Whether you're a Beatles fan or not, you can appreciate the fact that Sir George managed to overcome the limits of the technology at the time and produced startlingly good recordings. He did it because he had artistic vision (and awfully good musicians and songwriters to work with) and because he knew all the subtleties and intricacies of every piece of equipment he had to use.

However, Sir George today would probably be the first person to tell you, as a home recording artist, to take advantage of digital recording technology. Why? Because it's easier, it's cheaper, and the result is better than analog for a home studio. Although there are still a number of traditional analog or analog-digital hybrid studios all over the world that still churn out hit records, they have a few things you don't, including money, a full-time, dedicated engineering staff, and a whole lot of experience. And even with all that professional gear and experience, there are sometimes significant differences in recording quality from studio to studio.

Of course, going digital is not a license to ignore the fundamentals of sound recording, processing, and mixing; for example, whether you compress a bass track with the click of a mouse or you use a rack-mount unit, knowing what compression ratios to use, how to tweak input settings, delay times, and volume levels still applies. However, you will find that the learning curve is not so much a rock-climb as it is a few pushes in the right direction to get you going when it comes to a digital studio.

Digital is Cheaper, Much Cheaper

Make no mistake about it: The home recording revolution has not happened because professional 24-track mixing boards and 1-inch tape machines suddenly plummeted in price and ease of use. The reason a book like this one even exists is because of the advances made in digital recording technology using a computer or DAW (digital audio workstation), which have, in many cases, reduced a room full of audio equipment down to a handful of software plug-ins. This has enabled hundreds of thousands of home studio artists to produce high-quality recordings because they don't have to mortgage their lives to afford the equipment.

Why compare digital equipment to a professional studio? Isn't it more comparable to an 8-track cassette tape recorder or an inexpensive reel-to-reel 1/4-inch tape recorder? Not at all, for two reasons: First, a tape recorder doesn't record as accurately and noiselessly as a good quality sound card or DAW; second, with every generation of tape editing, the original quality of the recording drops significantly. This problem is nonexistent with a digital setup.

DIGITAL PRO/CONSUMER GAP IS SMALL

Analog multitrack cassette tape recorders also suffer from limited surface area on the tape itself, as well as much slower tape speeds than professional equipment. Contrast this with 16-bit, 44.1 kHz digital audio, which is the same whether you're using expensive professional equipment or inexpensive consumer equipment.

With that in mind, Tables 11.1 and 11.2 compare typical core equipment costs of a digital home studio setup with that of a professional studio. You don't have to be a math major to immediately see the difference (note that these figures are estimates at the time of this writing).

Table 11.1
The basic costs of a digital home studio

Equipment Type	Cost
Computer*	$799–3,500
Sound card	$150–1,000
Digital recording software	$300–600
Outboard mixer	$500
Common effects plug-ins	Cubase offers a wide variety to get you started
CD-RW drive for mastering	Most likely included in your Mac
CD-R or CD-RW media	$1–5 each

*Or good-quality consumer digital audio workstation

Table 11.2
The basic costs of a professional analog studio

Equipment Type	Cost
32-channel analog mixing board	$5,000
24-track 2-inch reel-to-reel tape	$5,000
Common effects boxes	$1,000 each
DAT machine for mastering	$700
2-inch tape reels	$200 each

It's worth noting that Table 11.1 is a liberal estimate: You could spend as little as $1,000 for a computer setup that will do a fair job and as little as $175 for a sound card. On the other hand, Table 11.2 is a minimal estimate: You could easily double or quadruple these costs depending on the quality of the components.

Digital is Easier

Although the raw recording itself is always important, producing a high-quality end product ultimately comes down to editing and mixing, and this is where digital recording really shines. Unlike recording tape, digital audio files are lossless—meaning the audio quality doesn't decrease with repeated editing, mixing, and rerecording—and the flexibility is enormous. You can perform editing feats in seconds that would require lots of skill, time, and experience using analog tape.

With software such as Cubase, it's easy to record an almost limitless number of tracks using a computer, and with audio plug-in software, you can easily add effects, clean up unwanted frequencies, speed up or slow down the music, even tune the vocals to virtual perfection during mixdown. In addition, you can copy and paste any number of recorded tracks with pinpoint accuracy, making it simple to replace a bad backing track in the second verse with that stellar performance in the first verse.

The bottom line is that the only kind of analog equipment comparable in price to a digital setup is multitrack cassette recording, yet the quality of digital is far better than cassette tape and, arguably, as good or better than reel-to-reel tape. In addition to being expensive, reel-to-reel tape requires a huge amount of maintenance, uses up a lot of tape at speeds of 15 inches per second, and is difficult to edit, requiring you to use a razor blade and editing block with precision. It can take years to get good at it.

Gearing Up

Even with all the advantages of digital technology, there are wide differences in equipment quality and features. To start, there are two routes you can take: computer-based digital recording using software and a sound card or a DAW.

DAW-Gonnit, Maw, I Need to Move

A digital audio workstation has one major advantage over a computer-based digital recording setup: It's much more portable. If portability is critical to you, then a DAW may be a better choice than a computer. In addition, several of today's DAWs include a digital mixer with analog inputs—some even have phantom power for mics that need it.

There are several disadvantages, though. A DAW typically has much smaller storage space available for your recordings, doesn't easily give you the ability to burn your own CDs without adding a computer or an expensive all-in-one CD recording unit, and can't be easily upgraded simply by buying a new sound card and/or software. It also lacks the visuals of a high-color computer screen.

It's not altogether uncommon for a DAW to be used in conjunction with a computer. Though it's virtually twice as expensive, it can provide portability but still afford you all the advantages of your computer. The key to a dual-setup is that both the DAW and your sound card support a digital input and output signal, rather than analog, so that you can transfer digital musical data in its original digital form. Converting to an analog signal, using an analog quarter-inch or eighth-inch jack, opens up the potential for more noise and lower frequency response in your recordings. You'll want to look for a DAW that supports digital transfer protocols, such as S/PDIF and/or TDIF.

Yamaha, Sony, Tascam, and several other companies offer digital-based DAWs with 8 tracks to 24 tracks or more that are full-featured and sell at consumer-level prices.

LOW-PRICED DAWS

For several years, 4-track DAW and DAW-like stand-alone units were popular and inexpensive, and there are still a few of them on the market at rock-bottom prices. The biggest disadvantage to these units is not their 4-track limit, because you can ping tracks back and forth (record three tracks, then record those three onto the one open track, opening up three more tracks, ad infinitum) for just about infinity on most of them. It's their general lack of editing, equalization, and effects, their small storage capacities, and their low recording quality. If you are on an ultraslim budget, Sony's 4- or 8-track Mini-Disc is probably still the best choice for price and capacity, though the trade-off is that mini-disc recorders end up using data compression to fit more audio into less storage space, using compression technology called ATRAC, which is a bit better than MP3. This results in lower audio quality for saving audio and/or mastering onto mini-discs.

Professional quality DAWs combine digital mixing, onboard hard disk recording, effects, higher-quality sampling (from 16-bit to 24-bit), and a large number of tracks. Yamaha, Tascam, Korg, and Roland have consistently been some of the most popular brands. You'll want to look for at least a 24-bit, 16-track hard disk recorder, 32-bit digital parametric EQ, compression and reverb effects, and at least 1 gigabyte of storage capacity to even approach the capability of a computer-based setup.

Real Power for the Home Studio: The Computer

With a computer, you will get the most bang for your buck, hands down. Using a computer as the center of your home recording setup affords you the ability to add limitless functionality to your studio, both in software upgrades as newer and better applications become available and storage for keeping all of the data you record accessible and archived for future use.

There are two popular platforms for setting up your digital studio on a computer: Macintosh and PC. In *Mac Home Recording Power!*, we are, of course, focusing on the Macintosh platform. For complete information about recording on the PC platform, see *Home Recording Power!* by Ben Milstead.

Real-World Hardware Choices

There are a number of components you'll need for Mac-based recording, and some are far more important than others. A monitor, for example, is not the most critical thing on your list, whereas a good hard drive is crucial. Here's the lowdown:

- A large and fast hard drive is probably the most important part of doing digital audio on a computer. Most new Macs come with a large and fast hard drive to start with. This is generally sufficient to get the ball rolling on your first recording. But as you have read many times in this book, *bigger is better*. Ask your Mac specialist about installing another hard drive in your computer. This second hard drive can either be installed directly inside your computer, or you can simply get yourself an external drive that is accessed via FireWire. This is a hot new technology that can pass large amounts of data through a very thin cable.

- Sound cards are as important as a good hard drive. It pays to do your homework—there are a number of cards on the market and there is also a lot of advertising hype and misrepresentation in the market. See the section, "Choosing and Installing a Sound Card" later in this chapter for more details.

CAN I USE IT FOR OTHER THINGS?

Although it is always ideal to have a dedicated system for audio recording, the speed of most of today's computers, even entry-level hardware, makes a dedicated audio computer unnecessary. There is no reason why you can't use the Mac for other applications—just keep in mind that, with every new piece of software or functionality you add to your computer, you increase the likelihood for things to go wrong, crashes to occur, data to be lost, and so on. You can also fill up your hard drive space much faster, which means you may have to add hard drives sooner than you would prefer.

- At the time of this writing, G4 processors are the rage. Where processors were once a problem when it came to solid audio recording on a Mac, this is simply not the case anymore. A G3-level processor clocked to at least 333 MHz or better will do the trick for some time to come. Just know that anything slower than a G3 333 MHz will make it hard to work on digital audio files for CD mastering.
- The more RAM you have, the better. The idea is simple, really: RAM is far faster than the fastest hard drive on the planet, and the more you have of it, the fewer trips your audio recording software has to make to the hard drive during actual recording. At the time of this writing, RAM is comparatively cheap: Go with a minimum of 256 MB of RAM or better—512 MB or more is ideal, as this will sustain your creativity for awhile before you will have to upgrade.
- An inexpensive 15-inch or 17-inch monitor will do just fine, because you need only a clean and simple window into the software you'll be using. There is no reason to pay thousands of dollars for a humongous Cinema Display flat screen or the newest LCD panel, unless you have money to burn or you plan on playing every new video game or running other graphics-intensive applications on the studio computer. Although, I have to admit, they are damn sexy looking.
- Chapter 16, "Pack It and Ship It," covers mastering and burning CDs in detail. Generally speaking, if you follow the guidelines in this book, you should already have a CD-RW included in your Mac. These drives are quite fast and will burn a CD before you can finish making a pot of coffee.

COMPATIBILITY ISSUES

If you're upgrading your system yourself, watch out for compatibility issues between components, and check the manufacturer's website for links to online forums or newsgroups (**http://discussions.info.apple.com** is an excellent resource), where you can read about other users' experiences. Also, a quick trip to the user forums at Steinberg's website (**www.steinberg.net**) will help answer more in-depth compatibility questions. A little research goes a long way when it comes to assembling Mac components. It is sure to save you from a few future headaches.

One more thing: Understand that the capabilities of computer hardware are going to change over time and get comfortable with the idea. Processors will get faster, hard drives bigger, monitors prettier, and so on. The difference today, compared to just a few years ago, however, is that affordable computer hardware is now fast enough to easily do audio recording on a Mac. In other words, if you set up a G4 500 MHz, 30 GB, 256 MB RAM system today running Mac OS X and Cubase SL, you have a system that, regardless of the advances that will be made next year or in the next 10 years in hardware, is fast enough to do the job comfortably.

Of course, as hardware gets better, so will software, and the capabilities of your Mac-based home studio will grow accordingly if you upgrade every few years. Cubase SL 18.0 will look as different from Cubase SL 1.0 as Cubase 18.0 does from the very first version of Cubase over a decade ago.

Choosing and Installing a Sound Card

The sound card in your home studio system is the heart of it all, and it's important that you choose a high-quality, fully supported sound card that is as noiseless as possible.

OS X

At the time of this writing, the recently released Mac OS X is a new operating system based on an entirely new set of code that differs greatly from previous Mac systems. That said, many audio card companies are trying to "keep up with the Joneses" by prereleasing their software drivers to make their audio cards work with OS X. These are what we call "beta drivers." They do not work at 100% quite yet, so you as a user are expected to try them out and report any problems to the manufacturer, essentially becoming a technical guinea pig. Unless you are a computer enthusiast who's interested in experimentation, make sure the audio card you select has an officially released driver for OS X. Do not, I repeat, *do not* use beta drivers.

Almost every sound card is made of the same basic components. The following is the core list:

- **Analog-to-Digital converters**. AD converters convert the incoming analog audio from your microphone and input signals into digital audio data. Most of the beginner level sound cards include a stereo pair of inputs and outputs (or I/Os in geek talk), but you'll probably want more than this.
- **Digital-to-Analog converters**. DA converters translate digital audio data from your PC into good old-fashioned analog audio that you can hear through speakers or headphones. DA converters are found in electronic keyboards, MIDI modules, Mini-Disc recorders, DAT recorders, and digital mixers.
- **Digital-to-Digital interface**. As you may already have a DAT recorder or another piece of gear that transmits a digital signal, sound card manufacturers generally include a digital interface so that you can transfer this information without losing any audio quality. The protocols that you will typically find will be either S/PDIF or ADAT. If this is something you are interested in, make sure to ask your music salesperson about it.
- **Mixer**. This is where crucial functions such as volume, input and output signals, and multichannel recording are handled.
- **Codec**. This is usually a dedicated audio chip that controls audio data, including compression, decompression, a mixer, and the AD/DA converters. Codecs can vary widely in quality.
- **MIDI ports**. Almost all sound cards have MIDI ports. Professional-level sound cards will come with MIDI interfaces sporting either standard 5-pin ports or USB ports.

So, what kind of sound card should you choose? In order to answer this question, you need to answer the following subquestions:

- How many inputs do you need on the sound card?
- What extra features do you want?

Let's examine these questions for a minute. Think about the kind of music you plan to record. If it's a typical rock 'n' roll setup, then you will need at least four individual inputs. This is so you can record a full drum kit without having to compromise your creativity. If you are planning to record just as a "singer/songwriter" for your own personal projects, then just a couple of inputs will be enough.

The extra features you will want to think about are a digital I/O and MIDI I/O. Are these really features that you need? Frankly, yes. As you have read at least a couple of times by now, you want to build a system that you can grow with over time, and that includes thinking about your future needs. This certainly includes the need for digital and MIDI I/Os.

Of course, after you answer these questions, then it just comes down to a matter of finances. Hopefully, you aren't pinched for cash as there are a number of ideal choices in the $150 to $1,000 price range, which are of superior quality. And like good hosts at a dinner party, we have provided a list of fantastic audio cards that are not only cost-efficient, but they are also ready and working well in both OS X and Cubase.

- M-Audio's Audiophile 2496 is a good first choice at about $149. It includes two channels of 24-bit AD and DA converters as well as S/PDIF. It also has a MIDI I/O for your sequencing needs.
- M-Audio also makes a great USB audio interface called the Quattro. This audio card supports 4 channels of 24-bit audio. It also has a MIDI I/O as well, but the best feature on this card is that it is a USB (Universal Serial Bus) audio card, so you won't have to open up your Mac to install it. If you look high and low, you can be sure to find this card for around $259.
- If you want a more hands-on approach to recording and mixing within Cubase, then the US428 from Tascam might be the solution for you. This card supports both analog and digital I/O, has MIDI support, and even sports a chromatic tuner for you guitarists. Best of all, it is a USB interface and the hardware interface acts as a mixing board that can be used within Cubase. If you look around, you will find the US428 for about $500.
- RME offers a very high-end audio solution called the Multiface that supports analog I/O, digital I/O, and MIDI. This card is special, because RME went to great lengths to write an extremely optimized ASIO driver. It's so optimized, in fact, that you can monitor audio live through the card with only 1.5 milliseconds of delay. But with a price tag of $1200, this will be sure to put a big hole in your pocketbook.

Sound Card Installation Notes

Just about all of the sound cards mentioned in the last section are PCI-based cards, meaning they plug into a PCI slot on your computer's motherboard. Physically installing a sound card in one of these slots is rarely a problem—it's about as technical as putting together a mic stand—but there are some general, good practices to prevent problems and make sure the installation goes as smoothly as possible:

- In order to put the card in the slot, you'll have to open your computer's case. Before doing anything inside the computer, always unplug the computer completely from its electrical socket—and it's a good rule to touch another piece of metal (such as a piece of metal furniture frame) to ground yourself to prevent damaging any of the components with static electricity.
- Proceed carefully and slowly, and read all of the manufacturer's directions for installing the sound card. Pay attention to the other devices in the case (it will usually be crowded and tight), being careful not to accidentally knock a hard drive cable loose.
- In rare cases when you have lots of other PCI devices already installed, particularly multiple sound cards, you may get clicks and pops in the audio due to simultaneous, heavy activity. If this happens, it may be possible to

give your main sound card a higher priority in the internal bus-mastering order by moving it to the slot closest to the AGP graphics slot or CPU.

- Handle the sound card, and any computer hardware for that matter, gently. You can unknowingly crack the circuit board if you flex it too much, which can cause almost untraceable and intermittent problems.
- In general, it's best to insert a PCI card by positioning one end of the connector first to get it started, then pushing the connector home with a gentle rocking action.
- All PCI cards are held in place by a single screw at the top of the backplate, and this should be tightened firmly to prevent a poor connection.
- If you have to use excessive force to get the sound card to fit, stop what you're doing and give the manufacturer a call; the circuit board itself could mistakenly have been cut too wide, and forcing it could damage the PCI slot.

Audio File Formats

For a Mac-based digital recording setup, there are a number of audio-based file formats you can deal with. Cubase, for example, handles three different formats.

With most of your recording projects, you'll be concerned with only three formats: MIDI files (.MID), Mac-based audio files (.AIFF), and whatever proprietary format the software application uses for storing MIDI and/or wave files with the software's other data.

In Cubase, the Cubase Project file (.CPR) is the format used. This format deals with MIDI data just like a MIDI file and digital audio data just like an AIFF file.

AIFF files are usually uncompressed audio files—meaning they are large (a typical three-minute song will take up a bit more than 30 MB of your hard drive) and they sound quite good. The sound quality of a wave file is determined by you when you record it and by the quality of the sound card you're using. Generally, you'll want to work with wave files at the same level of fidelity as the CD music standard, which is a bit depth (or "resolution") of 16 bits and a 44.1 kHz sampling rate.

BIT DEPTH

The idea of bit depth is not terribly complicated. Bit depth implies that the string of 0s and 1s representing a slice of audio data can't be more than 16 bits long (a pretty good-size number). Similarly, a sampling rate of 44.1 kHz means that the audio has been sampled 44,100 times per second. The result is that the sound reproduction is quite accurate, but the audio files take up a lot of space. That's why, at 16 bits and 44.1 kHz, you can't pack more than seventy-four minutes or so of audio onto a compact disc.

Bit depth also indicates the highest signal-to-noise ratio and frequency you can record. For example, at 16-bit, the highest signal-to-noise ratio is 96 dB and the highest frequency that can be recorded at 44.1 kHz is 22 kHz.

Figure 11.2 shows a typical Cubase project including both MIDI files and AIFF files. In this case, MIDI and audio files alike are recorded and played back as separate tracks. In addition to saving audio file data in a Cubase project file, you can export individual audio file tracks into separate files.

Figure 11.2
This Cubase project shows both digital audio files and MIDI files

Musicians use the MIDI file format extensively, as well as in many popular computer games and entertainment software, and there are loads of MIDI files available on the Internet. Chapter 9, "Wading in MIDI," covers the MIDI file format in detail.

Monitoring and Mixing with Headphones

In Chapter 2, "Choosing Your Space," you learned some techniques for positioning monitors and a bit about working toward effective, accurate monitor mixes. This section expands on this all-important aspect of your home studio by focusing on the headphone mix—which is critical not only for recording but also for monitoring your mixes during both mixdown and mastering.

There are a couple of things to realize about using headphones. First, they are absolutely necessary, and getting a decent pair is crucial. Second, the way you mix using headphones can be deceptive—even with excellent frequency response (in fact, sometimes because of excellent response) a headphone mix can sound quite different than the way your music will sound on a typical home or car stereo.

Choosing Headphones

Whether you're recording or mixing, you want as accurate a sound from your headphones as you can get. This is literally not as simple as it might sound. In one sense, you can evaluate the quality of headphones the same way you do monitors—by how good they sound. At the end of the day, this is more important than what the technical specifications say.

Unlike loudspeaker monitors, though, sound from headphones goes directly into your ears without the spatialization and acoustic shaping—also known as room coloration—that occurs when sound waves interact with your head and the space around you. And of course, no two heads (or ears, for that matter) are alike, so what sounds good to the drummer may not do it at all for the lead singer!

For these reasons, you should try a number of different brands of headphones before spending your money—don't just go on a friend's (or a book's) rote recommendations. When evaluating headphones, here are some important things to look for:

- Smooth, even overall frequency response—not too bright
- Deep bass response
- A good fit, because any discomfort at all will only get worse the longer you wear them
- Durability and ease of repair
- The cord length, because you'll need long cords for good mobility between instruments, the mixer, and the computer
- An ample power supply that should handle from 100 mw up to 1 W
- The frequency response—20 Hz to 20 kHz is the normal human hearing range, and anything lower or higher than that is unimportant to most music recording
- A low distortion factor—the lower, the better, usually less than 1 percent
- A sensitivity rating of 100 dB or greater

Comparative Headphone Mixing

Unlike monitors, which exist and create sound in a live acoustic space, headphones tend to sound a bit artificial because each audio channel is isolated to each of your ears. There is no room for sound waves to interact with each other, with your recording space, or with the rest of your head before they reach your eardrums. Therefore, headphone mixes can quickly become a mish-mash of complex phase-shifting, which may change, cancel, and/or delay frequencies. The bottom line is that an otherwise smooth headphone mix can sometimes sound downright rough when heard through your monitors.

In terms of panning, or effects such as reverb and delay, a headphone mix is generally accurate, unless you're using an excessive amount of phase-shifting effect. On the other hand, achieving any kind of accurate "3-D" type of effect is next to impossible using headphones, because standard headphones trap the entire soundfield in a straight line relative to each side of the stereo field to begin with.

Perhaps the simplest problem to avoid when choosing headphones is to find headphones with excellent bass response and flat frequency response across the entire spectrum. Bad bass response makes your monitor mix sound bad just about every time, and mixes made using headphones that are too bright tend to sound muddy coming from your speakers.

It's not easy to match a headphone mix with a monitor mix, but it can be done. Unfortunately, it's not something you can learn from another person or from a book. Good mixdowns with headphones are ultimately a matter of trial and error, which means you should always check the final result with the monitor mix.

HEADWIZE

Headwize (**www.headwize.com**) is an excellent resource on the Web for details about everything related to headphones. In particular, there are a number of good technical articles on psychoacoustics (how the brain processes sound) and effective studio headphone use.

Signal Processing Basics

Digital signal processing, or DSP, is simply a way of altering an audio signal. It's achieved electronically, through the use of an external piece of hardware that makes changes to the audio signal or through software plug-ins that do the trick using Cubase or other digital recording software.

Though Chapter 12, "Serious Audio," covers DSP and audio effects in detail, this section is a brief survey of the most common types of DSP you'll encounter during both recording and mixing, including reverb, compression, and delay.

Reverb

Generally speaking, reverb is how sound is reflected in any acoustic space; the rate, distance, and amplitude of that reflection is exactly what is simulated in a reverb box or reverb-capable plug-in. Reverb is all about timing between the original sound of your instrument or voice (or any other sound) and the sound that bounces off surfaces in the range of the original sound.

Because different spaces have different sizes (a football field vs. a shower stall, for example) and surfaces (grandstands vs. ceramic bathroom tile), there is an almost limitless number of types of reverb. A typical rack-mount device that can process reverb into your recording offers dozens of different settings, as do the software plug-ins.

Reverb can give music a whole new feel. For example, adding reverb to vocals helps the sound become fuller, more dimensional, and, in many cases, more natural than a straight-up "dry" vocal sound. (This is why most people sound better when they sing in the shower.)

Reverb can also be used to make string and percussion instruments sound larger than life or add ambience and spatial qualities that blend harmonies in beautiful ways.

Reverb consists of a number of different components that you typically control while recording or mixing; however, there are two fundamental pieces, which also happen to be the most important.

- The level of the original sound source itself
- Decay, which controls the length of time the reverb takes to stop sounding and the number of reverberations

The first component is probably too obvious: It's simply the original signal to which the reverb will respond. Reverb will sound different with different instruments and frequencies, as well as the sound's timbre and amplitude.

Decay is the rate at which the sound frequencies in the original sound reflect back, as well as how many times they do so. Depending on the types of frequencies in the original sound, the level of decay can be adjusted to a number of different settings. For example, if high-end frequencies roll off faster than the lower ones, you typically achieve a darker sound, while conversely, where the lowest frequencies take longer to reflect, you'll get a brighter sound.

The advantage of a good digital reverb processor is that it allows you to control the sound of your recording in so many different ways. You can control a variety of parameters, which run the gamut from tripped-out space effects to a concert hall to a warm, intimate-sounding club effect. Cubase SL comes with a reverb plug-in (Figure 11.3a) that lets you easily apply reverb to individual audio tracks and audition them before making changes to the tracks. If you have the extra money, the Reverb A plug-in found in Cubase SX (Figure 11.3b) is a much more robust and rich-sounding reverb that will be sure to turn heads.

Figure 11.3a
Cubase SL's Reverb B plug-in can add a new dimension to your recordings using reverb

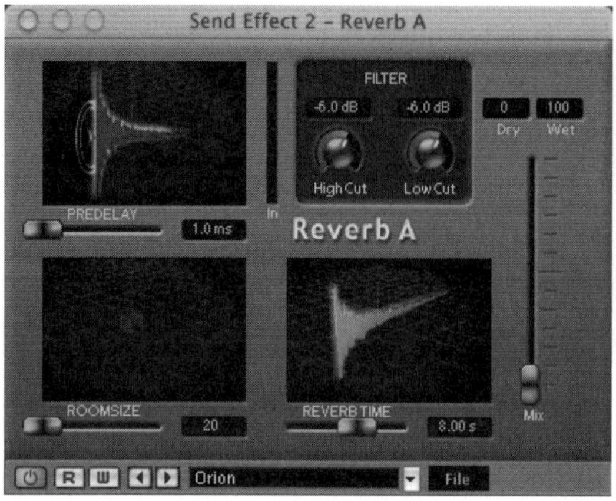

Figure 11.3b
Cubase SX's Reverb A plug-in is a high-quality 32-bit reverb that rivals most hardware reverbs

The downside to reverb is that it's notoriously easy to overuse, which often results in muddy or hard-to-EQ mixes. The best rule for reverb is never to record it to original tracks. Always record as dry and cleanly as you can, then you can add and tweak reverb later to your heart's content.

Compression

Compression restricts the volume of sound by attenuating signals that exceed a certain input, or threshold, level. By attenuating the louder signal levels, you limit the dynamic range of the sound, or the difference between the loudest and softest levels in sound. This has the effect of making compressed sounds a bit louder in the mix than the original, noncompressed frequencies; it's also very handy for ensuring that an input signal doesn't get too hot and cause digital distortion. There are four parts to compression:

- The level at which you want the compression to begin affecting the sound
- The attack time, which is the time it takes for the input gain to decrease to an amount you specify
- The release time, which is the time it takes for the gain to return to its original value (usually a 1:1 ratio to the attack time)
- The compression ratio itself, which is the increase of signal input in dBs needed to cause a 1 dB increase in the compressor's output signal

Most compressors have controls for all of these elements. Using different combinations, you can smooth out unevenness in volume, reduce vocal sibilance, increase or decrease sustain quality, and much more. One of the most frequently compressed instruments is the bass guitar; compressing a bass properly can bring up the lowest frequencies without losing the punctuation of the plucked bass strings, and add incredible sustain. Compression can also do wonders for overall mixes. With that in mind, your Uncle Steinberg has been kind enough to include the VST Dynamics plug-in, which includes a compressor (see Figure 11.4).

Figure 11.4
Cubase's VST Dynamics plug-in includes a compressor that can be used as a send or an insert effect

Delay

Delay can be a highly useful tool for fattening tracks, getting cool guitar effects, and augmenting reverb to increase spatialization and the "openness" of your sound. In fact, delay and reverb are often used together. There is really one important piece to controlling delay: its length. Delay lengths are always timed in milliseconds (ms). Recently though, delay plug-ins can also measure lengths according to note values, making it extremely easy to synchronize them to the tempo of your recording. Cubase provides a couple of great delay plug-ins for trippin' you out. The first one, called ModDelay (Figure 11.5a) is a mono-based delay that has the ability to sync to tempo or be a free-time based delay. The second plug-in, DoubleDelay (Figure 11.5b), is a fairly more complex effect, as it uses two individual delays to give you a completely unique result.

> **AVOIDING PHASE CANCELLATION**
>
> Be wary of using delay lengths below 5 ms or so. This almost always causes phase cancellation.

Figure 11.5a
Cubase's ModDelay plug-in is a mono delay that can sync to your song's tempo

Figure 11.5b
Cubase's DoubleDelay plug-in contains two independent delays that can create a fantastic ambience

Delays of 60 ms to 100 ms are commonly referred to as "slap echoes." These can make thin vocals sound a little fuller, whereas 40 ms to 60 ms delays "double" sound, which causes a vocal track, for example, to sound more like two singers than one. Be careful in both these ranges for vocals—and for any acoustic instrument for that matter. The downside is that a lot of the natural timbre can become unnatural rather quickly.

Lengths of more than 100 ms are usually heard as echoes. With longer delay, you should also be careful to make sure that the delay effect corresponds to the tempo of the music. If it doesn't fit the tempo, it can quickly throw off the timing of the song.

12

Serious Audio

Chapter 11, "Fun-Da-Mental Audio," covered the fundamentals of audio and is probably all most of you will ever need (maybe even a little more than you'll ever need). For the rest of you, this chapter dives even deeper into some of the more useful details behind digital audio. Warning: There's a little math and a sentence here and there that exists for the sole purpose of making the author sound like he invented the entire theory of digital audio (which, of course, he didn't—but don't tell anyone). The following topics are discussed:

- Audio buffer data
- Oversampling and dithering
- Reverb

It's a Pressure Cooker in There

If you've read Chapter 11, "Fun-Da-Mental Audio," you know that sound is, fundamentally, fluctuations in air pressure. Likewise, digital sound is a kind of graph or table of the changes in that air pressure over time.

This idea is easily illustrated. For instance, if you zoom in on an audio track in Cubase, as shown in Figure 12.1, you see a graphical representation of the audio data points, all sampled up and ready. All those wide, ragged edges indicate that there is a lot of air pressure, which your ear knows as loud audio. The wider the audio "graph" of the sounds, the higher the amplitude of the track's audio.

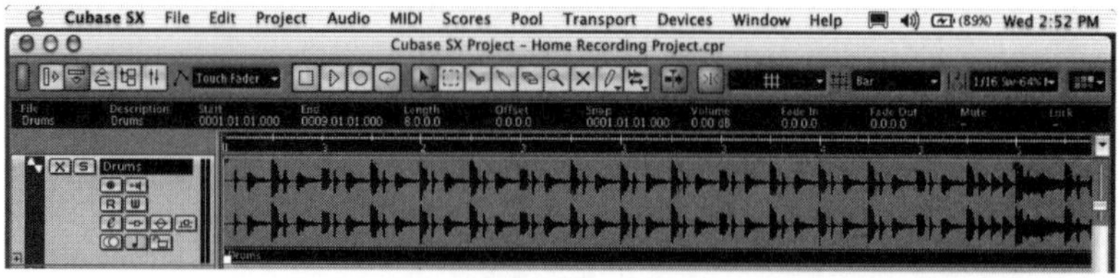

Figure 12.1
This one, Nigel, almost goes to 11

On the other hand, as shown in Figure 12.2, when you zoom in on an area where there is nothing but silence, the image is just a little line in the middle, indicating that there is no change in air pressure. Your ear correspondingly detects that as silence.

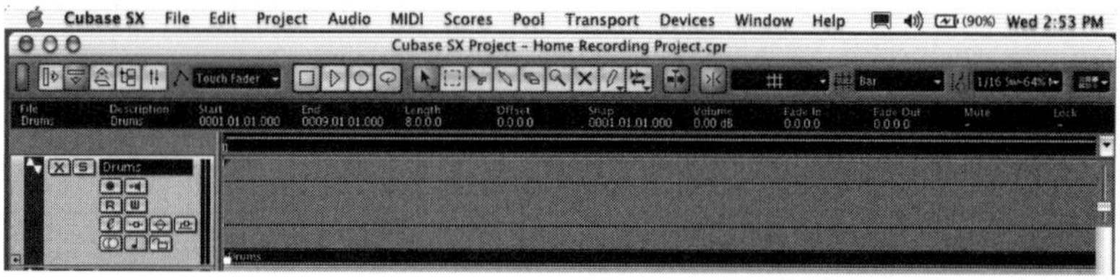

Figure 12.2
This one is the sound of silence

When you record sound, your computer's hardware knows how to process fluctuations in electrical voltage, which your sound card—by way of its A/D converter—measures so-many-times per second. A computer processor changes the signal into numbers, called samples. When you play sound, the whole process is reversed, so that the fluctuations in voltage go to your speakers, happily converted back to a waveform by your sound card's D/A converter.

SAMPLING RATE

The speed with which your sound card samples audio is called the sampling rate and is expressed in kilohertz (kHz). One kHz is 1,000 samples per second; 44.1 kHz is 44,100 samples per second, 96 kHz is 96,000 samples per second, and so on.

Pulse Code Modulation

The standard way of recording digital audio—the method used by both audio CDs and most Mac audio files (.AIFF files, for example)—is called PCM, or pulse code modulation. The process of PCM goes something like this in your computer's hardware:

- As discussed in the previous section, an electrical signal is sent down the path from your instrument or microphone.
- Your computer's A/D converter then precisely measures the signal at regular intervals—for example, 44,100 samples per second in the case of CD-quality audio.

- Each sample is converted into a 16-bit number and contains two channels of data, one for your left ear and one for your right, in order to produce stereo.
- The digital stereo image is recorded in an alternating fashion, in sequence: left, right, left, right, etc.

It seems almost magical that a sequence of millions of numbers can end up as an accurate audio recording. But it's not magic—it's air pressure (and mathematics!). All these numbers combine to re-create the same waveform that creates the same amount of air pressure over the same period of time, via a set of speakers, that you heard when the audio was first recorded.

Audio Data Storage

When you want to store an audio track or any other digital recording, you write it in some form to your hard drive. Well, you don't actually write it—your digital audio software does. Also, the file actually doesn't directly store anything about a sound's frequency, pitch, or amplitude; instead, it stores certain types of identifying information about the data and the digital samples themselves, in the form of audio buffer data.

A buffer is an area in the computer's memory reserved for data that is not logical code but is, instead, values representative of the audio's waveform. In the case of audio, these values are the samples taken when the audio was recorded—for example, 16-bit numbers for 16-bit audio—that translate into a description of what the audio is supposed to sound like.

A simple analogy is that nonfat latte you had at Starbucks last week: The physical cup itself is like a file, while the name on the cup identifies it as some kind of espresso-based concoction from Starbucks. The coffee itself is kind of like buffer data; opening the lid and taking a sip is analogous to opening an audio file.

Perfect Digital Audio

In 1928, the only way to record anything was to copy sound waves in wax. Harry Nyquist, an AT&T engineer, thought there might be a better way than wax, so he theorized that sound waves could be "sampled" and then read back to replot the original wave—perfectly reproducing the signal.

His idea was simple (the math was complex, though—you don't *want* to see the math): If you sample an analog signal at a rate of at least twice its highest frequency component, you can convert it back to analog, pass it through a low-pass filter, and get back the same thing you put in.

Though his theory was a stroke of genius, it turned out to be a frustrating thing for good old Harry at the time (and he was *good*, a prolific inventor who held more than 100 patents), because it needed at least 22,000 samples per second to really make it worthwhile. In the 1920s, nothing had been invented yet that could measure, record, and store that much information quickly, so Harry had to wait several decades for a binary language and integrated circuits—in other words, computers—to make digital recording and playback a reality.

Of course, there is theory, and there is, as always, reality:

- 16-bit samples, even 24-bit samples, are not the pure numbers of Nyquist's theorem, so digital sample values can never be completely accurate. For example, 16 bits is not a very big number when weighed against Nyquist's numbers, and though it ends up as a 96 dB dynamic range, the average level must be much lower than 96 dB in order to make up for peak frequencies. What's worse, at low amplitude, some signals tend to become distorted, causing the somewhat brittle or "cold" sound that some people associate with digital audio.
- Nyquist's theory uses samples that are instantaneous values, or "impulses," and reproducing a perfect impulse is impossible. The result is typically a loss of some high frequencies, though adjusting frequency response with filtering does help reduce this problem.
- Unfortunately, there is no such thing as the perfect low-pass filter required by Nyquist's theorem. A real filter has a finite, set slope—for instance, a steep filter can produce a lot of phase shift. A technique called "oversampling" was invented to try to overcome this problem.

Today, the audio on a compact disc is a realization of Nyquist's theory, but it is not perfect by any means. For any digital recording that sounds good, there is likely more than a little filtering, dithering, interpolating, slicing, dicing, and julienne fries behind it.

HOW GOOD IS GOOD?

The word "good" is a highly subjective term, especially when it comes to digital audio. For the purposes of this book, "good" digital audio is audio that accurately plays back that which it has recorded. The more accurate, the more "good."

Of course, that raises the question, "What exactly is accurate?" The long answer is, "Read the rest of the book." For those of you who want the short answer now: Accurate is "good."

The Big Julienne Fry: Oversampling

Take a look at the way a typical CD audio system plays back audio:

- Because the audio was recorded at 44.1 kHz, 16-bit audio samples are sent down the data stream at 44.1 kHz to an anti-aliasing, low-pass filter.
- Nyquist's theory says that the highest playback frequency is less than half the recorded rate, so the highest play-backable frequency you can hear is 22.05 kHz.

- Frequencies above 22.05 are "aliased" frequencies—essentially reflections of the original sampling frequency; the anti-aliasing filter attempts to block these reflections.

The biggest problem with this process is effectively blocking the reflections; the anti-aliasing filter's cutoff needs to go from around 0 dB attenuation at 20 kHz to somewhere near 90 dB at 22 kHz. This is a steep slope, and a filter this steep has a lot of phase shift as it nears the cutoff. This is not good, because it can produce less-than-stellar audio quality.

ATTENUATION

In the audio world, attenuation is how you affect the strength of an electrical signal; to "attenuate" a signal means to reduce its amplitude, hopefully with little or no distortion. Attenuating individual frequencies in a mix often means you end up reamplifying, or boosting, the overall mix (or other frequencies) to compensate, which can introduce distortion back into the mix all over again. It's a bit Zen-like, when you think about it.

The solution is to sample at a higher rate to begin with; because reflections of the audio image happen at near the sampling frequency (and multiples of it), sampling at a higher rate moves the reflections farther from the good, happy audio you want to keep.

This is called "oversampling" and is accomplished through interpolation. In mathematics, interpolation is simply estimating the value of something (usually a math function or a series of numbers) between two other, known values, and it's the same kind of thing here: Oversampling calculates the frequency spectrum as if the audio data were sampled with more than 44,100 samples.

For example, eight times as many samples running at eight times the rate is dubbed "8× oversampling," which produces a less-steep cutoff slope. For example, at a 44.1 kHz sampling rate, 8× oversampling generates 352,800 samples per second! This is almost a bit of magic, really, because oversampling effectively generates more samples from a waveform than what's there, and it works! The trade-off is that it takes more processing power to interpolate the audio.

WE'RE TALKING D/A

There is another type of oversampling, at the analog to digital stage, and it's far more complicated and far less interesting. "Oversampling" here refers to the digital to analog conversion stage.

Dithering

The fact is, you can't use 16 bits of data all the time; a digital recording must adjust to allow for peaks that use the full 16 bits, and that means most of the music is recorded at a lower volume using fewer than 16 bits. For instance, at 1 bit in amplitude, waveforms that are sine waves become square waves, a phenomenon that introduces a lot of very bad distortion into the equation. Points smaller than 1 bit don't make it into your recording at all.

This is where dithering can be a big help. Dithering is adding a little low-level noise to the audio signal, on purpose, in exchange for a huge reduction in distortion. The added noise spreads out most of the numeric errors, which would have produced distortion across the frequency spectrum, as broadband noise.

To illustrate this idea, think of sitting in the stands at the starting line of a racetrack. When the cars are all still and lined up before the race, it's impossible for you to look through them. You can't see the road beneath their wheels, or, if you're low enough to the ground, anything on the other side of them.

However, once the race begins, you can always see the road as well as the track's infield on the other side. When the cars come whizzing past you over the starting line, you see a little blur, but that's all. The blur is similar to the noise you get by dithering. You're trading a little bit of noise so that you can clearly and accurately hear what's really there.

Dithering Down

The most fundamental use of dithering is when you reduce the number of bits used to represent the signal—for example, "down-sampling" a recording from 16 bits to 8 bits. Instead of just rounding the 16-bit numbers to 8-bit numbers, which would by itself create unwanted amounts of distortion, dithering spreads the audio spectrum out to fit the samples into the smaller numbers. This decreases harmonic distortion and introduces a little broadband noise into the picture.

AKA TRUNCATING

Down-sampling has a more commonly known name in the digital audio domain, which is called "truncating." Although this is an alternative term, the function is still the same.

Dithering Everywhere

In addition to simply reducing the bit depth of a recording or audio file, there are other types of dithering going on all the time, behind the scenes.

For instance, the act of recording itself requires that the infinitely precise numbers of an analog audio signal be reduced to 16 bits, and dithering is going on at this stage, usually by way of the noise already present in your recording chain (the cables and equipment). Yes, that's right—the very presence of all your gear provides the noise necessary to do the dithering for you! Kind of ironic, isn't it?

In addition, almost all types of DSP (digital signal processing) require either some kind of reduction or multiplication of bits; for example, if you add that killer stadium reverb into your vocals, you're actually multiplying 16-bit values together, which results in 32-bit numbers, and you cannot round the extra bits without ruining the vocal, so you must dither.

Volume changes are yet another multiplication-heavy activity, and you do these all the time both during recording and mixdown.

NORMALIZING AND OVERNORMALIZING

Most audio software gives you the ability to normalize your audio. Normalizing is a simple process in which the software finds the peak amplitude in an audio file, and then boosts the entire file to that peak amplitude.

More sophisticated recording software, such as Cubase, allows you to normalize any range you specify in a given audio track. But beware: Don't get into the habit of normalizing every track after every edit you make! You're actually increasing noise and distortion, because the noise level is brought up along with the signal and the signal must be redithered. Never normalize—unless you know exactly what you're doing—until you have finished recording all of the elements of a composition.

UV22

Dithering is one of Cubase's strong points, as it uses the top standard in dithering algorithms (or processes) called the UV22. This dithering algorithm was developed and implemented by Apogee Technologies and has become one of the more commonly known pieces of hardware found in most mastering houses. The only drawback is that the UV22 in its hardware form costs around $6000, so it is more than just a mere drop in the bucket to us home recording guys.

To make the UV22 more accessible to end users, Apogee developed a software plug-in version of the hardware and made it available for licensing, which is where Steinberg came in. First, the UV22 was available only in Steinberg's most expensive version of Cubase, VST/32. When Cubase SX and SL were released in 2002, Steinberg was kind enough to provide the UV22 in both versions, but there is a small catch. In Cubase SX, the UV22 has the ability to dither your audio to variable bit rates (24, 20, 16, and 8) as SX has the ability to record up to 32 bits (see Figure 12.3). The SL version of the UV22 defaults simply to 16 bits. But before you SL users start to get that teary look in your eyes, just remember that your song is going to have to dither down to 16 bits anyway, so the rest of those bit rates are irrelevant to us.

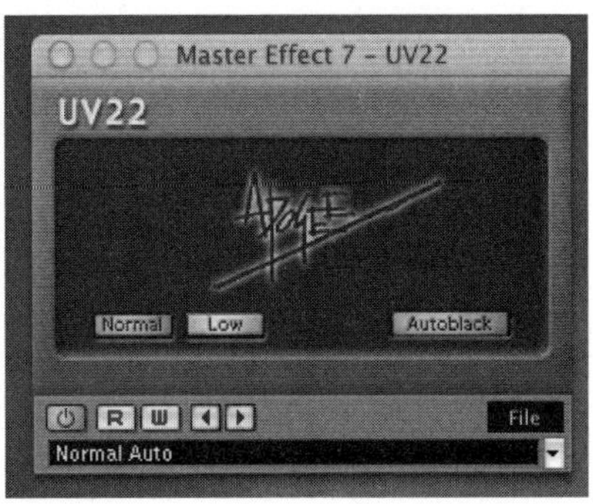

Figure 12.3
Both Cubase SX and SL contain a version of the Apogee UV22 dithering plug-in

Reverb Under the Covers

You undoubtedly already know that natural reverberation can have a great effect on music. Natural reverb is the result of sound reflecting off surfaces in a room; sound travels from its source and strikes walls, ceilings, and floors, reflecting off them at different angles. Some of the reflections find your ears immediately and are known as "early reflections." Other reflections may bounce a few more times off other surfaces in the room before finally vibrating your eardrums. A room's size, its contents and materials, and the density of its surfaces give any room its unique sound.

In the digital domain, reverb can be reproduced very effectively; the number of reflections and their frequencies are limited only by processing speed, whereas the delay of the reflections is limited only by the amount of your computer's memory.

Before digital processing, reverb was difficult to re-create well. "Plate" and "Spring" reverbs were created by emulating a speaker and a microphone at two ends of a metal spring or a suspended metal plate, but they weren't very portable or versatile.

FIR Filters

A finite impulse response (FIR) filter is a method of creating reverb that isn't dependent on time or frequency; it doesn't matter when you play a note, you'll get the same type of reverberation. This type of reverb is characterized by its response to a sound-generating event or its impulse response.

For instance, an F#9 on the guitar, a four-part harmony, even a handclap—any wave-producing action—is a sound-generating event. For FIR-based reverb, it turns out that each sample point of a sound event can be treated as little more than an echo of the event itself. So, any sound event becomes the sum of the other sound events for each individual sample at each of their respective times. This concept is called superposition.

The benefit is that room characteristics can easily be added to any dry digital mix in a fairly straightforward way, but it takes a lot of computing power. Each sample must be multiplied by each sample of the impulse response, then added to the mix. If you have x-number of samples to process, and a sound event itself is y-samples long, you need to perform $(x + y)$ multiplications and additions.

For example, if the impulse response to a sound event is two seconds long, and the song is two minutes long, your computer's processor winds up performing many, many trillions of multiplications and about the same number of additions at a 44.1 kHz sampling rate.

Even by today's standards, this method of reverb, while highly accurate, is processor-expensive. Thankfully, there are other ways.

Comb and Allpass Filters

Most digital reverbs today employ a different approach, through the use of multiple delays and feedback that build up a series of dense echoes. Much of this idea is based on the concept of a comb filter.

The impulse response of the comb filter—which gets its name from the comb-like notches in its frequency response pattern—is like a sound event bouncing around between two walls and growing weaker with each bounce—a very simple concept.

The problem is that it takes too many of these reflections to make a smooth reverb, and though a comb filter's phase cancellations can very easily mimic room effects, it can just as easily become harmonically unstable rather quickly and cause ringing.

A slightly better solution is called an allpass filter. In the case of an allpass, the impulse responses are fed both forward and backward to fill in the phase cancellations. Because all frequencies are passed equally, the result is a much smoother frequency response. However, an allpass still affects the phase of the signal, so it, too, can exhibit ringing, particularly with abrupt sound events.

Modern Reverb

Comb filters and allpass filters fall into a category all their own, called infinite impulse response filters, or IIR, and they are often combined to produce digital reverb. M.A. Schroeder, in the '70s, did a lot of the earliest work on digital reverb, and one of his best-known reverb designs used four comb filters and two allpass filters, as shown in Figure 12.4.

Figure 12.4
Schroeder's reverberator combined four comb filters and two allpass filters to create a very realistic reverb for its time.

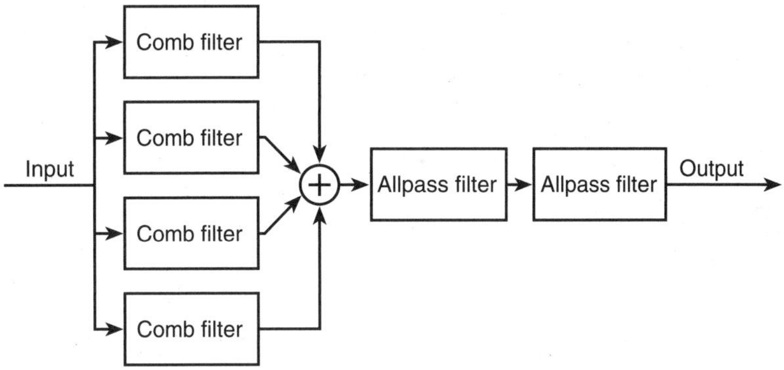

Schroeder's reverberator is a bit primitive when compared to modern reverb algorithms, in which room geometry, surface materials, and location can be taken into account by using both FIR and IIR filters together. For instance, a FIR filter might be used to create early reflections, and then IIR filters used to create diffuse reverberation of those reflections. Algorithms, which attempt to combine the best of both worlds, achieve more accurate results and are more versatile, while keeping an eye on processor use.

13

Recording and Mixing

Unlike in much of home recording's sordid past, you are no longer limited to a few noisy analog tracks and cheap equipment. Thanks to the advances made in digital recording software and sound cards, just like the big guys, you have virtually limitless tracks and very little noise to play with.

You've got it better than George Martin had it in the '60s.

But hold on, wait just a second, *caveat emptor*—or something like that: With all this rope, you could easily hang yourself if you don't understand how to turn your performances into high-quality master recordings. That's where the art and science of recording and mixing come in. It can still be a jungle in there if you don't know what you're doing.

We'll swing our machete in the following directions:

- Recording and mixing fundamentals
- Monitoring for fun and money
- Cabling and its role in the chain
- The mixing process
- EQ and more EQ
- Software mixing
- Understanding the mixing chain
- Using effects effectively

The Basics

Chapters 2 and 3 ("Choosing Your Space" and "Assembling Your Digital Studio," respectively) helped you get up and running with your studio room and equipment. If you're ready to start recording, where's the best place to begin? Just as with anything else in life, there are a few fundamentals—general skills and knowledge for keeping your nose clean and your frustration meter at low levels.

It Helps to Hear What You're Hearing

As it turns out, we humans don't hear low frequencies (bass frequencies) and high frequencies (treble frequencies) nearly as well at low volumes as we do at high volumes. This was demonstrated by a couple of Bell Labs' guys in the '30s, and is called the Fletcher-Munson Effect because of them.

> **FOR MORE ABOUT HUMAN HEARING**
> Chapter 11, "Fun-Da-Mental Audio," details much more about us humans and our hearing capabilities.

Fletcher and Munson measured human hearing and produced a set of curves (the Fletcher-Munson Curves) showing the human ear's sensitivity to loudness versus frequency. They showed that human hearing is extremely dependent upon loudness, and that the ear is most sensitive to sounds in the 3–4 kHz region.

Practically speaking, this means that sounds above and below 3–4 kHz must be louder in order to be heard at the same level. It also means that the lower the volume, the harder it is to hear the lows and highs. For example, bass frequencies in the 250 Hz and lower region (bass guitar, low toms, the kick drum) are roughly sixty times harder to hear at low levels than at high levels. In addition, high frequencies above 6 kHz or so (cymbals, vocal breath sounds) are about sixteen times harder to hear.

These facts should tell you something: Your recording and mixing levels will make a huge impact in how the end result sounds.

The best way to smooth out the impact is always to listen to your mix at different volumes and to shoot for a mix that works whether it's soft or loud or in-between. This usually means making some trade-offs when calibrating mix levels. For instance, to keep from losing the kick drum in the mix, you may have to pull back on some of its thunderous, snapping ear candy at middle to upper volume levels. Don't be afraid to make lots of adjustments to levels during both recording and mixing; it's virtually impossible to get a satisfying mix if you don't work extensively with levels.

The Mix Behind the Mask

Masking is another human ear limitation you will be dealing with on a regular basis. Masking is when the louder of two sounds around a given frequency keeps the lower of the two from being heard. It's the fundamental reason why individual instrument sounds, when soloed, sound different than they do all mixed together.

This problem isn't as prevalent these days as it was in the days of 4-track cassette recorders; because you've got a multitude of tracks to work with, you can monitor each of the instruments when recording and mixing. You have ample opportunity to adjust each performance's tone so that it works in the mix.

Masking can still rear its ugly head when monitoring while recording, though, if you don't take the time to fine-tune the level of the instrument you're on, as well as its tone.

Monitors

Good monitor speakers are an essential part of the home recording process. Like the selection of your home studio's cabling (covered later in this chapter), the value of making a proper choice in monitors is one of those things you can overlook up to a point, but when you reach that point, things can get ugly. In the end, it is your monitors that give an audible voice to the electrical signals that make up your music, and you shouldn't compromise those signals with a poor decision.

In fact, monitor speakers, more often than not, are the weakest link in the home studio chain. This is why it's not unusual for some home recording artists to spend almost as much on speakers as they do on their recording system, in order to achieve a proper balance of quality vs. total investment. Of course, on a practical level, just being able to afford the primary components of the studio (the space, computer, mixer, sound card, and so on) is hard enough, so it's best to regard speakers as one of those items that you should spend as much on as you can possibly afford. In the long run, you'll be happier.

Ideally, studio monitors should have an even or flat response across the frequency spectrum. Accuracy is the key objective here, and if your monitors inaccurately color a signal with frequency boosts or gaps, it'll make the mixing process very difficult, particularly EQ. When you start under- or overcompensating for bad monitors, your mixes can easily end up either bass or treble heavy on other loudspeakers, and you'll never know it.

Unfortunately, creating an unbiased monitoring setup at home means going through a little brush to get to the picnic; despite long bullet lists of technical claims made by monitor manufacturers, it's a random affair.

You should always compare different monitors with each other in the store, peruse the manufacturer's website, and read any reviews online you can find.

PROREC

ProRec, at **www.prorec.com**, is an excellent resource for reviews of studio equipment, and it's a good place to check for reviews of studio monitors. The site reviews high-quality equipment (and software) with an eye on value.

When comparing monitors, be careful to match levels as closely as possible, because louder music usually sounds better. Listen for clarity and a good tone across frequencies;

there should be no distortion or excessive buzz. Of course, after you've made a decision and you get your monitors home, you'll have to contend with the acoustics of your studio space. You can find more on this in Chapter 2, "Choosing Your Space."

Monitor Design

Most recipes for a monitor use only two or three ingredients: a speaker, a cabinet, and, in some cases, an amplifier. These aren't terribly complicated pieces of equipment in and of themselves, but their design can vary widely and involve a great deal of engineering.

The design of the cabinet can make a huge difference, and it's one of the most difficult design challenges for engineers who create monitors. For instance, you'll notice that professional-level studio monitors rarely contain sharp edges. This is because sharp edges on a cabinet can cause something known as *cabinet edge diffraction*. Sound likes smooth, lathed curves, whereas sharp edges cause sound waves to veer too sharply—which can be ruinous to your stereo mix.

EAR FATIGUE

Ear fatigue is what happens when the muscles that normally stabilize the tympanic membrane in your ears begin to tire as a result of contracting too much in response to repeated frequencies or loud noise. Ear fatigue can cause your ears to ring (after a loud concert, for example) and, more commonly, decreases the ability of your ears to accurately and consistently hear different frequencies.

The speakers themselves are designed to provide accurate representations of the sound sent to them. Beyond achieving accuracy, many studio monitors also take into account ear fatigue of a person who listens to them throughout the day. For example, tweeters might be covered in silk or other materials that soften the sound slightly, rather than plastic, which can cause a sharper tweeter sound but ultimately tire the ear.

Crossover

Because monitors usually have separate speakers for different frequencies (tweeters and woofers), monitors contain circuitry (called a crossover) to direct frequencies to the proper speaker.

You'll see information about the crossover circuitry of studio monitors in most manufacturers' literature. Most monitors are designed to "cross over" between speakers at or near the low range of the frequency response of the tweeter, around 2 kHz. The quality of the crossover circuitry affects sounds at or near this "crossover frequency," and monitors with less sophisticated circuitry or lower-quality parts cause the sound in that region to become vague or distorted.

Nearfield Monitors

Nearfield monitors, also called close-field monitors, are designed so that they sound best at a distance of 3 to 4 feet, and they are an excellent choice for your home studio.

The purpose of nearfields is to cut down on room reflections or other unwanted resonance, meaning that home studio spaces that are tight, rooms that sound bad, or rooms that haven't been acoustically treated can really benefit from a pair of nearfields. If you plan on purchasing nearfield monitors, bear in mind that the technology is not perfect. To get the most out of them, take the following into consideration:

- Position the monitors equidistant from the walls to each side of them.
- Make sure your ears are about the same distance from the monitors as the monitors are from each other. Think of an equilateral triangle, where the monitors are the two points of the base of the triangle and your head is the third point.
- Adjust the horizontal angle of the monitors to your ears. A tip for doing this is to place a mirror on the front of the speaker and have someone else vary the angle of the speaker until you see yourself. In other words, see what the speaker sees (make sure you look all pretty and stuff).

Tannoy makes good professional-quality nearfield monitors. Their System 600, with a frequency response of 52 to 20 kHz and power handling up to 160 watts, can be found (at the time of this writing) for around $500 per speaker, street. The System 600 is a pioneering design that actually puts the tweeter behind the center of the bass cone, causing all the sound to come from a single point, mimicking the way sound is created in nature.

HOW?

Remember—your home studio is not a venue for a Who concert; a range of 100–150 watts is generally sufficient for accurate monitoring in most home studios.

Yamaha NS-10s—if you can find them—have always been a solid choice, with a frequency response of 60 to 20 kHz and power handling up to 120 watts.

Passive Monitors

Both the Tannoy System 600 and Yamaha NS-10 are *passive* monitors, meaning they require an external amplifier to produce sound. Like most home stereo systems, passive monitors are connected to the amplifier via speaker cables.

IMPEDANCE MATCHING

For an amplifier to drive a passive speaker efficiently, proper impedance matching is important. Essentially, impedance is the electrical resistance in a circuit, measured in ohms. Every speaker has a rated impedance, generally 4, 8, or 16 ohms. A power amplifier needs to drive a certain amount of ohms per channel (two channels in a standard stereo setup); otherwise, the amp could overheat, distort audio, or not deliver wattage correctly.

Bottom line: Make sure you match impedances between your amplifier and monitors.

With any passive monitor setup, your amp can alter what you are hearing over your speakers by coloring the output sound. The trick is simply to match up the monitors with your amp so that any coloring is kept to a minimum. Some manufacturers have recommendations and even sell amplifiers that are already matched with monitors; a knowledgeable salesperson should also know what matches well and what doesn't. The ultimate decision is yours, of course, so compare combinations before you buy.

Active Monitors

Active monitors—monitors that come with their own built-in amp—are another option, but they are generally a bit more expensive and a bit less rugged. The Mackie HR 824 is an award-winning, killer-sounding choice and sells for a little less than $700 per speaker, street.

> **ACTIVE MONITORS ON A BUDGET**
> A budget-minded alternative to the Mackie HR 824 is the Alesis M1 Active, which currently sells for less than $500, street, per pair. Event and Yamaha also produce good-quality active monitors with more palatable price ranges for the budget conscious.

Because active monitors have a built-in amp, a host of potential problems with a passive configuration can be eliminated, giving you improved performance in some key areas:

- **Frequency response**. The internal circuitry of an active setup vastly improves its frequency response (the range of frequencies the monitor can handle without distortion). Onboard active electronic circuitry allows for precise control over crossover slope (how the monitor splits up the frequencies), while minimizing phase shifts and distortion.
- **Overload protection**. Passive monitors have no control over input power and usually rely on little more than a crude fuse to keep the speakers from toasting. An active system has sophisticated electronics that precisely control power going to the speakers.
- **Bi-amplification**. Most active systems, like the HR 824, for example, use separate amplifiers to drive each tweeter and woofer, greatly enhancing the monitor's damping (how well the monitor stops a sound when it has actually ended) and accuracy.

Subwoofers

Subwoofers deliver the deep driving bass sound into a sound landscape created by smaller or nearfield monitors. They can be used to supplement passive or active monitor configurations and typically handle frequencies in the 25–150 Hz range. If you use a subwoofer, configure your system, if possible, to keep the subwoofer's frequencies to below 100 Hz. This keeps the subwoofer omnidirectional.

Placement of subwoofers is less critical than nearfields. Bass frequencies are by nature omnidirectional and fill the room from just about any position. Just make sure the front of your subwoofer isn't fully obstructed by any of your larger gear or furniture.

Digital Monitors

A digital monitor is not strictly digital—the term "digital" in this case means that the monitor is an active system that takes digital inputs. While 24-bit/96 kHz digital inputs certainly go a ways toward eliminating noise and hum problems associated with analog cabling, really good analog cabling can do just about the same thing. Digital monitors are still a fairly new technology, so you may want to stay away from them until more manufacturers adopt the technology and the jury comes back with a verdict.

The Importance of Sound Cabling

With so many considerations to be made in assembling a functional home studio, it's easy to lose sight of something as seemingly minor as cables. But in reality, the quality of your studio's final output can only be as good as the cables used in it. It's not enough to just plug in whatever happens to be available. If you were looking for good string sounds on a module or keyboard, would you settle for the lowest end model?

An important factor to consider in cable selection is the conducting wire itself. Poor wire can contribute to degradations in harmonic structure, clarity, and frequency response.

A good-quality copper wire is the most cost-effective solution, whereas silver is costly enough that hooking up an entire studio with it could add up to a big investment.

OXYGEN FREE

Some manufacturers offer "oxygen-free" copper in their cables; by limiting the formation of trapped oxygen bubbles when the copper is extruded, internal corrosion is minimized, hence making the copper a better conductor of signal.

Whether a cable is silver or copper, long or short, analog or digital, it must have a quality termination. Examine a cable's termination before you purchase it. Check out the molding on the termination. If it has a metal termination, unscrew it and observe the soldering. If it looks or feels flimsy, you're better off without that cable. A poorly constructed termination can quickly lead to audio headaches down the line.

IS GOLD BETTER?

You'll often see gold used in cable connectors, but that's not because gold is a superior conductor—it's because gold is good for protecting connector terminals from corrosion. Non-gold connectors are not necessarily poorer in quality, although they might require a little more maintenance.

HOW TO PLUG/UNPLUG

When plugging in cables, use a firm grip around the termination. Never pull out a cable from beyond the termination along the regular insulated section. This can lead to damage of both the hardware and cable terminals. It will also damage your ego.

MORE ON CABLES

Cabling and connectors are discussed in excruciating detail in Chapter 3, "Assembling Your Digital Studio."

It's All in the Mix

The heart of any recording studio is its mixer—also referred to as a mixing board, the desk, the console, and, occasionally, your expletive of choice, depending on how well a session is going. A mixer pumps all of the various audio signals connected to it through its channels and blends them together into one single stereo signal. Mixers also serve as the place for enhancing your music with effects, DSP, equalization (EQ), and the like.

Mixers these days come in a wide range of sophistication and costs. Some mixers are more suited for live sound than studio recording, and recently, the digital mixer has been introduced with rave reviews, packing a powerful punch in a relatively small package. It's important to try and delineate precisely what you expect out of a mixer before you make the investment, whether it be a software-only solution or an external mixer/combination.

This section details the elements common to all mixers and shows you how to use one. Whether you're using your fingertips to turn knobs or your mouse to turn faders—or both—you'll be armed with the principles you'll need to do some great recording.

Preamps

Preamplifiers are used to boost the weak output levels of microphones to levels that are about line level (see the following note). A preamp, also sometimes called the "trim," is the first link in the mixing chain—the first circuit that processes a microphone signal connected to a mixer.

WHAT IS LINE LEVEL?

Practically speaking, "line level" is the signal level of the electrical signal running through your cables and gear. For inputs, it determines the sensitivity and loudness of your music, and for outputs, the loudness. The two most common types of line level settings are –10 dBV (consumer level, fine for home recording) and +4 dBV (professional, much hotter, and a little harder to work with).

Every input channel in a mixer has a gain control, which controls gain of the preamp. If you have a mic on a channel, you'll need a lot of the preamp, but if the channel is being used for a line level signal like the bass, synth, monitor mix, or DAT player, the preamp goes practically unused.

PREAMPS AND ATTENUATOR PADS

Preamps are designed to operate within a certain gain range. When you operate the gain or trim on a mixer's input channel, you generally are adjusting the gain of the preamplifier. If operated at unity gain (no amplification), many preamps will become unstable and may start to distort or tend to oscillate. Hence, designers of mixers usually provide attenuator pads before and/or after (usually before) the preamp, enabling the signal to be knocked down so that the preamp can always be operated with some gain.

For example, a microphone that puts out an audio signal level of –60 dBu is producing a weak signal by design: The diaphragm moves a little bit and a small current is produced. Without a preamp, the mixer just cannot work with this weak signal without introducing significant noise into the signal path. A DAT recorder, on the other hand, which produces an output level of +4 dBu, most likely doesn't need the preamp at all. Using a lot of preamp with a strong signal such as +4 dBu overloads the preamp and starts clipping like Edward Scissorhands. Clipping happens when the input signal is too strong for the device it is driving; the device "clips" the audio signal above this threshold and you get distortion.

Input Channels

You can plug a lot of stuff into a mixer: microphones, outputs of musical instruments, synthesizers, samplers, outboard effects, outputs of tape decks, TVs, DVDs, your computer's sound card—anything and everything that has an audio output. The mixer then allows you to control the volume of each input and do all sorts of things to change, enhance, or muck up the sound quality. You can route the signal back out to an effects processor or your software and back again into the mixer, blend all of the different sounds into an output for monitoring or recording to disk or tape, and do both at the same time.

The primary element of a mixer is where you plug in—the input channel. In fact, a mixer is characterized by how many input channels it has: A 32-channel mixer has double the input capacity of a 16-channel mixer, for example.

There are generally two types of physical input connections—balanced and unbalanced—and two types of signals—line level (as noted earlier) and mic-level. In pro-audio, mic-level connections are balanced connections that use an XLR connector. Line level connections may be either balanced or unbalanced, and typically use quarter-inch input connectors.

LO-Z, HI-Z

On some mixers, you may find the designation "Lo-Z" and "Hi-Z." These terms refer to impedance. Most professional-quality microphones are "Lo-Z," or low impedance, which means that you can have long lengths of balanced cable with little signal attenuation. Cheap microphones, and most "computer microphones," are "Hi-Z," or high impedance, which means that if your cable is longer than about 25 (unbalanced line) feet, you're going to get hum and some other nasty side effects. Stay away from Hi-Z mics, period. Unbalanced line level gear, on the other hand, is just fine.

Inputs are modular, meaning all the knobs and faders and buttons that control each input are typically organized together. So, although a 32-channel console may seem rather menacing at first, with hundreds of little knobs to turn, in reality, as soon as you've mastered one input module, you've got the other thirty-one down cold. Figure 13.1 shows the structure of a channel module or strip.

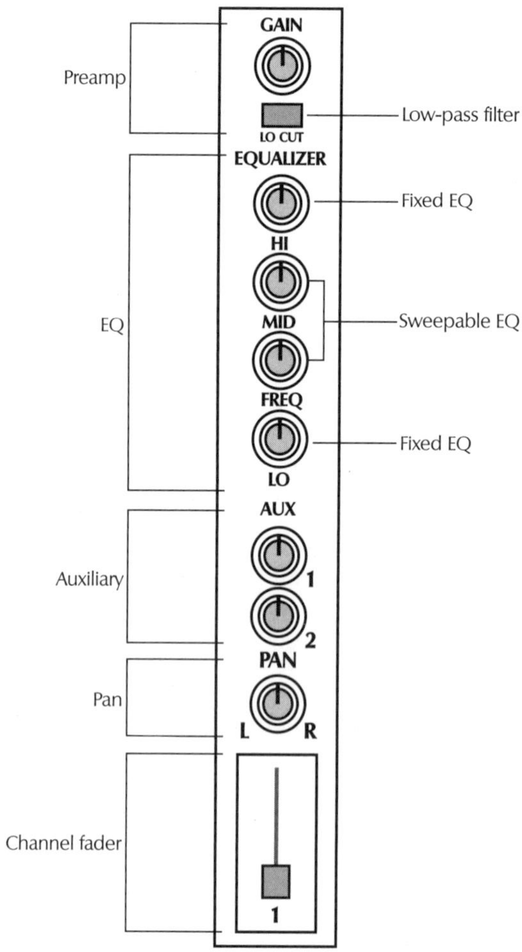

Figure 13.1
This basic anatomy of a channel strip includes the gain, EQ, aux, pan, and channel fader

The Mic Preamp

The mic preamp is the site on an input channel where microphones are connected. In general, microphones produce small voltage levels and require a special three-pronged XLR connector.

The mic preamp itself is a female XLR panel mount. XLR connectors (see Figure 13.2) are better quality than cable with quarter-inch standard connectors and are balanced, because the signal passes through a three-conductor cable and works with balanced input and output transformers on either end of the signal. They also use a screen between their conductors to reduce electronic interference.

Figure 13.2
XLR connectors make high-quality connections

XLR connectors can also accommodate microphones that utilize phantom power—a +48 volt DC signal that powers the microphone's internal amplifier. Condenser microphones that need power for charging their internal elements almost always need phantom power. Most modern mixers can provide phantom power to any one of its input channels and are usually engaged by depressing a button labeled "+48V" or "Phantom Power" elsewhere on the console.

USING PHANTOM POWER

Take special care when using phantom power. Serious microphone damage can result from improper use, especially with microphones that do not support phantom power (refer to your microphone and mixer manuals for proper use). In addition, phantom power can only be supplied over a balanced line.

A mic preamp performs an important amplifying function when a microphone is connected to it: Without it, the mic's signal is too weak and will be colored by unwanted ambient or circuit noise. Correspondingly, when the channel's fader is raised, the noise gets even worse.

The relationship between this kind of noise and the input signal is called the "signal-to-noise" ratio. Generally speaking, it's best to record with as strong or "hot" a signal as possible, to minimize unwanted noise by tipping the signal-to-noise ratio in favor of the input signal. If you listen carefully to older, pure analog recordings ("Stairway to Heaven" comes to mind—but you can't play it while reading this book!), you can clearly hear noise during sparse, dynamically soft passages where the signal-to-noise ratio is bad.

The amount of amplification, also called "gain," can be adjusted with the gain knob located on the channel strip.

> **HEADROOM**
>
> Every mixer has a nominal level at which it operates. But mixers are designed to handle fairly dynamic swings in level. When a signal's level "peaks," it means that it has gone beyond the mixer's audio capabilities. An excessive "peak" can cause clipping, and the results are rarely pretty.
>
> On any given mixer, the difference between the nominal operating level and the level at which clipping occurs is called headroom. There is usually an LED on most mixers that indicates when you're clipping, and, of course, you can hear it as well! You'll know it when you hear it.

Line Level Input

A line level input is used to connect equipment that carries the voltage level needed by the mixer to process the signal properly. This is typically –10 dB for most equipment, such as a keyboard or drum machine, for example.

Physically, the line level input is usually a female quarter-inch jack with its own dedicated gain, which lets you calibrate the level for best results. An unbalanced standard quarter-inch cable can be used to connect a piece of equipment to the line level input.

Filters

Near the XLR or quarter-inch input jacks, you are likely to find a filter button. A filter removes specific frequencies from an input signal. In particular, a high-pass filter is one that removes undesirable low frequency sounds and is often found on today's mixers. The filter may be labeled with a number, such as 70 or 90. This refers to the cutoff frequency; in other words, if it is labeled with a 70, all frequencies below 70 Hz will be filtered out. All of the frequencies above 70 Hz will be allowed to "pass" through, as discussed earlier in this chapter. This filter may also be referred to as a "lo cut" or "low pad."

Get on the Bus

Once an audio signal enters a mixer's domain by way of an input channel, it is assigned to a bus.

In electronics, a bus is defined as a connection that has three or more circuits in common. For all practical purposes, buses are what give a mixer its unique blending capabilities; the most basic type of bus on a mixer is the main output bus.

The main output is actually two buses—one for the left and one for the right. The Pan control found on any input channel can assign a signal to a point anywhere along the spectrum between these left and right output buses.

Of course, if blending a handful of external inputs to one stereo output were enough, this chapter would be smaller, and mixers a whole lot cheaper. But a good mixer must be capable of handling a variety of other studio needs. These could include the addition of a DAT (digital audio tape), an external effects processor, or a computer-based digital setup. To accomplish these tasks, most mixers are outfitted with supplemental busing systems.

For example, if one of the mixer's input channels were connected to a vocal microphone during a recording session, the ultimate destination wouldn't necessarily be the final mix; rather, the signal would probably need to be sent to one of the inputs of your hard-disk recorder or computer. By connecting the multitrack inputs to another bus' outputs, the same vocal signal could then be assigned to the new bus and be delivered to the multitrack. In fact, the flexible nature of the bus connection permits any signal assigned to it to be transported to the same destination.

Groups

The groups section of a mixer takes its busing capabilities a step further by providing special "group" faders. This means that all of the signals assigned to a particular bus can be manipulated by moving one volume control. This is especially valuable for mixing recordings that involve many tracks. For instance, if you were mixing a tune that featured a gospel choir backup, and you used three microphones to capture the group vocal and decided to double track them for an even bigger effect, you would be left with six faders to keep track of, let alone the rest of your instrumentation and lead vocal!

This is where group faders come in: By assigning the six choir tracks to a bus that feeds a couple of group faders, a stereo choir submix can be easily achieved. The original six faders can be adjusted to get just the right submix, and for the final mix, the group faders can be assigned to the main stereo output bus, rejoining the other vocals and instrumentation. The two group faders allow you to set the relative level of the choir as a whole to the rest of the tracks during final mixdown. Think of the whole process as ganging input channels together.

Auxiliary Buses

A good mixer offers a lot of flexibility for routing audio signals, almost like a good traffic cop. In addition to buses and groups, auxiliary buses, known simply as the "aux," transport one or more additional signals to the inputs of an external effects unit.

Most of the time, this means effects, from reverb to delay to flanging to compression. Effects are covered in more detail later in this chapter.

The number of auxes on a mixer vary, though most good mixers carry more than a handful. The outputs from the auxiliary buses are usually grouped together with corresponding knobs in the auxiliary section of each input channel. Each respective aux input connector introduces the processed signal back to the mixer and then can be reapplied to the main stereo output buses, joining all of the other music tracks before, ahem, "history is made."

EQ

Equalizing—or EQ—is the process of adjusting the signal levels of frequency ranges. Whether the capability is in your software or in the mixer (or both), equalization is the core audio tool you have for shaping your music during both recording and mixing.

Remember that the human ear can detect sounds falling within a range of 20 to 20,000 Hz. This makes for a formidable challenge when lots of different instruments and voices are combined. Each individual instrument has its own sonic characteristics that require equalizer modifications. Once these tracks are blended together at mixdown, more EQ decisions need to be made to achieve a balanced master recording.

Achieving that balance is the domain of EQ.

Cut and Boost

EQ got started way back in the days when a telephone was a piece of luxury equipment; in those days, a significant amount of signal loss was quite common, and though increasing the whole signal's amplitude could more or less make up for that loss, the loss was very frequency-dependent.

EQ was developed in response to that frequency-dependent signal loss, in order to boost only the frequencies that suffered the most attenuation. EQ effectively leveled out all the frequencies in the signal, hence the name "equalizer."

EQ circuitry then was strictly a matter a boosting frequencies, though; today, cutting a frequency is just as important in the process of "EQ'ing" a mix. Cutting—without boosting first—is achieved by using a filter, which is kind of the same thing as archaic EQ, but a bit different. By cutting frequencies, you are effectively boosting the frequencies you're not cutting, so the end result is a boost, but the process is not identical. For instance, a "low-pass" filter is not actually boosting anything—it's allowing all frequencies below a certain point, called the *cutoff frequency*, to pass without attenuation, while it cuts off all frequencies above the cutoff.

EQs VARY

Every mixer organizes its EQ section a little differently, with varying degrees of sophistication. At the very least, you will encounter low and high pots that will apply a boost or cut at a fixed frequency. The knob may be labeled with a number representing its setting. For example, a "60" refers to a low-end 60 Hertz setting. Whereas, a "12K" label refers to a much higher 12,000 Hertz setting.

Boosting and cutting combined make up most EQ devices today, whether in software, a mixing board, or a piece of other outboard gear. It's all a matter of boost and cut, cut and boost. The degree to which the boosts and cuts can be combined, layered, and ordered, and the range of frequencies they can operate on, have produced several basic types of EQ.

Fixed EQ

The most basic type of EQ is the tone control on an amplifier or car stereo. This type of EQ works with only two bands: bass and treble. When you turn up the bass, you get around 10 dB of boost near 100 Hz, with less and less effect above that frequency. Below 100 Hz, boosting and cutting doesn't vary too much, so that the slope of the changes in frequency is almost horizontal. In fact, it looks a bit like a shelf, which is why the term "shelving EQ" exists. Typical treble is a mirror image of the way simple bass EQ works, only on the other end of the frequency spectrum.

A typical mixer may have a two-band equalizer for each input channel, but better mixers are more likely to have more sophisticated, separate controls that work with three frequency bands or more, as illustrated in Figure 13.3.

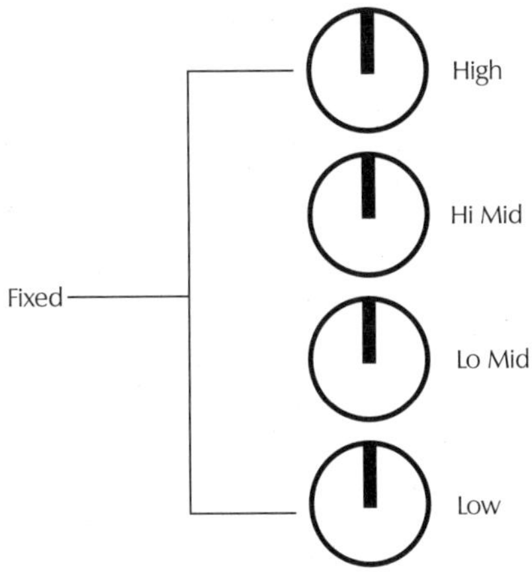

Figure 13.3
Many affordable mixing consoles use four bands of fixed EQ: High, Hi Mid, Low Mid, and Low

This type of simple equalization has its limits, though. Even a mixer that covers a few dozen discrete frequencies using a half-dozen different bands can have its limitations, which is why a few other types of EQ have been developed.

Sweepable EQ

A lot of consoles in the middle-of-the-road price range have a high and low fixed EQ and one or two mid, "sweepable" (sometimes called "semi-parametric") frequencies. Instead of having to cut or boost one set frequency as you do on a fixed EQ, sweepable EQ lets you target the frequency you want to adjust with one knob and cut or boost that frequency with another knob. Figure 13.4 shows a typical channel strip configuration.

CHANNEL STRIP TERMINOLOGY

The terminology for a channel strip (sometimes called a channel module) can be a bit different in the digital domain. A channel strip is analogous to a "control surface." You'll also see "control surface" sometimes used with analog/digital combo mixers.

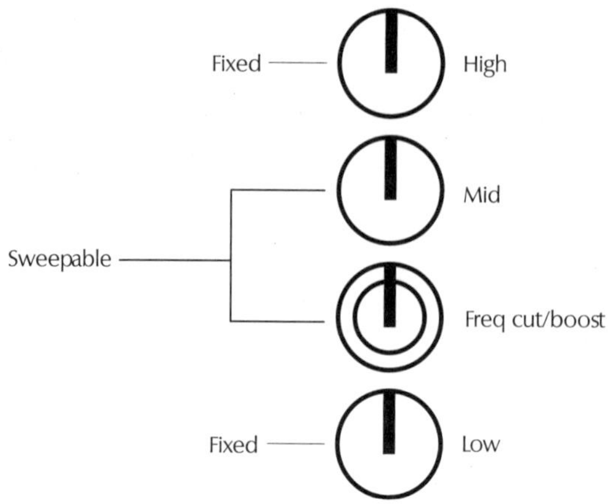

Figure 13.4
A sweepable EQ, in this case three bands, including one with sweepable midrange, gives you greater power to adjust frequencies across a given range

In fact, fixed/sweepable EQ is what you can expect these days for most analog mixers up to around $2,000 or a bit higher. The Behringer MX 2642A or Mackie 1642 VLZ Pro are both good examples in the $500 price range, and when used as a part of your digital recording setup, they provide solid, basic EQ alongside the greater capabilities of your recording software.

Parametric EQ

With both fixed and sweepable EQs, the steepness of the EQ curve is fixed. With any given boost or cut, the amount of the audio frequency that can be affected—whether it's fixed at one frequency or encompasses a specific range—has been set in the hardware and cannot be changed.

A parametric EQ goes beyond fixed and sweepables; all of its parameters can be adjusted to any amount, including:

- Center frequency
- The amount of boost or cut in gain
- The bandwidth

Most often, you'll find one or two sets of controls, labeled "High Mid" or "Low Mid" or possibly just "Mid." Although the natural sound spectrum is vast, having at least one parametric control paired with fixed High and Low knobs is an ideal way to handle even the most demanding audio signals.

The frequency value is the most elemental setting on a parametric control. Usually, High Mid can be set to a frequency center between 1000 and 20,000 Hertz (1–20 kHz), whereas Low Mid lies predictably between 45 and 3000 Hz.

The bandwidth, or "Q" setting, refers to how broad or narrow the EQ treatment will be. Bandwidth is measured in terms of octaves or fractions of one octave. On a piano, an octave is the distance from one "C" pitch to the next one. In Hertz, if a pitch comes in at

440 (A above Middle C), its octave would be 880. Most equalizers allow the user to select a bandwidth between 0.10 and 4 octave(s), where, a standard setting is 1 octave.

Finally, the amplitude of the EQ treatment is set via the cut/boost knob, which adds or subtracts the frequency plus bandwidth by decibels. Typically, the amplitude on a parametric EQ can be adjusted up to +/– 16–20 dB.

Graphic EQ

You are doubtless familiar with graphic EQ. A graphic equalizer can work simultaneously with eight or more frequency bands, usually with one octave or one-third octave band centers. Most graphic EQs employ both attenuation and boost filters.

A graphic EQ is called "graphic" because the sliders that represent each of the frequencies create a visual image that, when set, looks like the overall frequency response curve of the EQ taking place.

Graphic EQ reduces the effect of resonant peaks and dips in monitor response and, to a lesser degree, in the acoustic recording space itself, by reducing the tendency for acoustic feedback to occur.

As the overall gain of any sound system increases, feedback first occurs at peak frequencies, starting as a slight ringing, and then morphing into a loud, sometimes piercing howl. By using a graphic equalizer to attenuate the first peak, the overall system gain can be increased until the next lower peak begins to feedback. That peak can then be attenuated using another graphic EQ band and system gain can be increased a little more, until the peaks have all been leveled to the extent possible with all the bands. Using bands this way, with a graphic EQ, may increase overall gain from 6–10 dB above the initial gain.

Another use of graphic EQ is to model the contour of a mixer's frequency response to get the best overall response pattern for the mixer. In the real world, flat response is seldom what you will want. You'll probably tend to stay reasonably flat over the middle of the spectrum, but effects—especially reverb—will have you boosting the low end, and you'll roll off the high end to varying degrees, depending on the song.

Sometimes, the midrange (1–5 kHz) can be effective in increasing or decreasing sibilance, especially when sounds in this region have been masked by other, nearby frequencies.

SIBILANCE

Sibilance is noise associated with vocal sounding of words with, usually, "s," "sch," "ch," "z," and "j" sounds or syllables. The noise created by sibilance is a narrow band noise in the high frequency range (5–10 kHz).

Steinberg carries a VST plug-in to help combat this problem called the SPL De-Esser. It's a software emulation of the best hardware de-esser around, made by a company called SPL. One of its best features includes presets for male and female voices, because both are capable of typically producing the same kinds of noises at different frequencies.

Although this once was available as an optional plug-in, it is now included in the SX version of Cubase.

A graphic EQ is not something you'll typically find on board an analog mixing console, though most software setups (such as Cubase) do include a graphic EQ along with fixed, sweepable, and parametric EQs.

Auxiliary Section

Depending on how many auxiliary buses your mixer has, you'll find a corresponding knob for each one of them in the auxiliary (often simply called "Aux") section of each channel strip. These knobs are most commonly used to apply outboard effects to the audio signal of any given channel; by turning the aux pot clockwise, more signal is bused to the effects unit, and more effect is returned and blended into the final stereo mix. The relationship between the original signal and the affected signal is called the wet/dry balance. For example, a wet vocal is one that has a lot of reverb effect applied to it; and, a vocal with no effect whatsoever is considered very dry. In general, you'll make less use of auxes during recording, because you normally want the source tracks as dry as possible.

Many aux sends also have a pre-fader and post-fader switch that sends the exact amount of signal you dial in or the amount that tracks the fader, respectively. In addition to using auxes to set up effects subroutines, you can create a separate submix, for example.

Channel Inserts

Sometimes, an audio signal on a particular channel strip needs special processing apart from everything else. Many mixers are equipped with channel insert plugs that can be used in conjunction with another signal (an outboard processor, for example). Inserts don't function like auxiliary buses. Unlike an aux, the signal using a channel insert will be returned at the same point at which it was tapped.

Inserts are often used with compressors or noise gates to extend more control over certain signals during mixdown. You can also use them as extra single-channel outputs.

Mix B

When you're tracking, the performer (the instrumentalist or singer or you, if you're a one-person band) is monitoring everything with headphones—a very necessary thing to do unless he or she is John Cage.

The Mix B function of a mixer allows you to design a custom mix—also known as a cue or rollover mix—that can be assigned to the headphones' output without affecting the main mix. For instance, if you're tracking the singer in the band, using Mix B, you could assemble the perfect mix for his egotistical, self-serving needs in his headphones while independently manipulating the primary mix in your studio monitors. This lets you isolate the vocal and check for errors in performance, as well as make subtle adjustments without distracting the vocalist in mid-delivery.

In addition, if you're a one-stop shop, you may want to adjust Mix B to your own preferences according to each track you're laying down, while keeping the main mix you're working with piped out through the main bus. You might want to listen to your voice with 42 milliseconds of delay, for example, but not send it to disk that way.

USING MIX B FOR EXTRA INPUTS

Many mixers provide supplemental quarter-inch input jacks that feed Mix B fader knobs. This can be a handy feature when you find yourself running out of channel inputs.

Pan

The Pan control allows you to place the audio signal associated with its channel strip anywhere along the horizontal stereo panorama, from left to right. The Pan control is usually labeled "L" for left and "R" for right, where a straight up 12 o'clock setting results in no pan. This is similar to the left and right stereo control knobs found on just about every home stereo in the universe (except on Mars, because Martians, as it turns out, only have one ear).

The Pan control also plays an important role while tracking. Internal buses are typically organized into stereo pairs. So, when an input signal such as a bass guitar is bused to an external tape machine, the Pan control is used to select which one of the two buses will carry the signal. If buses 1 and 2 are connected to the first two inputs of your sound card, for instance, a hard left pan would send the signal to input 1 and a hard right pan to input 2.

Many tape machines can be set up to an input mode in which the remaining track inputs can be accessed in complementary pairs via inputs 1 and 2. On an 8-track tape machine, the Pan control selects whether a signal is bused to an odd numbered track (1, 3, 5, 7) or an even numbered track (2, 4, 6, 8). The same is true for a sound card, but the assignments are handled in software. Cubase, for example, lets you assign left and right signals to a track as well as the overall stereo image coming from any given channel.

Mute and Solo

The Mute and Solo buttons affect a channel and its surrounding modules in different ways. The Mute button, sometimes called Cut, completely silences a channel. This feature is an all-or-nothing "on" or "off" status without any gradation. The same applies to the Solo button; the only difference is that all surrounding channels are muted, effectively "soloing" the original channel's audio signal.

Solo can be a valuable tool for calibrating the gain amount on an input channel when many different signals are being managed. In this way, a signal can be carefully monitored for distortion and set to an ideal recording level. In addition, precise EQ modifications can be made so that the most ideal signal is sent to tape.

You'll also find solo and mute features on any respectable recording software.

The Fader

When people think of mixers, the piece most people envision first is the fader. A channel's fader is a vertical slider that allows you to continuously vary the signal level. This form and functionality has been around for decades and is very efficient at minimizing "cross talk"—the bleeding of audio from one channel to another.

Faders are usually present for individual channels, groups, and the main mix. They will sometimes be labeled with an "infinity" symbol, representing no signal or full fade, and a "0" or "U" for unity gain, representing no fade.

Faders are easy to use and many can be manipulated at the same time (also called "ganging" sliders). In fact, one of the coolest developments to come about in the last several years is the automation of faders (as well as all of the other controllers).

Automation is a really simple concept: Record the movements and settings of your controls and then "play" them back. It allows for an incredible amount of flexibility for a given mix and, most importantly, lets you take sequences of controller movements and settings from one situation and reapply them anywhere else.

In Cubase, for example, the process of automation is a breeze. To use automation in Mixer view, you simply:

1. Rewind to the beginning of a project.
2. Move the faders, pans, and any other controls to the initial settings you want.
3. Enable Automation recording by clicking on the Write All Automation button.
4. Begin playback and move the faders as needed so that the balance and mix you want is where you want it.

After you've stopped recording, you've now automated your mix. To listen to it again, and watch the faders move automatically:

1. Rewind to the beginning.
2. To make sure the faders show their current value, click the Read All Automation button.
3. Click Play. You'll see the faders move just the way they moved when you recorded their movements.

Of course, automation can get a bit more complicated than this, especially when you start dealing with real-time effects and complicated layouts. But you get the idea.

Bus Assignments

On mixers that have extended internal busing capabilities, you will encounter separate bus assignment buttons on each channel module. They are clearly marked with numbered pairs (1–2, 3–4, 5–6, 7–8). These are the assignment buttons used to group signals together or bus input signals, as discussed earlier. An "L/R" label found on most mixers represents the main stereo output bus. This assignment is used during final mixdown. The master fader controls the level of this signal.

Other Functions

More elaborate mixers come with additional functions that allow you to monitor signals in a host of other ways. One of these is the PFL, or pre-fade listen function.

PFL is always associated with a corresponding fader. When you enable it, the signal being fed to the fader can be bused to monitors or to headphones. This can allow you to:

- Check that the correct signal is being recorded
- Check the recording level
- Check the quality of a given signal

Another supplemental function is called "talkback." Talkback lets you communicate directly with other musicians in a separate room from your control room space. A lower quality in-line microphone installed directly on the mixer control surface makes the talkback utility possible; by hitting the talkback button, the mic signal can be bused to a pair of headphones.

COMMON CONTROLLER FUNCTIONS

Every switch, knob, and fader on a mixer performs at least one of three basic functions, as follows:

- A controller can select where a signal is coming from. These are known as source controllers and they determine the input source of a signal. A Mic/Line switch is an example of this controller, because it selects the source of the channel input.
- A controller can process the signal in some way. These are generally described according to the function they perform. EQ and gain controls are examples of this type of controller, because they alter the frequency response or set the gain of a signal, as opposed to determining its input or output.
- A controller can route where the signal is going. These are known as assign or routing switches, and they route signals to different buses or outputs. Channel Routing switches, for instance, route the channel signal to the Main Mix or Group buses.

Software Mixers

Computers have come a long way and are still newborns compared to the mixer. Yet, the computer and the mixer are two partner pieces of equipment that will only grow closer with time.

There are software programs available for some mixers that allow you to control each channel by manipulating images on a computer screen rather than physically moving the various controls yourself.

Most importantly, there are fully capable mixers within some software, such as Cubase, shown in Figure 13.5, which do an incredibly effective job of manipulating, routing, and busing your music.

Figure 13.5
Cubase's Console view emulates mixers in the physical world in software

Most software mixers have been designed to emulate mixers in the physical world, with many of the same functions. Some of them are simpler in design than Cubase but quite powerful behind the scenes, whereas some are limited only to faders that control each channel of input. The inputs to software mixers can come from your sound card or from any audio present on your system (such as CD-ROM or DVD-ROM).

Bias Peak is another example of an application that includes a unique software FX mixer of a sort, called vBox SE. Figure 13.6 shows the vBox mixer as individual FX modules that can be individually configured and routed to the stereo output. This allows for some really twisted sound design possibilities.

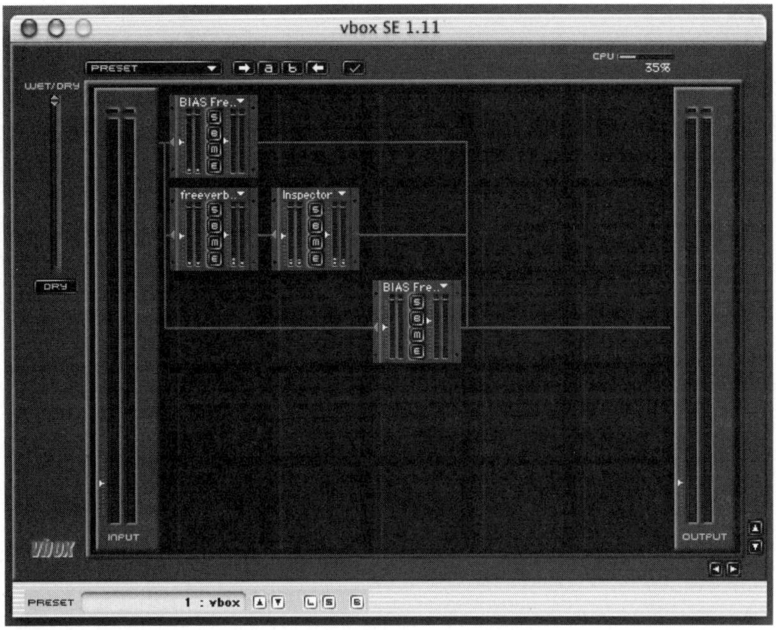

Figure 13.6
Bias' vBox SE comes included with Peak and produces endless possibilities in sound design

Don't be fooled by the simplicity of the vBox mixer. You can manipulate sound with an incredible assortment of FX by selecting them from the vBox pull-down menu.

- 4-band EQ
- AutoPan
- Degrade
- Detune
- Dither
- DubDelay
- Envelope
- Leslie
- Limiter
- Loudness
- Reverb
- RezFilter
- RoundPan
- Shepard
- Splitter
- SubSynth
- Tracker
- Vocoder

Rather than forcing you to go out and buy expensive effects processors, both Peak and Cubase allow you to integrate any VST plug-in effect. Figure 13.7 shows the detail of control you have with distortion, for example.

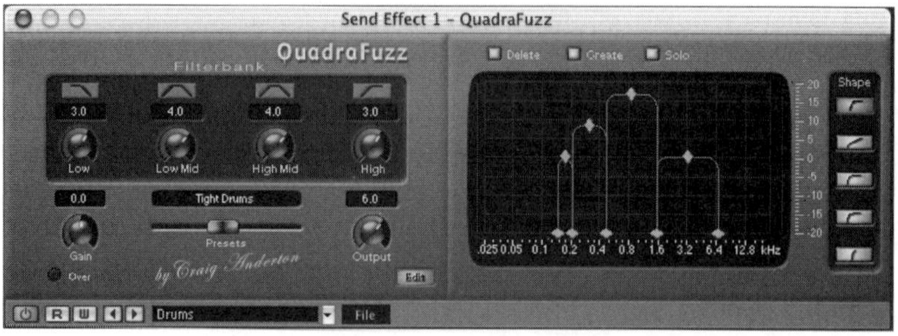

Figure 13.7
With the QuadraFuzz and having four independent bands of distortion, you'll be channeling Jimi in no time

Stepping Through the Mixing Chain

To recap, let's step through the mixing chain and attempt to picture the process of mixing as a series of steps. Of course, your mileage will vary, sometimes widely, because there are almost unlimited configurations and setups with a capable mixer. But there is a basic process behind the scenes at all times. We'll do it in seven steps—Input, EQ, Pan, Fade, Group, Aux, Listen—to keep it easy to remember.

1. **Input**. The mixer takes inputs, from a vocal microphone to your direct bass line to your synth—anything and everything capable of electrical audio signal. It is an input master. This is also where you set the trim.
2. **EQ**. EQs come in several flavors, from an external graphic EQ to a 2-pot tone control to Cubase's software mixing console. Most mixers have 3- or 4-band EQ, including a high band, which boosts or cuts around 1 kHz, a low band, which boosts or cuts around 100 Hz, and 1+ mid bands, which can either be fixed or sweepable. Better mixers and more capable software also employ parametric EQ, which gives you enormous control over most of the human ear's hearing spectrum.
3. **Pan**. The Pan control manages how much of the signal goes to the left bus vs. the right bus or any number of available buses, depending on the capability of the mixer. The pan pot (also known in tongue-twisting form as "panoramic potentiometer") directs the signal over left-right, like a traffic cop on a three-way street.
4. **Fade**. The audio signal next goes to individual channel faders, which control the level of the channel before it is routed to corresponding outputs. Sometimes, a channel strip also offers a mute switch and the very important PFL switch, which allows you to preview the channel through a monitor bus pre-fader.
5. **Group**. If present, special "group" faders take a mixer's busing capabilities a step further by giving you the ability to access all of the signals on a particular bus at once. Think of a group as an anal-retentive output.
6. **Aux**. Auxiliary buses are most commonly used to apply effects or other additive signals to an individual channel's signal.

7. **Listen**. Finally, the signal makes its way from the outputs into your monitor or headphones.

The previous steps can vary a bit, because most good-quality mixers have the added capability of being able to let you determine whether a signal is being routed pre-fade (before it hits the output bus(es)), or post-fade (after the signal passes through the output bus(es)). But you get the idea! Now go create art!

Using Effects Effectively

Wait a minute. Scratch the last sentence of the last section. You may want to use some effects in your mixes. In fact, if you're like most hot-blooded musicians and audiophiles on the planet, you can't live without a little reverb here, a little delay there, and some compression to top it all off.

Reverb, compression, and delay are all covered in Chapter 11, "Fun-Da-Mental Audio," with a more detailed look at reverb in Chapter 12, "Serious Audio." In the next section, we'll take a look at a few other, less fundamental—but very powerful—signal processors, or effects.

Noise Gates

A noise gate is a signal processor that turns down or turns off an audio signal when the level falls below where you set it. The idea is that the audio passes through and kind of leaves behind any low-level noise or leakage from other things in the mix you don't want. In this way, you can think of a noise gate as an adjustable noise housecleaner. You tell it how much house to clean and how much time to spend cleaning. How much cleaning a noise gate does is called its threshold.

Noise gates are good for temporarily muting mics. In complex, multichannel setups, the use of a noise gate can also improve the overall system sound without mucking up the mix. It's most effective if your groups use a separate noise gate for each group, and it's remarkably effective if you use a separate noise gate on individual input channels.

Noise gates are particularly suited to the guitar. Careful use of a noise gate in your guitar's signal chain is an ideal scenario: It keeps noise from the guitar at bay until it's time for you to put out and can save you from having to spend a lot of time muting parts of a track during mixdown.

Setting the threshold for a guitar is a by-ear proposition; generally, if you use a lot of gain or distortion and you're playing hard, you should start by setting a high threshold and work down from there until you hear the sweetest spot. With a high threshold, the noise gate is less sensitive to a little more banging and force.

If you're miking an acoustic, on the other hand, you can start with a much lower threshold, because, presumably, you won't be tempted to start having Pete Townshend flashbacks.

Phase Shifters

A phase shifter, or phaser, creates little notches at different frequencies that cut out sounds where the notches are. A phase shifter can control the number of notches, where each notch is located, and the size of the notches.

This is accomplished through the judicious use of deep, high "Q" filters; the source signal is split, with some of it going to the filter and some not. The actual shifting takes place mainly to either side of the notch. The notch is swept up and down the available frequencies in the mix, then mixed with the original signal, causing predictable phase cancellation.

Think of creating a paper airplane and then cutting tiny random notches where the wings are folded (nothing too elaborate, mind you, this is not quite a paper snowflake), then throwing the airplane. The resulting air flow around the notches is a bit like phase. (Note: If you try this example, you really won't hear anything—it's just an analogy. If you want to cut notches in a paper airplane anyway, just ensure that no one's watching. You could be perceived as being mentally phase-cancelled.)

Flanger and Chorus

Flangers turn out to be a special case of phase shifting. It also introduces phase cancellation into the signal path by mixing the output of a signal with a notched copy of itself, then retiming everything so that the original and copy are out of phase.

The big difference is that flanging notches are always equally spaced. Delay times are also usually in a range from 1–10 milliseconds; this is what produces a flanger's characteristic sweeping sound.

The idea has been around for a while, and the flanger actually takes its name from the flanges of a reel-to-reel tape. By using pressure against the flanges of the tape reel, early explorers of flanging were able to alter the timing of each machine's playback, causing all kinds of interesting, calculated phase cancellations.

It turned out to be a little math, actually: With equally-spaced notches, if one signal is delayed, then immediately mixed back differently (either as a completely different signal or a copy of the original), the result is cancellation at a frequency equal to about twice the delay time. Pretty cool, huh?

Chorus is similar to flanging, with two important differences:

- The delay is larger, usually between 20–30 milliseconds, so you don't get the sweeping sound of a flanger.
- Chorus makes no use of feedback.

The result is a type of delay that replicates not only the delay between sounds in a natural setting but also pitch differences. With the delay and pitch modulation together, you hear the unmistakable sound of a chorus effect.

Other Effects

There are lots of other effects you can use, and most of them can be had these days in the form of VST plug-in packages. Using VST plug-ins (or native plug-ins for your particular software) is a way to keep from spending enormous sums on separate external units, with an added bonus of having to run only a setup program, instead of physically hooking all this gear up.

It's really beyond the scope of this book to try to cover all the different signal processing permutations available these days. There are literally thousands of different effects and dozens of manufacturers. A good place to start online is **www.harmony-central.com**. The site has links, reviews, and loads of information about most of the plug-ins that have been released over the last several years. Many of the software companies also offer free demos of their plug-ins for download.

In addition, a well-equipped music retailer typically carries a large selection of VST plug-ins, and a knowledgeable salesperson should be more than happy to let you check them out.

Arboretum Software, online at **www.arboretum.com**, carries a VST plug-in suite called Hyperprism, which is a very strong offering in the let's-try-and-be-everything-to-everyone category; the package includes some killer effects, and lots of them for about $199 from the company's website. Hyperprism includes the following effects plug-ins:

- Band Pass Filter
- Band Reject Filter
- Bass Maximizer
- Chorus
- Compressor
- Echo
- Flanger
- Formant Pitch Shifter
- Frequency Shifter
- Granulator
- Hall Reverb
- Harmonic Exciter
- High Pass Filter
- HyperPhaser
- HyperVerb
- Limiter
- Low Pass Filter
- M-S Matrix
- More Stereo
- Multi Delay
- Noise Gate
- Pan
- Phaser
- Pitch Changer
- Quasi Stereo
- Ring Modulator
- Room Reverb
- Single Delay
- Sonic Decimator
- Stereo Dynamics
- Tremolo
- Tube/Tape Saturator
- Vibrato
- Vocoder

Ironically, the EQ and compressor plug-ins are the weakest parts of this package, but the rest is well worth taking a look at.

VST PLUG-IN EFFECTS

There is a long, long list of VST plug-ins that come included with Cubase SL/SX. Should you find yourself reaching the creative limit with these included plug-ins (as the saying goes, "He who dies with the most toys wins"), you need to be aware of the right kind of plug-in to purchase for your Cubase system.

First, you need to make sure that the plug-ins you are interested in buying are written for the VST platform, and you need to make sure that there is a Mac version included in the box.

Additionally, you need to also double-check to see if these plug-ins are *OS X ready*. The reason for this added precaution is to make sure that this is a piece of gear that you can use right out of the box. Otherwise, you could find yourself waiting for a long time while the plug-ins are updated and encoded for OS X.

Please do the research first by visiting the manufacturer's website or by asking your music store salesperson.

14

Step-By-Step: Your First 8-Track Song

This chapter steps you through recording, mixing, and mastering a simple 8-track song. Each section is a specific step in the process, from setting up your recording preferences to exporting the finished product as both an audio file master and an MP3 file.

This chapter discusses OS X and uses Cubase to handle recording, most of the mixing, and to master the song. If you use a different digital recording application, you should be able to follow along to some extent, but if you use an external mixing console and/or external hard drive exclusively, this won't be as valuable a chapter for you.

Your Operating System: The Lifeblood of Your Computer

Next to Cubase, your operating system has already or is going to become your best friend as you start your new career as a Hit-Charting Producer. The history of the operating systems for the Macintosh is a long and lengthy work in itself. It could take the contents of an entire book to cover how Apple's OS has evolved over the years, but it would quickly put you to sleep. Seriously though, if you want to see the ultimate cheat sheet movie, just rent *The Pirates of Silicon Valley* to learn the inner workings of Apple and Microsoft, as there is nothing quite as funny as seeing Anthony Michael Hall's portrayal of Bill Gates.

With earlier editions of the Mac OS, the two main concerns that loomed over the heads of many a wannabe computer geek were "Extensions" and "Preferences." Extensions are subapplications that operate within the Mac OS and allow usage of third-party software or hardware that can be installed in a Macintosh computer. Preferences are simply the custom settings that you can assign to the Mac's software and hardware. That said, the next two phrases that any Mac user would certainly come to know soon would be "confliction" and "corruption," plus other colorful three- and four-letter words used often in computing but that we can't mention here.

Simply put, like children on a playground, not all extensions play well with each other, and this caused inexplicable crashes. The easiest way to solve this was to go through a very long list of active extensions and systematically turn them off one by one until the crashes stopped occurring.

Preferences, on the other hand, would sometimes become corrupted, so that the computer and programs could not read or use them. This also caused mysterious crashes, in turn causing users to spontaneously start ripping the hair out of their heads while shouting those other colorful words I mentioned before. A pretty common fix to this was to move the preferences for the program in trouble into the virtual trash can, commonly known as "trashing the prefs." Upon restarting the program, the Mac OS instantly created a new set of preferences for that program and, with luck, the problem was solved.

So why am I telling you this? The main reason is to assure you that these problems are a thing of the past, as Mac OS X has solved many of these problems. There are no more extensions to worry about, as this operating system is completely new code—not just another quick fix over an older operating system. If you bought a new Mac after January 2003, OS X should be the only operating system on it. The other reason I'm telling you this...well, let's just say it will make you sound smarter at parties.

And just as I hear the PC crowd heckling us and jumping with glee, let me assure you that Microsoft Windows had just as many computer crashing drawbacks in the previous OS and are now pretty much on the same playing field as us with their Windows XP operating system.

Step 1: Installing Cubase SX/SL

Although this is not strictly a Cubase book, I feel that it is important to go over the basic installation of Cubase on your computer, as problems can occur if it's not properly installed. With a Mac, the installation procedure is, thankfully, a painless one as you need only three things:

1. Your Cubase SX/SL CD-ROM.
2. Your Cubase SX/SL copy protection key or "dongle." This copy protection key is blue and has a USB tip on the end of it.
3. Your Cubase SX/SL serial number. This is located on a registration card that can be found in your Cubase box.

GO AHEAD AND REGISTER

It is very important that you fill out your registration card and send it to the manufacturer for a couple of reasons. First, you want to make sure you get the most up-to-date information on your software as it's updated. Second, at some point you are going to need help from an expert, and you will require technical support from the manufacturer. Without your registration, you will not be qualified for either of these.

Before we begin the installation, it is important to remember not to attach the copy protection key to one of your Mac's USB ports. Instead just put it aside for a few minutes. So let's begin:

1. Pop the Cubase CD-ROM into your tray and wait until the Cubase icon shows up on your desktop.
2. Double-click on the Cubase icon to display the contents of the Cubase CD-ROM.
3. Double-click on the Cubase installer and follow the instructions. If you are computer-savvy, you can install the program in any location on the hard drive that you want (in a folder called "Music" for example). However, if this is your first time, the default location will do just fine.
4. After it starts to install, the program will ask you for a serial number. Just whip out that Cubase registration card and use the serial number printed on it. Just remember, this is your personal serial number. No one else should have it except you.
5. The program will then go through the installation process, which can take a few minutes; be patient.
6. After Cubase has finished installing, just restart your Mac and you are ready to go. As the computer is restarting, you can plug your copy protection key into any available USB port.

WHERE'S THE ICON?

After your Mac has restarted, you will undoubtedly want to start Cubase right away. The only problem is that you can't seem to locate the Cubase program icon anywhere on your desktop. This is a quick and easy fix that just takes a second to complete. Assuming that you installed Cubase in the default location:

1. Double-click the Macintosh HD icon to view the contents of the Mac HD.
2. Double-click the Applications folder.
3. Double-click the Cubase folder.
4. Click the Cubase SX/SL icon once. This just highlights the program without launching it.
5. Drag the Cubase icon onto your dock and release the mouse. You should now see a shortcut of the Cubase icon on your dock. This is simply an easier way to find and launch the program. You can do this with any program on your system.

JUST SAY NO

If this is your first computer, you will certainly discover the Internet sooner or later. There are many useful information resources on the Net—sources such as **www.cubase.net** or **www.harmony-central.com**. You will also find virtual bulletin boards where users log in and share questions and tips on various topics related to the software you are using. Although these forums can be quite useful in getting information and help, you will undoubtedly see topics about using

(continued)

illegal copies of the software, or "cracked versions" as we call them in geek world. If you read through these strings, upset users will attempt to justify using these cracked versions of the software over buying it. Let me just tell you, whatever their reasons may be, it *is* illegal to use cracked software. The companies that develop these incredible programs spend thousands of dollars and man-hours conceiving, coding, and testing the software so users like us can enjoy and use them for years to come. They all have lives to lead and families to look after and feed (I think I just rhymed). Frankly speaking, the users who want to compel you to use cracked software are pathetic individuals who are probably just too cheap to buy the software in the first place.

So Young Jedi, do not be tempted by the Dark Side of the Virtual Force. If you are reading this passage and want to learn how you can help support our cause, just visit **www.be-cool.org** to learn how.

Step 2: A Little Preparation

In the world of professional recording studios, good recording engineers maintain fairly detailed records most of the time about setups, settings, mix levels, and so on. A "track sheet" is their primary means of documentation.

It makes sense that you should have your own track sheet of sorts, too, but yours need not be quite as detailed, because most of it is virtually done for you in Cubase. You could also keep handwritten records if you prefer, though having them is not strictly necessary. You can also create a virtual track sheet in the Notepad program that comes embedded in Cubase.

1. The first thing to do is really easy: Launch Cubase by clicking the Cubase icon on the dock.
2. Every time Cubase is first launched, you will see the Transport Control at the bottom of the screen and the menu bar at the top of the screen, but nothing in between. Don't panic, this just means you have to create a new project. Go to the File menu and select New Project. You will be prompted with a list of session templates, as shown in Figure 14.1. Select the Empty option and click OK. You will then need to create and select a folder in which to store your project. Because this is your first project, I suggest placing the folder on your desktop so you can find it easily.

Figure 14.1
Cubase provides a list of templates for different recording studios

3. You will now see the default layout for Cubase, called the Project window, which consists of a blank screen, as shown in Figure 14.2. Go to the Project menu and select the Add Track submenu. You then have many choices of kinds of tracks to insert into your project. We will be sure to play around with a MIDI track or two later, but for now, we will want to create seven audio tracks (six mono tracks of audio and one stereo track, giving us a total of eight audio tracks). If you want to do it the long way, you can add one track at a time by just selecting audio. Just remember that speed is the name of the game here, so select the Multiple option, as shown in Figure 14.3. Next, you will be prompted to tell Cubase what type of track you want to create and how many, as shown in Figure 14.4. Select Audio and type in the number 7 under the track count. You should now see seven tracks of audio on your Project window, as shown in Figure 14.5.

Figure 14.2
Cubase's empty Project window

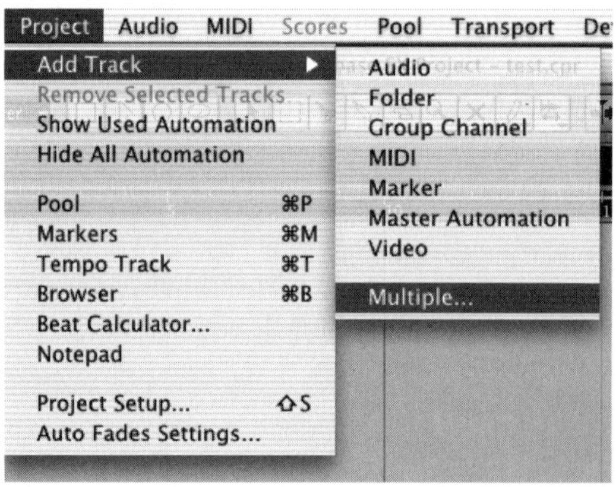

Figure 14.3
The Project menu can help to create numerous tracks

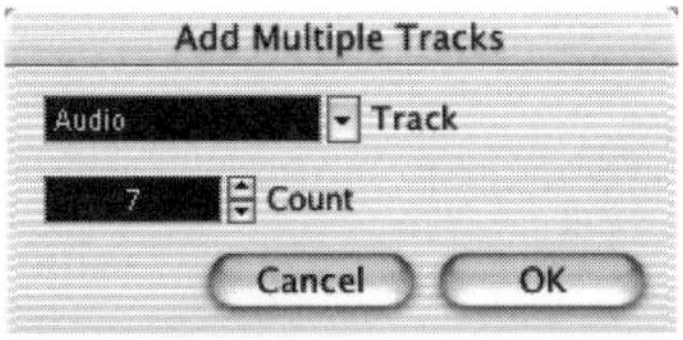

Figure 14.4
Start by adding seven audio tracks

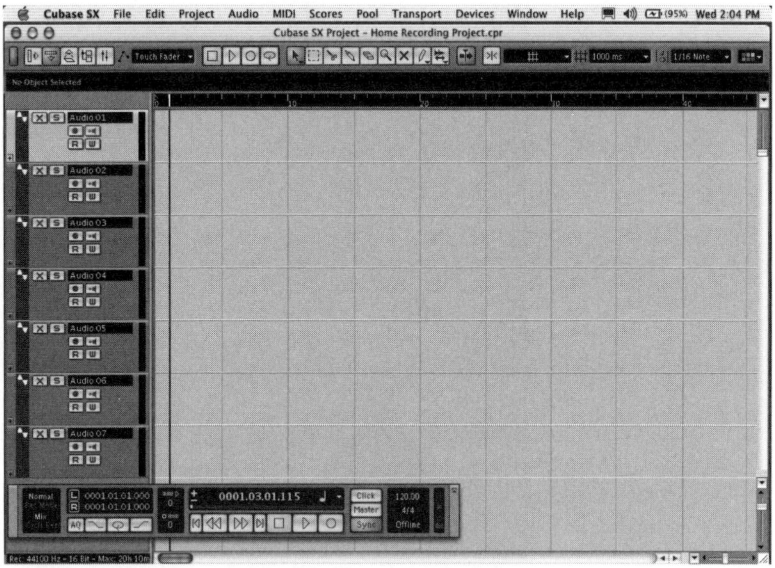

Figure 14.5
You now have seven blank audio tracks

4. After you've added the tracks, give each one a name. You can do this by double-clicking the default names and typing in new names at the cursor. For this session, we'll use a stereo track for drums, one track for bass guitar, two tracks for guitars, one for a keyboard, and two for vocals, as shown in Figure 14.6.

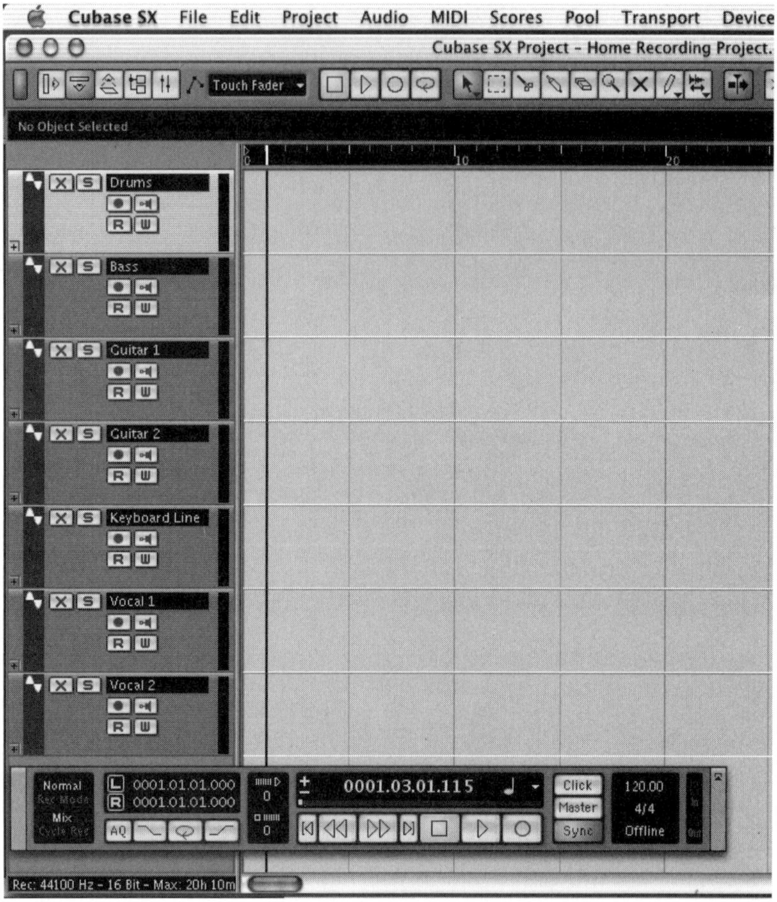

Figure 14.6
Name your tracks

5. Next, you will want to save your work up to this point. Just select the Save option from the File menu. You can also save this layout as a customized template so that when you start Cubase again for another project, you won't have to set up the Project window again. This is done by selecting the Save as Template option in the File menu, as shown in Figure 14.7.

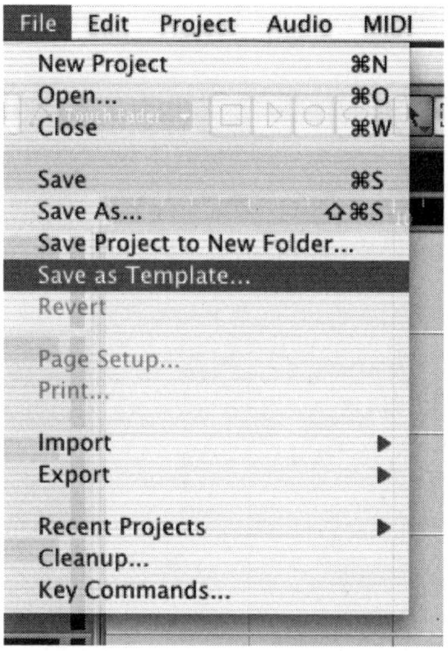

Figure 14.7
After you create your custom project, you can save it as a template

Step 3: Setting Up Cubase

Step 3 involves making sure that the global audio settings for Cubase are set up properly.

Selecting Your Audio Card

When you are using a Macintosh, keep in mind that you already have an audio card, regardless of whether you installed an additional audio card. That said, Cubase needs to know which audio card to use in your project. This only takes a minute to do and after it is done, Cubase remembers this setting from that point on.

To select your audio card:

1. Click the Devices menu and select Device Setup (see Figure 14.8).
2. The Device Setup window then appears. Select the VST Multitrack option from the left side of the window. The information for the audio card should now appear on the right side of the window (see Figure 14.9).

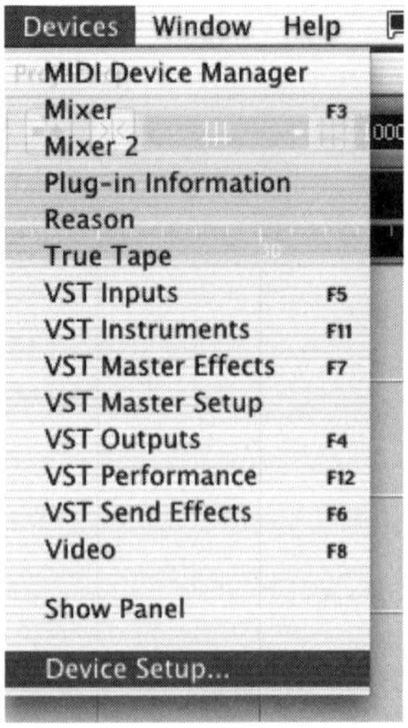

Figure 14.8
Select Device Setup from the Devices menu

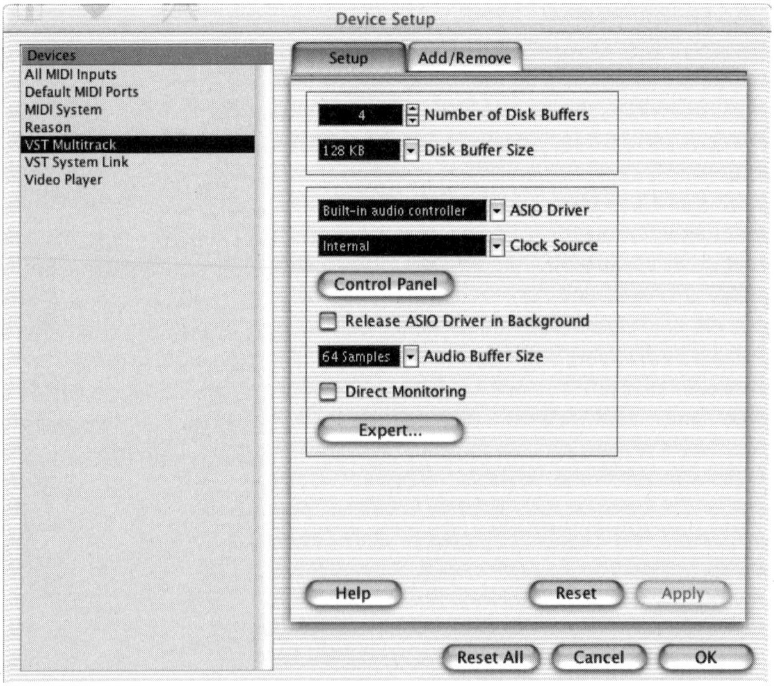

Figure 14.9
The Device Setup window

3. Under the ASIO Driver option, you should see the "Built-in Audio Controller" option listed. This is the driver for the internal audio card in your Macintosh. Click on this and change it to the audio card you have installed in your system (see Figure 14.10).

Figure 14.10
Select your audio card

4. Click OK to close the Device Setup window.

Setting the Sampling Rate

A fundamental aspect of doing digital audio involves setting the sampling rate. Simply put, the sampling rate is how many times an audio signal is sampled. You can't have different sample rates for different tracks; one setting does it all. What should you set it to? First, you're limited by your sound card: You can't set your sampling rate any higher than the hardware supports. For CD-quality sound, use 44.1 kHz. But remember: The higher the sampling rate, the more hard drive space will be used when recording and playing back audio. If this is your first recording project, it is probably best to record at 44.1 kHz. When you get a little more accustomed to the process of recording in Cubase, you can consider using a higher sampling rate. One of the immediate benefits is the ability to accurately capture instruments with a broad frequency range. A good example of this is a cymbal on a drum kit, which produces a very wide range of frequencies, or an acoustic piano.

To set the sampling rate and bit depth:

1. Click the Project menu and select Project Setup (see Figure 14.11). You can also access this window by holding down both the Shift and S keys.
2. The Project Setup window then appears (see Figure 14.12). As you can see, this project already has the correct sampling rate, so there is no need to change it.
3. Under Record Format, 16 bits is the default setting. If your audio card supports a greater bit depth, you can select it here.
4. Click OK.

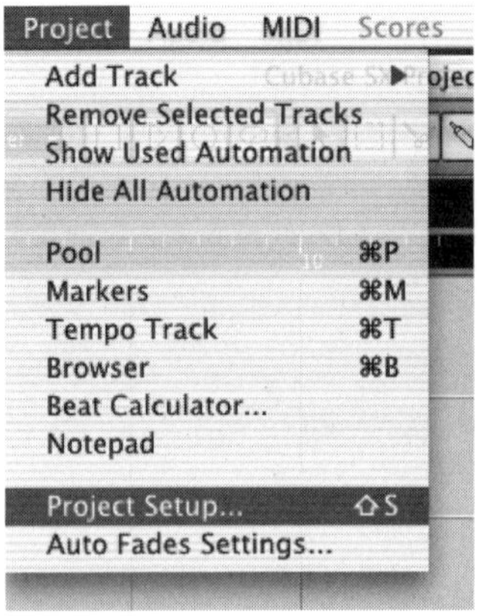

Figure 14.11
Click the Project menu to access the Project Setup window

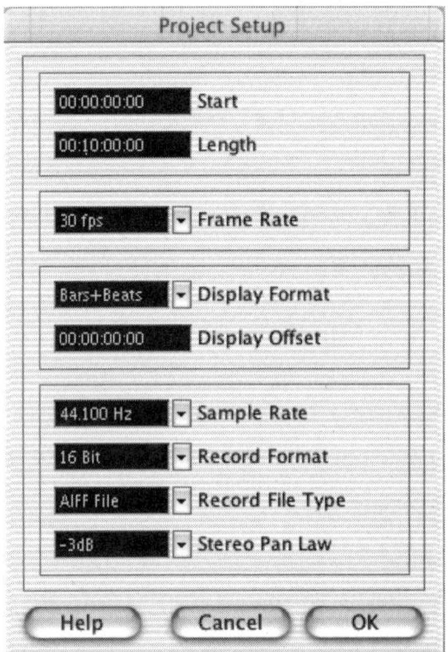

Figure 14.12
The Project Setup window is where you can make changes to the bit depth and sampling rate

UNDERSTANDING BIT DEPTH

We've seen that a higher sampling rate allows us to more accurately capture an audio signal with a wider frequency range, but what are the benefits of recording at a greater bit depth? All information created and stored on a computer exists, at its most basic level, as a binary code consisting of a series of zeros and ones (zero=off, one=on). Sixteen bits of audio data is represented by a specific number of these zeros and ones in intervals of four bits. For example, a binary representation of a 16-bit recording is 1010 1111 0110 1101. Once these bits have all reached 1, this means that you will have recorded at the maximum potential that 16-bit recording can offer. In recording terms, this means that you have recorded at the highest volume potential and you cannot record any louder, or your signal will distort. With 24-bit recording, a greater number of zeros and ones are now introduced into your recording system, which in turn gives you a greater volume threshold—and greater waveform accuracy—with which to record.

The bad news is that because you can use a 24-bit audio card, there is still a potential to distort your signal, as you can record a 24-bit signal into Cubase at its full potential amplitude. Steinberg has a great solution for this problem in the top-of-the-line version of Cubase called SX. This version can record at 32 bits, which simply means that you now get a virtually infinite number of zeros and ones to record with; but more importantly, you also get a greater dynamic range with which to work. This means that you could have all of your gear turned up to 10 (or 11 if you are a Spinal Tap fan) and your recording will not distort because it is mathematically impossible to do so.

Step 4: Recording a Track

Now, it's time to record something. What you record is, of course, completely up to you. For the purposes of this tutorial, we're using a couple of drum tracks, bass, guitars, a simple keyboard line, and vocals, as mentioned earlier.

Before you can start really performing, however, there is one more thing you need to do.

Checking Input Levels

Before you record for real, you'll need to check and/or calibrate your input levels. This is a critical step no matter what kind of setup you're using.

If your audio input is too low, it will be lost in the background noise, whereas if it's too high, it will overload the input channel and cause distortion. To check input levels, follow these steps:

1. In the Project window, arm the first track you are going to record on by clicking the Record Enable button. Once clicked, the program is now ready to record a signal, as shown in Figure 14.13.

Figure 14.13
To record an audio signal, you must first arm or "Record Enable" the track

2. Do a test performance, concentrating just on volume with no regard for making the performance perfect. Watch the meter: It should be moving with your test performance (see Figure 14.14). If it isn't, raise the volume of your source sound (the instrument or vocal) and try to get the meter as high as possible without it reaching maximum (the red area).

Figure 14.14
After the track is armed, you can monitor the signal you are going to record

AM I GETTING THROUGH?

If you see absolutely no meter movement of any kind, there is most likely an audio routing problem with the physical audio input itself or possibly an audio routing issue inside of Cubase. To troubleshoot this, you will need to "be the signal" and trace out your steps to see how you are getting your audio into Cubase. If you are using a guitar preamp or a microphone preamp, just connect its output to the input of your audio card. This is the bone-dry simple way of routing audio to your recording system. If you now arm the audio track and you still do not see an audio signal, make sure you have the right audio card selected.

If all else fails, give Steinberg's technical support a call and I'm sure they will sort you out quickly.

Rolling Tape—Er, Disk, That Is

It's time to record for real. For this session, a drum machine will be handling the stereo drum track. Bass will be recorded on one mono track, as will the guitars, keys, and vocals.

Which instrument you lay down first has everything to do with your songwriting style and instrument preferences. We'll pretend that this song is a typical techno tune, so we'll lay down the basic drum beat first, on the Drums track.

1. First, we'll change the Drums track into a stereo track. Make sure you have the Drums track highlighted, and click the Show Inspector button at the top-left of the Project window (see Figure 14.15).

Figure 14.15
Click the Show Inspector button to display the information for the Drums track

2. Change the Drums track from mono to stereo by clicking the Stereo Switch button, which is located under the "R" button (see Figures 14.16a and 14.16b).

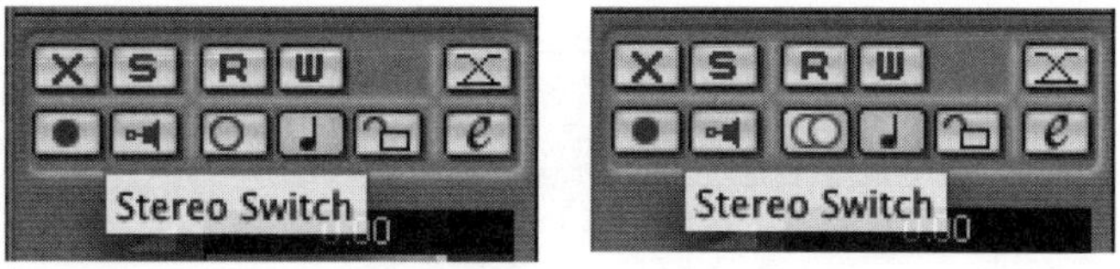

Figure 14.16a and 14.16b
To record a stereo audio track, we need to change the Drums track into a stereo track

3. Arm the track for recording.
4. On the Transport bar, select the Click button. This activates the metronome.
5. Click the Record button on the Transport bar when you are ready to record. The 2 bar count-in will begin immediately.
6. Play something—anything.
7. When you're finished laying down the track, press the space bar or click the Stop button on the toolbar.

Your recorded track will show up in the Cubase Project window (see Figure 14.17).

Figure 14.17
Your first drum track—it's got a beat and you can dance to it

Although you just recorded a stereo track of drums, further down the line you might consider recording each different drum sound onto a different track (kick track, snare track, hi-hat track, and so on). The idea behind this technique is flexibility; by recording multiple mono tracks for an instrument like drums, you will have a greater degree of flexibility when mixdown arrives.

The final step is to lay down the other instruments, in this case one at a time (because you're working along for this tutorial). Obviously, as you record each new track, the tracks you've already recorded will play back and their individual track meters will indicate that they're playing.

When you're done with tracking the other six instruments, you'll have something similar to Figure 14.18 on your screen.

Figure 14.18
Your first 8-track hard disk recording is sure to sound better than your typical porta-studio results

When you're ready to play it back, simply press the space bar or click the Play button on the toolbar. This is a good time to take a close look at the level meters again and make sure you're getting hot signal across all the tracks.

INPUT MONITORING: WHAT GOES IN THERE?

Cubase, and most good-quality recording software for that matter, has an *input monitoring* feature that mimics the live monitoring you can do with an analog board. In other words, you can hear any instrument that is plugged into your sound card whether you're recording it or not.

This includes any plug-in effects as well. You can enable input monitoring in Cubase by clicking on the Monitoring button to the right of the Record Enable button, which looks like a little speaker.

Of course, if you're routing your instruments through an external mixing console, mic, or line mixer, you can monitor everything live in any case; Cubase's input monitoring is pertinent only in cases in which you are running directly from the output of the sound card to one external monitoring bus.

A word of caution: Input monitoring can cause feedback if you are routing the outputs of your sound card back into an external mixer, so use the feature carefully.

Step 5: Using Looping

One of the beauties of digital software is the ability to easily loop tracks in real time. Loop recording, or looping, is a natural for computers, and it lets you start recording and record as many takes as you like, all in a single step.

Cubase loops between "loop start" and "loop end" times, letting you record one take during each loop range. The program creates a new clip for each take, and the clips can be stored either in a single track, or automatically overwrite everything each go-round.

To use looping:

1. Choose the last vocal track and arm the track.
2. Set the loop start and end times in the Transport bar.
3. On the Transport bar, select the loop option. This shades the section that will be looped.
4. Under the Cubase SX or SL menu, select Preferences.
5. In the Preferences window, select the Audio Preferences and set the Cycle Record Mode to "Create Events" (see Figure 14.19).

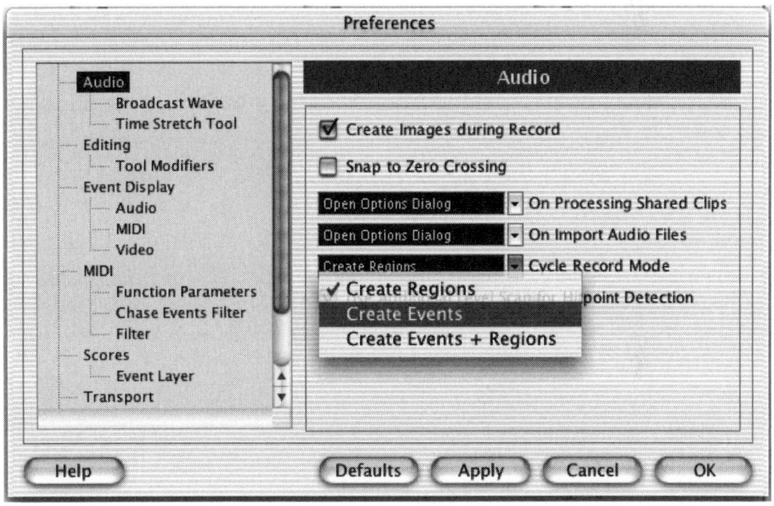

Figure 14.19
You can set up Cubase to record a new take every time the loop recycles

6. Click OK to close the Preferences window and set the cursor back to zero.
7. Click the Record button on the Transport bar and start singing! At the end of each end time in the loop, Cubase will return to the start of the loop and you can record the next take. This waveform will be drawn in real time as it is creating a new take.
8. Press the space bar when you're ready to stop.

Step 6: Punch-In Edits

Punch-in is a technique that is essential to recording—it gives you the flexibility to replace any section in a track without having to rerecord the entire track.

WHY "PUNCH-IN"?

The term "punch-in" comes from the days when recording engineers had to physically punch the Record button, while the tape was rolling.

In this session, pretend that during the fourth measure of the lead vocal you went flat when you were singing—but the rest of the track is more than acceptable. With the song rolling, we are going to punch-in, i.e., go into Record mode, just before the bum note. The trick is to remember to punch-out before you accidentally record over the acceptable part.

By punching-in, you can play the entire vocal performance over, so that you're into the song and melody, then sing over the area you need to correct. It's really very simple: Cubase simply records a new clip over the previous performance between the start and stop times.

To use punch recording, follow these steps:

1. Just like the loop points, set up your start time and end time to perform the punch-in and -out.
2. Select the Punch In and Punch Out tools on the Transport bar, as shown in Figure 14.20.

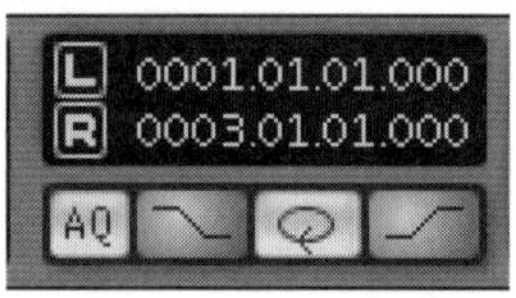

Figure 14.20
Use punch-in to correct mistakes

3. Start recording. Once the cursor reaches the stop time of the punch points, Cubase automatically stops recording.

When punch recording is enabled, the punch times are indicated by the Left and Right locator points. Figure 14.21 shows both the markers and the end result of punching-in between measures 3 and 5 in the Drums track for the session.

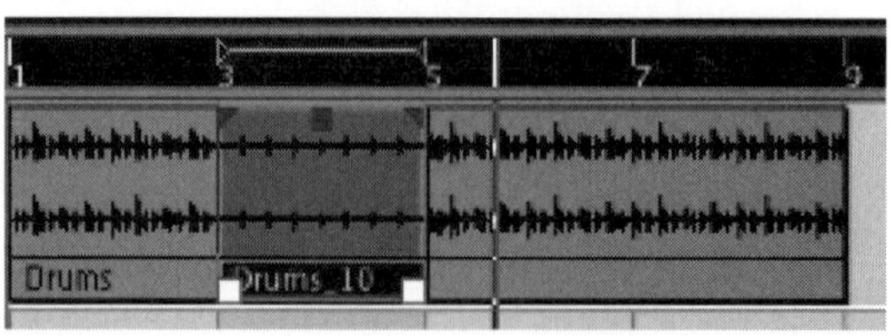

Figure 14.21
The punch-in was a success

EDITING WITH A CROSSFADE

Cubase has the ability to create what is called a crossfade. For example, if you want one guitar track to fade out while another guitar track fades in, Cubase can do this quickly and gives you many different fade options. For this example, we will use two stereo guitar tracks and show how to crossfade them.

1. Click the Snap to Grid button to turn off Snap to Grid. The tool to do this is located in the top-right corner of the Project window, as shown in Figure 14.22. The Snap to Grid settings control slip editing as well as drag-and-drop.

Figure 14.22
Turn off the Snap to Grid function

2. Click and drag one audio clip onto another. This displays a shaded area in between the clips, as shown in Figure 14.23.

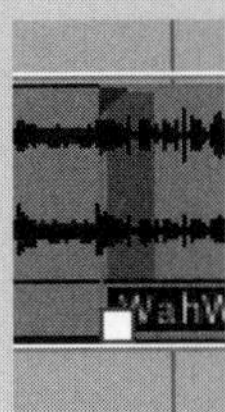

Figure 14.23
After dragging one clip onto another, a shaded area shows that the crossfade is ready to be made

3. From the Audio menu, select the Crossfade option. You can also just press the X key on your computer keyboard.
4. The Crossfade window should now open and you can customize the fade in and fade out to your liking. See Figure 14.24.

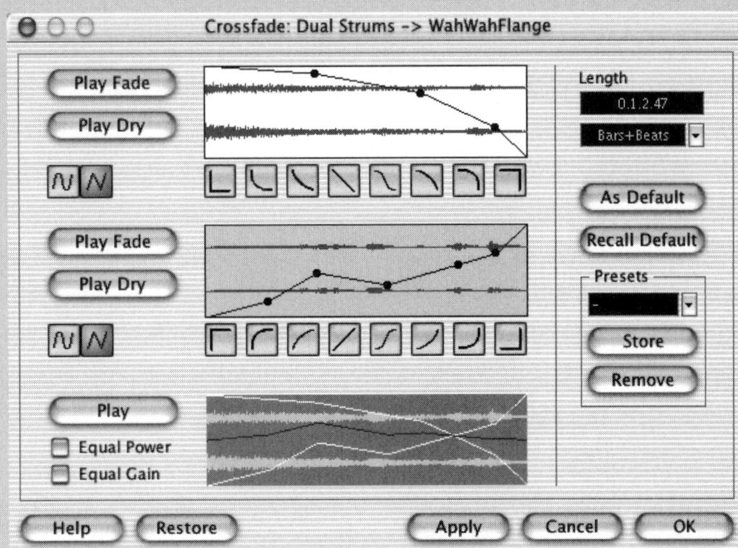

Figure 14.24
The Crossfade window

5. Click the Apply button and you should now see a graphical representation of the crossfade you just created. See Figure 14.25.

Figure 14.25
The crossfade has now been made

6. After the crossfade is created, you can stretch the fade out as far as you want, which sustains the effect, as shown in Figure 14.26.

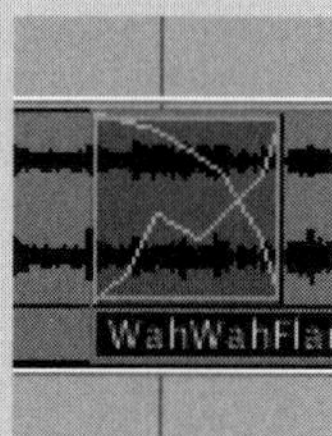

Figure 14.26
After creating the crossfade, you can stretch it out over a larger portion of the clip

Step 7: Mixing Some Effects In

For this session, we'll limit our mixing activities to the basic task of introducing some effects into the mix. First, we'll add some flange to a guitar track, and then add a little reverb to a vocal track.

1. In the Project window, select the guitar track, and then click the Show Inspector button. This displays all of the information for the guitar track.
2. Click the Show Effects Rack and this launches the Virtual FX Rack.
3. Load up the Flanger and the Reverb VST FX. These are included in both versions of Cubase.
4. You're almost there. Now just assign some signal from the guitar to the Flanger and you should hear the swirling bliss of your first VST effect.
5. For the vocal track, repeat Steps 1–4. Note that the Cubase Reverb contains the settings you'd find on any external reverb unit: dry mix, wet mix, decay, and low- and high-pass filter. Experiment with the different settings just as you would with a piece of outboard gear.

When you're finished tinkering with all of the effects, listen closely to the overall mix. A tried-and-true method for auditioning individual effects is to first audition the whole song, then solo each track to check noise level and saturation, and then try different combinations of the effected tracks with other tracks in the mix by selectively muting.

KEEP IT CLEAN

As discussed in Chapter 11, "Fun-Da-Mental Audio," and elsewhere in the book, in general, don't get carried away with effects. For example, using a different reverb on several tracks at once can cause some nasty harmonic modulation. You want *moderation*—not modulation!

Step 8: Mastering to a File

In a very short amount of time, you've recorded eight tracks of audio, crossfaded a couple of tracks together, corrected a mistake or two, and added some basic effects to individual tracks.

Normally, you'd obviously spend more time than this, not only getting the performances the way you want them, but with EQ both during recording and mixing, as well as backup tracks, doubling tracks, quantization for MIDI tracks, and much more.

Now, let's complete this session by mastering the project to an AIFF file.

FORMATS

Cubase also gives you the ability to save to the WAV and Sound Designer II formats.

To export the song as an AIFF file:

1. First, set your Right and Left Locators to the start and end of your song.
2. Choose File > Export > Audio Mixdown to display the Export Audio dialog box, as shown in Figure 14.27.
3. Select a folder to save to, and name your file "SteppingThrough8".
4. Choose AIFF from the Format drop-down list (this should be the default setting if this is your first mixdown).
5. In the Channels field, select Stereo Interleaved.
6. In the Bit Depth field, select the bit depth that you want your exported file to use.
7. In the Include field, select the features you want to include in your export. In our case today, you will want to include the Effects.
8. Click Export.

EXPORTING AUTOMATION

Selecting the Include Automation function will export any automation moves made or recorded in the mixer or the Project window. For more information on this, be sure to check out *Cubase SX Power!* at your local bookstore.

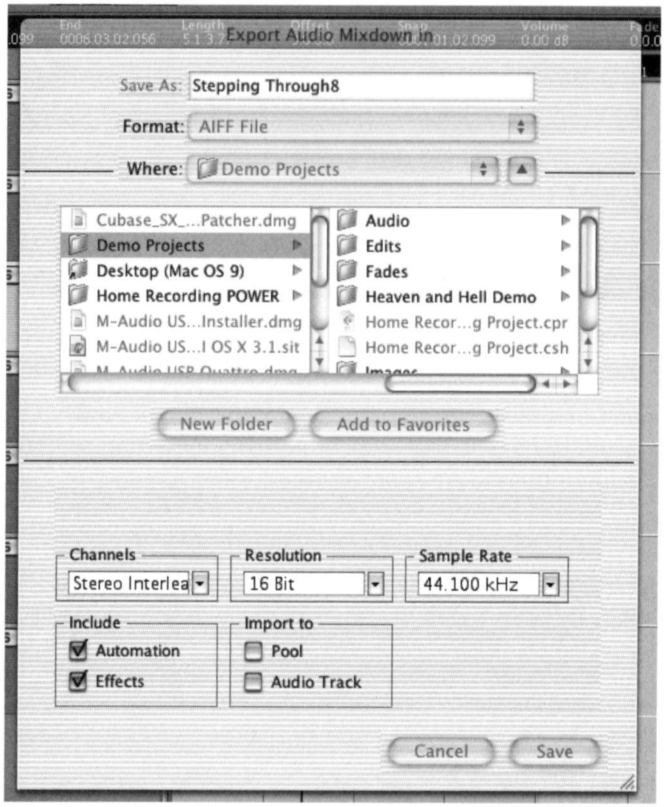

Figure 14.27
Mastering your song to an AIFF file involves a few clicks of the mouse button—not much more

You're done! After a few seconds, Cubase saves the file as an AIFF file on your computer's hard drive. From here, you can prepare the file to be permanently mastered as an audio track onto disk, convert it to yet another file format, open it in QuickTime Player or any other audio player to listen to it, or even import it back into Cubase. Note that if you do import it back into Cubase, it will appear as one stereo track.

GETTING TO MP3

For some reason, Cubase SX/SL does not include an MP3 encoder. But before you reach for the phone to launch a complaint to your local music store, here comes Apple to the rescue!

In Mac OS X, Apple has provided an MP3 program called iTunes. This program can rip audio from music CDs, and can create and play MP3 files in minutes.

So, even though there's a bit of a hoop to jump through to create MP3s, at least there is a cost-free solution.

Maybe we'll be lucky and Steinberg will release an MP3 encoder in a future edition of Cubase.

15

Tracking Tips and Techniques

Sometimes, it takes a lot of mistakes and costs a lot of money (that wasn't there to begin with) to learn how to be good at something. Double that for home recording. It's not hard to get tripped up, move a bit too fast, or head in the wrong direction with a project.

In that spirit, this chapter offers some of those tidbits of information that come only with lots of late nights and black coffee.

Plan the Session

It's not exactly most musicians' penchant to plan. Nor do most musicians consider much more than a set list a useful way to plan anything.

This is wrong. All wrong. It always pays to put some forethought into a project. Whether your aim is to record a slew of songs and get a roster up on MP3.com or cut demo CDs and selectively try to get them in the hands of the recording industry, going to the trouble of planning the recording session will save you time in the long run, and you'll produce better work. By forcing yourself to sit down and list what you hope to accomplish and envisioning what the result will be, you're making yourself focus on the task of finishing the song.

Suppose your goal is to record enough material to release your own homegrown CD, but the catch is that you need a little help in the rhythm section. There are several preproduction tasks that make sense:

- Record a demo first, rather than going right into the first "real" session, to familiarize the other musicians with the material. Unless your gig is avant-garde or free jazz, you don't want to waste sessions teaching everybody else the song.

- The flavor of the demo should be about the song, not the sound. Don't try to get a great sound or spend time mixing tracks; the demo should be a general sketch of each arrangement and rhythm.
- Think about how you will record the first session. If each instrument needs its own track, you need to configure your mixing console or software beforehand. You may need to double up on some tracks due to limited equipment, for example, so plan for it; don't figure you'll fix it in the mix. In fact, never count on fixing *anything* in the mix. Writing down a pre-track list that spells out each instrument and where it goes in the song will really keep you focused.
- Zeroing out all of the knobs and faders on your equipment is also good practice to give you a fresh session each time and avoid mistakenly using settings from the last session. Do the same for your software: For example, you can set up a basic template in Cubase by saving the track and instrument configurations you use most often to a template.
- Keep any first session with other musicians open and relaxed, by having something to drink on hand, for instance. Have a schedule. Plan a specific block of time—that's what the pros do—and stick to that timeframe. If someone is going off in a direction you don't like, say simply, "I like what you're doing, but we really need to keep to the original arrangement" and move on. If your fellow musician has a problem with that, he has no business being within a mile of your music.

Quick Basic EQ Settings

Although EQ can, in many cases, be a highly subjective aspect of recording, it helps to have a quick and dirty, basic configuration to start with and, most importantly, to learn from.

> **FOR MORE ON MIXING**
> Chapter 13,"Recording and Mixing," has all the gory details for getting the most out of your mixes.

Table 15.1 represents some fundamental EQ settings for a typical instrument setup: drums, guitar, bass, and vocals. This is not by any means the only way to EQ—in fact, your mileage will vary greatly, especially with the guitars and vocals.

These recommendations give you a place to start, however, by giving you a feel for which instruments typically respond to which frequency ranges the most. The emphasis is on a warmer, more balanced mix.

Table 15.1
Example basic EQ settings

Instrument	Value	Frequency Range
Drums	+6 dB –8 dB +10 dB	High Midrange Low
Bass Guitar	+2 dB +4 dB at 250 Hz	Low Midrange
Rhythm Guitar	+6 dB at 2.5 kHz +1.5 dB	Midrange Low
Lead Guitar	+3 dB +6 dB	High Midrange
Lead Vocal	+3 dB at 3–4 kHz +3 dB	High Midrange
Backing Vocals	+2 dB –6 dB at 2.5 kHz +0.5 dB	High Midrange Low

Cut, Copy, and Paste

One of the most effective and time-honored ways (it's been happening almost since a multitrack studio was in existence) to save time and get the best recording possible is to reuse material whenever and wherever you can.

For example, in Cubase (and any other digital recording software worth its salt), you accomplish this by moving or copying clips to new tracks or existing tracks by cutting or copying and then pasting—just like moving text around in a word processor. There are a couple of different ways to do it.

The first way is great for pinpoint accuracy: Use the Snap functions (see Figures 15.1, 15.2, and 15.3) in Cubase and a couple of easy keyboard commands.

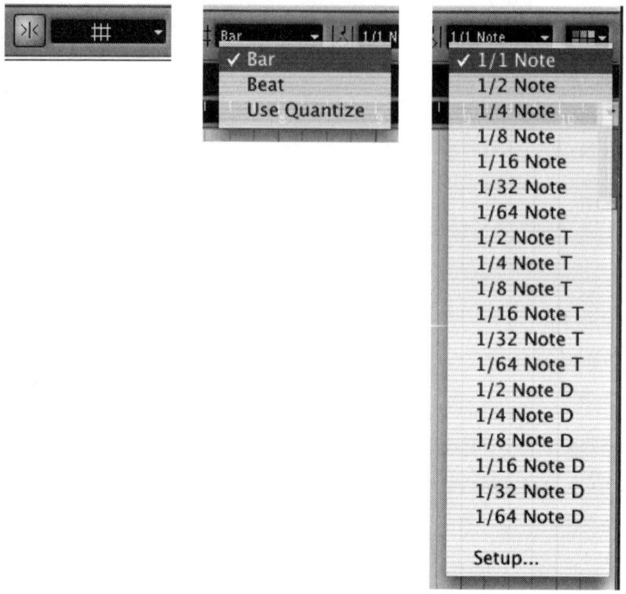

Figure 15.1, Figure 15.2, and Figure 15.3
The Snap function allows you to move clips by large subdivisions (whole measures) or smaller subdivisions (32nd notes)

After setting your snap values, let's start by looking at a MIDI clip we're going to copy and paste (see Figure 15.4).

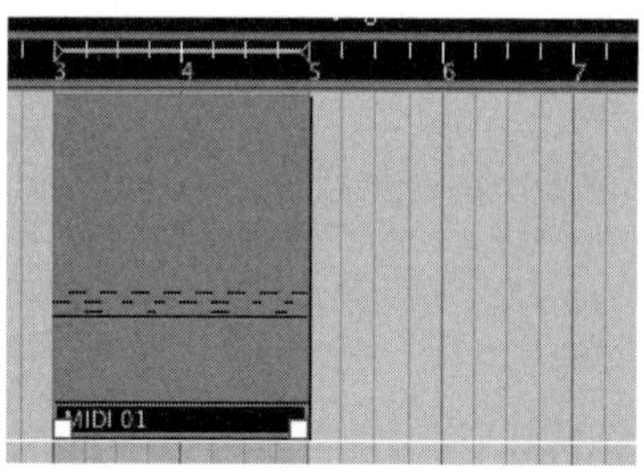

Figure 15.4
Here's the MIDI clip we're going to copy and paste

Next, hold down the Option key (located between the Apple key and Control key) with your left hand. Then use your right hand to click and drag the clip one measure to the right (see Figure 15.5). While you are dragging it, you should see the new clip with a "+" next to it, signifying that you are making a copy of the selected clip.

Figure 15.5
Making a copy in Cubase is quick and easy

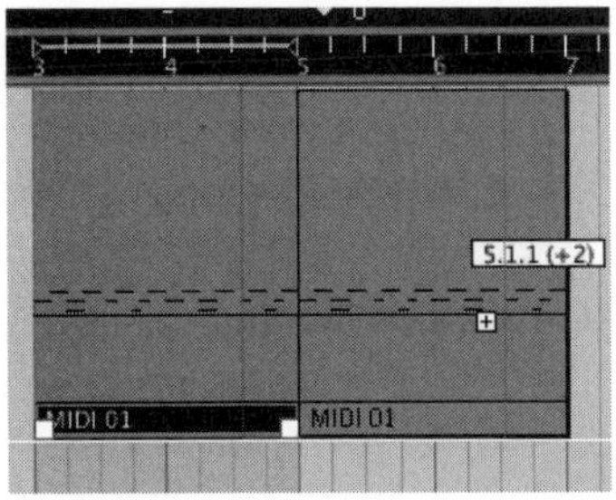

When you've finished dragging the clip to the right, release the mouse and you should now see the copied clip one measure to the right of the original (see Figure 15.6).

Figure 15.6
Now you are the King of Copies

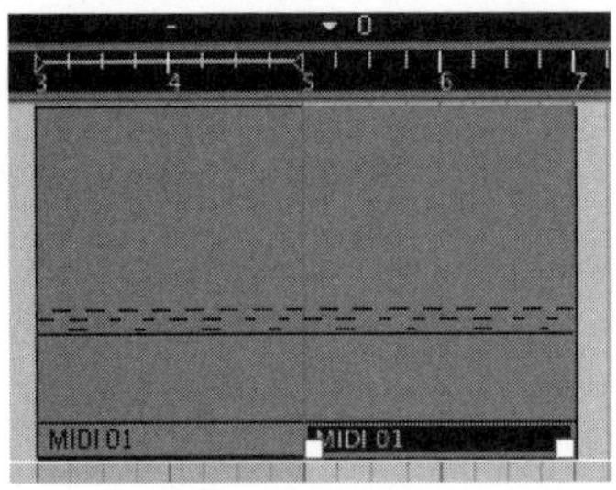

What makes this method of copying so great is that you can quickly and easily create a single copy for just one clip, or even a group of clips at one time by selecting everything at once. But, what if you need to make multiple copies of this clip? Clicking and dragging is all fine and good, but it can become tedious and time-consuming.

There is a very cool solution that is just a keyboard shortcut away. Let's start with the same clip from our previous example and select it by just clicking on it once with your mouse. Then select "Repeat" from the Edit menu, or hold down your Apple key and "K" to launch the same window (see Figure 15.7).

Figure 15.7
Cubase's Repeat function

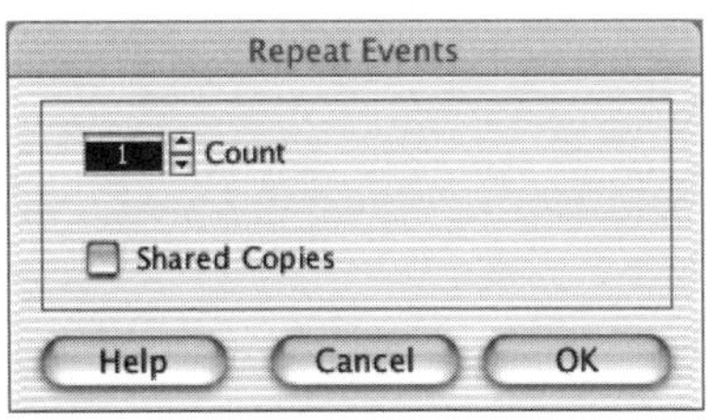

At this point, you will need to type in the number of repeats you want for this clip. For this example, let's just stick with one copy. Click OK and now you should see the original clip plus a duplicate right after it.

SHARED COPIES

Below the Count field, where you specify the number of copies, is an option called "Shared Copies." If selected, the new MIDI clips that are created are thought of as "Ghost Copies." This means that they are still linked to the original MIDI clip. Furthermore, if you make any changes to the copies, the original MIDI clip is also affected. If this is a function you had in mind, turn on the Shared Copies. Otherwise, you will want to keep it turned off.

Note: When you make a copy of an audio clip in Cubase with either of the methods posted here, the new audio clips are always shared copies by default. This is to help save hard drive space on your computer. The good news is that you can convert these repeated copies into their own separate clips by selecting "Convert to Real Copy" from the Edit menu.

Cutting clips in Cubase is also a snap. Just select the Scissors tool from the toolbar at the top of the Project window. Then select your clip and click the mouse button anywhere along the clip to make a cut (see Figures 15.8 and 15.9). Just be aware that the Snap tool is linked to this function just as the copy function was; that is, if your Snap is set to a whole measure, then the cuts that you make are measured in whole measures. This is easily changed by just selecting a smaller division in the Snap menu.

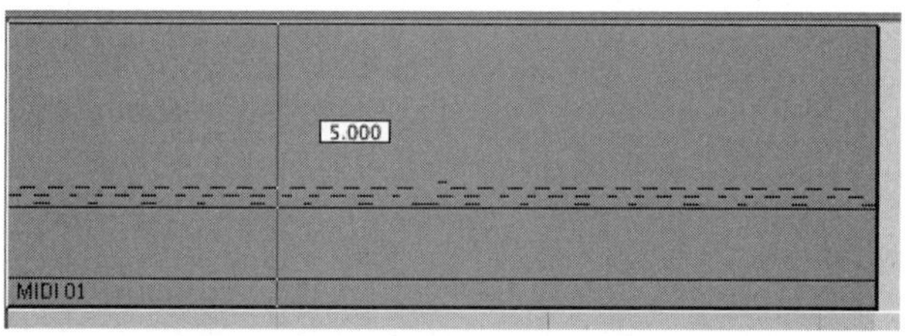

Figure 15.8
Here's our clip before the cut...

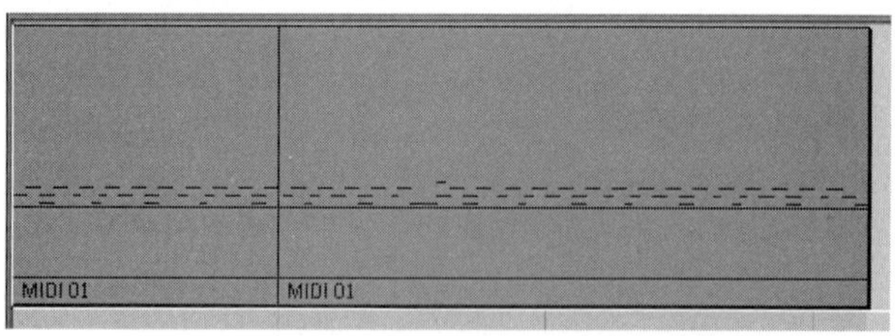

Figure 15.9
...and after the cut

As you can see, in Cubase, the process of reusing your music in different locations throughout your song is particularly easy. Not too many years ago, it was a bit more difficult with analog equipment (that's an understatement), but the result was still the same. It's a huge time-saver!

Using a Patchbay

A patchbay is a very effective way to cut down on frustration as well as time when connecting all of your studio equipment. A patchbay is a rack-mountable piece of gear with front and back cable jacks, which help you easily direct the signals to and from each piece of gear in your setup. It's the best way to keep your cables organized.

Most patchbays align rows of sixteen to twenty-four jacks in two columns, so that you can permanently plug in all the inputs and outputs of your gear, rather than having to repatch cables each time a session requires a change of instrument or track on the mixer.

There is no hard-and-fast rule as to how you set up a patchbay. The traditional way uses the top row for outputs and the bottom for inputs, but you *can* roll your own. However, there are three types of jacks that a patchbay uses, and you should be aware of their differences before you go hooking things up:

- **Denormaled jacks**. Simply send input from the top and bottom back jacks directly to the front jacks.
- **Normaled jacks**. Route a top jack in the back of the patchbay to a bottom jack in the back when the front jacks aren't being used. These are for times when you don't need the front jacks—with aux returns from your mixer, for example.
- **Half-normaled jacks**. Essentially allow you to have two copies of the signal from a given output jack, which is very useful for processing two different EQ configurations at the same time.

There are a lot of patchbay models you can buy, and you can even buy plans to build your own or build one from scratch. Switchcraft, Tascam, and Fostex all make affordable and good-quality models, usually in the $200–400 price range. Patchbay cables are also cheap and plentiful.

Master Your Destiny

In the professional recording world, mastering is actually a wholly separate art and science unto itself. Mastering engineers have a different type of process—and even different (usually very expensive) types of equipment, for example, compressors that can control the highs and lows independently and EQ that can affect both right and left channels independently as well as relative to the audio signal. You can really hear a difference when you listen to a well-mastered CD by someone who has a long list of credits, a great set of ears, and is always up-to-date with the best equipment and technology.

In the home studio, you can still master, even if your equipment is more limited, especially when you consider the availability of great mastering software for your Mac (Bias Peak, for example). You should go through a mastering process: Fix glitches, clean up fades, order your songs correctly, and set the timing between tracks on CDs if you're cutting a CD.

This is also the time to pay attention to the dynamics of the song(s) you're mastering. Normalizing, for example, should be done at this stage. By the same token, noise reduction is just as important, and you ideally shouldn't normalize more than once or twice to keep noise at a minimum.

Mastering is your final stab at making the compositions as clear and full of impact as possible. It's the polish. How much time should you spend on it? Depending on what you have to work with (the quality, dynamics, and clarity of the mix), you should plan at least an evening to two evenings just for mastering. You should also get as many people as you can to listen to your mixes closely to see if there is something missing in the mix before you master. Take notes: If you get many of the same comments, it's probably something you should fix or an area of the song that needs attention. If you get a lot of varied input, however, you can pretty safely ignore all of it.

In general, keep these goals in mind when mastering:

- Don't master right after the "final" take. Give your ears at least a 24-hour break before a mastering session. It's kind of like eating a rich dessert on a full stomach: You have no idea how the dessert really tastes, and there's a good chance you'll get sick!
- Stay away from limiters, and, in general, don't compress an entire mix.
- If you do use compression, think "well-balanced" performance. Use only as much compression as you absolutely need to make tweaks to the sound.
- In general, keep the vocals, bass, and kick near the center of the mix, and pay close attention to how the high frequencies sit next to each other in the stereo field—guitars and cymbals, for example.
- Don't use aural exciters: Their harmonic additive and enhancing abilities are great for putting new life into a recording, but not as a piece of mastering equipment.
- Get as hot as you can with the mastered signal. For a digital setup, signals tend to clip badly past 0 dB.

THE BUDDY SYSTEM

If you aren't the only home studio aficionado on the block and you trust a friend or someone else who is, get together to exchange producing and mastering tips and tricks. A fresh pair of ears is probably the single most important advantage the big studios have over you when it comes to mastering. Many musicians/producers rely on a few friends to listen to new material and provide straightforward feedback. A good friend can be very blunt and honest with you, which is essential to helping anyone grow as an artist.

Track Sheets

After you've got a final mix and a master, then cut it to CD or DAT (hopefully, using the techniques in Chapter 18, "Promoting and Marketing Your Music")—you're finished, right? The answer is "just about."

If you ever have a problem with a master or need to fix mistakes, you may find it difficult to re-create all the settings you used without a "record" of your mix—a track sheet. Even with recording software like Cubase, it's really a good idea to have a track sheet in Microsoft Word or another word processing program. It's ultimately up to you, but if you don't want to find yourself in a frustrating situation down the road, spend a few minutes documenting the recording.

> **NOTEPAD**
> Steinberg has already thought ahead by providing a simple word processing program called Notepad. Although it is not as sexy as Microsoft Word, it comes through in a pinch. Just select Notepad from the Project menu and you're stylin'.

So what should you write on your track sheets? At a minimum, you should always document the following information:

- Performer(s)
- Song title
- Master title
- Positions
- Fader values
- EQ settings
- Pan, effects, and send/return settings

It's particularly easy to get used to not using track sheets with digital recording software; your mix and the audio are always automatically stored for you. Doesn't matter: Take the extra precaution of double-documenting. Fifteen extra minutes now could mean saving a few days sometime in the future.

> **BACK IT UP**
> If it hasn't been said enough in this book, make a backup of your work. If you are in the middle of a serious audio and MIDI production, you should back up your work every night. Blank CDs are cheap, and that half hour you spend backing up could save you from losing the entire project!

16

Pack It and Ship It

It wasn't too long ago that CD recorders were expensive toys for software creators. Not any more: These days, CD-R and CD-RW drives alike are capable of creating CD audio disks and CD-ROMs at consumer prices. This chapter guides you through selecting and using a CD recording drive and provides you with some tips and tricks for creating and packaging your CDs. This chapter focuses on:

- Burning your music to a CD
- Mixing your audio tracks with other data
- Creating sleeves, liner notes, and graphics

Putting Your Music on CD

Creating your own audio CDs has become quite popular now that the hardware is affordable. In fact, more and more consumers are using them because they're cheap and easy to install. Instead of having to continually insert CDs just to play particular songs, users are buying economical CD-R drives and a few software tools, and, voila: They've got a higher-tech version of a compilation tape!

Of course, you can do the same thing—but as a recording artist, you can also put a CD recording drive to real use. Even if your primary goal is to distribute your music via the Internet, a CD "burner" can save you time and money by enabling you to archive your performances and recordings instead of buying more expensive and less reliable hard drives.

The Technology is Better and Faster

Not long ago, burning a CD was a frustrating exercise in patience. Buffer-underrun problems, slow recording speeds, and inferior software turned a lot of well-intentioned CD mastering projects into coasters.

BUFFER UNDERRUN

A buffer underrun used to be an all-too-common problem. A buffer underrun is what occurs when the data stream from the computer to the CD recording drive is interrupted. Though it can still happen, these days it's less likely, thanks to bigger buffers to hold incoming data, faster computers, and better-designed software to manage high-speed CD recording drives.

There are dozens of CD drive models on the market, produced by companies such as Sony, Philips, and Toshiba. At the time of this writing, prices for these drives range anywhere from $150 to $300, and most of them include basic software to get you up and running. Two types of drives exist—CD-R and CD-RW.

IT'S INCLUDED

Most off-the-shelf Macintosh systems already have a CD-RW drive included in the package. Only the cheapest basic model Macs come with a standard CD-ROM drive. This is where you can begin to see why you should consider spending a little more on your purchase of a new Mac.

THE CUTTING EDGE: DVD

Actually, there is a third type of drive in the consumer market: DVD-R. DVD (digital versatile disc) recordable technology does the same thing with DVDs that CD recording technology does with CDs. DVD-R is a write-once medium that can hold any type of information normally stored on DVD discs, such as video, audio, images, data files, and multimedia programs. Depending on the type of information you record, DVD-R discs are usable on virtually any compatible DVD playback device, including most DVD-ROM drives and DVD video players.

Top-of-the-line new Macintosh systems generally include a DVD-R drive. Although these drives are a little more expensive than the now traditional CD-RW drives, Apple DVD-R drives have the ability to record onto both blank DVDs and CDs, making it a perfect solution for musicians. As blank CDs only hold a maximum of 800 MB of data per disc, this pales in comparison to the storage space of a blank DVD that holds up to 4.7 GB! So, not only can you burn CDs that you can pop in your stereo system, but you can also effectively back up the data files for your songs onto DVD.

Finally, DVD-audio—which has been up in the air for a number of years—has emerged, with a first run of DVD-audio releases and rereleases of those artists and albums that we hold near and dear. The format holds a lot of promise, and artists such as Neil Young are reportedly getting behind the format because of its larger bit rates and higher sampling rates (which is ironic considering how much he bad-mouthed digital recording in past years). DVD-audio also supports full multichannel (2, 4, 5.1, or 7.1 channels) at a full PCM bit rate (rather than the compressed Dolby Digital). DVD-audio discs support a highly flexible format structure, including bit rates that range from 16 to 24 bits and sampling rates of

44.1, 48, 88.2, 96, 176.4, and even 192 kHz! Hello! This means you could choose, for example, 2-channel stereo, 24-bit audio at 192 kHz for the highest fidelity—or go with 6-channel, surround sound, 24-bit audio at 96 kHz for multichannel surround (such as 5.1). You can even mix and match three front channels at 24-bit, 96 kHz and surround channels at 20-bit, 48 kHz, as well as store video clips, graphics, lyrics, bios, games, and other data.

Although DVD-audio has not quite taken off yet, there are a few noteworthy releases that demand our attention. Most importantly, the DVD-audio rerelease of Queen's "A Night at the Opera" is a pure testament to the rebirth of a classic album. "Bohemian Rhapsody" mixed in surround is something not to be missed and you'll be sure to hear new elements and textures of that song that you never heard before, even if you saw *Wayne's World* a couple thousand times. Look for great things to come with the DVD-audio format.

CD-R

"CD-R" stands for compact disk-recordable. It is a type of disk drive that can create CD-ROMs and audio CDs once and once only—meaning that you can't reuse the disk once you've written data to it.

Although CD-R drives were very popular in the mid to late '90s, you'll find it virtually impossible to locate a new CD-R drive, as they are based on older technology. You'll get more for your mileage with a CD-rewritable (CD-RW).

CD-RW

CD-RW drives are dual function, offering both CD-R and CD-RW recording, so you can choose which method works best according to what you want to record. CD-RW differs from CD-R in that it uses a different type of disk that can be reused, or rewritten.

CD-RW disks are not writable by CD-R drives; although most new CD-ROM drives do support CD-RW, not all of them read CD-RW disks at full speed. The important thing to know is that, although many new audio CD players can handle CD-RW discs, most older ones cannot. If you want to create audio CDs using CD-RW disks, you're taking chances with it working successfully.

The best bet is to use CD-R disks with a CD-RW drive. That way you're assured of compatibility with most CD players, but you still have the advantage of being able to use CD-RW disks for storage, archiving, and testing.

The best drives are capable of writing CD-RW/CD-R media at 24×/52× (respectively) and they read at 52× or even higher. It's typical to find a CD-RW at about 24×/48×/48× these days for less than $100!

CD Recording Software

Nearly all CD-RW drives sold today are bundled with some kind of CD recording software. Some of the bundled software works fine for burning audio CDs, whereas some of it may not work consistently or very well. We'll use Toast from Roxio in this chapter to walk you through the process of burning an audio CD, because it comes with many of the drives on the market and has proven to be reliable and easy to use.

If you don't have Toast, it can be purchased through your local software or on the Web from **www.roxio.com/**. At the time of this writing, it can be bought for around $89—a reasonable price considering its quality and many features.

> **OS X CAN BURN!**
> One of the lesser-known features of Mac OS X is that it has the ability to burn CDs on its own. Although it doesn't offer the bells and whistles of Toast, such as mixed mode CDs, video CDs, and disc images you can store on your hard drive, if you're on the strictest of budgets, it will do the trick.

> **HARD DRIVE ELBOW ROOM**
> The files you create as you go through the process of burning CDs are very big and take up a lot of space on your hard drive. Before you get started, make sure you have at least 600 MB free on your hard drive.

Installing Toast is simple and fast, as the Roxio installer places the Toast folder in your Applications folder.

After you've installed Toast, you can launch the program by double-clicking the Toast icon in the system tray. At this point, you are asked for your Name, Company, and CD Key code, which can be found on the cover of the Toast CD.

Figure 16.1 shows the startup screen you'll see when the program launches. You're presented with four options: Data, Audio, Copy, and Other.

- **Data CD**. The option for creating CD-ROMs. CD-ROMs are useful for backing up your important files or archiving source music tracks. A CD-ROM is used for data storage only and cannot be played on a CD player.
- **Audio**. An option that points to two different programs—the standard CD audio recording application and Spin Doctor, a program that records audio CDs but also gives you options for recording files to your hard drive as well as the ability to remove clicks, pops, and hisses from the audio source.
- **Copy**. The quick and dirty method for making backup copies of any type of CD supported by your CD recording drive.
- **Other**. A series of other burning options, including MP3 CDs, Video CDs, DVD, and a slew of other Macintosh proprietary formats.

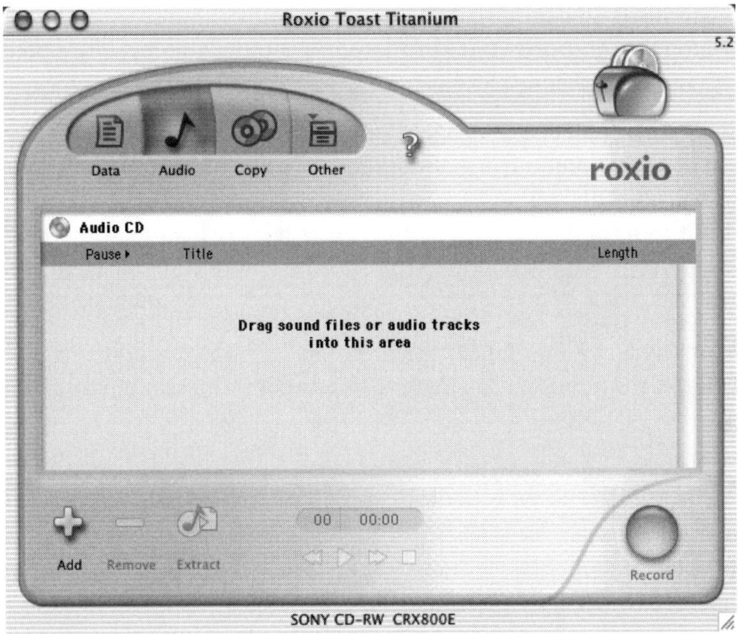

Figure 16.1
Roxio Toast has a simple yet complete graphical interface

The Audio option is the one you want to select. When you click on it, the menu prompts you to place audio files in the workspace so it can burn a CD (see Figure 16.2). If you have any AIFF or WAV files on your hard drive, drag and drop a couple into the workspace.

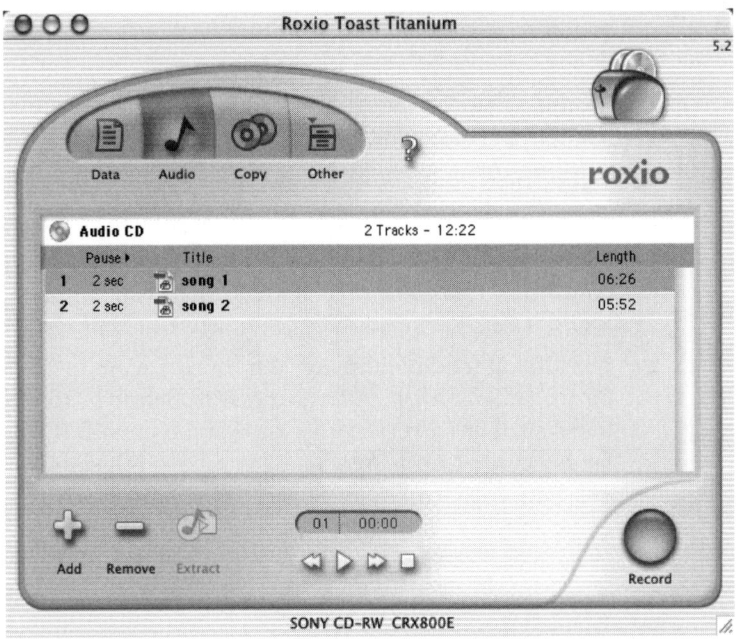

Figure 16.2
You can burn audio CDs in Toast by just dragging and dropping your files into the workspace

After you drop files into the workspace, a couple of new features are ready for you to use—the pause time and the most important button in Toast, the Record button.

Toast has the ability to change the pause time between tracks, which is a fairly new feature to the program. Toast used to place a default, two-second pause time between tracks in earlier versions, so this addition to the program is a welcome one and easy to grasp. You can assign a pause time between zero and eight seconds on each track. That way, if you want to have the CD start immediately as it is inserted into your player, you can set the pause time of track one to zero seconds; whereas if you want the next song to have a five-second pause before it plays, set its pause time to five.

After you have your audio CD tracks listed in the right order, just pop in a blank CD and click the Record button. The Record window then pops up and lists a few different burning options (see Figure 16.3).

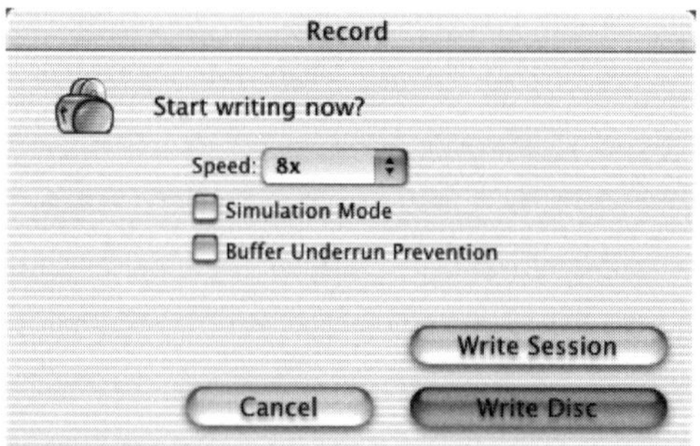

Figure 16.3
Just a couple of options to choose before you burn your first audio CD

- **Writing speed**. Allows you to select the speed of your burner. As you can see, the maximum burn speed on this Macintosh iBook is "eight speed," meaning that it will be burned at eight times the standard burn time. An example of this is an audio CD that is sixty minutes long. If you burn the CD at the slowest burn speed, it will take sixty minutes to burn the disc before it is ready. If you burn that same length CD at "two speed," it will take thirty minutes. That said, if the same length CD is burned at eight speed, your audio CD will be ready in seven and a half minutes. In other words, pretty damn fast! The speed you select is up to you, but if you are using a newer Mac, it's safe to say that you can burn the CD as fast as you want.
- **Simulation mode**. Simulates a burn of the audio CD before it actually burns a disc. This is to ensure that if there are any problems with the burn, such as corrupted files or a problem with the burner itself, they can be detected prior to burning. If you have extremely vital information and you have the time, it is suggested that you select to burn in this mode. Otherwise, just leave it blank.

- **Buffer underrun prevention**. Refers to the same discussed earlier in this chapter. To review, a buffer underrun happens when the data stream from the Mac to the burner is interrupted. Although it's become less of a problem these days, Roxio includes this option to prevent it from happening. It does not slow the burning process down, so go ahead and check it if you cherish your data.
- **Write session**. Allows you to use the blank CD more than once if you are just burning information. This is a fantastic solution for doing a daily back up of smaller files of different formats.
- **Write disc**. Is another name for a function referred to as "Disc at Once," in which the disc being used can only be used once after the initial burn. If you select this mode and burn the CD, that's all folks!

After you have selected your burning options, just click on either Write Session or Write Disc, and on you go to burn your first audio CD. Crack open the champagne and let the royalty checks begin!

Toast's Other Formats

Let's have a quick look at some of the different formats you can burn with Toast:

- Data CDs
- Other formats

Data Discs

Besides the burning of Mac data CDs, Toast has a number of different types of data templates that will certainly become more and more useful to you over time as you learn to use them.

- **Mac OS CD**. Is the basic setting, which allows the CD that is burned to be used on any Macintosh computer with a CD-ROM drive.
- **Mac OS and PC Hybrid**. Burns a CD that is readable in either a Macintosh or a Windows-based PC. Although this doesn't sound all that exciting, it was a real pain to do this back when Toast was at version 3 (about four years ago).
- **Mac OS Extended CD**. Refers to a newer Mac information format called "HFS+," which is a filing system found in Mac OS 8.1 or later. If you plan on using any of these burned CDs in an older Mac, it is recommended that you do not use this template.
- **Mac OS Extended and PC Hybrid**. Is the same as the previous hybrid template, except that the Mac information is written using the HFS+ format. Once again, if it is not necessary for you to use it, you don't have to.

Other Formats

Let's take a quick look at some of the other types of discs that Toast is capable of burning.

- **Video**. Is another format that has been popular for some time and is supported by Toast. A video CD works much like a DVD, except the quality of the video is nowhere near the quality of a video on a DVD. Video CDs can hold about seventy minutes of video data and Toast can prepare them in a way that allows you to access the different video files much like a DVD or VHS player. A new feature allows you to burn movies created in iMovie as a Video CD.
- **MP3**. Can be played on any computer or compact disc player that reads MP3-formatted CDs.
- **DVD**. If you are one of those lucky duckies that shelled out the extra money for the DVD-R/RW drive in your new Macintosh, Toast can be used to burn data to blank DVDs. Additionally, Toast can prepare DVD video for DLT, which is the platform that duplication houses use to mass-produce mastered DVDs.
- **Disc image**. Makes an exact disc image of any CD placed in your tray. Although it sounds similar to the Disc Copy function mentioned earlier, Toast does not burn a new CD after creating a disc image. Rather, it is stored on your computer desktop as a virtual copy of the CD.
- **Enhanced music**. Is a very popular format whereby an audio CD can be given additional multimedia features. This can include virtual menus, additional audio and video material, lyric sheets, or links to websites. Adding this feature to your final project is certainly something that can help set you apart from all of the other bedroom musicians out there.

Spin Doctor

Spin Doctor is an additional program that is included with the latest version of Toast (see Figure 16.4). It has two primary functions:

- Record audio material such as old records and tapes in order to burn them to CD. Spin Doctor opens up AIFF files as well.
- Clean up and enhance recorded material by removing noise and hiss and increasing clarity and dynamic range with included effects.

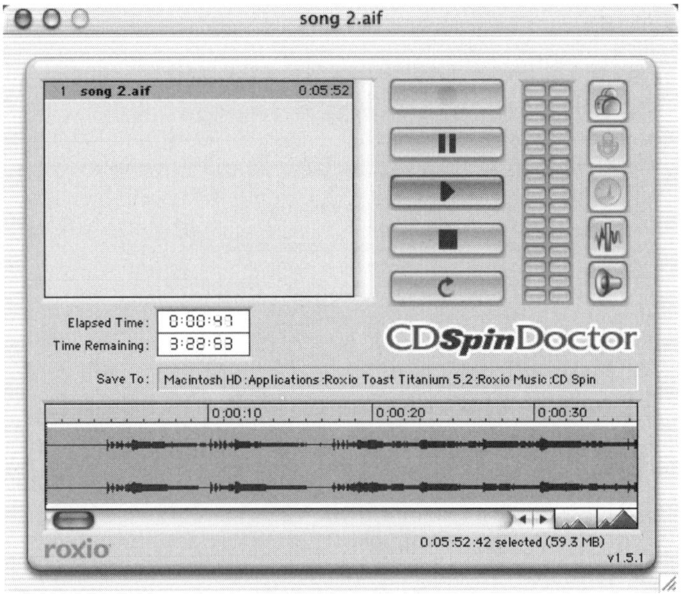

Figure 16.4
Cleaning up old records and tapes is just what the Spin Doctor ordered

Starting off with Spin Doctor is easy and just takes a few minutes to master. Let's have a quick look at how to record and clean up an old audio file.

1. First, let's assume that you have an old record player or tape deck. You need to route your signal into your Mac through an amplifier. You can use an old AM/FM receiver to achieve this, or you could spend twenty bucks at Radio Shack and pick up a phono preamp. Inside the Toast Titanium box, you'll find an audio cable to help route the signal to your internal audio card on your Mac.
2. Play some of your record or tape to verify that you are getting signal into Spin Doctor. If you are not seeing any signal, select the appropriate input source from the Inputs menu.
3. Click on the Record button and start playing your source music.
4. When you are finished recording, click the Stop button and Spin Doctor asks you to name the file. Once named, the file is placed in the Spin Doctor program folder.
5. When the recording is finished, it appears in the Project window. You can now highlight the audio file by clicking on it. Select the Filters button, on the far right of the interface, to bring up the Filters dialog box (see Figure 16.5).

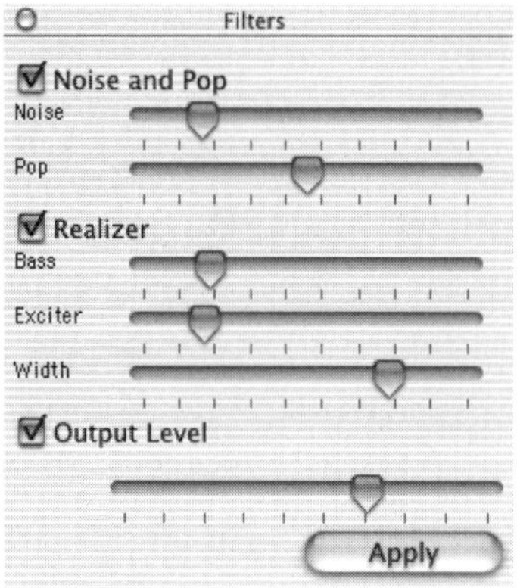

Figure 16.5
Spin Doctor has filters to take away pops and clicks

6. After you have made your adjustments, click the Apply button and Spin Doctor creates a new file. It's important to note that once you have applied the process to your audio, it is a permanent alteration of the file. Simply put, you can't go back.
7. After the new file has been created, you can send the file to Toast to be burned by clicking on the Toast icon in the graphical interface.

Sleeves, Liner Notes, and Graphics

Creating a package design for your audio CD can be straightforward with the right software—or quite difficult if you intend to produce sparkling, professional-looking materials.

This section focuses on DIY—doing it yourself—because it's the most cost-effective route for a starving artist. Unless you have no visual sense whatsoever, doing your own design and printing will give you acceptable results.

The biggest expense to doing it yourself is a good-quality color printer—typically an inkjet device—which can range in price from $50 to $500. At the time of this writing, the price for a color inkjet with a reasonable dpi (dots per inch) rating of at least 1200 × 1200 averages less than $100.

Aside from that, you'll need to purchase the paper supplies (labels and glossy insert stock), as well as the CD-R media itself. The paper supplies *can* get expensive, but generally speaking, they are a minor expense, available from most office-supply stores.

If you truly don't have any visual sense to speak of, you may want to consider hiring a graphic artist to do the design work for you. If you go this route, you will still need to communicate your own sense of design and expectations about the art that will accompany your music. Here are some tips:

- If you have any kind of design concept in mind, try to sketch it out, regardless of how bad you might think it looks. Even a page of doodles will help.
- Browse your own music collection, select covers that you like the most, and take note of the things you like about them, such as the type of design and use of color and text.
- Browse through recent releases in your music genre at the music store. Write down what you think works and what doesn't.
- Talk to other musicians and see if they have used a graphic artist they will recommend. Of course, before you use their recommendation, take a look at their CDs and see if you like the design!

Discus RE

Discus RE (Really Easy) is a great program for quickly creating your CD's sleeve and label. It's a matter of changing text, dropping in a graphics file, and moving everything around to position it the way you want. You can also use forty-two prebuilt themes—graphics and layouts—and simply fill in the blanks. Discus also has these templates made for different sizes of blank CDs, including mini CDs and business card CDs.

But the program does have some drawbacks. For example, though you can define a front cover and an inside cover, any graphics you insert for either one automatically gets used for both, meaning you cannot choose a different image for the front cover and another image for the inside cover. You'll also notice that any images you add are resized and their color depth is set to a limit of 256 colors.

However, keep in mind that this is a light version of the full-blown Discus program, which can be purchased and downloaded through a built-in link within the program.

Included CD Templates

For more features and better functionality, Roxio also supplies premade templates for more professional applications, such as Appleworks (comes included with OS X), Macromedia Freehand, and QuarkXPress (the standard in desktop publishing). If you have any of these programs already, then you are already playing with the big boys rather than the beginners.

Because you already have Appleworks installed on your Mac, have a look at the template provided by Roxio (see Figure 16.6). Notice that Appleworks gives you a lot of additional editing options that you wouldn't find in most other free applications that come with a computer. Once again, this is yet another reason to love Apple.

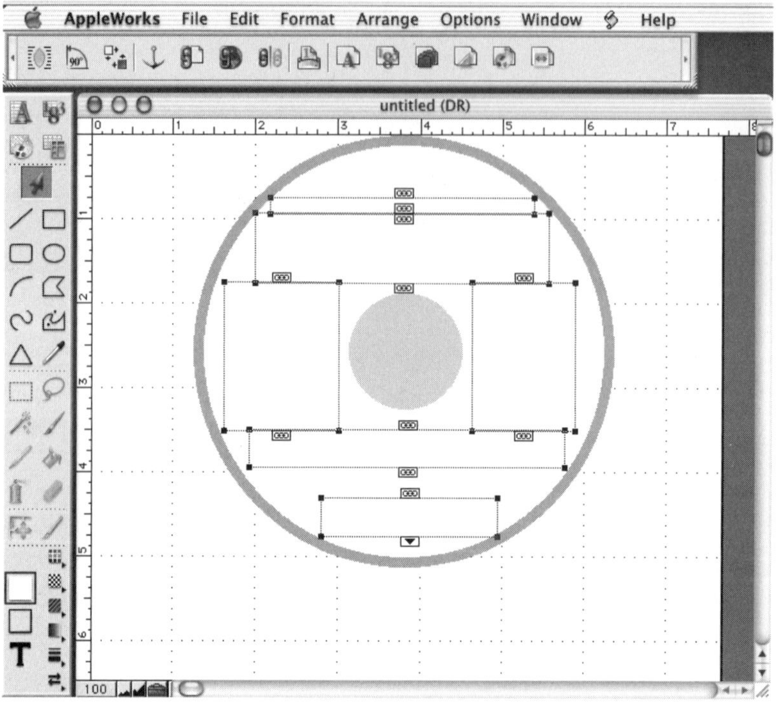

Figure 16.6
The supplied CD template for Appleworks gives you an excellent way of customizing a CD cover

> **PHOTOSHOP**
> A graphics program such as Photoshop is the ultimate choice for complete control over your own designs. However, getting the correct sizes for the jewel case insert and CD label will be difficult (for example, a standard-size jewel case is 5½ × 4⅞ inches) and time-consuming with these professional-level image-authoring applications.

Doing a Big Burn

If you're burning even a dozen CDs a day, a CD recording drive will handle the load with relative ease. But if you find yourself in the enviable position of needing to produce CDs in higher quantities (like hundreds, or thousands), you may want to look into using a professional shop to burn your CDs from one master.

A short- to medium-sized run of CDs—or CD-ROMs—is not as expensive as it used to be. Many vendors advertise rates as low as $1 per disk, which usually includes two-color labeling. Though CD-R disks and label supplies are relatively cheap, you will save a lot of time and wear on your equipment by using a shop to burn large quantities.

17

Wired for Sound: The Internet

Quite simply, the Internet is the biggest thing to happen to music in a long time. For the first time in "recorded" history, artists have a cheap and easy outlet for getting their music heard by millions of potential listeners.

Whether you've already decided you're second in line for a direct Web-jack into your brain or you're just getting good at e-mail, this chapter is for you. You'll learn:

- The differences between online audio file formats
- How to package your music for the Internet
- Tips for the design and setup of your own website
- How to protect your intellectual property

The Internet Music Craze

It's hard not to have heard about MP3, Real Audio, file sharing, streaming audio, and QuickTime. These technologies are rapidly becoming almost ubiquitous parts of the popular music experience.

Not convinced? Take a trip down to your local software chain store and check out the music software section: A couple of years ago, you would have been hard-pressed to find even a handful of titles there—and you would have been lucky if more than one of them was in stock. Today, hundreds of boxes representing dozens of available titles line the shelf. This is because software makers are responding to the huge numbers of online music lovers—and musicians—that have grown because of the Internet.

At the time of this writing, MP3 remains the most used, transferred, shared, encoded, decoded, copied—you name it—music format on the Internet. MP3 became popular so quickly because, around the time it was introduced, online music was either 1) delivered in small files but of very poor playback quality; or 2) of good sound fidelity but unacceptably slow to download because of huge file sizes.

Unless you had the patience of a saint, listening to music then was like listening to a song that had been recorded off an AM radio station—not a very compelling prospect to say the least. MP3 changed all that by providing much higher quality sound while keeping the average file size manageable.

So how does it work? To understand how MP3 works, you have to first understand a little about audio file formats.

MORE ON AUDIO FILE FORMATS

Although this chapter focuses on the handful of audio file formats that are popular on the Internet, there are many other audio file formats. See Chapter 11, "Fun-Da-Mental Audio," for general coverage of file formats as well as digital audio.

How Audio File Formats Work

An audio file isn't much different than any other file on a computer: It's a piece of data that adheres to a specific set of rules defining how all the data bits (the 0s and 1s) should be stored on your hard drive. A "format" is simply the set of rules.

Of course, there is more than one set of rules. For example, CD music always follows the rule that audio data must be stored using a bit depth (or "resolution") of 16 bits and a 44.1 kHz sampling rate. This means that a string of 0s and 1s representing a slice of audio data can't be more than 16 bits long (a pretty good-size number), and that the music has been sampled 44,100 times per second. The result is that the sound reproduction is quite accurate, but the audio files take up a lot of space. That's why, at 16 bits and 44.1 kHz, you can't pack more than seventy-four minutes or so of audio onto a CD.

AUDIO CD DATA

The seventy-four minutes of audio data on an audio CD, or "Red Book" audio (named after the color of the cover on the original audio CD specification) is stored in a special PCM audio data format—not in an .AIFF file or any other standard Mac audio file format.

In fact, downloading one three-minute song on a 56 K modem from a CD takes a long time—nearly two hours. For all but the most discerning owners of a very high bandwidth Internet connection, this is unacceptable.

HOW MUCH WILL IT HOLD?

The way you determine how much music can be stored on a compact disc is actually quite simple. It's a matter of figuring out the number of bits all the pieces add up to. This is done by multiplying the number of samples per second by the number of bits per sample by the number of channels (in the case of CD audio, separate samples are taken for both the left and right speakers to provide stereo, so the number of channels is two). Here's how it tallies up for CD audio:

44,100 × 16 × 2 = 1,411,200 (bits per second)

Because 8 bits equal one byte, and a kilobyte is 1,000 bytes, 1.4 million bits per second is 176 KB per second. If a song is three minutes long, then it consumes almost 32 MB of space on the CD!

A FEW OTHER FORMATS

We don't cover AIFF, WAV, or MIDI files in this chapter—you can find all of the excruciating details in Chapters 9 and 10 ("Wading in MIDI" and "Diving Deeper into MIDI," respectively), as well as numerous other places in the book. But just in case you're skipping around, here's the quick skinny:

AIFF files are practically the Macintosh twin of a WAV file, and you'll see them with both the .AIF and .SND file extensions. It's an excellent all-purpose file format and almost all sound and music software for the Macintosh platform employs it. You'll probably use the AIFF format for the majority of your audio work, and almost all Mac-based sound and music software use this format. AIFF files have the .AIF file extension and are as good as or better than CD-quality sound.

WAV files are the highly popular Windows-based, noncompressed audio format. The WAV file format supports many types of audio data including 8-bit and 16-bit, mono and stereo audio.

The MIDI file format is used by musicians extensively, as well as in many popular computer games and entertainment software, and there are loads of MIDI files available on the Internet. A MIDI file does not capture and store audio data; instead, it manages a list of events, which describes the specific steps that your sound card or computer must take to generate the music. MIDI files are tiny compared to digital audio files and are easy to edit, allowing the music to easily be rearranged, recorded, and played in real time. For more on MIDI, see Chapters 9 and 10.

MP3: It's All in the Algorithm

With the MP3 file format, it takes less than ten minutes to download an average three-minute song at a modem speed of around 50 Kbps, which doesn't require the patience of a saint! MP3 does this by using an algorithm that compresses, or *encodes*, the audio data, wadding up the entire chunk of audio data kind of like the way you might crumple a sheet of paper into a ball.

Of course, in order to listen to the music once your download is complete, it must be decompressed, or *decoded*, on your computer—kind of like unwadding that paper ball.

This is done with an MP3 player, such as iTunes, Real Player, MusicMatch—the list goes on and on. The kicker is that decoded audio does not sound quite as good as the original, uncompressed recording. Think of that paper ball: When you unfold it, it has creases in it, so that anything written on the paper is not quite as clear as it was when the paper was smooth and crease-free.

In the case of MP3, there are enough creases to keep the file size manageable, but not so many that the audio quality suffers too much. An average MP3 file actually compresses at a ratio of about 12 to 1, so think of twelve creases. This is not far from CD-quality.

A NICKEL TOUR OF MP3 HISTORY

MP3 stands for "Moving Picture Experts Group, Audio Layer 3." It began as far back as the 1980s, when the German Fraunhofer Institut set out to create a high-quality, highly compressed audio file format. Fraunhofer was granted a patent for MP3 in Germany in 1989 and subsequently submitted MP3 to the International Standards Organization (ISO).

It wasn't until around 1997, however, that a commercially acceptable MP3 player was created. Dubbed the "AMP MP3 Playback Engine," it quickly became the basis for the creation of Winamp, the first widely adopted MP3 player to hit the Internet. Winamp was developed by two university students, Justin Frankel and Dmitry Boldyrev.

Since then, there have been many new versions of Winamp, while a slew of other players have emerged offering different playback options, EQs, effects, graphic visualizations, and other features and improvements. New tools, encoders, and CD rippers have also been developed, spurring an exciting—and competitive—marketplace. "MP3" has become the most popular search term at search engine sites, and portable MP3 players now let music lovers take their music with them wherever they go.

If that weren't enough, there was Napster—the tool that allowed users to connect to each other's hard drives to share MP3 files. Shortly after Napster was released in 1999, it spawned a community of music junkies that grew like gangbusters. This brought about a huge protest by a number of famous musicians and led to the eventual shutting down of Napster in 2001.

Another compelling aspect of the history of MP3 (you *could* arguably call it the revolution of MP3) is the fact that music in MP3 format has always been free and void of security features. This has in no small way attracted the attention of the RIAA (the Recording Industry Association of America), which represents the major recording labels. The RIAA views MP3 as a significant piracy threat and has tried more than once to stop its unsecured use, including filing successful lawsuits against Napster, MP3.com, and other file-sharing services.

MP3 Encoding

So, how do you get your music made into an MP3 file? How do you go about encoding it? There are numerous tools available, and it is not the aim of this chapter to cover them all. Table 17.1 lists some of the most popular programs that encode MP3 files.

Table 17.1
MP3 encoding software

Name	Website	Platform(s)
iTunes	apple.com	Mac
MusicMatch 6.0	musicmatch.com	PC/Mac/Linux
Audion	panic.com/audion/	Mac
Cabrio	melonsoft.com/products/cabrio/	Mac

Table 17.1 is by no means a definitive list, and the features of these programs vary widely. iTunes and MusicMatch, for example, are full-featured MP3 players in their own right.

In addition, most of the digital audio recording software available provides the ability to encode MP3 files, such as Bias Peak. With Peak, the process is handled by simply exporting the file to the MP3 format, as shown in Figure 17.1. All you have to do is select File > Save As from the menu bar and choose MP3 from the Files of Type drop-down list. At this point, you can also include an ID tag for your music so that listeners will know who the composer is and what style of music it is.

Figure 17.1
MP3-encoding your composition in Peak is straightforward and easy

Peak cannot encode MP3s immediately after you install the program. Bias supplies a link in the Peak program folder that takes you to a website where you can download a library file to install in your Peak program folder. Upon starting Peak again, you will be encoding MP3s in no time.

MP3 ENCODERS

One can only speculate as to why Cubase SL (at the time of this writing selling for around $399 street) does not include MP3 encoding for free. With the earlier version of Cubase, called VST, Steinberg required Mac users to purchase an MP3 encoder for an additional $20 just to encode MP3.

But the quick and easy way around this is just to use iTunes, as it is a free program that is already included with your Mac.

Introduced in 2000, iTunes (see Figure 17.2) is Apple's premiere MP3 audio application. It easily rips and converts audio from CDs, creates customized play lists, and streams audio from MP3 websites with simplicity. Heck, it even burns audio CDs. And for a price tag of *zero*, it seems pretty pointless to worry about MP3 encoding in other Mac applications.

Figure 17.2
iTunes suits the needs of any MP3 junkie

Bit Rates and Compression Techniques

Good MP3 encoding software actually gives you more than one option for converting your music to MP3. The reason for this is that the format itself was designed to support different degrees of compression, as shown in Table 17.2.

Table 17.2
MP3 performance comparison

Sound Quality	Bandwidth	Mode	Bit Rate	Compression Ratio
CD	16 kHz	Stereo	112–128 Kbps	12:1
Near-CD	15 kHz	Stereo	96 Kbps	16:1
FM radio	11 kHz	Stereo	64 Kbps	24:1
AM radio	7.5 kHz	Mono	32 Kbps	24:1
Short-wave	4.5 kHz	Mono	16 Kbps	48:1
Telephone	2.5 kHz	Mono	8 Kbps	96:1

IS IT TRULY CD QUALITY?

Technically speaking, 96–128 Kbps is not strictly CD quality, though it sounds so close in most common listening environments that for popular music, it is, practically speaking, CD quality. The ambient noise characteristic of listening outdoors, in your car, or on a CD Walkman masks the deficiencies. However, for highly dynamic genres such as classical music, compression is less suitable.

Note the numbers in the Compression Ratio column. These are in reality approximations—the actual compression rate that can be achieved during encoding can vary by a few digits higher or lower. For example, although 12:1 is an average compression rate to maintain CD quality, it could wind up anywhere from 11:1 to 14:1.

That's the reason for the numbers in the Bit Rate column: Because compression ratios are not always an exact measurement, a bit rate is calculated to accurately track compression strength. A bit rate is the average number of Kilobits (Kbps) that 1 second of audio data will consume. One Kilobit is 1,024 bits.

We learned earlier that a digital audio signal from a CD runs at 1,378,125 bits per second. Translated into a bit rate, this is approximately 1,378 Kbps! With MP3, CD-like sound quality can be achieved by compressing the audio down to a bit rate of 96 Kbps.

The question is: How far can you go without sacrificing too much quality? This is not an unusual question in the online world. For instance, Web designers struggle with optimizing images and image formats all the time. The two most widely used image files are the GIF and JPEG formats, and each of them uses compression algorithms. For that matter, if you've ever downloaded a Stuffit file, you've encountered compression as well—a Stuffit file format can compress just about anything, from text to binary executable files to images, as well as audio files.

96 OR BETTER

There aren't really that many instances in which you'll want to go below 96 Kbps. If you are doing a lot of singing and/or have a lot going on musically, anything lower than 96 Kbps will not sound good. Also, some of the websites that allow you to post your MP3s require that the bit rate be at least 128 Kbps, including MP3.com.

In a few cases, lowering the bit rate might make sense; for example, if you're doing a lot of spoken word or if instrumentation is sparse, you may not lose any noticeable quality while reducing the file size. The best way to find out is to experiment with different bit rates.

For audio, to make a good compression algorithm technique, the MP3 format uses something called *perceptual noise shaping*. The idea is simple: The encoding algorithm uses psychoacoustic modeling—certain known facts about how humans hear—to determine how to compress the data.

PSYCHOACOUSTICS

The psychoacoustic model of the human auditory system is more or less a description of the sensitivity of the human ear to sound frequencies. With some variation, most of us are very sensitive to frequencies between 2.5 and 5 kHz, and our perception drops pretty rapidly for frequencies lower or higher than this range.

For example, sound frequencies that the human ear can barely detect or not hear at all can be eliminated during the compression process, while sound frequencies that are heard better than others are "punctuated"—especially if two sounds occur at the same time, in which case the loudest frequencies can be left untouched at the expense of softer frequency levels.

The bottom line is that, by eliminating some of the less common frequencies and inaudible elements of an audio signal, audio can be scrunched up into a manageable size.

Other compressed audio file formats work in a similar fashion, and when it comes to Macintosh there is only one other format worth mentioning—Real Audio.

Real Audio

If you spend any time at all surfing the Internet, you've certainly heard of Real Audio. As the audio-only part of the RealMedia file format, Real Audio is well-suited to very high compression rates and streaming audio.

This means that even on a slow modem you can almost immediately start listening to a song as it downloads rather than having to wait for the whole file to download to your computer's hard drive. This makes Real Audio ideal for previewing songs online, but less than desirable if you want to provide near-CD quality—unless you use Real's newer G2 format, which provides more options and much better quality compression. To find out more about Real Audio, surf on over to **www.real.com**.

Getting Your Music Out There

You understand how MP3 files and other Internet audio file formats work now. You've downloaded a suitable MP3 encoder and converted all your recordings to MP3.

You're ready for the next step—getting the music up there, out there, and online-there—and it's only a matter of time before Amazon.com picks up your music for distribution.

Sound far-fetched? Maybe. Maybe not—artists are starting to make money and are truly getting exposure on the Internet now. Go read some of the success stories over at MP3.com if you're skeptical.

It is going to take some work, though. You need to put the guitar down, don your marketing hat, think of what you want to say about your music and the "image" you want to project, and decide where you want your music to be available online. The rest of this chapter guides you through these steps, starting with setting up your own website.

If you want to be noticed, you need a dedicated Web presence for your music. No bones about it, and there's no objection you can make that holds water, unless you don't have the money—and that one almost doesn't cut it, because websites are mighty cheap these days.

Even if your strategy is only to get your music hosted on other websites (such as MP3.com), you still need a "home base." Why? Let's look at few reasons.

Timing Is Everything

Internet time is very similar to an MP3 file, in that it's highly compressed. News, events, new content—these things *can* happen almost instantly when you have the ability to communicate almost instantly. With your own website, you can post new music whenever you want, as quickly as you want. You can upload news about the band, your lyrics, gig dates—anything and everything you want to say about the music—in less time than it takes to make your morning coffee. You can also get feedback on your music through the use of a bulletin board, guest book, or your own online chat.

You can do these things through a music site that will host your music—and many of them do a very good job of providing these kinds of services. However, it's not instant: A professional music host site has to accommodate thousands of artists and will need to categorize, verify, and read whatever changes you make to your site. This takes time—from hours to days.

The Look Is Important

With your own site, you are completely in charge of the look and feel—the image you want to project to the world. Now, this could be a bad thing if your visual sense is only slightly better than a bat's, but it can be a very good thing if you have a good feel for color and design—or someone you love does!

Alternatively—presuming you don't have the money to hire a working designer—there are lots of artists on the Web who are looking to add to their resumes. Go to Google Groups (you can get to them from **www.google.com**) and search the discussion areas for Web designers. Make a pot of coffee. By the time you've finished the brew, you'll probably have located a half-dozen students or fledgling designers willing to talk about lending you their expertise for cheap.

Don't Limit Yourself

Another downside to keeping your music hosted with an online music service is size. You are limited to how many pages you can have and what formats you can use. Although having your own site comes with some limitations, too, they are far less restrictive than what you'll find at MP3.com or Garageband.com, for example.

A Little Remuneration, Please

There's also the potential for earning some money from your site. If you choose, you can charge money for downloads, or, more likely, you can participate in link exchange programs, merchandise selling programs, or paid advertisements. You won't get rich by any means, but you may make a few bucks—enough to offset the purchase of that new effects box or VST plug-in you've been wanting.

Designing a Website

There are very large books—many of them completely worthless and a handful of them very useful—that say an awful lot about Web design. There are books on color theory, user interfaces, understanding the user path, optimizing graphics, and Web programming. There are books on designing in Shockwave, Flash, Dynamic HTML, and JavaScript. There are books on using client-side Java, and there are books on using HTML. Amend that: There are a *ton* of books on both Java and HTML.

Suffice it to say, all those books exist because a well-designed website is not the easiest thing in the world to, well, design. Therefore, this section is not going to attempt to teach you how to create a decent-looking Web page without having to become a professional Web designer. What it does do is provide you with a quick, cheap, useful roadmap for putting together your own site by showing you the tools you'll need and a little bit about how to use them.

Cracking the Code

First things first. If you have a burning desire to understand the inner-workings of Figure 17.3, then you do not need to read this section. You may skip it and instead purchase the book *HTML for the World Wide Web with XHTML and CSS: Visual QuickStart Guide, Fifth Edition*, by Elizabeth Castro (ISBN: 0321130073).

The figure shows an example of the source code behind a typical Web page—in this case, a small part of the HTML source code behind one of the pages on Jethro Tull's website **www.jtull.com**; followed up by a shot of the actual Web page itself (see Figures 17.3 and 17.4).

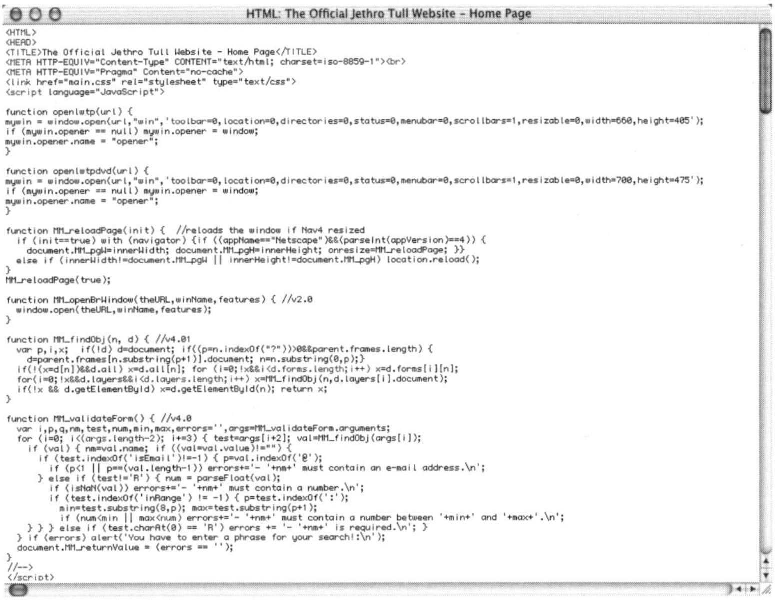

Figure 17.3
This is a small part of the HTML source code for Jethro Tull's home page

Tools for Building a Website

You'll need to decide on the tools you will use to build your website. There are many Mac-based HTML editors that are OS X ready, such as Dreamweaver MX (see the following Note). These programs can be rather expensive (at least $200), to say nothing of the learning curve required to create a website. Sure, there are ways around the monetary problems, such as purchasing educational editions if you are a student or faculty, but Apple has a solution for everyone; it's called *.mac* (see Figure 17.5).

Figure 17.4
And here is what that same code looks like in your Web browser

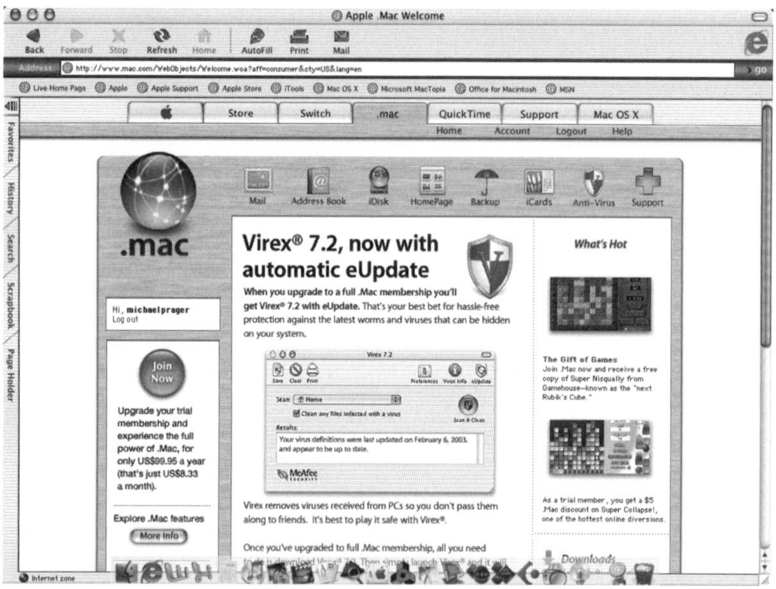

Figure 17.5
.mac is Apple's solution for creating a Web page in minutes

.mac is a subscription service that Apple provides for Mac users that offers the following services:

- A .mac e-mail address that can be checked via the Web. For example, recordingdork@mac.com.
- Tools to create and build a good-looking Web page without ever looking at a line of code.

- A backup solution (iDisk) that lets you archive vital information on your own virtual hard drive on the Apple server.
- Antivirus software by McAfee that helps protect your computer against viruses.
- The ability to create customized virtual greeting cards. This could be a good way to announce future gigs and record releases to your friends, family, and hopefully fans.

The best thing about .mac is that you can try it out for a month for free before you decide if you want to purchase it. Granted, it is a stripped down version, with limited disc space. But hey, free is free, right? If you like the service, you can then pay $99 to upgrade your account to full user status.

DREAMWEAVER

If .mac is not your "cup of meat" (to quote Bob Dylan), then you might want to have a look at Dreamweaver MX as a solution. Dreamweaver has a lot of very complex functions for creating a Web page that looks professional, and the learning curve isn't as hard as you might think.

The price tag is pretty steep ($399 at the time of this writing). You can try before you buy by downloading a thirty-day demo from **www.macromedia.com**.

An Overview of .mac

Let's have a look at what home page goodies Apple has cooked up for us with .mac. At this point, let's assume that you have signed up for your free trial account.

First, we need to log in, so type in your user name and password, as shown in Figure 17.6.

Figure 17.6
Remember to write down your account information so you can log in anytime and on any computer

.mac Mail

When you first create your .mac account, you are given a choice of user names, which will also become your e-mail address name.

When you log in and check your e-mail, you will see an inbox that looks a lot like Figure 17.7.

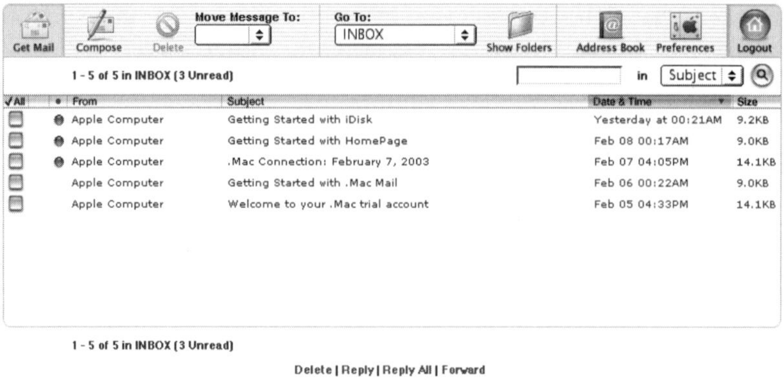

Figure 17.7
.mac's inbox

Creating Your First Web Page with .mac

Apple has made it as simple as 1-2-3 to create your first Web page. To start creating our page, we first need to select a "theme." This theme is selected from a preexisting list provided by Apple. Because this is our first time out, let's keep it simple by selecting the "Events" theme, which is located in the Newsletter subdirectory (see Figure 17.8).

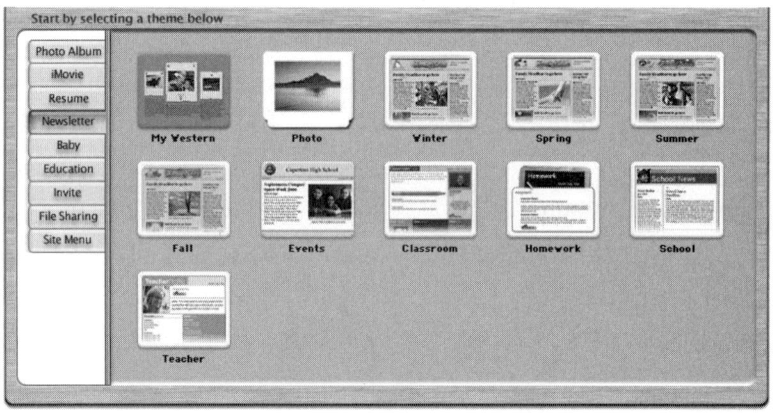

Figure 17.8
Premade themes are supplied by Apple

After you select the theme you want, the template for that theme appears. At first, the template doesn't look so cool, because the content is the standard content provided with the template to show you how it will look. Don't panic, just click the Edit button, which is found in the upper-right corner. Now, you can begin to edit your Web page (see Figure 17.9).

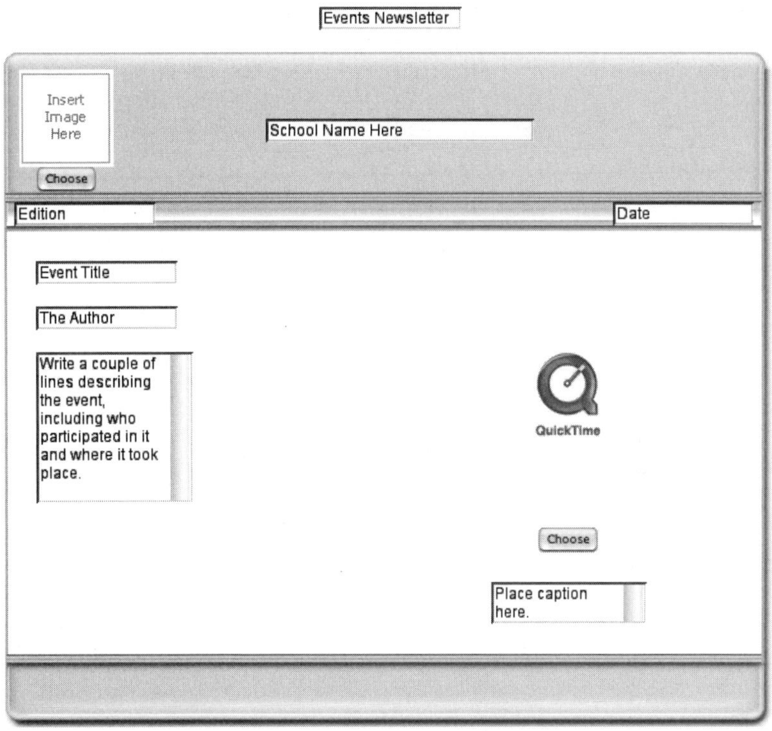

Figure 17.9
Editing your Web page is just a click away

Let's start with the title of your page. Obviously, you don't want to call it "Events Newsletter." Rather, you probably want to call it something like "What's New?"

After that, it's just a matter of filling in the blanks. When you finish, your page might look something like Figure 17.10.

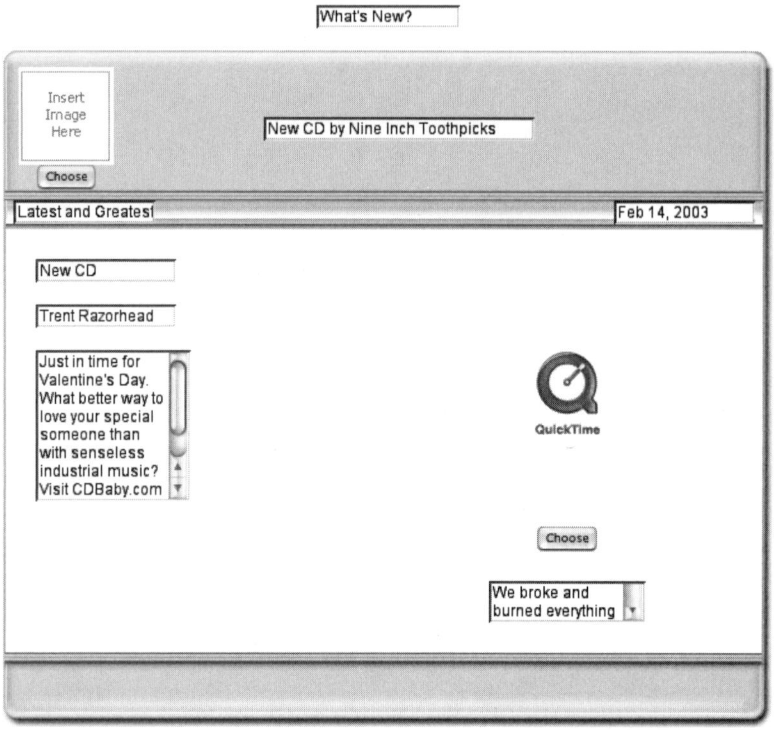

Figure 17.10
Nine Inch Toothpicks has a new CD out? Cool!

Next, you will need to place some pictures into that template. If you happen to have any artwork in JPG or GIF format on your computer, you can upload it to your iDisk, at which point you can then add it to your page (see Figure 17.11). And if you don't happen to have any spare artwork lying around, you can always try out some of Apple's demo artwork, which is accessed in the same way.

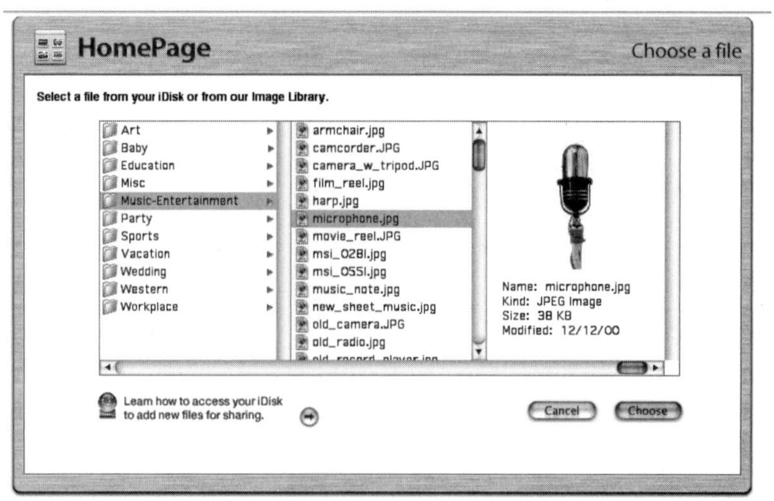

Figure 17.11
Select a couple of demo images to place on your Web page; you can change them later

After you have selected images for your page, you can then have a look at what your page is going to look like. Make sure everything is spelled correctly (see Figure 17.12), and click the "Publish" button in the upper-right corner, and .mac then gives you a link to your page. You can also send out an announcement to let your waiting fans know your CD is out (see Figure 17.13).

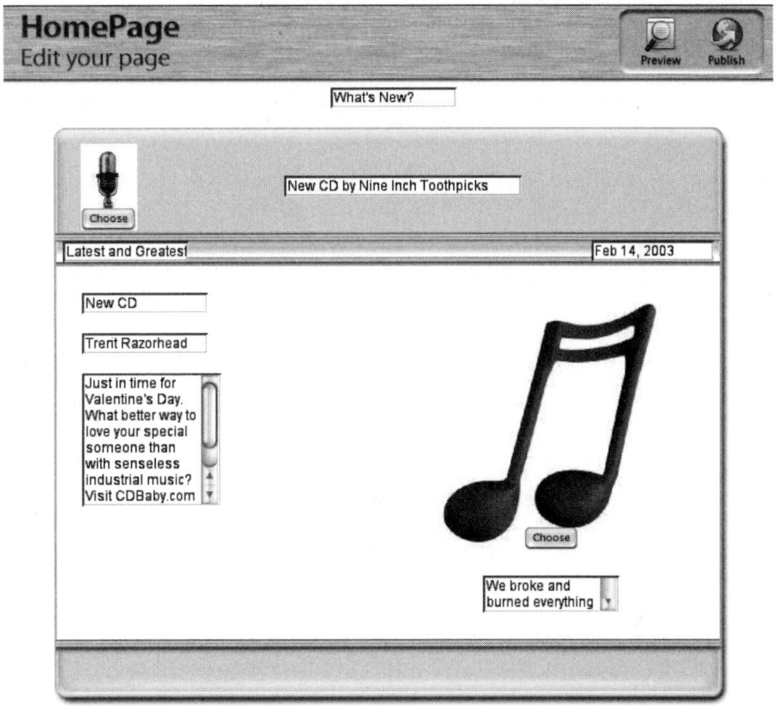

Figure 17.12
You are one click away from publishing your first home page; just make sure you "dot your I's and cross your T's" by double-checking the spelling

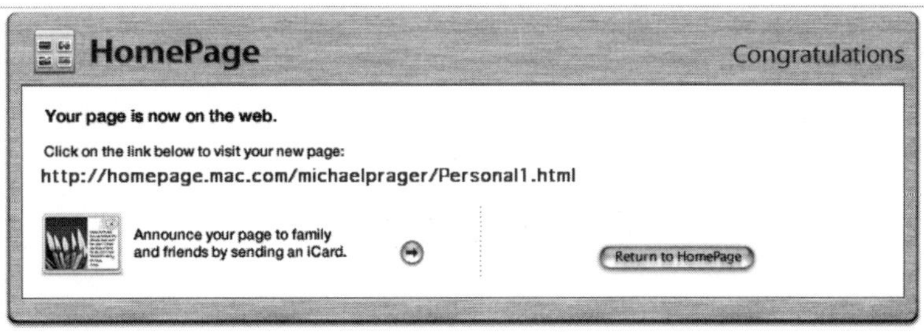

Figure 17.13
You have now created and launched your first Web page; click on the link to check it out!

TAKING IT FURTHER

.mac is great for creating simple Web pages, but if you want to set up an online store or another complex function, you will need to either bite the bullet and pick up Web development software such as Dreamweaver MX or find a Web designer who will do the job for a reasonable price.

Let's now assume that you have not subscribed to .mac and that instead you've created a Web page using Dreamweaver. Next, you'll need to register your desired Web address, find a server to host your site, and upload your files.

Web Hosting

When you create a Web page using .mac, you don't need to worry about hosting, because your creation is stored on Apple's server. But if you've created a Web page using other tools, you need to find a server where you can store your Web page so it can be accessed by anyone with an Internet connection.

This process involves several steps. The first one is to locate a reputable hosting company that you can afford. The second step is to decide if you need your own Web page address or if you're happy using the base Web address of the hosting company. The third step is to learn how to upload your files to your new site.

Hosting Services

Web hosting is simply paying for space on another computer that has a Web server and a high-speed connection to the Internet. The host computer "serves" your Web page to your adoring fans.

There are hundreds of reputable Web hosting services these days and perhaps a few that aren't so reputable. Plans and prices can sometimes vary by quite a bit, so it's worth doing some research to see what kinds of deals are available.

At the time of this writing, a typical plan costs about $20 per month and looks something like this:

- 200 MB of disk storage
- 10 GB data transfer per month
- 20+ e-mail accounts
- 24-hr FTP access
- CGI-BIN + free scripts
- Graphical statistics and raw logs
- Real Audio/Video support
- 99.9 percent uptime guarantee

As you can see, an average plan gives you some limitations on how much storage space you can have for Web pages, how active your site can be (for example, no more than 3 gigabytes of data transfer—or "throughput"—per month is allowed), how many e-mail accounts you can have, and so on.

The best approach is to start off small and see where it leads. In the previous example, 200 MB of disk space and 10 GB of throughput is plenty of storage and bandwidth to get you started, and you'll probably have to think for awhile to figure out how you can use twenty-five e-mail accounts.

Probably the most important thing to look for is reputation. What you want to avoid is hosting with a company that has a lot of technical problems, uses substandard equipment, or has bad customer service.

Budgetweb.com and The Ultimate Web Host List (**webhostlist.internetlist.com**) are both excellent sites for researching Web-hosting services, and Yahoo! also maintains a long list of companies.

Search the discussions area of Deja (**www.deja.com**) for information about different Web hosting companies. In addition to being a consumer product review site, Deja publishes and updates messages from thousands of newsgroups, and you're very likely to find information on the companies you're curious about.

There are also a number of free hosting services available. The most used are:

- GeoCities (**www.geocities.com**)
- Tripod (**www.tripod.com**)
- Angelfire (**www.angelfire.com**)
- FreeTown (**www.freetown.com**)
- ACMEcity (**www.acmecity.com**)

Free hosting services typically offer chat, e-mail, and Web pages, but they have far greater limitations on space and bandwidth, and like to throw any number of ads up on your pages without your permission.

Domain Names

A domain name is the descriptive Web address visitors to your site will type in to get there (it's also called a URL, or Uniform Resource Locator, but you need not memorize that one). When it comes to a domain name, there are essentially two choices:

- Your site can have its own unique domain name, e.g., www.yourname.com, which you purchase through a domain name provider. A list of all the domain name providers is available at **www.icann.org**. Many Web hosting companies will also register the domain for you. The cost is currently around $35 per year or less.
- Your site can have a "piggyback" URL, for example, www.yourwebhost.com/yourname, or possibly yourname.yourwebhost.com. A URL of this sort doesn't require registration and can be set up on virtually any Web host. This is the format that free Web-hosting companies use as well.

It almost goes without saying that if you can afford it, go with a unique domain name.

Uploading Your Site

After you've enlisted a Web hosting company to host your site, you'll typically be given an FTP account with which to upload and manage the files for your site. FTP stands for file transfer protocol, and it's the standard for uploading and downloading files to and from a website.

> **DREAMWEAVER CAN FTP**
> Dreamweaver MX also includes an alternative to using stand-alone FTP software, by allowing you to "publish" your site directly to the server. The process is very simple and as easy as drag and drop!

Intellectual Property

This chapter wouldn't be complete without a few words concerning intellectual property rights as they pertain to the Internet. It's a bit of a touchy subject, for a couple reasons.

First, just how concerned should you be? Do you need to worry about someone making claim to your work—or making money from it—once it's available to anyone with a connection? Second, how do you protect your work, and what kind of protection do you need?

The Law

You may be aware of the changes made to U.S. copyright law in 1978. On January 1 of that year, a completely new copyright statute, the Copyright Act of 1976 (Public Law 94-553), came into effect in the United States, superseding the Copyright Act of 1909. The law applies to creators of "original works of authorship," including literary, dramatic, musical, artistic, and certain other intellectual works.

The law protects both published and unpublished works, and the protection exists from the time the work is created in fixed form; that is, it is an "incidence of the process of authorship." The copyright in the work of authorship immediately becomes the property of the author who created it. Only the author or those deriving their rights can rightfully claim copyright.

So, the bottom line is that, technically speaking, U.S. law provides the ability for you to establish grounds with which to seek redress if someone rips off your work.

The Reality

You can practically throw copyright law out the door when it comes to the Internet and your music. To begin with, although a number of other countries (Japan, the U.K., and Germany, for example) do recognize copyrights—even if the copyright for a particular work is not registered in their home country—not every country does. So that's one risk: On the Internet, your work is available to the whole world.

The reality is that, once your music is online, you'll be hard-pressed to decide who can download it and who can't—and even then, you ultimately have no idea where it will end up. And if that weren't enough, there is a lot of debate going on right now about what is legal and what is not in the online music world. Recent lawsuits over the rights of recording artists, the RIAA, Napster, and MP3.com have shown that there are no clear answers yet.

You'll need to decide how much the issue of protecting your own work means to you. Perhaps the best advice is to not worry about it—to just let it happen—it's hard enough just to get the music noticed, let alone worry about who "owns" it and who doesn't. On the other hand, you may not feel comfortable with the openness of the Internet—in which case, about the only thing you can truly do is not participate at all.

If you do participate, here are a few tips for watching your music's backside:

- Post copyright notices on your website, using the © symbol and specifying that you own your own work.
- Make sure that when you encode your music for the Internet, your name and the copyright mark © are included. This is done through the ID3 tagging format for MP3 files—almost all of the MP3 software available allows you to tag your music with ID3.
- Read the license agreements carefully when you sign up to post your music on other websites. If you feel uncomfortable at all about the legalese, get a lawyer to check the verbiage for you.
- Check the sites where your music is available on a regular basis. See how they're approaching the delivery of the site's content and ensure that you're comfortable with their practices and policies.

18

Promoting and Marketing Your Music

If you want your music to be heard, you'll have to know a thing or two about marketing and promoting it. This chapter shows you the basic ropes and dives into the details where it makes sense, including coverage of these topics:

- The basics of promoting your music
- Marketing your music using the Internet
- Using search engines and directories
- Advertising and affiliate programs

Promoting Your Music

Promoting your music is a big topic, and there are several good books that have been written on it. *All You Need to Know About the Music Business*, by Donald S. Passman and Randy Glass (Simon & Schuster, 2000, ISBN 0684870649) is excellent, as is *This Business of Music Marketing and Promotion*, by Tad Lathrop and Jim Pettigrew (Billboard Books, 1999, ISBN 082307711X).

Although it would be impossible to try to distill the kinds of insights and details these books bring to the table, we'll touch on some fundamental tips for how to promote your music.

Have a Marketing Plan

You don't have to be a marketing manager at Procter & Gamble to know the basics. First, write down some clear and practical goals you have for distributing your work. You'll be amazed at how useful writing it all down can be: It brings into focus the reasons you want to promote your work.

Think about your own "hot buttons" as a consumer of music: What makes you spend your own money on a new recording? What attracts you most to music you'll pay money for? Is it the radio, television, the *Rolling Stone* review, live performances, or the Internet? Write down the areas in which your CDs will have the best chance of being noticed, and then prioritize which ones you can tackle.

If you live near a college town, for example, getting a little radio time may not be all that difficult. Many college towns set aside time to play local artists on a fairly regular basis. The same is true for college newspapers—in fact, if you have any writing skills at all, penning an article about the CD and your music yourself and pitching it to the paper could be the slight edge you need to get the word out.

A Little Airplay Would Be Nice!

Radio airplay remains the defacto method for promoting popular music. Do a little research and find out where the radio stations in your area are located. Prepare a CD and print a bio sheet describing your music and either mail or hand-deliver your music to stations that you think would be interested in playing your style.

Local radio stations sometimes do compilation CDs of local artists as well. Look at the checkout counters of local music stores to see if any have been offered in your area, or ask the stations themselves.

Another option is public broadcasting. Many public television stations still set aside TV airtime for local announcements as well as locally produced programs. It wouldn't be unusual to get a music video played on one of these stations.

BREAKING IN VIA COLLEGE RADIO

College radio (public broadcasting) stations might be a more positive direction than you think. Local station KCRW 89.9 in Santa Monica, CA is renowned for their ability to find unsigned artists and launch the careers of signed artists with great success. A couple of names to throw in the hat are the Cranberries, Weezer, Tori Amos (whose recording career, incidentally, had a disastrous beginning), and Sixpence None the Richer. All of these bands had little or no airplay until they were *discovered* by KCRW; and now commercial radio stations can't seem to stop playing them.

Send Press Releases

Send press releases to all local media about your new CD. Talk about the CD, talk about the tracks, and give a short bio about yourself. Keep press releases short and to the point. Even small radio and TV stations receive a slew of press releases every day, so a pithy, well-written release stands a greater chance of being used. Send a copy of your CD along with the press release, and if you're playing gigs, note any upcoming live performances.

Believe it or not, large books have been written about press releases. Take a trip down to the library and get a handle on standard press release formats—you'll stand a much better chance of getting them noticed by the media.

> **A DIY SUCCESS**
>
> Do-It-Yourself success Laurie Z has managed to sell over 20,000 CDs worldwide on her own without the need for a record label. Although that might not sound like a lot of sales, remember that independent musicians usually make a lot more money per CD if they're sold independently rather than through a record label. And how many people can say they had film legend Jack Palance sing on their Christmas CD?
>
> Seriously though, Laurie has all of the insider tips to record promotion, and you can get the knowledge by checking out her video titled *The 'Do it Yourself' Guide to Releasing an Independent CD!* (Zebra Productions Inc, 1998). Check it out at her website (**www.lauriez.com**), or just find her products at CD Baby (**www.cdbaby.com**).

Marketing Your Music

Guess what? After you establish your Web presence, transfer your website's files to the host server, and choose a Web address, you're halfway home! Okay—maybe a little more than halfway—but that depends on how much stock you put in the idea of marketing and advertising your music online.

One thing's for sure—if you don't take the time to advertise yourself, you're not going to create a lot of fans. It's the irony of being a home recording artist rearing its ugly head again: Sometimes, you have to spend so much time doing things that have nothing to do with the music that the music almost becomes secondary.

Still, using the Internet to boost your audience is not difficult—only time-consuming. All of the resources in this section are easy to grasp and many of them are free or cheap, so the only thing that can potentially keep you from making yourself known is how much time you can devote to it. And that's a long way from where home studio enthusiasts were a few years ago, when there was a lot more time than money (and there wasn't much money, then, either).

Music Sites That Want You

There are a number of websites that want to make your music available to their listeners, and many of them attract huge numbers of visitors per day—far more listeners than you'll likely ever get to your home site.

These sites are your number-one source for online marketing, and they represent the best kind of marketing, because the focus is almost always on the music.

MP3.com

MP3.com is still the mother of all music websites for getting your music heard. Make no mistake about it—if you're a home recording artist, you should be on MP3.com. Because of its huge traffic, joining MP3.com is almost a guarantee that your music will be heard by thousands of music lovers (potentially millions).

MP3.com also has a number of tools—from online radio stations to a daily ranking system—to help you market yourself effectively online as well as earn money. It's free to join, and there are no maintenance fees.

MP3.com provides Web pages for your music (see Figure 18.1), showcases tunes on a daily (sometimes hourly) basis, allows for pictures and other artist information, and allows you to update your pages fairly quickly. The site also has a large and very active online bulletin board system, so getting feedback on your latest recording can be very swift.

MP3.com also has a unique program that enables it to make CDs of your music and sell them online. So far, the deal has always been a straight-up 50/50 split, which is very reasonable, considering that they cut and manufacture the CDs, market them, and handle all of the accounting. Most artists get a check for a few dozen dollars every quarter—but some have made thousands, and a few have made hundreds of thousands of dollars from the online sale of their CDs.

Figure 18.1
Your fame and fortune could be just a click away with MP3.com—just ask Red Delicious

Broadjam.com

In early 2000, Roy Elkins, who was a big part of the marketing team at Sonic Foundry, decided to find his calling elsewhere. With his extensive knowledge of the music industry, Roy founded and launched Broadjam, a website dedicated to promote the independent artist but with a few twists and turns that set it apart from everyone else in this list.

Through affiliations with companies such as Taxi and New Line Cinema, Broadjam is able to build a community by offering services for independent artists that include building websites for them on popular pages such as MP3.com, and submitting them to independent A&R companies such as Taxi, who have helped a lot of indies get off the ground.

Plus, the Broadjam website is extremely easy to get around in and very streamlined, so you won't spend all of your time downloading graphics, as shown in Figure 18.2.

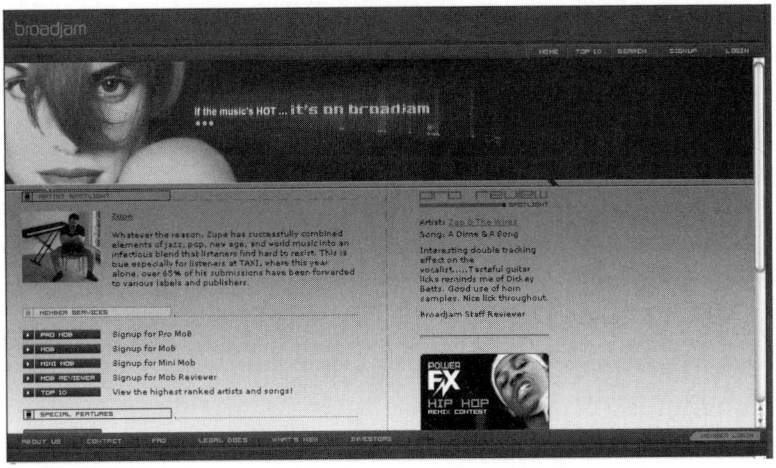

Figure 18.2
Broadjam is an essential website to help you succeed with Internet marketing

Garageband.com

Garageband.com is a fascinatingly cool concept: You can upload your tunes only after you've reviewed other songs. In turn, other artists review your tunes for the same reason. Pretty neat, eh? The result is that you get a lot of constructive (and occasionally not-so-constructive) criticism about your music, the mix, the lyrics—everything—from other musicians as well as the listening public, who may also do reviews.

Songs that consistently get high rankings may get promoted to "The Final Countdown," a final round of reviewing to determine a winning artist, who will earn a $250,000 recording contract from Garageband.com for a stated review period.

The process claims to be 100 percent merit-based and 100 percent driven by the reviews of music lovers, and it appears to be a very fair way to decide which new artists get big breaks.

Oh, yeah, one other thing: Garageband.com also claims that there's always the potential for one of its advisory board members to jump in and offer a deal to an artist on the spot. This is not necessarily an impressive claim, until you look at their list of advisory board members, which reads like a Who's Who list of recording producers and engineers. Names like Sir George Martin, Brian Eno, and Steve Earle are enough to make you think twice about the possibilities.

And if that isn't proof enough, check out the end credits for the movie *Little Nicky*, starring Adam Sandler. Aside from the classic rock source music that they used on the sound track, a lot of the other music was selected via Garageband.com.

IUMA (iuma.com)

The Internet Underground Music Archive is an excellent place to gain exposure for your music. You get a Web address with your band name first (for example, daisies.iuma.com for the band "The Daisies") and a custom Web page where you can post all your band information and MP3s, sell CDs, create message boards and fan lists, and get e-mail from fans. The service is free.

The IUMA interface is very well-designed, and navigating the site is intuitive and easy. Artists are categorized by the musical genres you'd expect. Visitors can do a full-text search, sample tunes in Real Audio, and then download the MP3s when they find something they like. There is also a large community and message board area, as well as streaming IUMA Radio.

CMJ (www.cmj.com)

CMJ (which stands for College Media Journal) offers a wide array of services for artists, including your own website, e-mail, a personalized domain name, and subscription discounts for their magazines. The site is well-designed and quick to load.

Though you're limited to uploading three songs, CMJ claims that your uploads will be reviewed by their A&R staff who have "solid contacts throughout the music industry."

It definitely can't hurt.

Search Engines and Directories

Sites that specialize in searching and cataloging the Web are, themselves, some of the most heavily used websites. In fact, most "top ten" lists of the largest websites include many of the search engine and directory sites.

This is no surprise, really—the Web comprises millions of Web pages and it's hard to know what's out there without someone to index it all for you. The great thing about these sites is that you can get listed on them—thereby increasing traffic to your site—and in most cases, it's totally free.

This section lists the sites you'll want to register with, and they fall into two categories: search engines and directories.

A search engine site employs applications (often called "spiders" or "Web bots") that crawl websites twenty-four hours a day, following links and taking notes. These spiders then funnel the information back to the search engine site to be index and published. A directory doesn't use spiders; instead, real people surf the sites, follow links, and write summaries about them to be indexed. The advantage to search engines is that they uncover more pages and are more up-to-date. Directories, on the other hand (Yahoo!, for example), generally do a better job describing what a website is really all about.

Although search engines and directories have different approaches to how they index the Web, they don't vary nearly as much in their submission practices and requirements.

Almost all of them expect you to have a few key things before you submit your Web address.

- **Describe yourself**. Write a brief description of your site that reflects what it's about. Spend some time on this, and keep it short—less than twenty-five words. Though you'll want to accurately describe what's on the site and make your site appealing to users, stay away from clichés and "marketing" words, such as "the future of rock and roll" or "amazing musical sound quality" and the like. Get to the heart of what your site—and your music—is.
- **Keywords and keyword phrases**. Submit or suggest keywords that describe the site. These are words that a prospective visitor would type in to find you. For example, if your songs are country songs that sound like Johnny Cash, your keyword phrases might include the name of your band, "Johnny Cash," "Country Music," and so forth. In general, try to keep the list of keyword phrases a short one. Four to six phrases are plenty for a given Web page.
- **Make the page match the content**. Write copy on your pages that accurately reflects the content. For example, if you have a lyrics page, preface the lyrics with a paragraph or two explicitly describing what's on the page and where the lyrics come from. Though it may seem like overkill, the search engines love it—which makes sense, because search engines need to be able to describe the page before a new user gets to it.

META TAGS

Web pages can also contain things called "meta tags," which are really just hidden keywords and a description of the page to help spiders when they index it. It's a good idea to put meta tags in all of your Web pages, and include the same description and keywords you might submit to the search engine and directory sites.

If you're using Dreamweaver MX, adding meta tags is easy:

1. In Page view, click Insert > Head > Meta.
2. Under the Attributes box, specify the Name, or the HTTP Equivalent. If this is your first time using meta tags, select Name.
3. In the Value box, type the word "Keywords."
4. In the Content box, type in your keywords. Make sure that you separate your keywords with a comma between each word. When you are finished adding your keywords, click OK and you are set to go.

Yahoo! (www.yahoo.com)

Yahoo! is the Web's most popular directory service and has a well-deserved reputation for helping users find information easily. Yahoo! is the largest human-compiled guide to the Web and employs hundreds of editors in its efforts. With more than one million sites listed, Yahoo! is one of the best, and you definitely want a listing here.

Yahoo! is the oldest major website directory, having launched in late 1994, so the site has had a lot of time to figure out what works and what doesn't. The number one rule when submitting to Yahoo!—submit only your primary domain name or main page, and do it only once.

Open Directory (www.dmoz.org)

Open Directory uses volunteer editors to catalog the Web, and the company pledges that anyone and everyone may use information from the directory through an open license arrangement. Several sites, including Lycos, AOL Search, AltaVista, and Hotbot, currently feature Open Directory categories within their results pages.

Open Directory is less picky than Yahoo! about the strength of your site, its description, and your keywords, but a listing in the Open Directory is just as important because of its open license approach.

GoTo (www.goto.com)

Unlike the other search engines, GoTo sells its listings, meaning you can pay money to be placed higher in the search results, which GoTo feels improves relevancy. It does have nonpaid search results, however. GoTo launched in 1997 and incorporated the former University of Colorado-based World Wide Web Worm.

GoTo is listed here because it garners a large amount of traffic, but you may want to put this one on the shelf until you see how well you do with the other, free services.

AltaVista (www.altavista.com)

AltaVista is one of the largest search engines on the Web in terms of quantity. Its comprehensive coverage and power searching capabilities have made it particularly popular among experienced Web users. It also offers a number of features designed to appeal to basic users, such as "Ask AltaVista" results, and it also provides directory listings from the Open Directory.

If you only have time to list with one search engine, this is the one.

Excite (www.excite.com)

Excite is one of the most popular search services on the Web. It has a medium-sized index and integrates non-Web material such as secondary sources of information and sports scores into its results to provide more descriptive listings. Excite was launched in late 1995 and grew quickly in prominence, even buying two of its competitors (Magellan in July 1996 and WebCrawler in November 1996).

Go.com (www.go.com)

Go is mainly a portal site produced by Infoseek and Disney, but it also provides search services. Go is very good at providing high-quality and relevant search results, thanks to the type of search algorithms it uses, but it also has an impressive human-compiled directory of websites as well.

LookSmart (www.looksmart.com)

LookSmart is yet another human-compiled directory of websites. In addition to being its own independent Web service, the company provides directory results to MSN Search, Excite, and other partners. AltaVista provides LookSmart with search results when a search fails to find a match from among LookSmart's reviews.

Google (www.google.com)

Google is a search engine that makes heavy use of "link popularity" to rank websites. The idea is that the more popular a site is, the more other pages will link to it. This can be especially helpful in finding good sites in response to general searches for music, because users across the Web have upped the results rankings by linking to them.

The success of Google is a good reason to get your site listed on as many other services and websites as possible.

HotBot (www.hotbot.com)

HotBot is similar to AltaVista, and is revered for its large index of the Web and its power-search options. The site also gets directory information from the Open Directory. HotBot was purchased by Lycos in 1998 but continues to be run as a separate search service.

Lycos (www.lycos.com)

Lycos started out as an independent search engine, indexing its own search results. In 1999, it shifted to a directory model similar to Yahoo!'s. Its main listings come from the Open Directory, but secondary results come from its own spidering of the Web.

Lycos is very popular and well worth a listing. It's a good site to list multiple pages, provided each page has distinct content.

Northern Light (www.northernlight.com)

Northern Light features a very large index, can categorize documents by topic, and is very well-designed. When you submit to Northern Light, you submit only your top-level or primary domain name, and no other pages. Their spider is good enough to find all of the pages on your site.

Northern Light also sells pay-per-view information that is not typically accessible to search engine spiders. These are documents from other sources, such as newswires and magazines. You can search the collection for free, but, at the time of this writing, Northern Light charges up to $4 to see individual documents.

Search Engine Watch (www.searchenginewatch.com)

Search Engine Watch is not actually a search service, but it is listed here because it is far and away the best place on the Web to learn more about the whole business of search engines and directories. The site keeps up with everything that's happening in the search engine "community" on a daily basis and offers a number of informative, detailed articles about how to use search services more effectively. The site is maintained by Danny Sullivan, an experienced editor and professional journalist.

Advertising

As your website grows, there are a few things you can do to earn revenue from it—and there are a number of opportunities to spend money getting the word out.

You may have heard about "ad engines" or ad services such as Double-Click or AdForce. Although buying and selling advertising to support your music is a beautiful idea, the reality that it's big business, big money, and not something you should invest any brain cells in until your site is well over the 10,000-visitor-per-day mark. And unless you're planning on launching your own dot-com, that isn't going to happen any time soon.

Still, there are a few things you can do. One of them is looking for inexpensive banner space deals on small- to midsized sites that might be happy to take anything you can offer. They might even offer you banner space in exchange for a link or banner on your site.

This can be an effective means of advertising if you can get exposure across many sites—and it will also help your rankings on Google.com, as discussed in the last section. Look for small- to midsized websites that have visitors who would be interested in your site's content. Sometimes, this means more than just your music. For example, if you are a highly lyrical songwriter, cross-listing your site with poetry websites by pointing to your lyrics page could be a clever way to get new listeners interested in your music. And there are a large number of small zine and journal sites that focus on poetry.

Another example might be the kind of recording equipment you use. If you've become the definitive expert on your DAW setup, why not write an article about it and post it on your website? Sites that do equipment reviews (such as **www.harmony-central.com**, for example) or sites that sell gear (**www.audiomidi.com** or **www.musiciansfriend.com**) might just find your article interesting enough to link to you, and this ultimately means more exposure to your recordings.

If you do any linking or advertising on other sites, it pays to put together some banner ads to put on those sites. Having a banner ad is much more effective than just a text-based link.

> **E-MAIL PROMOS**
>
> E-mail is one of the most powerful (and cheap) online tools available to you. An excellent way to advertise is through the use of an e-mail newsletter, either your own homegrown, periodic updates (using any e-mail software) or by buying ad space in an existing newsletter that reaches people in your audience. E-mail advertising typically generates a higher response than any other online advertising method.

Banner Ads

Although you can hire a designer to create a banner ad for you, if you've acquired even basic Web or graphics skills, creating your own banner isn't too difficult. In fact, there is even ad creation software that can make it easy for you to create banners whether you're artistic or not.

Banner ads can vary widely in their design, but most sites require that the banner be one of several specific sizes, as shown in Table 18.1. In addition, banner ads almost always have technical requirements. For example, a banner ad is typically several frames of animation, so its format must be the GIF file format (the JPEG format doesn't support animation). There are also limitations on the size of the GIF: Generally, it should be less than 15 Kb for a full-sized banner to less than 3 Kb for a button-sized ad, though many sites have even tighter file size restrictions.

Table 18.1
Banner ad sizes

Banner Type	Pixel Size
Full banner	468×60
Half banner	234×60
Square button	125×125
Button style	120×90 or 120×60
Small button	88×31
Vertical banner	120×240

What Makes a Good Banner Ad?

Just like a memorable pop song that has a "hook," a well-designed banner ad should also hook viewers into wanting to click it. For example, you could feature your most creative song title in the ad, or your most interesting band photo.

The graphics should generally be bold and clear—not subtle and muted. This is because your ad will be competing with all the other content on a given page, and possibly other ads as well. Try to keep the animation limited to three or four frames, but pause the frames long enough so that the viewer has plenty of time to read them or to "get it."

Here are some other tips:

- Obtain some good GIF animation software for creating banner ads. At this time, there are a couple of free GIF building programs ready for Mac OS X, such as GIFBuilder, which can be found at the Version Tracker website (**www.versiontracker.com**). Another good choice is Adobe's ImageReady application, which works on both Mac and Windows (**www.adobe.com**).
- Use simple, readable fonts—not fancy spaced-out characters.
- Always include your Web address in the ad. If the viewer doesn't click-through to your site, you at least want her to remember the address!
- Create a static version in addition to the animated one, because some sites don't accept animated ads (usually due to file size).

FLASH

Another banner format that has really become popular over the last couple of years is Flash, which was developed by Macromedia (**www.macromedia.com**). Flash is a much simpler way of developing animation effects due to its intuitive graphical interface and user-friendly tech support. The only drawback to Flash is cost ($199 at the time of this writing), so if you are doing this on a budget, it may not be *the* solution for you.

But there are always solutions and workarounds to these financial woes. One solution is to find a program that converts GIF files to the Flash format, such as Gif2Swf 2.5 for OS X. This utility program is only $15 and can be purchased from Crazy Ivan Productions (**www.gfx2swf.com/**). But if you must have the Flash program and you are a current student at your local high school or college, you are eligible to purchase an educational edition of Flash for around $99 at your local college bookstore. You can also contact Macromedia for further details about this offer.

THE MEDIUM IS THE MESSAGE: AUDIO ADVERTISING

An increasingly interesting option these days is audio and radio advertising via the Internet. It's getting to be popular, and is particularly well-suited to online music.

The simplest example of doing audio advertising is to mix an audio message referring to your website in the song itself—either at the beginning or end of the song. Something like, "Visit sitename.com to hear more!" works just fine. Then, as you sign up with music sites and make your material more widely available, listeners have an immediate reference to where to find more. Of course, this approach could also be potentially irritating to the listener—it's up to you to decide how far you can go with it.

There are also a slew of Internet broadcasting sites that do audio advertising, usually inserting ads that run for 10–15 seconds before the music starts. Broadcast.com, for example, has been doing this for some time.

These "lead-in" advertisements can be implemented in any file format, but the tools that come with both RealMedia and Windows Media are better suited for it. In fact, RealMedia has created an extension to their RealServer product for this purpose. See **www.realnetworks.com/products/advertising/index.html** for details.

ONLINE BROADCASTING POWER!

For a comprehensive primer on online broadcasting, see the book, *Online Broadcasting Power!*, by Ben Sawyer and Dave Greely (Muska & Lipman, 2001, ISBN 0-9662889-8-X). The book discusses everything from the technical aspects of broadcasting online to the legal issues, teaches you how to promote your station, and covers the latest software, such as SHOUTcast, icecast, RealAudio, Windows Media Audio, and myCaster.

Bringing in a Little Income

It's worth mentioning that you can bring in some extra income from your website by participating in affiliate programs. Affiliate programs—or "associate stores" as they're sometimes called—allow you to earn a commission by sending visitors from your site to the Web retailer sponsoring the affiliate program. If one of your site's viewers ends up making a purchase, you get the commission, usually a small percentage of the sale.

But What About the Music, Man?

Affiliate stores are not everybody's gig. Some people feel funny about making-over their site into a virtual storefront, just to make a few extra bucks. And, you will ultimately be giving your listeners one more reason to jump from your site to somewhere else—potentially before they've decided to bookmark it.

On the plus side, you may need a way to help pay your monthly Web hosting fees, or offset the cost of your Internet connection or the upgrades you invariably will have to make to your computer.

The most obvious route to consider, since your gig is music, is to offer links to online music stores. You can put up direct links to artists' pages or even to specific albums, which isn't a bad thing if you're a music enthusiast and you want to encourage other people to check out what you think is hot.

You can also add some legitimacy to your links by doing album reviews and making recommendations. In this way, you're not only increasing the likelihood that you'll pick up a sale, but also adding something to the dialogue by providing useful information to your visitors in any case.

Join affiliate programs that you like—sites that you respect, have used yourself, and that have good customer service. You want every visitor to be a return visitor, and becoming an associate store for a site with a questionable reputation or bad customer service will ultimately reflect poorly on your website.

The technical aspects of joining an affiliate program are fairly simple: You typically provide the URL of your website and receive pieces of HTML code to embed in the links that go to the retailer's site. These pieces of code contain a unique ID that lets the retailers know that it was you who sent them the customer.

Most affiliate programs pay you up to fifteen percent of the sale, though you are usually required to earn a minimum amount per month (or per quarter) before they cut you a check. That said, the following sections list some of the better programs available.

Amazon.com (www.amazon.com)

Amazon.com, originally a small online bookstore, is now the largest e-commerce site on the Web. Though their core business is still books (and to an increasing degree music), they now sell or broker just about everything from toys to new cars to home improvement tools.

Amazon handles all of the customer service, fulfillment, shipping, and tracking of sales. You can link to Amazon by recommending specific products, by placing an Amazon search box on your site, or by linking to the Amazon home page. There is no charge to join and you can earn up to fifteen percent on books featured on your site and five percent on all other items. You can check your earnings and traffic reports online at any time.

CD Baby (www.cdbaby.com)

Although Amazon is the biggest online bookstore around, the biggest problem with relying solely on their site is that with all of the products they carry, your CD will surely get lost in the shuffle. The same can be said for any of the other online record shops listed here. So ideally, you will want to concentrate your efforts on the type of online CD shop that features and supports independent musicians.

CD Baby is probably one of the only online CD shops that really promotes the independent musician. You just sign up with them, send them five finished CDs to start, and they provide a couple of key services for you. They build a website for you featuring your CD, and they encode a couple of songs in the Real Audio format, so there is no need to worry about sending them additional information.

The service does come with a price though, as they take $4 per CD as their profit for every CD sold (that's nearly 30% if you are selling a CD for $15). But speaking honestly, for the amount of advertising that they do in magazines and on the Web, it is a good deal for you. Plus, if you were an artist on a major record label, the most money you could expect to get from a record deal would be $1–2 per disc.

Barnes & Noble (www.bn.com)

Barnes & Noble has been selling books for years and now has a thriving online business. They pay five percent for sales of music, software, videos, and gift certificates and up to seven percent on books and magazines. You can link to the Barnes & Noble main page, featured subject areas, Bargain Book Store, Music Store, and specific title pages or put a Barnes & Noble search box on your site.

Tracking your progress is easy with a number of online reports that allow you to see impressions (how many people viewed your Web page and how often), click-through (people who actually clicked on your ad), orders, shipments, and your commissions.

Borders (www.borders.com)

Borders is yet another bookstore that has established an online component to their business. Borders pays up to seven percent of sales, though you have to produce one million dollars in sales to reach the seven percent mark. They start paying you when your commissions exceed $50.

TowerRecords.com (www.towerrecords.com)

Tower Records is one of the largest record chains in the country, and they are also fast becoming a large online retailer of music and video. TowerRecords.com pays you a straight-up four percent on CDs, videos, and DVDs and have no sales quotas. You can recommend titles, add a TowerRecords.com search box to your site, or use a TowerRecords.com banner to link directly to their home page.

Appendix A
Home Studio Recording Resources on the Web

The focus of this book has been to get your home studio up and running in a real-world, practical way. The aim has been to show the reality of setting up a home studio and making it all work so that you can start recording, mixing, and distributing your work as soon as possible. The book is comprehensive, but it doesn't—and doesn't attempt to—cover everything.

If you want to take your skill and knowledge further, stay up on the newest equipment and techniques, and communicate with other home recording artists—you'll find several comprehensive places on the Internet for doing just that. This appendix lists several of the best sites at the time of this writing.

Apple Computers

http://www.apple.com

Figure A.1

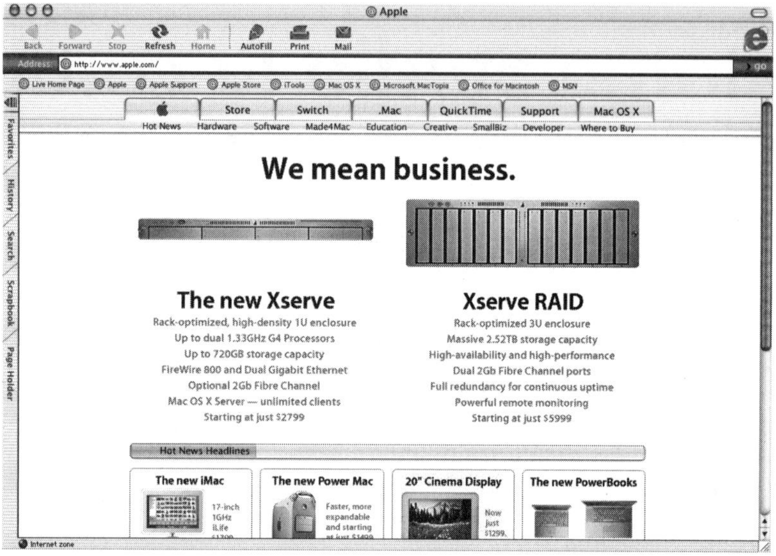

Because this book focuses on Macintosh computers, it seems only right that we point out the Apple home page. The mother of all Apple resources can be found at this site, including support for older Mac users. There is also an online store where you can customize and create your own specialized G4 system for music and multimedia creation.

Harmony Central

http://www.harmony-central.com/

Figure A.2

Harmony Central is probably the single best source of information for musicians on the Web right now. Especially popular is its extensive (highly extensive—it would take you weeks to go through their databases) equipment reviews from regular musicians.

The site is very well maintained and updated, just as it has been from its inception in 1995. Harmony Central also reports daily on the music and recording industry. The site is divided into departments: Guitar, Bass, Effects, Software, Recording, MIDI, Keyboard and Synths, Drums and Percussion, Computers and Music, and Bands. It will take you about five minutes to figure out that you need to bookmark this site.

KvR Instruments Resources

http://www.kvr-vst.com

Figure A.3

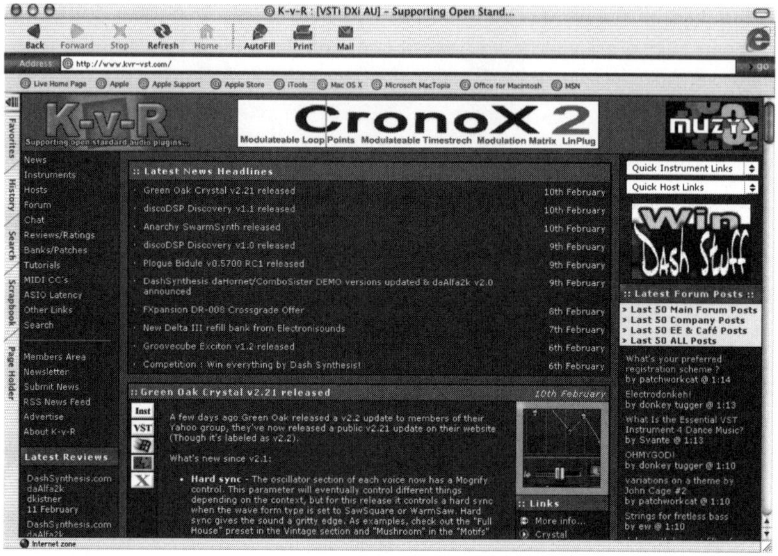

KvR Instruments Resources is probably one of the best places to find information on the growing popularity of virtual instruments. This site is dedicated to bringing users the latest information on virtual instruments of every format (VSTi/AudioUnits/Dxi). Fantastic user forums on this site are maintained by people who would rather be productive in music than start senseless debates (or flame wars as we call them in the virtual world).

MP3.com

http://www.mp3.com/

Figure A.4

MP3.com is still the mother of all online resources for the homegrown recording artist. If you're a home recordist, it's almost a given that your work should be presented here, and it's still free.

MP3.com's message boards boast some of the heaviest activity on the Internet, and they offer free artist pages, Web radio stations, and the cost-free means to market, distribute, and collect real money for your music.

Broadjam

http://www.broadjam.com/

Figure A.5

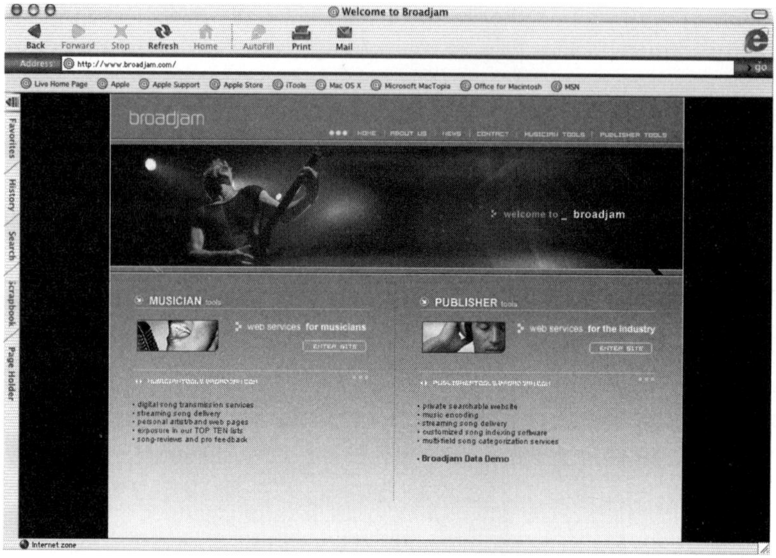

If you are ready to be taken seriously as a musician and not get lost in the endless ocean of bad MP3 files on the Web, Broadjam is a good place to start. They act both as a good forum for other musicians and publishers to hear and critique your music, and they will also create MP3 pages for your music on popular music pages, such as MP3.com.

What sets Broadjam apart from the rest of the endless MP3 pages is that they don't just give your music away. The MP3 pages that Broadjam creates entail providing "stream only" MP3 pages, so people can hear your music, but they cannot simply download it for free.

Home Recording at About.com

http://homerecording.about.com/

Figure A.6

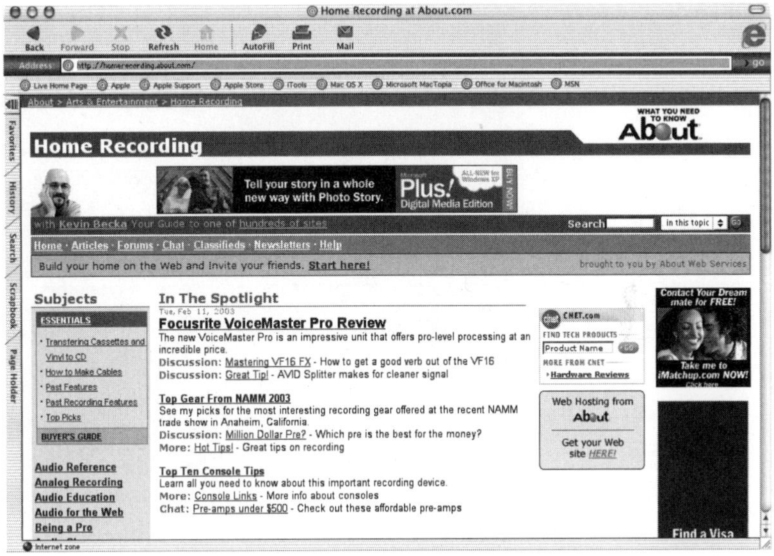

Kevin Becka, a recording engineer, writer, editor, and musician, maintains About.com's comprehensive website on Home Recording. According to Kevin:

> The recording scene has changed dramatically in the last ten years, with modular digital multitrack and hard disk recording decentralizing the industry. The line between consumer and pro audio gear is getting hazier each day, and it's becoming easier to have a great recording studio on a tight budget. I base the site around cutting edge recording techniques along with user reviews, news, an active forum, and a great chat room.

The nice thing about Kevin's comment is that he's right on. The site is updated frequently and provides a large number of home recording articles, online forums, chat, and a newsletter. An excellent resource!

Synth Zone

http://www.synthzone.com/

Figure A.7

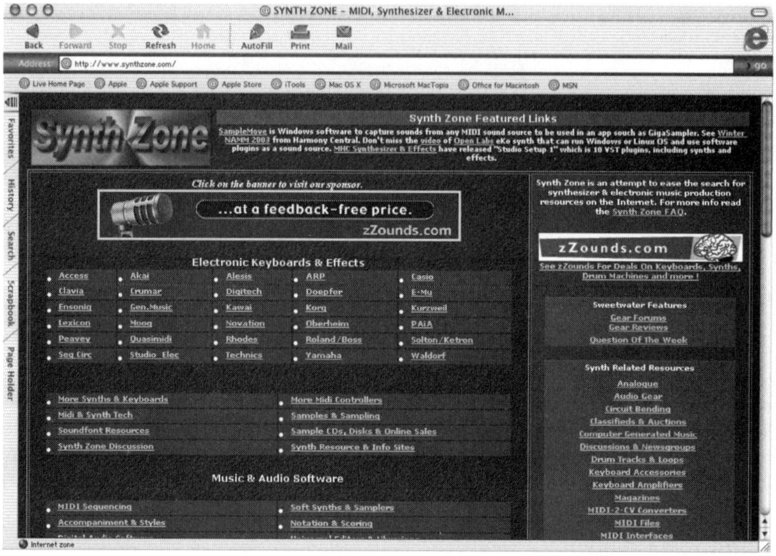

Synth Zone has been around almost since the Web began and contains rich sources of information about MIDI, synthesizer, and music production. The site is especially well-known for its links to synthesizer software patches, manuals, and additional software. There's at least one active link for just about any synth you can name, as well as links to discussion groups, classifieds, auctions, and software downloads.

APPENDIX A

The Recording Website

http://www.recordingwebsite.com/

Figure A.8

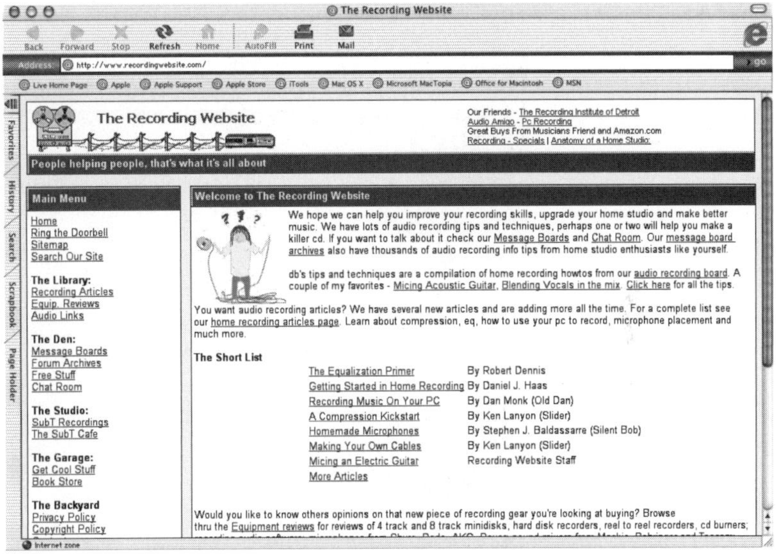

The Recording Website is a growing collection of articles and equipment reviews. The site has an active message board with tons of posts. The articles on the site tend to be fairly short but are well worth reading for their accuracy and level of detail.

What is a Synthesizer?

http://hem.passagen.se/tkolb/art/synth/intro_e.htm

Figure A.9

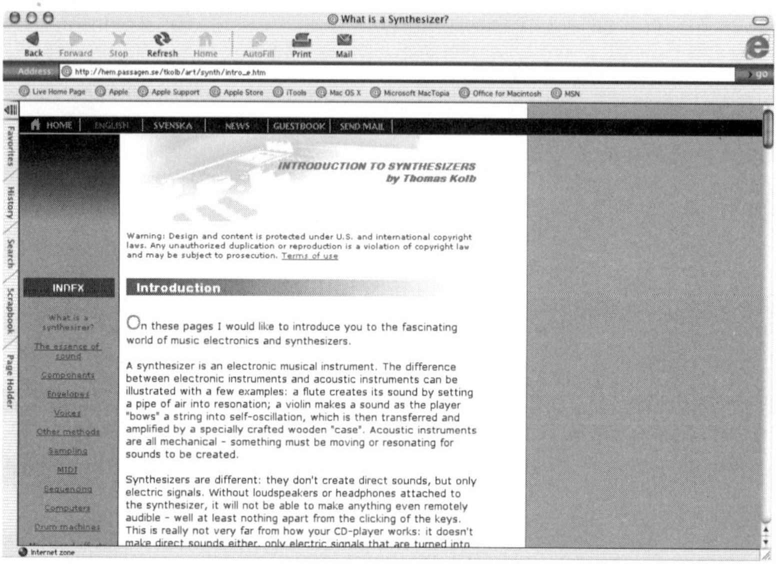

This Sweden-based website (the English is excellent), written and maintained by Thomas Kolb, is a wonderful exploration of details behind synth components, sampling, MIDI, computer-based recording, mixing, and effects. The articles are rich and well written.

Streamworksaudio.com

http://www.streamworksaudio.com

Figure A.10

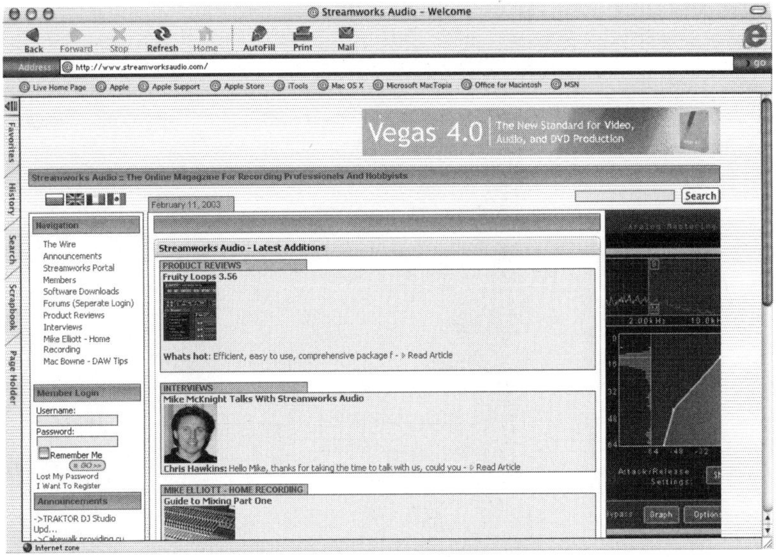

Streamworksaudio.com is an E-zine and news site for anyone interested in virtual studios. The site has articles, reviews, interviews, and registered user forums. It is a good source of information for virtual studio junkies.

Steinberg

http://www.steinberg.net/

Figure A.11

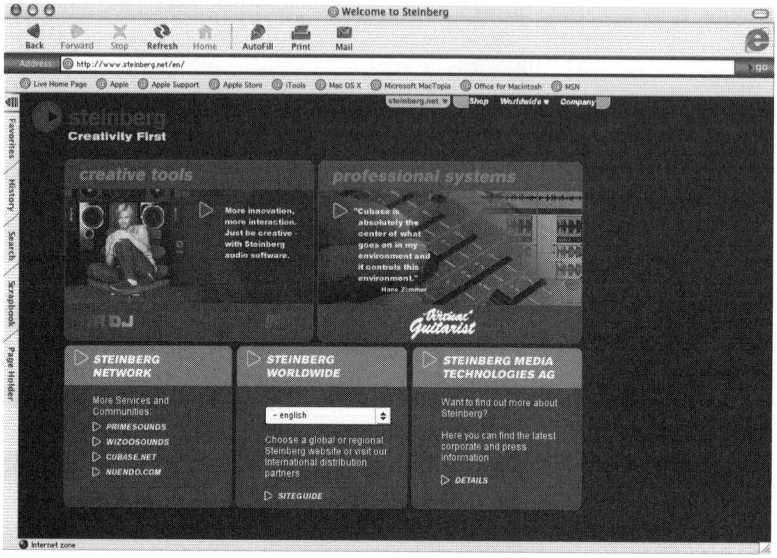

The Steinberg home page is the first place to look for more information on Cubase. The site contains a lot of information, with extensive FAQs (frequently asked questions), product updates, and technical specifications.

You also can find tips, techniques, and tricks and hook up with the Cubase.net user forums. You can also find support for the software and get in touch with Steinberg's Tech Support group from the site.

Bias

http://www.bias-inc.com/

Figure A.12

For updates, discussion, product information, and specifications, Bias, the makers of Peak, has developed a well-designed and deep website. In addition to excellent support of Peak, it also provides support and documentation for all of its other products—including Deck and VBox.

VirSyn

http://www.virsyn.com

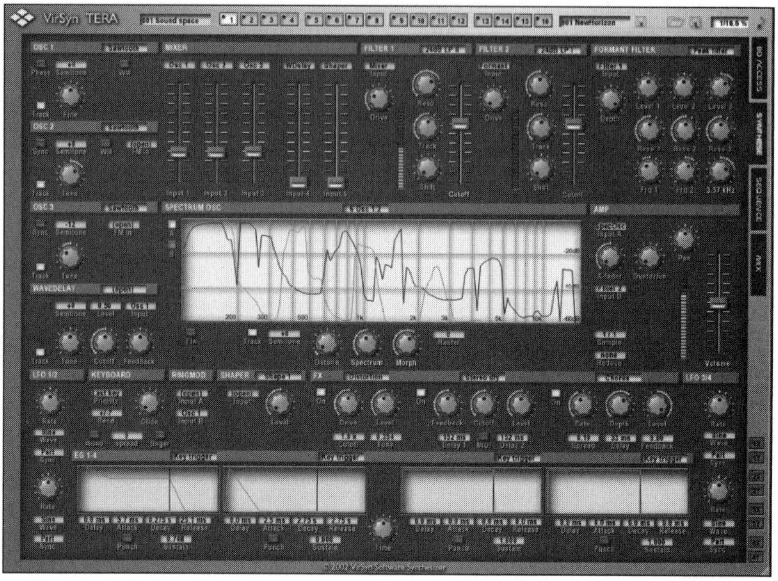

Figure A.13

VirSyn is the maker of one of the best virtual synths on the market called the TERA. Not only is it a VST Instrument, but it is also supported for OS X and Audio Units for Emagic's Logic program. According to the developer, the TERA is always being updated.

MIDIman

http://www.midiman.com

Figure A.14

Throughout the development of the audio recording portion of this book, audio hardware made by MIDIman was used to perform the examples. They produce some of the best-known audio cards, called the Delta Series, which not only have fantastic support for Cubase SL/SX and OS X, but also price tags that won't destroy your budget.

Index

Note: Italicized page numbers refer to illustrations or tables.

NUMBERS

A

D

E

F

INDEX

N

O

P

Q

R

S

INDEX

T

U

V

W

X

Y